DARK TIMES DECENT MEN

C000258639

STORIES OF IRISHMEN IN WWII

INSPIRATION FOR THE TITLE:

Raymond Wall from Loughrea, County Galway, a former flight mechanic (engines) with RAF Bomber Command, was once asked by his son, Cyril Wall – who many Dubliners might remember as the owner of *Yesteryear Antiques* on North Frederick Street – why he had volunteered to join the British forces during the Second World War. Cyril was confused, since he knew his father as a devout pacifist who condoned no violence of any kind. It made absolutely no sense to Cyril that his father had ever willingly put on a military uniform. Raymond took a breath, turned to Cyril, and replied:

> *Those were different times then. They were dark times. There was an insidious evil rampaging across Europe, and decent men were needed to stop it.*

RAF ground crew working on an Avro Lancaster four-engine heavy bomber of No 90 Squadron RAF during 1944/45. Aircraftman Raymond Wall from Loughrea, County Galway is one of those pictured.

Neil Richardson studied philosophy in University College Dublin before writing his first book, *A Coward If I Return, A Hero If I Fall: Stories of Irishmen in WWI*, which won the Argosy Non-Fiction Book of the Year Award at the 2010 Irish Book Awards. Neil is also a member of the Reserve Defence Forces, and his family have a long military tradition stretching back over 150 years. Neil's ancestors served in India and Africa, in the Boer War, and during both world wars.

Praise for *A COWARD IF I RETURN, A HERO IF I FALL*

'Remarkable ... insightful. A moving collection of stories about Irishmen who fought in that war, backed up by photos, diaries and documents that bring us closer to these men than any book I have read before.' Eoghan Harris, *Sunday Independent*

'This very rich text will be read with interest by all those seeking to understand the impact of the war on Ireland and the Irish ... One of the great achievements of the book is to present to the public some truly new material which has not been available before.' *www.warbooksreview.com*

'Given that the first casualty of any war is the truth, any attempt to honour the Irish who fought in The Great War can only be welcomed. *A Coward If I Return, A Hero If I Fall* is arguably the finest modern effort to record the tales of the Irish who fought in the greatest concentrated slaughter in human history.' *Munster Express*

'Heart-rending stories about bravery, family sacrifice, lucky escapes and tragic ends.' *Irish Post*

This book adds another dimension to the books on the Irish experience during the conflict ... I would recommend it most strongly.' *Books Ireland*

'Ireland's deliberate amnesia surrounding World War One is at last being punctured and a fine book such as this serves a key role in humanising the suffering.' *The Westmeath Independent*

DARK TIMES, DECENT MEN

STORIES OF IRISHMEN IN WORLD WAR II

NEIL RICHARDSON

IRISH BOOK AWARD WINNER

THE O'BRIEN PRESS
DUBLIN

First published 2012 by
The O'Brien Press Ltd.,
12 Terenure Road East, Rathgar, Dublin 6, Ireland.
Tel: +353 1 4923333; Fax: +353 1 4922777
E-mail: books@obrien.ie
Website: www.obrien.ie

ISBN: 978-1-84717-297-6

A catalogue record for this title is available from The British Library.

1 2 3 4 5 6 7 8 9 10

12 13 14 15 16 17 18

Typesetting, editing, layout and design: The O'Brien Press Ltd

Printed and bound by MPG Books Ltd.
The paper in this book is produced using pulp from managed forests.

For Caroline, for making it happen,
and for Cyril Wall, who helped me fill a lot of pages

This book is dedicated to every Irish soldier in every army
– past, present, and future

Acknowledgements

My wonderful editor Susan Houlden and all the fantastic staff at The O'Brien Press.

Hubert 'Pat' Barron, Michael Coleman, Joseph Dunne, Phil Farrington, Paddy Gillen, Joseph Hardaker, Don Harkin, John Hemingway, Ted Johnson, Sam Kendrick, Owen 'Tony' Larney, Lawrence Lee, Reggie Lee, Max Levitas, Sol Levitas, Martin Lynch, Patrick O'Connor, John O'Sullivan, Christopher Robinson, William Upington.

Republic of Ireland Royal British Legion; Northern Ireland Royal British Legion; Republic of Ireland Royal Air Forces Association; Yvonne Altman O'Connor, Howard Freeman and the Irish Jewish Museum; Michael McDonagh and the Navan Travellers' Centre; William McDonagh and *Voice of the Traveller* Magazine; Gearóid O'Brien, Lorraine Francis and all the staff at the Athlone Library; UK National Archives; Janice Bovill, Margaret Kinnie, Joyce Carlyle and the British Army Personnel Centre (Historical Disclosures Section); Julia Burgess and RAF Disclosures; Simon Gaskin and Royal Navy Records Management; Diane Flanagan and the Irish Guards Association; National Archives of Australia; Ricky Phillips, Jessie Webb, Krissy Kraljevic, Beau Cooper and the Australian War Memorial; Michael A Blum and the Marine Corps League; James Hunniford and the National Museum of the Marine Corps; Annette Amerman and the Marine Corps History Division; Randall E Dawson, Miguel A Barrera and the National Personnel Records Center (USA); Susan Ward and the Miami Veterans' Administration; Hoyt Bruce Moore and the 506th Association; Tara Lichterman and Casemate Publishing; Emer Hogan and Grub Street Publishing; *Anglo Celt, Argus, Athlone Advertiser, Avondhu, Carlow Nationalist, Clare Champion, Connacht Telegraph, Connacht Tribune, Drogheda Independent, Dublin People, Evening Echo, Fingal Independent, Galway Advertiser, Irish Examiner, Kerry's Eye, Kildare Nationalist, Kilkenny Advertiser, Kilkenny People, Laois Nationalist, Leinster Express, Limerick Leader, Limerick Post, Mayo Advertiser, Mayo Echo, Mayo News, Meath Chronicle, Metro Herald, Mullingar Advertiser, Munster Express, Nenagh Guardian, Offaly Express, Offaly Topic, Roscommon Champion, Roscommon Herald, Sligo Champion, Sligo Weekender, Southern Star, The Corkman, The Echo, The Kerryman, The Kingdom, Tuam Herald, Tullamore Tribune, Waterford Today, Western People, Westmeath Examiner,* Tadhg Carey and *The Westmeath Independent, Westmeath Topic.*

Richard Adams, John Alvey, Ray Barry, Kathy Bateson, Patricia Brien, Carol Briscoe, Joe Briscoe, Noel Broderick, Conor Cahalane, Dean Callaghan, Olivia Callan, Nuala Carr, Pat Casey, Donal Cassidy, Sarah Cassidy, Lorraine Chambers, Noelle Clery, Josie Cole, Dermot Collins, Tom Collins, William Collins, Colm Connaughton, Bridget Connolly, Pauline Conway, Benny Cooney, Louise

Crivon, Quentin Crivon, Peter Cunningham, David Davin-Power, John Donohoe, Eric Doran, Brian Duffy, Michael Duffy, Rory Duffy, Caroline Emerson, Frances Farrell, John Feeney, Richard Finan, Alison Finlay, Leonie Finn, Edward Fleming, Richard Franklin, Stephen Frayne, Tony Gaffey, Dorothy Gilchrist, Paddy Gillen, Robin Gillen, Donna Harkin, Josie Harkin, Rita Harris, Patrick Holden, Tommy Holohan, Shane Horkan, Ian Hueston, Kevin Hynes, Suzanne Igoe, Cllr Ruth Illingworth, Eileen Kavanagh, Jimmy Kearns, Kenneth Kelly, Mary Kelly, Tony Kelly, Mary-Anne Kieran, Mary Kilcullen, Tony King, Brian Kinsey, John Kirke, Eric Knight, Keith Lee, Lawrence Lee, Malcolm Lee, Mary Lennon, Ben Levitas, Ruth Levitas, Anne Loughlin, Carmel Lynch, Patrick Lynch, Marie Maher, Barbara Maloney, Kenneth Martin, Michael Martin, Sarah McBride, John McCullen, Gerard McDonnell, Jim McIlmurray, Pete McWilliams, Richard Moles, Neil Mongey, Henry Mooney, Laurence K Moore, Micheál Moore, John Moriarty, Rosemary Mullen, Jim Mulvey, Dennis Murnane, Michael Murray, Rois Ní Dhochartaigh, Tony Nolan, Gabriel O'Brien, Bernie O'Connor, Ronnie O'Dea, Paddy Phelan, Paddy Reid, Gordon Revington, Joan Richardson, John Robertson, Greg Rogers, James Rogers, Gail Sackloff, Anne Sands, Tadhg Sexton, Colman Shaughnessy, William Shorten, Lucita Shorter, David Sterritt, Robert Stewart, Eric Strange, Pádraig Sweeney, Warwick H Taylor, Su Topping, Mark Vivian, Anna Walsh, Emer Walsh, Peter Walsh, Dr Hugh Weir, Martin Whelan, William Whelan, Alex Wogan, Finola Young.

CONTENTS

Hitler, flanked by the massed ranks of the Sturmabteilung *(SA) – the Nazi party's early paramilitary wing – ascends the steps to the speaker's podium during the 1934 Nazi Party Rally at Nuremberg.*

INTRODUCTION

'The only thing necessary for the triumph of evil
is for good men to do nothing.'
Attributed to Edmund Burke, Irish philosopher

Twenty-one years between the ending of one world war and the beginning of another. Enough time for a new generation of soldiers to be born and grow to adulthood. Enough time for economic and industrial forces to recover to fight again. But not enough time for the memories of past horrors to have faded, or for the bitterness of the defeated to have dissipated.

Part of me decided to write this book as a natural follow-on to *A Coward If I Return, A Hero If I Fall: Stories of Irishmen in WWI*, because I had family who also served with the British forces during the Second World War, and because I believed that – like our involvement in the First World War – the Irish participation in the Second World War was equally forgotten about, if not *doubly* forgotten about.

With the recent increase in books on the subject of the Irish in the First World War, and the return of annual commemorations, modern Irish people are steadily becoming more and more aware that 200,000 of their countrymen served in the British Army in the trenches during 1914–1918. They were joined by 300,000 Irish emigrants, or sons born to Irish parents, who served in other armies around the world, bringing the total Irish contribution to roughly half a million men. Out of those who served in the British Army, at least 35,000 never came home.

However, with regard to the Second World War, the stories that most southern Irish people have to tell revolve around the 'Emergency', and tales about rationing or the hated 'glimmer man' – whose job it was to make sure that a home or business was not using gas outside of regulation hours – are usually what is remembered. Occasionally, there might be a memory of receiving gas masks in case of air raids, or cardboard shoes – introduced to deal

*Above and opposite: Two cards made up by men from Lurgan, County Armagh, and sent to their families back home. **Above:** Eric McClure is pictured, while opposite is Frederick Mathews from Carnegie Street. McClure survived the war; Mathews was killed in action on 28 June 1942 in North Africa, aged thirty-four, while serving as a driver with the New Zealand Army Service Corps.*

with leather shortages – that disintegrated as soon as they came into contact with the Irish weather, or about the absence of cars on city roads due to the lack of petrol, but the stories usually end there. Even the memories about anything military invariably only ever involve the Irish Army – and usually focus on a family member who enlisted as the army expanded after war broke out, or who served as a reservist with the Local Defence Force (LDF). Mentions of men in other armies are normally confined to the British or German aircrews that bailed out over Ireland or crash landed before ending up in internment camps on the Curragh. And so, as the southern twenty-six counties of Ireland were independent and neutral during the Second World War – as opposed to being a part of the United Kingdom and officially at war – the Second World War is not considered to have concerned southern Ireland.

As a result, the majority of modern Irish people are still unaware that during the Second World War, at least 130,000 Irish served in the British forces – the 20,000 Irish already serving in the British forces when war broke out being joined by approximately 110,000 wartime volunteers (roughly 66,000 from southern Ireland and 64,000 from Northern Ireland). However, this figure is only a conservative estimate based on bottom line academic consensus. Some researchers have quoted figures of 150,000 and 200,000, and one source – First World War General Sir Hubert Gough in a letter to *The Times* in August 1944 – suggested that over 165,000 volunteers from southern Ireland *alone* had joined the British forces by that time (which, when added to the 64,000 volunteers from Northern Ireland known to have enlisted, would total 229,000). Furthermore, these are the numbers for the British forces *alone* – they do not include the Irish who are known to have served with the US, Canadian, Australian and New Zealand militaries. Based on this, the numbers of Irish who served in combatant armies during the Second World War might be very close to the numbers who fought during the First World War. Finally, in the British forces alone, at least 7,500 Irish are known to have died during the Second World War.

I felt that the experiences of these Irish soldiers, sailors, and airmen must also be preserved, especially those who kept no diaries and were never written about in official histories – the people whose stories and experiences were known only to themselves or their families, stories that would vanish forever if not recorded.

Once again I submitted articles to national newspapers and websites appealing for Irish Second World War veterans – from anywhere on the island of Ireland – or their families, to contact me and pass on their accounts. Hundreds of people did so, and I am extremely grateful to all of them.

However, another part of me wanted to write a book on the subject of the Irish in the Second World War because in so many ways this was a very different war to the conflict of 1914–1918. Trench warfare, waves and waves of infantry walking towards walls of machine gun bullets, thousands of artillery pieces pounding mile after mile of territory into a cratered no-man's-land, a thousand yards of progress taking a year to achieve, and death tolls like the 60,000 British casualties incurred on the first day of the Battle of the Somme in 1916 – they were now a thing of the past. But replacing these features of an old war were a new set of horrors: rocket technology and the large-scale bombing of cities, *Blitzkrieg* ('Lightning War') and the true mechanisation of warfare – where the plane and the tank became a terrifying and dominating force on the battlefield – the fight against fanatical units like the *Schutzstaffel* (SS) and *Hitler-Jugend* ('Hitler

Youth') or the soldiers of the Imperial Japanese Army, inhumane treatment in POW camps, the Holocaust and human experimentation, and, ultimately, the advent of atomic weapons.

There was no patriotic rush to the recruiting offices this time – people knew the terrifying cost of twentieth century warfare – but, in retrospect, this new war could also be labelled as a just war. Unlike the 1914–1918 conflict, the Second World War could be considered an ultimately necessary struggle to stop a very real force of evil. And so, the Irish who fought in the Second World War experienced something very different to their fathers in the trenches and, for that reason, their story must be told also.

Furthermore, the Irish who served in the combatant armies of the Second World War grew up in an Ireland, and a world, that had changed drastically since the end of 1918. While their fathers had been raised in an Ireland that was still a part of Britain – where, aside from political tensions between nationalists and unionists, the country had been pre-dominantly peaceful – many of the new generation were born during the War of Inde-pendence of 1919–1921 or the Irish Civil War of 1922–1923, or in the aftermath when Ireland was divided into the southern twenty-six counties of the Irish Free State and the six northern counties of Ulster that became known as Northern Ireland and remained a part of the United Kingdom (a division that was only finalised and made official on 3 December 1925). While the 1916 Rising was, for the most part, history to Irish Second World War soldiers, many were born into an Ireland that was actively at war at the time of their birth.

This was true in the case of James Murray – who was born during the War of Independ-ence in a one-room tenement on South William Street, Dublin in 1921. The night James was born, there was a curfew in effect in Dublin. But when his mother went into labour, James' father – a driver for Jacob's biscuits – was forced to go outside in order to fetch the midwife. British forces saw him running through the streets and, thinking he was an IRA man, opened fire. Luckily, James' father was not hurt, and James Murray went on to land on Sword Beach on D-Day while serving in 2nd King's Own Shropshire Light Infantry.

However, being born during a violent period in Irish history was not the only difficulty that Irish Second World War soldiers had to face before 1939 and the start of their war. The so-called Spanish Flu pandemic of 1918 took the lives of 280,000 people in Ireland and Britain in a one-year period and 50 million people worldwide – an event which killed the parents of many Irish children, including the mother of Eamonn 'Ed' O'Dea from Kildimo, County Limerick. She died of the flu in 1919 when Ed was only four years old, leaving him to be raised by his father and two aunts – Ed later served as a Stoker Petty Officer with the Royal Navy during the war.

Modernity and the ideals of a new leading class had also changed Ireland in many ways since 1918. On 3 July 1924, Eoin MacNeill – then minister for education – made the teach-ing of the Irish language compulsory in all schools, and in 1928, for the first time in over a hundred years, an Irish currency began circulating again. Several organisations with roots in Irish nationalism also began enforcing their ideals. After attending a 'foreign sport' rugby match between Ennis and Nenagh in 1931, sixteen members of the Ennis Dalcassian Gaelic Athletic Association (GAA) were expelled from their club, and in 1934, the Gaelic League wrote to Dublin Corporation that it was 'determined to crush ... [the] denationalising ... present day instrument of social degradation ...' that was jazz music, a campaign that was fully supported by Irish bishops.

With regards to the strengthening of the bond between Church and State that was also taking place during this time, in 1925 a resolution was passed in the Dáil (Irish parliament) making it illegal for an Irish citizen to divorce and then re-marry in the State. By 1931, the first Saint Patrick's Day parade was held in the Free State, and over the following two years, two pontifical masses were held in the Phoenix Park – one in 1932, attended by over a million people, to celebrate the close of the thirty-first Eucharistic Congress, and another in 1933, where 300,000 people gathered to celebrate a hundred years of Catholic emancipation. This Church-State relationship ultimately led to the 'special position' given to the Catholic Church in the 1937 Irish Constitution. Furthermore, while for a Catholic to attend Trinity College Dublin remained, at the very least, frowned-upon, at worst, a crime worthy of excommunication (official Church disapproval of Catholic attendance at the university was only lifted in 1970), it was considered a mortal sin to be a communist. Meanwhile, reflecting the recent political division of the country, work began on the construction of the Northern Ireland Parliament Buildings, in the Stormont area of Belfast, on 19 May 1928. It was opened four years later on 22 November 1932, giving Northern Ireland its own seat of government.

As for the modern world bringing change to Ireland, the BBC made its first broadcast in Northern Ireland on 14 September 1924 with the station 2BE. Two years later on 1 January 1926, the Irish Free State's own new broadcasting service – 2RN – began transmitting. Electricity came to the Free State with the opening of the Shannon hydro-electric scheme at Ardnacrusha, County Clare, in 1929. At the time, it was the largest hydro-electric station in the world and was built by the German engineering firm Siemens – who attempted to raise the wages of under-paid workers on site, but were overruled by the Irish government (Just over ten years later, Siemens would have factories in the vicinity of Nazi concentration camps where forced-labour was used to manufacture electrical switches for the German military.) And so, with broadcasting and electricity, the 'wireless' radio soon became a central feature of Irish home life, providing a new form of entertainment and access to news. There was also a growth in the number of cinemas in Ireland during this time, with Ireland's first talking film being Al Jolson's *The Singing Fool*, shown at the Capitol Theatre off O'Connell Street, Dublin in 1929. In many ways, Irish life was starting to become more international.

By the time of the Second World War, there were only nine surviving Irish regiments in the British Army. During the First World War, there had been fifteen. **Top Row, left to right:** *Cap badges of the Royal Inniskilling Fusiliers, Royal Irish Fusiliers, Royal Ulster Rifles.* **Middle Row, left to right:** *Irish Guards, Liverpool Irish (TA), London Irish Rifles (TA).* **Bottom Row, left to right:** *5th Royal Inniskilling Dragoon Guards, 8th King's Royal Irish Hussars, North Irish Horse.*

However, while many things had changed since the days of their fathers' youth, some aspects of life in Ireland remained exactly the same. Before fighting in the trenches, many Irishmen had known terrible poverty – living in dilapidated city tenements or barely surviving on a tiny rural farm – and the Great Depression that began with the Wall Street stock market crash ensured that their sons and daughters would be familiar with it as well. In 1929, when most soon-to-be Irish Second World War soldiers were in their early teens, unemployment rose sharply all around the world, with the heavy industry, construction and farming sectors being particularly hard hit. In Ireland, around the same time that many young men were approaching the age when they would leave school and be expected to get their first job, there were now simply no jobs to be had. Approximately 250,000 out of a population of 4.2 million were soon unemployed across the island.

In Northern Ireland, construction in the Belfast shipyards nearly came to a complete halt. The city had once been known as the largest producer of linen in the world – now, 8,000 linen workers were unemployed – and it was not long before the Belfast Executive Committee noted that 20,000 children living in the city's slums were suffering from malnutrition. Meanwhile, in the Free State, infant mortality was high (a figure that was, as noted in a Department of Local Government and Public Health report, still on the rise by 1938) and in Limerick – in a three month period in late 1932 – 108 cases of diphtheria and sixty-eight cases of scarlet fever in children were admitted to Limerick City Hospital. Grants to initiate public works schemes that could provide employment, housing schemes, and welfare or benefit programmes were widely requested, with 'We Want Work' being the slogan of a march through Listowel, County Kerry by members of the local Workers' Union. Similar protest marches, along with work strikes, soon became regular occurences across the island.

The economic and social situation was grim across Ireland, but due to the worldwide effects of the Wall Street Crash, emigration was no longer a solution to unemployment. Irish people never stopped leaving the country to find work – travelling to places like Britain, the US, Canada, Australia, or New Zealand – but after 1929, the numbers were nothing like they used to be. While just under 21,000 Irish people a year had emigrated to America between 1920 and 1930, during the period 1931 to 1940, the number dropped to roughly 1,500 a year. There were simply no jobs to be had on the other side of the Atlantic. Emigration to Australia and New Zealand similarly dropped to 2,500 a year during this time. In fact, the economic situation was so bad, that between 1931 and 1938, while Ireland had 8,480 people leave the country, 15,859 actually emigrated *into* Ireland – desperate former-emigrants who were coming home, hoping to escape the new poverty in America.

And so, well into the 1930s, the economic situation in Ireland was certainly bleak. This would ultimately be a deciding factor in many (but certainly not all) men's decision to join the British Army during the Second World War.

Similarly, in the way that Irish First World War soldiers had grown up in a politically changing world, so too did the Irish who went on to fight in the Second World War. But while their fathers had known the struggle between nationalist and unionist, they experienced the clash of socialism/communism and fascism. In a devastated post-war Europe, many turned to either the political left or the political right in an attempt to replace the styles of government that had led to the war and its aftermath. For the Irish, the Spanish Civil War was the first war that dealt with this divide of political ideals.

In 1932, Éamon de Valera and Fianna Fáil came to power for the first time. The party had a strong anti-Treaty heritage and replaced the pro-Treaty Cumann na nGaedheal government which had been in power since 1922. One of de Valera's first acts as President of the Executive Council of the Irish Free State (the future position of Taoiseach) was to lift the ban on the Irish Republican Army (IRA), which had been illegal up to this point and was now a completely anti-Treaty organisation, and release many political prisoners from jail. The IRA immediately started disrupting Cumann na nGaedheal events, which brought them into violent clashes with the Army Comrades Association – also known as the National Guard, or by their nickname the 'Blueshirts', for their Saint Patrick's blue uniform shirt. Many of the Blueshirts were former Free State soldiers who had fought the anti-Treaty IRA during the Irish Civil War, and they firmly supported Cumann na nGaedheal. Suddenly, the old anti-Treaty versus pro-Treaty struggle of the Irish Civil War period was brought back to life.

In 1933, de Valera declared the Blueshirts illegal, and so they merged with Cumann na nGaedheal and the National Centre Party to form Fine Gael on 3 September that year. However, former Blueshirt leader Eoin O'Duffy – also the first leader of Fine Gael – soon left this new party as the majority of its members did not support his strongly right-wing views. He then founded the openly fascist National Corporate Party in 1935, whose military wing became known as the 'Greenshirts'. In terms of political opinion, they were completely opposed to Ireland's other main paramilitary group – the IRA.

When the Spanish Civil War broke out in 1936, the IRA and the National Corporate Party/Greenshirts saw a conflict that seemed to mirror their own in Ireland. The IRA had become more left-wing and socialist since the Irish Civil War, which brought them to empathise with the Spanish republicans, while the right-wing, conservative National Corporate Party/Greenshirts identified with the pro-Catholic, anti-communist aims of Franco's nationalists. Soon, both sides sent troops to fight in the war – many from the IRA, along with other Irish socialists, formed the left-wing 'Connolly Column', named after 1916 martyr James Connolly, and served on the republican side, while 700 men who supported Eoin O'Duffy fought in the right-wing 'Irish Brigade' on the nationalist side.

In fact, several Irishmen who would go on to serve during the Second World War were involved in the Spanish Civil War. From Morley's Bridge, near Kilgarvan in County Kerry, Michael Lehane was a student at Darrara Agricultural College – near Clonakilty in County Cork – until hard times forced him to move to Dublin where he found work as a builder's labourer. He fought on the republican side during the Spanish Civil War – at Cordoba in 1936, at Las Rozas de Madrid during the Battle of the Corunna Road and at the Battle of Brunete (where he was wounded) during 1937, and at the Battle of the Ebro (where he was again wounded) in 1938 – before serving in the Norwegian Merchant Navy during the Second World War. He disagreed with wearing a British uniform, but still felt that it was his duty to do something to stop Hitler and Nazi Germany.

Michael Lehane was not the only Irish republican veteran of the Spanish Civil War to fight in the Second World War. Patrick O'Daire from Glenties, County Donegal – who initially served in and then later commanded the Major Attlee Company of the British Battalion, 15th International Brigade (pictured here on the Ebro front in 1938) – went on to become a major in the Pioneer Corps during the Second World War. Ironically, he had started his soldiering career by fighting with the IRA against the British during the War of Independence when he was only sixteen years old, making his story a particularly unique one – he went from Irish rebel to British officer during his lifetime. O'Daire later settled in Llanberis, Wales and died in 1981 – aged seventy-six.

Lehane's ship – SS *Brant County* – set sail from Halifax, Nova Scotia on 2 March 1943 carrying 670 tons of explosives and a large quantity of carbide. Michael Lehane was killed when the ship was torpedoed and sunk by *U-86* on 11 March. He was on duty in the engine room at the time and died in the initial explosion. Having previously served in the Connolly Column throughout the Spanish Civil War, Michael Lehane had insisted on continuing the fight against fascism. He was only thirty-four years old at the time of his death. With no known grave, today he is commemorated on the Halifax Memorial.

However, whereas Spain might have been the place where many Irishmen first came into contact with fascism, Nazi Germany was the real threat. The 1919 Treaty of Versailles had forced Germany to accept full responsibility for starting the First World War, while stripping her of territories, significantly reducing the size of her military, and ordering her to pay 11.3 billion pounds in reparations fees (taken at 1919 value). Germany was bankrupted and there was soon widespread civil unrest. But by 1936 and the start of the Spanish Civil War, Germany's chancellor – a charismatic and energetic former First World War corporal named Adolf Hitler – and the *Nationalsozialistische Deutsche Arbeiterpartei* (or 'Nazi' party) had turned the country around. As employment and industry grew and grew, Hitler trebled the size of the army between 1933 and 1935 before introducing conscription and expanding it to half a million men. Meanwhile, new military technologies were developed – including modern tanks – and the *Luftwaffe* (Air Force) and the *Kriegsmarine* (Navy) were rebuilt, moves that were strictly forbidden under the Treaty of Versailles. In 1935, the industrially important Saar region – separated from Germany by the Treaty of Versailles – voted to rejoin the Fatherland. Then, in 1936, the first of Hitler's moves to retake other lost territories began when the German Army illegally occupied the demilitarised Rhineland.

However, there was a terrible price for the speed at which the Nazis rebuilt a desolate Germany. The first concentration camp – Dachau – was opened in 1933. Communists, socialists, anti-Nazi journalists and any other perceived enemies of the party were interred. Of course, they were joined by thousands of German Jews. Hitler had instilled strong anti-Semitism in the German people, while teaching his non-Jewish countrymen and women that they were true 'Aryans' – a 'master race'. It was not long before Eastern Europeans, Slavs, Romani gypsies, homosexuals, physically and mentally disabled persons, Jehovah's Witnesses, Catholic clergy, and anti-Nazi intellectuals were also being interred in large numbers.

The outside world was shocked at these developments, but as the Nazis began holding book burnings, destroying trade unions, banning the freedoms of the press and abolishing civil liberties, no one made any moves to stop them. Intellectuals and Jews fled the country in their thousands as Hitler cemented his place, and that of the Nazi party, in German society. Through a mixture of voter coercion and ruthless behaviour, Hitler turned the country into a one-party state, and with Nazi imagery and their symbol – the swastika – soon everywhere, Nazi activities dominated everyday German life. Then, after combining the office of President and Chancellor on the death of President Paul von Hindenburg in 1934, Hitler became *Führer* (Leader) of Germany and Supreme Commander of the Armed Forces (he later took over personal control of the armed forces) – essentially a fascist dictator. The German military were now forced to swear their oath of allegiance to Hitler personally, as opposed to the office of Supreme Commander, and the common greeting 'Heil Hitler!' even contained his name.

Nazi Germany might not have been the only fascist dictatorship operating in the world – with Mussolini's Italy and Emperor Hirohito's fascist-like Empire of Japan also posing a threat – but with Germany's resurrected military and industrial might, Hitler was the greatest danger. Given that Hitler wanted to undo the injustices inflicted on Germany by the Treaty of Versailles, the world knew that another war was possible long before it actually started in 1939. After his Rhineland occupation in 1936, Hitler pressed on to form *Anschluss* (Union) with Austria in March 1938 – another forbidden move. 'Appeasement' and the ceding of the Czechoslovakian Sudetenland to Germany in September 1938 failed to stop him, and then the world knew that another war was certainly on its way. After the Sudetenland, six months later the Nazis took the rest of Czechoslovakia in May 1939, then demanded the Baltic-coast city of Danzig and access to it through Poland, before making a secret deal with Stalin's Russia to actually invade Poland and divide it between them. It was obvious now that Hitler could never be appeased, only military force could stop him. In August 1939, Britain finally promised to go to war with Germany if it invaded Poland. On 1 September 1939, this is exactly what happened. British Prime Minister Neville Chamberlain subsequently issued an ultimatum to the German government. The Germans did not reply. And so for the second time in the twentieth century, Britain was at war with Germany. By the time the Second World War ended, six years later, 70 million people had been killed – nearly four times as many dead as during the First World War – and out of this 70 million, over sixty percent of them were civilians, not soldiers.

It is now time to turn to the Irish soldiers, sailors and airmen – from all across the island of Ireland – who went to war. Unlike their fathers' generation, most of the infantry soldiers would serve in non-Irish regiments (the five southern Irish infantry regiments and one of cavalry had been disbanded on the formation of the Irish Free State in 1922), although many from north and south of the border would still go on to serve in the surviving Irish units during the war – units such as the Royal Inniskilling Fusiliers, Royal Irish Fusiliers, Royal Ulster Rifles (formerly the Royal Irish Rifles), Irish Guards, North Irish Horse, 8th King's Royal Irish Hussars and the recently created 5th Royal Inniskilling Dragoon Guards, as well as in the London Irish Rifles and Liverpool Irish (both Territorial Army units), and in other units with past Irish links, such as the 4th/7th Royal Dragoon Guards and the 16th/5th Lancers. Also, service in the RAF — which had been in its infancy during the last year of the First World War — was very popular with the Irish during 1939–1945, often because it was seen as the most glamorous arm of the British forces, and because it allowed men to learn a technical trade which could prove useful in finding employment after the war.

Before we turn to the Irish reasons for joining, it is necessary that a few myths are dispelled. Firstly, no Irish person could be conscripted into the British forces during the Second World War without their consent — conscription was never introduced in Northern Ireland, and as for Irish people living in Britain, they could be called up for service, but if they were from Ireland, they were given a choice; they could either join the British forces as requested, or return home to Ireland. Therefore, they all had to volunteer freely.

Secondly, and far more importantly, the reason for joining up varied with each person. Irish Second World War soldiers, sailors and airmen did not *all* enlist in the British Army, Royal Navy or the Royal Air Force because they were penniless — because there were no jobs to be had in Ireland and because they had no other choice but to choose the British uniform. It is true that life in Ireland was tough at the time, but as the next few paragraphs will show, economic necessity was nowhere near the only factor that made men enter the recruiting offices.

George Francis Loughlin from Fermoy, County Cork had emigrated to England in 1932, aged sixteen, to start an apprenticeship as a carpenter with his uncle in Wiltshire — he had previously had a job emptying spittoons in the Fermoy TB hospital. When the war broke out, George saw it as an opportunity to see the world, travel, and experience adventure, so he enlisted in the army, going on to serve in the 7th Armoured Division (the famous 'Desert Rats') in North Africa. From nearby Limerick, Martin Lynch also joined for adventure, and as he recalled in a short memoir that he wrote for the Limerick branch of the Royal British Legion:

> I am unlikely to forget the date of my enlistment in the Royal Air Force, if only because it was my birthday, 20 October 1943. I was an enthusiastic eighteen at the time and long had ambitions to join after hearing stories from friends who might be called veterans ...

Family tradition also played a huge part in many men's decision to join. Given the fact that Irishmen had served with distinction in the British Army for as long as it had existed, with there being more Irish in the British Army than English, Scots and Welsh combined during certain periods of the nineteenth century, it was not unusual for many young Irishmen in 1939 to be descended from or related to soldiers who had fought in the Peninsular War, in the Crimea, in India, against the Boers in South Africa, or in the trenches of the

First World War. One such young Irishman was Patrick O'Hara from Cork city. His father was an old British soldier, and in 1942, he gave the seventeen-year-old Patrick the train fare from Cork to Belfast so he could enlist. Patrick wanted to do his bit, as his father had before him, and after lying about his age, Patrick joined the Royal Navy and served aboard HMS *Teviot* in the Atlantic, the Mediterranean, and in the Far East.

However, while there were those who were joining up, others were continuing on in uniform, or in some cases, even being recalled to active service. William Joseph 'Joe' Fleming – a former lobster fisherman from Dunmore East, County Waterford – was a merchant sailor when war broke out. The captain of the ship that Joe was currently on gave all the Irish crew members the option of leaving the ship (as southern Ireland was neutral), but the Irish sailors chose to remain on board. Joe Fleming later sailed in the Atlantic convoys, and also participated in rescuing British troops during the evacuation of Dunkirk.

Meanwhile, Christopher James 'Jimmy' McLoughlin from Enfield, County Meath, was a retired Royal Engineers sapper, First World War veteran and recipient of the Distinguished Conduct Medal (DCM) when the Second World War broke out. Aged forty-six in 1939 and then working in the post office engineering section in Edinburgh, Scotland, he was recalled to active service and served with the British Expeditionary Force (BEF) in France and Belgium before being evacuated at Dunkirk and going on to serve in North Africa where he contracted malaria. He survived the war and in 1953 – aged sixty – Jimmy finally retired from his work with the post office and returned home to live in Ireland, settling in Mullingar in 1954. Sadly however, veteran of two world wars and recipient of the DCM Christopher James 'Jimmy' McLoughlin did not get to enjoy his retirement for very long. He passed away on 25 June 1956 – aged sixty-three – and now lies buried in Ballyglass Cemetery, Mullingar.

For others, failing to get into (or stay in) the Irish Army, due to being underage, is what drove them north of the border to enlist in the British forces. After enlisting at Ballymullen Barracks in 1940 with a friend named Seamus Raymond, Anthony Moriarty from Tralee, County Kerry was thwarted by his mother – she went down to the barracks and spoke to an officer, a Captain Brown, and told him that her son and his friend were both sixteen and so underage. The pair were immediately discharged, but determined to experience the military life, they travelled to Northern Ireland and enlisted in the RAF. Seamus served as aircrew with RAF Bomber Command and survived the war, only to die in a plane crash in 1947 – while Anthony later transferred into the British Army and joined 3rd Irish Guards. Then, on 4 March 1945 – while north of Hamb, Germany – Anthony Moriarty was killed in action when his unit came under German machine gun and anti-tank fire (a comrade named Callaghan later visited Anthony's mother and explained that Anthony had been riding on a tank when it took a direct hit from a mortar shell. Callaghan assured Bridget Moriarty that her son had died instantly and had felt no pain). Anthony Moriarty was

The last photograph ever taken of Guardsman Anthony Moriarty from Tralee, County Kerry.

twenty-one years old when he died, and today lies buried in Reichswald Forest War Cemetery.

Of course, there were other serving soldiers in the Irish Army who deserted it or left it of their own free will. William Holohan from Athy, County Kildare was one such man. While serving in Renmore Barracks, Galway, he became friendly with a local girl named Peg. When she suddenly emigrated to England with a friend, William was determined to follow her. So he deserted the Irish Army, took the bus to Enniskillen, and joined the Royal Engineers. Within a week, he was back in touch with Peg and soon going out with her, and he went on to serve in the Middle East, North Africa, and France.

Other men deserted or left the Irish Defences Forces due to the (often only slightly) higher pay offered in the British forces, or due to the fact that – after being motivated to enlist by patriotism or a desire to defend Ireland from Nazi Germany – they were put to work cutting turf on the Irish bogs in an effort to save money for the government. Many viewed this as monotonous, boring, 'inglorious' work – and subsequently deserted to seek a more active role in stopping Hitler. In fact, approximately 5,500 Irish soldiers deserted the Irish Defence Forces during the war, the vast majority of them doing so in order to join the British forces.

Then there was conscription in the USA. Michael Rogers from Tulsk, County Roscommon – who was living in New Jersey when America entered the war – was conscripted into the US Army and landed on the Normandy beaches as part of the D-Day invasion, 6 June 1944. His family have a story of how, after being wounded, Michael saved an injured comrade from drowning that day by carrying him out of the sea while under fire – an act of bravery for which he was later decorated.

Mark Craig – while still a corporal – from Portnoo, County Donegal, and some comrades from Anti-Tank Company, 114th Infantry Regiment, US Army in France. Craig is seated centre with right hand on the sling of his rifle.

However, while many Irish were surely drafted into the US forces, many are known to have enlisted of their own free will. Mark Craig falls into this category. Originally from Portnoo, County Donegal – he enlisted in New York City and served as a technical sergeant with the 114th Infantry Regiment of the 44th Infantry Division in France. Craig commanded a gun crew in the regiment's Anti-Tank Company, and after landing in France in September 1944 he was subsequently engaged in heavy fighting in the Rhineland. Then – after several days of fierce battles against German panzers and panzergrenadiers in the vicinity of Schalbach, France – at approximately 0300hrs on 26 November 1944, the barn that Craig and his gun crew were sleeping in suffered a direct hit from enemy shellfire. Thirty-four-year-old Technical Sergeant Mark Craig was killed instantly and today lies buried in Epinal American Cemetery. He was posthumously awarded the Purple Heart.

As for economic necessity, this was obviously a factor which drove many to enlist, although it was not always because a man simply had no job. Sometimes, it was a cruel twist of fate that made a man suddenly poor, as was the case with Christopher Green. From Bow Street in Dublin, Christy was a sheep dealer who ran into debt when foot-and-mouth

Above*: Technical Sergeant Mark Craig's grave (closest on the right) in Epinal American Cemetery.*
Below*: Certificate of the awarding of a posthumous Purple Heart medal to Technical Sergeant Mark Craig.*

THE UNITED STATES OF AMERICA

TO ALL WHO SHALL SEE THESE PRESENTS, GREETING:

THIS IS TO CERTIFY THAT
THE PRESIDENT OF THE UNITED STATES OF AMERICA
PURSUANT TO AUTHORITY VESTED IN HIM BY CONGRESS
HAS AWARDED THE

PURPLE HEART

ESTABLISHED BY GENERAL GEORGE WASHINGTON
AT NEWBURGH, NEW YORK, AUGUST 7, 1782
TO

Technical Sergeant Marc J. Craig, A.S.No. 32002275,

FOR MILITARY MERIT AND FOR WOUNDS RECEIVED
IN ACTION

resulting in his death November 26, 1944.

OFFICIAL: GIVEN UNDER MY HAND IN THE CITY OF WASHINGTON
                   THIS   18th   DAY OF   January   19 45

                                                    Henry L. Stimson
MAJOR GENERAL   SECRETARY OF WAR
THE ADJUTANT GENERAL

disease broke out in Ireland. Owing money to the bank, he was forced to travel to Belfast to enlist. Nearly forty years old, he joined the Royal Artillery and was posted to Singapore by early 1942.

Finally, idealism and the knowledge that Nazism was a threat that must be stopped motivated many Irish to join the Allied forces. Michael Lehane, mentioned previously – the Spanish Civil War veteran who went on to serve with the Norwegian Merchant Navy – was one such man, but there were also others who did serve in British uniform, men like Raymond Wall from Loughrea, County Galway. Raymond served as a flight mechanic (engines) with RAF Bomber Command because:

> Those were different times then. They were dark times. There was an insidious evil
> rampaging across Europe, and decent men were needed to stop it.

Ultimately, the southern twenty-six counties of Ireland remained officially neutral during 1939–1945, a move made possible by Éamon de Valera and Fianna Fáil's various amendments to the Free State Constitution and then the introduction of a new Irish Constitution in 1937 – after which the Free State ceased to exist and the twenty-six counties became officially known as Ireland or Éire – along with the return of the Spike Island, Berehaven and Lough Swilly treaty ports to the Irish state and the ending of the Anglo-Irish Trade War (or 'Economic War') in 1938.

However, the purpose of this book is not to debate the subject of Irish neutrality, or focus on the experiences of soldiers in the Irish Army, Navy or Air Corps, but to remember the Irish who served in the combatant armies of the Second World War, as it is their stories that have largely gone untold.

Alongside the individuals mentioned in this introduction (whose full stories are told in later chapters), there were other Irish links to the Second World War and to the personalities and events of 1939–1945. Hitler might not have even been alive by the time of the Second World War if it was not for the actions of Irishman Michael Keogh. From Tullow, County Carlow, Michael Keogh was a great-nephew of Myles Keogh – Colonel Custer's second-in-command who was killed along with him at the Battle of the Little Bighorn in 1876. By the time of the First World War, Michael Keogh was a soldier in the Royal Irish Regiment, having previously served in the US Army. He was captured by the Germans during the early years of the war, and then volunteered (one of only fifty-three men to do so) to serve in Roger Casement's Irish Brigade of POWs that would return to Ireland and fight in the upcoming Easter Rising. Keogh was a man with strong republican views, but after the Germans decided to scrap the idea of an Irish Brigade, Keogh joined the German Army. He fought on the German side for the rest of the war, staying in the German military after the armistice was declared.

As his memoir *With Casement's Irish Brigade* recalled, in 1919, now a captain in the

German Army, Keogh 'was the officer of the day in the Turken Strasse barracks [Munich] when I got an urgent call at about eight in the evening. A riot had broken out over two political agents in the gymnasium. These "political officers" were allowed to approach the men for votes and support. I ordered out a sergeant and six men and, with fixed bayonets, led them off. There were about 200 men in the gymnasium, among them some tough Tyrolean troops ... Bayonets were beginning to flash ... The two on the floor were in danger of being kicked to death. I ordered the guard to fire one round over the heads of the rioters. It stopped the commotion ... The crowd around muttered and growled, boiling for blood ...' One of the two politicians who had suffered the wrath of the mob was Adolf Hitler. Although cut, bleeding and beaten, he was still alive, having been saved by Michael Keogh.

Then there was Irish communist John Desmond Bernal – from Nenagh, County Tipperary – who was responsible for mapping the D-Day beaches and for developing the artificial 'Mulberry' harbours which allowed the Allies to pour men, vehicles and supplies into France in the immediate aftermath of the invasion, while Irish playwright Samuel Beckett was involved with the French Resistance during the war – earning the *Croix de Guerre* and the *Médaille de la Résistance*.

Finally, the last battle ever fought against a foreign invader on mainland British soil was fought by the 1st London Irish Rifles against the crew of a downed German Junkers JU 88 bomber on 27 September 1940 in Kent, in an event that became known as the Battle of Graveney Marsh.

Irish-born fighter pilots flew in the Battle of Britain. Eight Irishmen also won the Victoria Cross – Britain and the Commonwealth's highest award for valour in the face of the enemy – and out of these eight, seven were from, or had strong family links to, the south. There was an Irishman who helped train the famous Easy Company of the 506th Parachute Infantry Regiment (PIR), 101st Airborne Division, and another who was decorated and earned a battlefield commission fighting the Japanese on Guadalcanal and Cape Gloucester while serving in the United States Marine Corps (USMC).

Meanwhile, 634,000 Irish emigrated to Britain during the war or in the immediate post-war years in order to work as munitions workers or in other war-related industries, as construction workers and labourers in the rebuilding of destroyed cities, or as nurses in the military and civilian hospitals.

Irishmen also worked as 'Bevin Boys' – named after Ernest Bevin, the wartime British Minister of Labour and National Service. They were men who initially volunteered for or were conscripted into the Armed Forces, but who were then trained as miners (though some did volunteer) and sent down the English coalmines in order to meet the demand for fuel.

The Germans tried to decorate some Irish with medals; others were executed by the

SS. There were Irishmen who lost limbs, who were starved and tortured as POWs, and thousands who lost their lives. Irish minorities also fought to stop the Axis forces – including Irish Jews and Irish travellers. There were young men who had never seen war before, and older men who had previously served in the trenches or who had fought in Spain. Others served in the new special forces Commando units, Special Boat Section (SBS), or the Special Air Service (SAS) – the legendary Lieutenant-Colonel Robert Blair 'Paddy' Mayne from Newtownards, County Down was one of the earliest members of the latter; his amazing story has filled several books by itself – and one of the most incredible spies of the Second World War was Maureen Patricia 'Paddy' O'Sullivan, a woman from Dublin who parachuted into France in March 1944.

The Irish were involved in the D-Day landings of 6 June 1944; they served in every major land campaign in Europe; they fought in the deserts of North Africa against Rommel and the Afrika Korps, and in the jungles of Asia and the Pacific against the Japanese and against the disease and rot of those tropical places; as sailors they hunted enemy vessels and protected convoys in U-Boat infested waters; as airmen they defended Britain and attacked the Germans behind their lines; while thousands suffered in POW camps around the world.

The stories of the fighting Irish, those 'decent men', are all contained in the pages of this book as a tribute to their memory and to their sacrifices.

May we never forget what they did for us.

Happening all over again: 17 October 1939, looking almost indistinguishable from their First World War counterparts, 1ˢᵗ Royal Ulster Rifles march, in the pouring rain, through Gavrelle – scene of intense fighting during 1917.

CHAPTER 1

ONCE MORE UNTO THE BREACH

– THE BATTLE OF FRANCE AND THE DUNKIRK EVACUATION

'I wouldn't mind it a bit if it weren't for the damn rain & mud. I
heard about it from fellows in the last war,
but seeing is believing.'
**Technical Sergeant Mark Craig from Portnoo,
County Donegal, 114th Infantry Regiment, US Army.
Letter to his mother, 23 October 1944**

Within a month of the war breaking out, the Polish military had suffered 904,000 casualties – nearly seventy-seven percent of which had been taken POW – and the country had fallen to the Nazis and the Soviets. Back in Ireland, on 3 September, the Irish government introduced the Emergency Powers Act 1939, having declared a state of emergency in the country two days earlier. Determined to preserve Irish neutrality, the Act introduced government censorship of the media and of mail, gave the State control over the economy, ordered the compulsory farming of land, and gave the Garda Síochána (Irish police) new powers of search, arrest and internment. Petrol rationing was also introduced and air raid sirens were soon set up by Dublin Corporation across the city. Meanwhile, in Britain, as preparations were made for the German air raids that would surely come soon, night-time blackouts were ordered, hospitals across the country were told to expect 1 million casualties in the next two months, and 1.5 million women and children were evacuated from the major cities. Three British Army divisions were immediately shipped over to France – the second BEF (British Expeditionary Force) to land there in twenty-five years, which included many Irishmen – and by October, the total number of British troops in France was 158,000.

But nothing happened. With their focus still on Poland, the Nazis did not rush west to attack France or Britain, and paralysed by memories of the First World War, the British and the French did not go on the offensive. Both nations were actually fearful of provoking the Nazis, even though they currently outnumbered and outgunned the German Army in the West. And so, while 500,000 French soon manned the Maginot Line – the most sophisticated line of forts ever constructed – which defended France's border with Germany from

Belgium to Switzerland, the BEF – assuming that when the German attack finally came, it would come through northern Belgium as it had during the last war – dug in on the Belgian border and waited. And still nothing happened, creating a period that has become known as the 'Phoney War'.

However, back in Ireland, the war made itself known very quickly. The survivors of SS *Athenia* – the first British ship to be torpedoed by a German U-boat during the Second World War – were landed in Galway, soon after the vessel sunk on 4 September. A week later on 11 September, a ship actually flying the Irish tricolour – the tanker *Inverliffey*, en route from Trinidad to Coryton Refinery in Essex – was shelled and sunk by *U-38*. However, what probably prevented this event being seen as an act of aggression towards the Irish State was the fact that, unbeknownst to the German U-boat commander, the *Inverliffey* had actually been transferred from the Irish registry of ships to the British registry two days before the sinking. And so, although the ship had still been flying the Irish tricolour, she had technically been a British vessel.

Christmas 1939 came, and there was still no activity in France. In Ireland pro-Nazi elements of the IRA – who ultimately hoped to see a German landing in Ireland, along with German assistance in retaking the six counties of Northern Ireland – stole approximately 1 million rounds of ammunition from the national arsenal in the Phoenix Park, Dublin, on 23 December. This element of the IRA would come to represent a serious concern for the Irish government as the war progressed; they were a very real threat to Irish neutrality (the IRA had previously declared war on Britain in January 1939, and the same month that the war broke out – August 1939 – an IRA bomb in Coventry killed five and injured sixty).

1940 finally brought the British Army into contact with the German Army, although not initially in France. Britain, along with French and Polish forces, invaded Norway on 9 April – the British forces included 1st Irish Guards – to try and stop the flow of iron ore from Sweden that was being sent to Germany through Norwegian ports. It was seen as a peripheral battle – one that might not incur the full wrath of the German Army – but the operation was a disaster. Poor equipment, bad preparation, and lack of air support resulted in just under 4,500 British casualties in two months, and after lists of the Irish dead from the Norwegian Campaign appeared in the papers back in Ireland, the Irish government banned the media from publishing any further mentions of Irish war dead (from then on, when the names of Irish soldiers killed in the war appeared in the papers, it was stated that they died while 'working in Britain'). The Allies would finally evacuate Norway on 8 June 1940.

Then word started spreading in France of an impending German attack. These reports were immediately ignored, simply because they claimed that the Germans were not planning to come through northern Belgium – they were planning to come through the supposedly impenetrable Ardennes Forest to the south. A further intelligence report even included a date of attack – 10 May 1940. It too was ignored.

On that exact day, the Western Front was opened when the Germans invaded Luxembourg, Holland, Belgium and France. This effectively ended the Phoney War and started what became known as the Battle of France. To the Allies, it looked as though they had been right all along – the main German thrust was coming from the north, not through the Ardennes. The ten divisions of the BEF (it now numbered 316,000 men), and France's forty best divisions, were ordered to enter Belgium immediately. Meanwhile, the *Luftwaffe* took to the air, and while Allied aircraft were busy supporting the push into Belgium, the German pilots attacked Allied airfields behind the lines, destroying Allied planes on the ground. At the same time, in the Ardennes, forty-five German divisions – including the 41,000 vehicles of Kleist's Panzer Group (1ˢᵗ Panzer Army) – began making its way through the forest and towards France. By 12 May, the lead elements were through and had reached the banks of the River Meuse. This area – having been considered impenetrable – was defended by the weakest and poorest equipped of France's divisions. Within a few days, the German's panzers were across the Meuse and were pouring into France. Within a week, they have advanced over 200 miles.

It was not long before word reached the BEF in Belgium that they had been lured into a trap. The real battle had been far to the south of them, and now the Germans were in France and were approaching them from the rear. As 12 million refugees fled in the face of the German invasion, the BEF knew that they had to withdraw. There was no chance of performing another feat like the 1914 Battle of the Marne – when the British and French had stopped the German advance on Paris and sent the Kaiser's men retreating back towards Belgium. Now, in 1940, the Nazis had the BEF cut off from the rest of France, so the only option was to evacuate.

THE BATTLE OF FRANCE

A CRUEL TWIST OF FATE

JOSEPH FAHY

Joseph Fahy was born in September 1919 in Rahan, County Offaly. He came from a farming background and his father, Thomas, had died when Joseph was only ten years old (he had also lost a brother, Bryan, in infancy). The family home was right beside the local bog and they 'burned bricks' at the back of the house, meaning they had a brick kiln. The bricks that they made were known as 'Pullough Yellow-Brick', named after a nearby town. With the Grand Canal not far away, the Fahys used to ship the brick by barge to Dublin.

In adult life, Joseph Fahy and his older brother Matthew drove a turf delivery truck for a living. One day in Ballyboy, near Kilcormac, Joseph crashed into a cow with his truck. The cow died, and Joseph was forced to sell his truck to pay the farmer – a man named Lynch – for damages (ironically, the relative who provided me with Joseph's story – Carmel Lynch nee Fahy, Joseph's niece – says that she would never have met her husband if it was not for Joseph Fahy crashing into the Lynch's cow in the late 1930s and putting the two families in contact). With his livelihood gone, Joseph was forced to emigrate to England to get work. Then, when Germany invaded Poland – 1 September 1939 – and it seemed as though it would only be a matter of days before Britain would be at war, Joseph enlisted in the army and soon ended up serving as a private in the 2nd Royal Warwickshire Regiment.

This unit was part of 144th Infantry Brigade, 48th (South Midland) Infantry Division – one of the BEF divisions in France by 1940.

Private Joseph Fahy, 2nd Royal Warwickshire Regiment, from Rahan, County Offaly. He took up boxing when he enlisted – a sport that was extremely popular in the army. On 15 January 1940, with Joseph in France, his mother died back home in Ireland. His family made the decision not to inform Joseph about his mother's death and he was probably still unaware of it by the time the Germans finally invaded France.

When the Germans finally invaded on 10 May, Private Joseph Fahy and 2nd Royal Warwickshire Regiment initially advanced into Belgium, but then four days later, on 14 May, they received the first of many subsequent orders to withdraw. The Allies had finally realised that the real German threat was far to the south, and as Joseph and his comrades fell back towards France, they soon came under attack from the enemy, while also having to deal with possible German spies in the villages through which they were retreating. By 22 May, the exhausted battalion had returned to France but they still had no idea what was really going on.

However, while southwest of Lille – as recorded in the battalion war diary (a day-to-day account of a unit's activities):

> Column was halted just before Seclin and told that immediately on arrival at
> Aubers, orders would be received to proceed direct to Dunkirk. This was a shock.

The order had been given to evacuate France, but while 2nd Royal Warwickshire Regiment initially began to head north towards the Dunkirk beaches, on 26 May 1940 – after nine days of retreating – Private Joseph Fahy and his comrades were instructed to turn and make a stand at Wormhoudt, twelve miles south of Dunkirk. The Dunkirk evacuation had already begun, and since Wormhoudt was on the main road to Dunkirk, the British had to prevent German panzers from getting onto the road and reaching the beaches for as long as they could. And so, the various companies of the 2nd Royal Warwickshire Regiment dug in to the west of Wormhoudt.

On 28 May, elements of the 3rd Panzer Division and 2nd Battalion of the 1st Waffen-SS Division *Leibstandarte Adolf Hitler* – Hitler's personal SS bodyguard – attacked the 2nd Royal Warwickshire Regiment. The fighting was intense and as an intelligence summary for the battle recorded:

> Enemy attacked with large numbers of tanks from every direction. Tanks were large
> and were closely followed, and in many cases, actually accompanied by infantry. Tanks
> advanced at a slow pace firing continually with machine guns using tracer bullets, and
> also from a larger gun firing small shells ... Infantry attacked in large numbers, and,
> in some cases, shoulder to shoulder. In rear they were urged on by the cry of 'Heil
> Hitler!' Large numbers were undoubtedly mown down by our fire. At one point a
> charge was made with fixed bayonets ... Many of the enemy were dressed in civilian
> clothes, others wore uniform of the British, French and Belgian armies. As they came
> they shouted 'Hullo, boys! We're here! Don't fire!'

Ultimately, the British had to retreat northwards, but many from the 2nd Royal Warwickshire Regiment – along with others from the Cheshire Regiment, Royal Artillery, and some French troops – were surrounded and forced to surrender to the Germans. However, incorrectly believing that his divisional commander had been killed in the battle, SS-*Hauptsturmführer* Wilhelm Mohnke – commanding officer of the 2nd Battalion of the 1st Waffen-SS

Division *Leibstandarte Adolf Hitler* – ordered that the prisoners, totalling 100 men, be packed tight into a tiny cowshed nearby. He then had twelve of his soldiers throw five grenades into the barn. The grenades exploded in amongst the terrified crowd of men, killing many of them instantly. Chaos soon erupted, with two prisoners – Captain John Lynn-Allen and the badly injured Private Bert Evans, whose arm had nearly been severed by one of the grenade explosions – making a run for it (Captain Lynn-Allen was caught and executed minutes later while Private Evans survived to be recaptured). As some SS soldiers pursued the escapees, others grabbed ten of the survivors in the barn, dragged them outside, and shot them in the back. The SS then started firing wildly at the remaining survivors in the cowshed. Once finished, they simply walked away.

In all, eighty-five men had been murdered in cold blood – in an event that became known as the Wormhoudt Massacre. Three days after the killings, it was discovered that fifteen of the 100 men in the barn were still alive (there had been other survivors, but they had died after three days without medical attention). These men were immediately removed and their wounds were tended to, but unfortunately, Private Joseph Fahy from Rahan, County Offaly was not one of them. Having survived the retreat from Belgium and the Battle of Wormhoudt, he had died, along with eighty-four other men, in or around the cowshed – a victim of either German grenade or bullet. He was only twenty-one years old, and he died never knowing that his mother had passed away back home in Ireland in January. However, Joseph was not the only Irishman to die while serving in 2nd Royal Warwickshire Regiment during the Battle of Wormhoudt, and twenty-three-year-old Private Thomas Hanna from Billy, County Antrim was also killed during the fighting. With no known grave, today he is commemorated on the Dunkirk Memorial. Meanwhile, Joseph Fahy's remains lie in Wormhoudt Communal Cemetery, buried alongside his murdered comrades.

TO SLOW THE ENEMY ADVANCE

HUBERT 'PAT' BARRON

Irish airmen were also involved in the Battle of France, and one man whose war effectively started and stopped with the opening of the battle was Sergeant Hubert 'Pat' Barron. Pat was born in 1917 in Swansea, Wales to Irish parents. That same year, his father was seriously wounded on the Western Front, and then in 1919, Pat's mother passed away. A few years later, with Pat's father finding it hard to cope with two young children, Pat and his sister were sent to live with their grandparents in Ireland. And so, Pat grew up in Ballinameela, County Waterford – situated about halfway between Cappoquin and Dungarvan.

In later life, Pat wrote a privately published memoir, called *At the Going Down of the Sun*, and in it he recalled:

> One of my childhood memories during this time, was of sitting on my grandpa's shoulders at early nightfall and staring in awe at the towering flames, as the police barracks in Cappoquin burned to the ground ... My grandfather referred to those episodes as 'The Troubles'.

As a teenager, Pat developed a passion for airplanes:

> I read – perhaps 'devoured' is a more accurate word – every story in any magazine I could find which dealt with the airplane. I revered the great aces of WWI; Bishop, Mannock, Richtofen, Collishaw, Cobham, and others ... Then it happened! National Aviation Day was announced to be coming to Dungarvan, Co. Waterford, Ireland. Newspaper banner headline, street banners, and many pamphlets spelled out that Sir Alan Cobham was bringing his 'Aviation Circus' to town, on the 14th September 1933 ... It was Indian Summer weather and I was 16 years old. On that day in the meadow beside the river in Dungarvan, a young boy's dream came true. Even though I did not have the five shillings for a flight, I could see and feel that I was there ... 'I danced the skies on laughter-silvered wings' along with the intrepid 'bird men'. My decision for my future was firmed, come what may, I would be an air pilot.

Pat's father thought he was mad. "'What, join the Royal Flying Corps and break your ruddy neck?" From the trenches of WWI dad had watched the RFC and *Luftwaffe* pilots crash and "break their ruddy necks"'. But Pat was determined, and so, needing high marks in his leaving certificate exams in order to be accepted into RAF pilot training, Pat began studying hard. Two years later, in 1935, he applied to join the RAF and was accepted – he began flight training on 17 July 1936, aged nineteen, at Yatesbury in Wiltshire.

Pat initially learned to fly in a de Havilland DH 82 Tiger Moth, before going on to fly Hawker Hart, Audax and Fury aircraft, and graduated from flight school on 25 May 1937. He was posted to No 226 Bomber Squadron RAF, stationed at the recently opened RAF Harwell in Berkshire, and soon found himself flying Fairey Battle aircraft, a two-seater light bomber. In 1938 he married and then in July 1939, Pat and his wife had a daughter. Two months later, Britain was at war.

No 226 Bomber Squadron RAF departed RAF Harwell on 2 September 1939 bound for Reims. The following day, Britain declared war on Germany. No 226 Bomber Squadron RAF was therefore one of the original squadrons attached to the BEF, and formed No 72 Wing of the Advanced Air Striking Force.

> [During the Phoney War] the freezing, dreary first months of 1940 kept us grounded for days. During that period, the squadron received a special assignment from On High. We were ordered to initiate and complete a Line-Overlap series of photographs of a portion of the Rhine River. Intelligence had provided information re heavy barge

traffic on that part of the river. The supplies were originating from neutral Switzerland for shipment to the Ruhr industrial area. Based on the photo evidence, decisions would be made if the shipping traffic should be bombed.

When the Battle of France finally began on 10 May 1940, the sixteen planes of No 226 Bomber Squadron RAF were still based at Reims. They were ordered to slow the German advance by bombing motor transport columns and any other targets of tactical value, but before Sergeant Pat Barron could even get into an aircraft and into the air, the *Luftwaffe* began attacking Allied airbases.

The noise of bursting bombs, anti-aircraft fire, exploding aircraft and petrol tankers, along with the ripping, chattering sound of machine-gun and cannon fire was sometimes deafening. Pillars of smoke rose into the sky from aircraft and tankers burning on the ground. Vapour trails and the black smoke of falling aircraft formed strange patterns, crisscrossing the blue summer sky.

Fairey Battles *of Sergeant Hubert 'Pat' Barron's No 226 Bomber Squadron RAF undergoing servicing on the flight line at Reims-Champagne. The aircraft on the right, K9183 MQ-R, was shot down by ground fire – while flying at an altitude of only five feet – during an attack against enemy columns south-west of Luxembourg on 10 May 1940, in which Pat Barron also took part. The pilot died of his wounds, but the other two crew members survived.*

Shortly after noon, the air raids let up and the 'Battles' with delayed-action bombs in the bomb bays, started taking off in pairs for assigned targets to the northeast. No fighters could be spared for escort ... As we sped over the lush meadows and woods of north-eastern France at tree-top height, our grey-green aircraft blended with the terrain. Not to be seen was our one and only defence from the faster, superior gunned and more manoeuvrable Luftwaffe fighters.

Soon in sight of Luxembourg city, Pat's plane came under intense enemy anti-aircraft fire and Flight Lieutenant Brian Kerridge's plane (Pat's flight commander) was shot down. As Pat recalled, an 'ugly orange blossom of fire grew on Brian's left wing, and they crashed onto the field ahead, ploughing into the hedgerow of a suburban garden'. Unbeknownst to Pat, Kerridge and his crew survived the crash. However, Kerridge died five days later in a Luxembourg hospital. He was twenty-seven years old.

Pat's was now the only British plane left in the air, and after being wounded by ground fire just above his left knee, he suddenly spotted his target, 'a column of enemy tanks and armoured vehicles on a road east of the city'. He armed his bombs, dived on the lead vehicle – firing the Fairey Battle's machine guns as he went – and released his payload of bombs before circling around the column to strafe it with more machine gun fire. Soon low on ammunition, but with 'at least two or three tanks and some other vehicles ... blazing and out of action', Pat turned back for Reims. However, he soon began to feel faint from blood loss.

When Pat finally spotted Champagne Airport at Reims and brought his plane in to land, 'the undercarriage collapsed [on touchdown], and we skidded along on the belly in a huge cloud of dust ... we came literally to a "screeching halt".' Fire engines and ambulances rushed over to his plane and Pat was pulled from the cockpit as his fellow crewmembers jumped out and ran for safety. 'As we ran, now dragged along by two others, I heard and felt the explosion, as the aircraft burst into flames ... Then all went black for me.'

Pat woke up in Epernay, France, with an Irish surgeon looking down on him and smiling. A few days later, when the British had no choice but to start evacuating their forces from France, Pat was moved to a hospital in England, and so avoided being taken POW by the Germans. Having the stitches in his leg removed too early – which made the wound tear open – Pat was still in hospital when he learned that he had been awarded the Distinguished Flying Medal. The citation appeared in the *London Gazette* on 7 June 1940 and read:

In May, 1940, this airman was the leader of a half section of aircraft engaged on a low-level bombing attack against enemy columns advancing through Luxemburg. In spite of exceptionally heavy opposition by enemy machine gun and pom-pom fire he pressed home his attack and all his bombs were observed to burst on or near the target. During this attack Sergeant Barron was wounded, but he brought his aircraft and crew back safely.

Once Pat had recovered to the point where he only needed a walking stick to help him move about (having previously been wheelchair-bound and then reliant on crutches), he travelled to Hove – a town just west of Brighton in East Sussex – and was reunited with his wife and daughter. They had moved to Hove after Pat had been deployed to France in September 1939. However, a Nazi invasion of southern England was now a genuine possibility, and so Pat soon moved his family to live with friends in Oxford. Then, one day before Pat left Hove himself, he was sitting alone in a local pub when another man walked in. The man looked somehow familiar to Pat, and when the barmaid went over to serve him, the newcomer asked her a question while looking in Pat's direction. The barmaid then came over to Pat, and told him that this man would like to speak to him.

When Pat approached, the man began:

'Excuse my appearance. I've just come off night duty. Home Guard, y'know. Now I know better than to ask questions, but these I must. Were you in France?'

'Yes, sir!' [replied Pat]

'Were you flying Battles?'

'Yes, sir!'

His hand began to tremble and he placed it on the polished mahogany bar top and he grasped it, before asking the next question. 'Did you, by chance, know Brian Kerridge?'

'Yes, sir! I did.'

'How well?'

'We flew together. I was his No. 2.'

His mouth was visibly working, as he asked the next question. 'Did you see him go?'

'Yes, sir.'

'Is there any hope?'

'No. I'm afraid not, sir.'

'I ... I am ... Brian Kerridge's father.' The tears streamed down his face. He shook my hand. He tried to say 'thank you' but could not. Turning he walked, stoop-shouldered, slowly out the door. I had never seen him before. I have not seen him since.

During the Battle of Britain – in which the *Luftwaffe* tried to pave the way for a German invasion of Britain, but were beaten back by the RAF – Pat was near RAF Biggin Hill in Bromley, London when it was bombed on 31 August 1940. He witnessed British and German planes fighting in the skies above the base. Following this, in October 1940, Pat was posted to RAF Netheravon in Wiltshire as a flight instructor. Pilots in combat had a life expectancy of fifty hours, and for this reason the RAF were unwilling to risk the lives of the few experienced pilots they had left, so Pat was put to work training new pilots in order to help bring the RAF back up to strength.

After transferring to RAF Peterborough, Cambridgeshire, in January 1941, Pat was soon sent across the Atlantic to Kingston, Ontario in Canada, as part of the British Commonwealth Air Training Plan. With Britain considered a potentially unsafe place to train pilots, men were sent to safer skies in Commonwealth countries in order to earn their wings, and men like Sergeant Pat Barron were sent to train them. His family soon followed him.

By mid-1942, Pat was a flight officer, and now an instructor at the No 34 Operational Training Unit in Penfield Ridge, New Brunswick, where he instructed on heavy twin-engine aircraft. Early the following year, he was promoted to flight lieutenant and sent to Ferry Command, Dorval, Montreal, 'the base from which the large aircraft made in Canada and the USA were flown across the Atlantic Ocean to the U.K. Squadrons ... It was an airman's dream come true. On the Tarmac were "Lancasters", "Liberators", "Fortresses", "Mosquitoes", "Mitchells", "Venturas", "Hudsons", "Dakotas" (DC-3s), and "Baltimores" – all for delivery across the Atlantic Ocean.'

In between his subsequent delivery trips across the Atlantic, and then some flights across the Pacific, Pat was given the job of flying (Royal Canadian Air Force) Air Marshal William Avery 'Billy' Bishop from Montreal to Nassau. During the First World War, Bishop had been Canada's top fighter ace, and he was one of Pat's boyhood heroes. 'I told him how, as a boy, I read about him and his great achievements. He smiled and asked what my plans were for the future. I told him I hoped to fly long distance on the International airlines.'

Finally, in 1945, Pat was sent as part of an RAF detachment to Pacific Ferry, Lindbergh Field, San Diego, California. The detachment's main role was to deliver B-24 Liberator aircraft to Australia. Pat, now aged twenty-eight, was still at this station when the war ended.

Post-war, Pat flew for several international airline companies, then in 1960 – while flying for Seven Seas Airlines – he returned to Luxembourg for the first time since 1940 and the Battle of France. 'The memories flooded back as if it had all happened the previous week.' After visiting two local war cemeteries, Pat had another chance encounter while 'sipping on a beer in [a] cafe'. A young man – who had obviously learned about Pat's history – approached Pat, introduced himself, and then went on to tell Pat that, back when he had been a boy in 1940, he and his sister had helped pull the fatally injured Brian Kerridge and his crew from their crashed Fairey Battle after it was shot down on 10 May. In fact, the plane had actually crashed into this man's front garden. Pat was stunned, and was then brought by this local man to see Brian Kerridge's grave in Luxembourg (Hollerich) Communal Cemetery.

Pat later found himself in the Congo, in late 1960, and during this time he flew Dr Conor Cruise O'Brien – Ireland's special representative to the Secretary General of the United Nations – on several occasions. Then, when nine Irish soldiers were killed in Niemba, Northern Katanga on 8 November 1960 – the first Irish Defence Forces peacekeepers to die on active service – Pat ignored his bosses' demands to return with his aircraft to Luxembourg.

Instead, he remained behind, at the request of an Irish Army officer, in order to fly the bodies of the nine dead soldiers back to Ireland. As Pat recalled:

> The caskets were loaded, and we took off for Dublin, Ireland. It was night when we landed at Baldonnel Airport, and it was raining heavily ... in keeping with the sad occasion. Over 7,000 mourners, sheltering under their black umbrellas, gave witness to the national grief.

After seven years living in Mondorf-les-Bains, Luxembourg, while working for Seven Seas Airlines, Pat Barron and his family returned to live permanently in Canada. On 10 September 1994 – the fiftieth anniversary of Luxembourg's liberation from the Nazis – seventy-seven-year-old Pat was invited back to Luxembourg as an official guest for the celebrations. At the same time, he was made a *Citoyen d'Honneur* of Mondorf-les-Bains, in recognition of his wartime service to the country. In fact, during the commemoration ceremony, when Pat and other veterans were formed up to be reviewed by the Grand Duke and Grand Duchess of Luxembourg, the Grand Duchess stopped and spoke to Pat, discovering that he had first flown over the country on 10 May 1940. "'But that was the first day of our being invaded. We called, and they [the RAF] came ...'"

Ninety-four-year-old Hubert 'Pat' Barron is now retired, and at the time of writing, he still lives in his adopted home of Canada.

DUNKIRK

THE CHOICE

WILLIAM JOSEPH 'JOE' FLEMING

Born in November 1913, William Joseph 'Joe' Fleming – along with his two brothers, John and James – had worked as a lobster fisherman in his native Dunmore East, County Waterford, before all three of them joined the Merchant Navy (Cunard Line) some time before the outbreak of the Second World War. Joe's early claim to fame was that he had a cousin named Ryan who had been a steward aboard the *Carpathia* on the night that she had picked up survivors from the *Titanic*.

In the months leading up to the war, Joe sailed almost exclusively aboard the *Aquitania* on voyages between Southampton and New York, and he was at sea aboard the *Aquitania* when word reached the ship that Britain was now at war with Germany. The ship was to join the war effort, but as Ireland was remaining neutral, the Irish crewmen could choose to leave. The ship's captain assembled the Irish crewmembers and gave them the choice:

'Any man that wishes to leave should take one step forward.' None of the Irish crew took the captain up on his offer; they all decided to stay onboard.

Aquitania went on to serve as a troop transport in the Far East while Joe Fleming – aged twenty-five – was transferred to the *St Julien*, a former Weymouth-Channel Islands ferry owned by Great Western Railway, now a hospital carrier. During the period of the Phoney War, Joe made trips aboard the *St Julien* to France, evacuating sick troops back to England. Then, on 29 May 1940, two days after the evacuations from Dunkirk had begun, *St Julien* was involved in the rescue operation – codenamed Operation Dynamo. While thousands of British and French troops were wading out to sea from the Dunkirk beaches – in order to be ferried out to waiting larger vessels – and others were being picked up by the 700-strong famous flotilla of 'little ships of Dunkirk', others were being evacuated straight onto the larger vessels via Dunkirk harbour. En route to Dunkirk harbour, the crew of the *St Julien* suddenly spotted a *Luftwaffe* bomber diving on their position. As Captain Richardson of the *St Julien* ordered evasive action, the German pilot strafed the ship with machine gun fire and dropped two bombs towards the hospital carrier – which was painted white with giant red crosses to mark her as a non-combatant. The bombs missed the vessel, though they

Men of the Royal Ulster Rifles awaiting evacuation at Bray Dunes about five miles from Dunkirk, 26–29 May 1940.

detonated in the sea very close by. The *Luftwaffe* bomber circled back around to strafe again and drop the rest of his bomb payload. The bombs dropped on the second run also missed the *St Julien* – although the ship rocked from the nearby explosions.

Regarding the attack, WJR Gardner – in the book, *The Evacuation from Dunkirk: Operation Dynamo, 26 May–4 June 1940* – recorded:

> At 1700 also, the H/C [Hospital Carrier] *St. Julien, en route* for Dunkirk harbour, was deliberately bombed 'for a considerable period' in the vicinity of Nieuport Bank buoy; she was slightly damaged by near misses. The *St. Julien* lay off Dunkirk harbour for about ½ an hour waiting for an opportunity to enter; when air attacks recommenced, however, she sailed for Dover without having entered the harbour.

That day, the *St Julien* made six trips to and from Dunkirk harbour. However, on four of these six trips, they were unable to get near the harbour and therefore unable to load any casualties. But on the other two trips, the ship sailed back to England with its decks packed with wounded soldiers – men who might have ended up as POWs, or perhaps died, if it was not for the *St Julien* (Joe Fleming sailed to Dunkirk five more times aboard the *St Julien* during Operation Dynamo – which made eleven trips in all for him – and on one trip he had a chance meeting with his brother, James). 47,310 troops were rescued from Dunkirk that day, 29 May 1940 – 338,226 soldiers in total (198,229 British and 139,997 French) by the end of the evacuation on 3 June. It was an operation that saved the veteran core of the British Army from annihilation.

As for Joe Fleming, he was soon transferred off the *St Julien* – in fact, his transfer took place before the Dunkirk evacuation had even ended. On 1 June 1940, he left the hospital carrier and ended up being reassigned to the *Empress of Canada* – a troopship that carried ANZAC (Australia and New Zealand Army Corps) troops to Europe. Joe was still serving aboard her on 13 March 1943 when the *Empress of Canada* was torpedoed and sunk by the Italian submarine *Leonardo Da Vinci* while 400 miles south of Cape Palmas, Liberia. There were 1,800 people on board, 392 of whom died in the sinking. Ironically, nearly fifty percent of those killed were Italian POWs.

Joe Fleming spent three days floating in the water before he was rescued. In order to recover from his ordeal, he was sent to a rest camp in South Africa for a month. When he was well enough to sail again, he joined the crew of the *Queen Mary*. Joe remained aboard this vessel until well after the end of the war – he stayed in the Merchant Navy after the fighting ended – and one of his memories of his time aboard the *Queen Mary* was of transporting thousands of American soldiers over to Europe in the lead up to D-Day. By the time he retired in 1967, Joe was a bosun and had also sailed aboard the *Queen Elizabeth*, *Ascania*, *Scythia*, *Saxonia*, *Carmania*, and *Sylvania* – the latter being the last Cunard vessel ever built for transatlantic crossings. Aged fifty-three, Joe retired to live in Southampton, and as his son Edward recalled, 'He used to become very upset talking about the war because he had lost so many friends and "so many good men" during those years.'

William Joseph 'Joe' Fleming lived in Southampton for the rest of his life. He died in 2004, aged ninety.

PLAYING POSSUM

WILLIAM JOHN 'JOHN PAT' McCREADY

One man who actually stood on the Dunkirk beaches was William John McCready from Lurgan, County Armagh. Born to a Protestant father and a Catholic mother, McCready was raised a Catholic. Because of this, and with Lurgan being a nationalist town within Northern Ireland, he never went by the name William and instead preferred to be called 'John Pat'. However, his Catholic and nationalist background did not stop him from joining the British Army as a young man, and when the Second World War broke out, John Pat was a Fusilier (Private) in the 2nd Royal Inniskilling Fusiliers. One of the few Irish units which comprised the BEF, when the Battle of France began the 2nd Royal Inniskilling Fusiliers were a part of 13th Infantry Brigade, 5th Infantry Division.

After days of retreating, John Pat was one of a group of soldiers who finally made it to the Dunkirk beaches where they would hopefully be evacuated back to Britain. John Pat remembered that, when he first arrived at the beaches, there was no enemy to be seen, but, before long, German Messerschmitt Bf109s (also known as Me109s) appeared in the skies overhead. A formation of three enemy fighters dived low and performed a flypast of the beach, but did not fire. However, once they had finished their run, they circled back around and lined themselves back up with the beach. This time, they raked the sand with their 20mm cannons – flying so low and close that John Pat could see the pilot of one of the planes turning his head to look at the men on the beach as he swooped past.

It was chaos on the beach. With no British anti-aircraft guns available, soldiers were torn apart by large calibre bullets, wounded men began screaming for help, while others – panicking and terrified – ran for the nearest cover they could find. Some men upturned a few old nearby fishing boats and others dived behind rocky outcrops. Then there were those who, with no cover that they could reach before the next attack, simply formed a mass of men and huddled together in a futile attempt to stay safe.

The Bf109s strafed the beach again, once more chewing men to pieces. Time after time, they simply lined up for a run, fired along the length of the beach, then circled round to attack again. Then, on one strafe, John Pat saw distant puffs of sand as 20mm bullets began hitting the beach about a half a mile away. In a microsecond, the fire from the Bf109 – travelling at 300mph – tore its way down the beach and he was hit by the same aircraft. John Pat looked down at his upper left arm to see that the round had badly ripped him up. He could see shattered bone and shredded muscle tissue. Bleeding heavily, John Pat dropped to the ground, but then, remembering what he had been told in training about keeping wounds free of dirt, he instinctively jumped back up and start trying to brush the sand out of his wound. Nearby, a fellow soldier shouted, 'What are you doing? Get down! Get down!' John Pat came to his senses and dived onto the sand.

Some time later – the Bf109s having finally flown away – the beach was full of dead and wounded men and there was now no hope of being rescued by British forces. Unlike thousands of his luckier comrades elsewhere, Fusilier John Pat McCready would not be evacuated back to Britain. A truck of German soldiers arrived and an immaculately dressed German officer got out and started walking towards the British wounded. As he neared the closest wounded man, the officer drew his Luger pistol. John Pat later remembered that the officer was a handsome young man, that the peak of his cap was turned up because he had obviously removed the strengthening wire from it, and that his boots were incredibly well polished. The officer, who John Pat would always later refer to as 'Shiny Boots', then stood over a wounded British soldier and shot him in the head, before starting to move amongst the dead and dying and shooting other wounded men in the same way.

Suddenly, John Pat realised that Shiny Boots was heading in his direction, and so – absolutely terrified – John Pat started turning as slowly as he could away from the German officer. He then tried to lie in such a way as to expose his shredded left arm, his chest and legs – now soaked in his own blood, which actually made him look like he had been hit by a bomb. He then opened his mouth in a contorted fashion and closed his eyes almost shut – closed enough to look shut from a few feet away, but open enough so that he could still see through his eyelashes. All of a sudden, Shiny Boots appeared right in front of him. It must have been a horrifying moment for John Pat, but after several extremely tense seconds, Shiny Boots suddenly moved off. Satisfied that John Pat must already be dead – the act of 'playing possum' having saved John Pat's life – the German officer moved on to another wounded soldier a few feet away and shot the man in the head. John Pat was close enough to hear the wounded man cry out as he was executed. This officer's actions were completely barbaric, but John Pat recalled that no enlisted German soldiers were executing any wounded – it was just this officer.

Later, after Shiny Boots had left the beach, the enlisted German soldiers started going around, checking the British bodies for intelligence, souvenirs, or anything of use. Suddenly, John Pat felt one of them tugging on his legs and he let out a cry. Startled, the German soldier called some of his comrades over and the badly wounded Fusilier McCready was immediately loaded onto a truck along with other wounded who had obviously also escaped the wrath of the German officer. Taken to a dressing station in a barn, an English-speaking German surgeon looked over John Pat's wounds and then asked him his name. John Pat simply tried to show the doctor his identity tags but the doctor said, in a kind voice, 'No, I want you to tell me your name.' So John Pat did. Then the doctor asked John Pat where he was from and replied that he had never been to Ireland. Finally, he asked John Pat if he liked being in the army. At this stage, John Pat realised that the doctor was trying to put him at ease. The German doctor took a deep breath and said, 'I'm sorry, but I'm going to have to take your arm.' By that point, John Pat had already known full well that amputation was probably the only way he would survive, and he readily accepted.

After being transferred to a field hospital and operated on, which resulted in his left arm being fully amputated, John Pat ended up in the German POW camp Stalag III-A, where he remained for the rest of the war. Here, he spoke to other men who had been on other beaches, and all had the same tale to tell – German officers had gone around summarily executing wounded British soldiers, but no enlisted German soldiers had taken part in these killings, which suggested that there must have been no general order to do so and that, therefore, those officers must have been acting on their own.

While in the POW camp, John Pat learned to play the drum one-handed, and when he finally returned to his native Lurgan after the war, he continued to play in a local band. However, John Pat McCready refused to accept any disability pension from the army, and instead started work in an optical factory in Lurgan as a specialist lens fitter. Nor did he ever wear a prosthetic arm, he just tucked his loose sleeve into his trouser pocket, and he could regularly be seen cycling around on a bike that had been customised for him – it had one brake-lever that controlled both brakes. John Pat simply refused to let the war dictate the remainder of his life.

1,793 DAYS

RICHARD 'DICKY' ADAMS

Finally, like 'John Pat' McCready mentioned above, Richard 'Dicky' Adams from Dublin was one of the thousands of Allied soldiers who did not escape from Dunkirk during Operation Dynamo, and instead spent the rest of the war in a German POW camp. Dicky was born in 1900 and grew up in Gloucester Diamond, Dublin – a decrepit and overcrowded tenement area of the north inner city. His family were in the livery business, and one night

A view of the huts and compound at a typical German POW camp during the Second World War, similar to the Stalag III-A POW camp, in which John Pat McCready and Dicky Adams spent five years. This particular camp is Stalag Luft III, scene of the Great Escape *in 1944.*

during the War of Independence, after finally putting the horses away after a long day's work, Dicky found himself walking home in the dark after curfew. Suddenly, an armoured car came around the corner and Dicky's instinctive reaction was to run. Seeing a young man dart away from them, the Black and Tans (British auxiliary soldiers) in the armoured car sped after him. Dicky jumped down a flight of twenty-seven steps 'in a single gallop', as his son – Richard Adams Jnr – recalled, and then raced into Gloucester Diamond and home. But the Tans followed him in and immediately ordered every man from the tenement to come out into the street. Dicky did not want to get anyone else into trouble, so he stepped forward and said that he was the man they were looking for. The Tans asked him why he ran and Dicky explained that he had been working late and had not wanted to be caught out after curfew. With that, the Tans grabbed him, threw him in the armoured car, and drove him around for the night, letting him out the next morning with a warning to just stop the next time. In later life, Dicky recalled that they could have simply opened fire and shot him, but as a younger man, he had never thought about it like that.

When the Irish Civil War broke out, Dicky Adams joined the National (Free State) Army and served in Cork. On one occasion, his unit was captured by anti-Treaty forces and their boots and weapons were taken from them. He always remembered that the army wage at the time was good, but he was discharged after the war ended due to peacetime reductions. Dicky returned to the livery business and ended up working as a manager with Brooks Thomas – a builders' merchant firm – in Dublin, which was still horse-drawn at the time. Dicky loved horses, and he used to rent out horse-drawn hearses as a side business. At some point prior to the outbreak of the Second World War, he also served in the Mounted Escort, more commonly known as the 'Blue Hussars'. This was an Irish ceremonial cavalry unit set up in 1931 to provide escorts at state functions and to the President of the Executive Council of the Irish Free State – their first role was as guard of honour for the Papal Legate during the 1932 Eucharistic Congress – before they became the Irish President's escort from 1938 until they were disbanded ten years later.

With the outbreak of war in 1939, Dicky Adams decided to enlist in the British Army. As an older recruit – he was thirty-nine at this stage – he was posted to the Auxiliary Military Pioneer Corps (soon to be renamed the Pioneer Corps), a combatant corps that performed light engineering tasks in the field, including construction of roads, bridges and airfields, track laying, transporting stores and stretcher-bearing. Many soldiers in the Auxiliary Military Pioneer Corps were African, Indian or Mauritian, but, surprisingly, there were also a large number of Germans and Austrians in the corps. These men were either Jews or strongly anti-Nazi, men who had fled to Britain from their homelands prior to the war – they were soldiers who risked almost certain execution if captured by *Wehrmacht* forces. Dicky remembered that he was treated very well by the British since, as an Irish recruit and therefore a willing volunteer, he and others like him were seen as good men to have and dependable.

Like so many other Irishmen in the British Army, Private Richard 'Dicky' Adams soon became involved in army boxing – the sport was also extremely popular in Dublin at the time – and then on 13 April 1940, while his Auxiliary Military Pioneer Corps unit was attached to a unit of Royal Engineers, Dicky found himself coming ashore in Norway. During the landing, he actually fell out of the boat into the freezing, icy waters. But he was lucky, he was only in the water for a few minutes before a comrade pulled him out.

Dicky did not stay long in Norway and was soon withdrawn and posted to an Auxiliary Military Pioneer Corps unit in France, just in time for the German invasion of 10 May. Like the rest of the BEF, he and his comrades pressed on into Belgium – it was his job to demolish bridges in order to halt the German advance – and until his commanders received word that the Germans had pushed through the Ardennes and were now threatening the rear of the BEF, Dicky actually thought that 'my side had been winning.' After all, the bulk of the German Army had been far to the south – the enemy in northern Belgium had merely been a distraction.

All of a sudden, the order was given to retreat, and Dicky's unit began blowing bridges to protect the flank of the withdrawing BEF. On the same day that the Dunkirk evacuation began – 26 May – Private Richard 'Dicky' Adams and his unit were surrounded by the Germans in the town of Albert, France. Albert sits on the banks of the River Ancre, just north of the River Somme, and was in the centre of the bloody 1916 Battle of the Somme. Now, in 1940 however, there would be no 'Big Push' against the Germans. The British in Albert surrendered, and Dicky Adams became another of Hitler's POWs.

After the fall of France and the surrender of 22 June – where Hitler made the French sign an armistice in the same railway carriage in Compiègne Forest that had been used by the French to receive the German surrender of 1918 – Dicky Adams and his group of fellow POWs were forced to walk to their camp, a journey of several hundred miles. While other POW groups were transported by rail, or sometimes by barge, Richard Adams Jnr recalled that it actually took his father nearly a year to march to the gates of Stalag III-A in Luckenwalde, Brandenburg. During this time, while Dicky and the other POWs were generally mistreated by SS guards and poorly supplied with food, Dicky learned to speak fluent German. So when he finally reached the camp in 1941, he was soon employed as an interpreter by the camp commandant.

Unbeknownst to Dicky in Luckenwalde, his family back home in Dublin had received a telegram not long after Dunkirk to say that he was missing, presumed dead. Now, a year later, his distraught wife was working hard by herself to support the family, while his children believed that they no longer had a father. In fact, it was not until 1943 that Dicky managed to get a letter out of the camp to his family, via the Red Cross in Switzerland, to say that he was still alive. Soon after, his extremely relieved family began writing back to him.

Stalag III-A was a miserable place. Situated in eastern Germany, close to the Polish border, it was bitterly cold in winter. Supplies for prisoners were non-existent, with barely any blankets provided and only tiny amounts of food (the German guards themselves were poorly provided for, with POW camps being low on the Nazi list of supply priorities). The daily ration generally consisted of a slice of black bread and some grass soup, so most POWs had to rely on Red Cross parcels in order to get enough food to stay alive. At one point during the war, the camp housed 4,000 US prisoners, 4,000 French colonial troops, as well as containing other compounds for Belgian, British, French, Italian, Russian and Serbian soldiers, and for all of these men, there were only two taps that provided drinking water. Prisoners were frequently infested with lice, showers were extremely rare, and the POWs in Stalag III-A were treated horrendously – the Russians especially. Beatings were commonplace. By the end of the war, approximately 200,000 Allied soldiers had been imprisoned within the camp at one time or another, and out of these, 5,000 POWs had died in Stalag

III-A of starvation, disease, mistreatment by the guards, or had frozen to death during the harsh winters.

The camp was a work camp, with the inmates of Stalag III-A regularly forming work parties and marching to nearby towns to perform jobs for local civilian households, businesses or farmers. On one such work party in December 1941, Dicky stole a piglet from a farmer. This act should have landed him in trouble, but while the farm's sow had had eleven piglets, the farmer had only recorded nine born in an attempt to try and keep two for himself (any piglet born on this farm was supposed to be allocated for the camp). When the farmer started complaining angrily to Dicky and the rest of the work party that one of his piglets was missing, Dicky stopped the man and said, in fluent German, 'Look, you've got ten there. It says here that only nine were born. There's not one missing. You've actually got one extra!' And so, with the farmer having been caught out, he had to leave Dicky with the piglet. That Christmas Day, the men in Dicky's hut had pork stew for dinner.

Around the same time, Dicky was out on another work party where he had a completely different experience. One day, he and a group of prisoners were being marched past a frozen lake with two German children out playing on the ice. Suddenly, the ice broke beneath them and the two children fell into the freezing water. While German guards stood around, unsure of what to do, Dicky reacted immediately and grabbed a piece of broken fence that was lying on the ground nearby. He laid the fence on the ice and used it to support his weight so he could crawl out and reach the children. He managed to pull both of them out of the lake, thereby saving their lives. As a father himself, his first reaction had been to try and help.

When the camp authorities found out what had happened, Dicky was summoned before the camp commandant. The Germans believed that an act of bravery by a soldier – on or off the battlefield – must be rewarded by a military medal, and so they tried to award Private Dicky Adams with the Iron Cross. However, he turned down their offer, fearing that his comrades would view him as a collaborator – if not his fellow 'kriegies' (a nickname for POWs, taken from the German word *Kriegsgefangener*, meaning 'war prisoner'), then perhaps people back home after the war. It would have made for a unique collection of medals for a British soldier if he had accepted it, and Dicky's son recently lamented 'that dad hadn't just taken it, said nothing, and put it in his pocket.' After that, Dicky and the men in his hut received better treatment from the guards, out of respect for what he had done. But that was not the only lasting effect of Dicky Adams' brave act – just over three years later in 1945, his life was saved because of it.

One day towards the end of the war, two of the camp's Alsatian guard dogs went missing. The camp commandant was furious and threatened to shoot prisoners unless the dogs were returned. The next day, the skins of the two dogs were found draped across the camp fence. Unbeknownst to the Germans, several Russian prisoners in the camp had caught them, butchered them, and eaten them. Russia was not a signatory of the Geneva Convention, and coupled with the fact that the Nazis viewed the Slavic peoples as a lesser race, this meant that Russian POWs suffered worse treatment than their British counterparts (when a Russian soldier died in the camp, his comrades were given a stretcher made out of a brown-paper-like material to carry his corpse on for burial. Returning without this flimsy stretcher was a shooting offence). So the Russians often had to take drastic action in order to have enough to eat.

Enraged by the death of the two guard dogs, and looking for a way to vent his frustration, a German officer went looking for a small dog that he knew one of the British POWs was keeping as a pet. When he found the dog, he shot it on the spot. As it happened, the small dog was Dicky Adams' pet, and was actually shot and killed while it was yapping around Dicky's feet. Once again, Dicky reacted instinctively and punched the officer, knocking the German unconscious to the ground. He was arrested immediately, and what probably saved him from being shot on the spot was the fact that he had knocked the German officer out cold. Dicky was put on trial – during which he was actually defended by another German officer – and because he had previously saved the lives of two German children, the charges were dropped.

However, this was not the only reason behind Dicky getting off the hook. In Spring 1945, there was a shift in attitude towards POWs in Stalag III-A. Hitler's Ardennes Offensive had failed, and the Allies were closing in on Germany from west and east. It was only a matter of time before the war would end, and Germany no longer had any hopes of winning it. With this obviously in the back of their minds, the camp authorities had begun to adopt a policy of treating the prisoners as best they could, in the hopes that, when they were inevitably arrested themselves by the Allies, they would be treated fairly. Dicky could well have been exonerated because executing a British soldier just weeks before the Allies reached the gates of Stalag III-A would not have done the camp authorities any favours.

Outside of the camp, German civilians living on surrounding farms had been ordered to provide as much food as possible for the POWs. The local bakery had been instructed to supply all the bread that it could bake, and on one occasion, Private Dicky Adams and Private Owen 'Tony' Larney – another Dubliner (from the Conker Hill area of Clontarf) – were sent with a donkey and cart to bring the bread back to the camp. Tony had been one of the first men to volunteer for the Commandos in 1940 and had been there for the construction of the Achnacarry Commando Training Centre in the Lochaber region of Scotland. He fought during the Battle of Crete in 1941 to rescue the Greek royal family – where he had been involved in a bloody, close-quarter rearguard action against the Germans with bayonet and grenades – before being wounded and captured during 1945. Described as an athletic, 6'6" man 'as tough as nails', Tony hated the Germans with a vengeance.

During the trip back from the bakery, the pair kept coming across hungry German chil-dren by the roadside – children who were getting little or no food due to rationing and supply shortages – and every time he saw one, Dicky picked up a loaf of bread off the cart and threw it to the child. Tony Larney, on the other hand, had no love for Germans or the German people, and so while Dicky kept throwing bread to German children, Tony kept hitting the donkey to make it go faster, complaining that if the donkey did not hurry up, there would be no bread left for the POWs by the time they returned to the camp.

Ironically, Tony Larney was not the only other Dublin-man that Dicky encountered while in Stalag III-A. He was also reunited with his brother-in-law, 'Mattie' Leyden – a sol-dier in the Durham Light Infantry – who had been captured by the Italians while fighting near Tobruk in North Africa. Mattie had been mistreated by his Italian captors, and after being initially put to work in an Italian salt mine, he was transferred to Stalag III-A when the Allies invaded Italy. Like Tony Larney with the Germans, Mattie Leyden had a hatred for Italians that lasted long after the war ended.

Then, at 6am on 6 April 1945, good news spread quickly through the camp. The Rus-sians had arrived outside; Stalag III-A had finally been liberated. Another prisoner, RAF Flight Sergeant David Berrie (who had been, ironically, taken prisoner after bailing out from a damaged Lancaster bomber piloted by Irishman Don Harkin, who is mentioned in the next chapter) from Stirling in Scotland, recorded what happened next:

> It was an officer in a staff car who carried out an inspection of the camp then returned to his H.Q. Between 8am and 9am we were visited by an armoured column who were loudly cheered by all American and British personnel. The Russian P.O.W.'s left the camp to join their own forces whilst we stayed in our compounds awaiting developments. Our C.O. General Ruger [Norwegian] left camp to arrange matters with the Russian authorities. Wing Commander Collard was thus left in charge. British and American personnel behaved in an orderly manner, but French and Italians were a disgusting mob causing our authorities no end of trouble. Gunfire continued all day and German aircraft put in several appearances but did no damage as fire from the woods close by quickly chased them away. Went to bed expecting to be awake all night.

After 1,793 days in captivity, Dicky Adams was no longer a POW.

Dicky recalled that the Russians wanted to arm the non-Russian POWs and set them free to aid the Soviet advance into Germany, but that the former prisoners chose to stay in the camp instead. The reason for this was that many men – especially those captured in the early years of the war before Russia had joined the Allies – had very little regard for the Soviet Union. They viewed the Russians as just another foreign army, and what most older veterans remembered about Russia was that she had divided Poland with Germany in

1939 before starting a war with Finland. And so, the bulk of the POWs insisted that they be allowed to remain within Stalag III-A until the Russians could provide sufficient transport to bring them back to their own armies. Other accounts suggest that the Russians tried to disperse some of the prisoners out of the camp, while some make mention of non-Russian POWs who did not want to wait any longer for freedom, and who left the camp in small groups in order to make their way west to British, American or French lines.

In the days that followed, fighting continued in the area until the war moved westwards. Then the food ration improved, and with the camp now being administered by a Russian staff, word soon reached the POWs that the Soviets had linked up with US troops. It was not long before US trucks arrived at the camp, and along with Russian transport, began shipping the prisoners out and back to their respective armies. Private Richard 'Dicky' Adams was finally free, and he was discharged from the British Army in January 1946. His service was recorded as 'exemplary'.

However, his return home showed him just how long he had been gone, and being reunited with his family after a five year absence came as a shock to the now-forty-five-year-old veteran. When Dicky got off the train in Dublin and met his wife and daughters on the platform, he had brought dolls as presents for the two girls. But his daughters had grown up while he was away, having turned from young girls into young women, and Dicky was embarrassed at having bought them toys meant for young children. It was not long before his life in Stalag III-A also began to affect his health, and he was soon hospitalised in Leopardstown Hospital for two years, suffering with chest difficulties. He always remembered that in Leopardstown, the quality of care that ex-soldiers received was excellent, and that men who were suffering from post-traumatic stress disorder (shellshock) or other mental problems were treated very humanely and with great dignity.

On discharge from hospital – which Dicky unfortunately had to return to every twelve to eighteen months – he returned to his old job as manager in Brooks Thomas, and he started his 'second family', as his children born after the war – who were much younger than their siblings born pre-war – came to call themselves. However, he never really spoke of the war, except on rare occasions. During one of these, Richard Adams Jnr asked his father if he had ever shot anyone. Dicky replied, 'I don't know, they would be just in the distance and you'd be firing at them ... I hope I didn't.' Another time, he spoke about how he believed that the Germans were good people overall, and that, like the outside world, the ordinary German citizen was equally terrified of Nazi fanatics. However, when Éamon de Valera's name would be mentioned in conversation, Dicky would immediately become annoyed and complain that, 'the rest of the world had a world war, and we just had an Emergency.' Another lasting sign that he had been incarcerated in a POW camp for five years was the fact that he would eat anything left behind on a plate after a meal, and would always complain about 'this waste of food', even if it was only a crust of bread that had been left uneaten.

Richard Adams Jnr always knew his father as a quiet man, and only learned about his father's experiences during the war after a chance meeting with Dicky's fellow POW, Tony Larney. It was an emotional meeting for both men – with Richard Jnr learning so much that he had never known about his father, including the accounts of him saving the German children, punching the German officer, and throwing bread to the starving Germans while returning to the camp on the donkey and cart. Tony Larney actually told Richard Jnr that 'Dicky Adams was the most principled man I ever met, but with the fieriest temper for a fella his size.' It was a side to his father that Richard Jnr knew nothing about.

Richard 'Dicky' Adams retired from Brooks Thomas in the 1960s. He passed away in the 1970s.

The Allies were squarely beaten during the Battle of France. It was a battle in which several Irish units fought, including the infantry of 1st Royal Irish Fusiliers, 2nd Royal Inniskilling Fusiliers, and 2nd Royal Ulster Rifles, with 2nd Irish Guards arriving after 10 May as part of 1st Armoured Division sent to reinforce the BEF. The armoured 5th Royal Inniskilling Dragoon Guards also fought during this time, as did the 3rd (Ulster) Anti-Aircraft Brigade. Part of the Royal Artillery, it was one of only two Irish brigades that served during the war.

The Battle of France also saw the awarding of the first Irish Victoria Cross of the Second World War. On 12 May 1940, Flying Officer Donald Garland from Ballinacor, County Wicklow, was ordered to lead his flight of five Fairey Battle bombers from No 12 Squadron RAF and destroy the Veldwezelt and Vroenhoven bridges over the Albert Canal to prevent the enemy advancing. The bridges were protected by German fighters and anti-aircraft guns, but after attacking the Veldwezelt Bridge in the face of intense enemy fire, Donald Garland was shot down and killed (only one Fairey Battle managed to return from the mission). Garland was only twenty-one years old, and he was posthumously awarded the first Irish Victoria Cross of the war. Today his remains lie buried in Heverlee War Cemetery.

Sadly, he was not the only member of his family to die during the war. His brother, twenty-seven-year-old Pilot Officer Desmond Garland, No 50 Squadron RAF, died on 5 June 1942 and is today commemorated on the Runnymede Memorial. The following year, another brother – Flight Lieutenant John Garland, RAF – died on 28 February 1943. He is buried in Midhurst Cemetery, Sussex. Finally, during the last year of the war, a third brother – Flight Lieutenant Patrick Garland, No 2 Squadron RAF – was killed on New Year's Day 1945. Aged thirty-six, his remains lie buried in Bergen-Op-Zoom War Cemetery.

The British and French had prepared, trained, and equipped themselves to fight the last war, while Germany – defeated in the last war – had learned from its mistakes. While the British and French had been complacent in victory – entering the Second World War as if they had just finished fighting the First – the Germans had developed modern tanks, focused on attaining air superiority, and had developed a system that allowed aircraft, tanks and infantry to be used together for maximum effect. In forty-six days, they had captured Belgium, Holland, Luxembourg, and most important of all, France. The Germans soon occupied the north of the country, while the puppet Vichy Government was set up to control the south.

However, 198,229 British and 139,997 French troops had been evacuated from Dunkirk during Operation Dynamo, and along with thousands of other Allied soldiers who were rescued from western France during Operation Ariel and from Le Havre during Operation Cycle, 536,155 soldiers in total were ultimately saved from the Nazis – veteran, experienced men who could form the core of new Allied armies.

That said, there was an extremely high cost to the Battle of France. In all, the Allies of Britain, France, Belgium, Holland, Luxembourg, Canada, Poland and Czechoslovakia had suffered 360,000 casualties, and had lost a further 1.9 million men to Nazi POW camps. Meanwhile, the Germans had lost approximately 158,000 killed or wounded. In terms of British fatalities, the BEF had lost nearly 4,500 killed in action, and out of this number, almost 400 (nearly ten percent of the total British dead) were Irishmen, from both north and south of the island – many of whom had lost their lives in an attempt to keep the Germans away from Dunkirk and the evacuating troops.

Furthermore, out of the BEF fatalities suffered during the Battle of France, one third of them were tragically incurred in a single day when RMS *Lancastria*, which was in the process of evacuating British troops from St Nazaire, was bombed by a German Junkers JU 88 bomber on 17 June 1940 and sank within twenty minutes. The ship was overcrowded – the captain having been instructed to rescue as many men from France as possible – and 1,738 men were either shot in the water by strafing German aircraft or drowned in the sinking, which included at least twenty-five Irishmen.

In terms of equipment, the BEF had to abandon 2,472 guns and 85,000 vehicles in France, along with 68,000 tons of ammunition, 147,000 tons of fuel, and 377,000 tons of other stores. More than 200 Allied ships were sunk, a further 200 damaged, while the RAF lost 959 aircraft in May and June 1940 (the fighter losses accounted for nearly fifty percent of RAF Fighter Command's total strength). Many Allied soldiers actually believed that the RAF had done little to help them during the evacuation, but the truth was that the RAF had always pushed inland to fight its battles with the *Luftwaffe*, thereby keeping the German Air Force away from the beaches and the troops on the ground.

However, probably the least known story surrounding the Dunkirk evacuation – from an Irish perspective – is that an Irish naval vessel actually took part in the rescuing of British troops from the beaches.

In May 1939, the Irish government ordered two Motor Torpedo Boats (MTBs) from Britain – the order was later increased to six – in order to form the Marine and Coast-watching Service in September that year. The Marine Service (as it was soon redesignated) was tasked with mine laying in Cork and Waterford harbours, regulation of merchant ships, upkeep of navigational aids and fisheries protection during the war. However, when an Irish naval crew was sent to Southampton to collect *MTB2* in 1940, they arrived at the same time as the Dunkirk evacuation. As recorded in Robert Widders' *Spitting on a Soldier's Grave*, the captain of *MTB2* – a former member of the Royal Navy – wanted to help with the evacuation. He asked his crew to volunteer, which they did, and so the Irish naval vessel set sail for Dunkirk.

They actually made two trips to rescue British soldiers from the beaches, but were then advised against returning for a third for political reasons. Instead, they returned to Ireland, and, as Widders states, 'When MTB2 returned to the naval base at Hawlbowline, in Cork, the crew were sworn to secrecy about their Dunkirk escapade.' If word had spread that an official Irish naval vessel, with the crew in Irish naval uniform, had aided the British in the evacuation of their troops from France, it would have seriously damaged Ireland's neutrality, and perhaps even resulted in retaliation from Nazi Germany. But word did not get out, and the story of Ireland's direct involvement in Dunkirk was forgotten. A few weeks later, on 4 July, Éamon de Valera confirmed that Ireland – having declared itself neutral when the war began – would stay neutral. (It was only revealed in 1970 that British Prime Minister Neville Chamberlain had earlier offered to try and bring an end to Irish partition if the southern government would join Britain and declare war on Germany, but that de Valera had turned down the offer, believing that he might never be able to reach an agreement with Northern Irish unionists.)

And so, with France firmly under Nazi control, Hitler now turned his attention to Britain and his plan – Operation Sealion – to invade the country. Meanwhile in Ireland, on 23 June, Minister for the Co-Ordination of Defence Measures Frank Aiken began urging Irish people to stock up on food and water and prepare shelters in case of bombing. However, Operation Sealion would soon go down in history as a Nazi failure and as Britain's 'finest hour'. This was the Battle of Britain, where the RAF would ultimately beat the *Luftwaffe* in the skies over England and halt Hitler's seemingly unstoppable advance. Many Irish pilots would play a part in winning this victory.

CHAPTER 2

THE DANGEROUS SKIES

– THE WAR IN THE AIR

Personnel of a Home Guard Motor Transport Company in Ulster, pictured in an army lorry, 1 November 1942. Members of this company did some of their training with the Royal Army Service Corps in Northern Ireland, and they are believed to have been the only Home Guard Motor Transport Company in the United Kingdom.

'In those days you flew singly, there weren't pairs flying, nor were there really squadrons. Squadrons got you into the battle, but in the battle you did your own fighting.'
Battle of Britain pilot John Hemingway from Dublin.
Interview with Zampano Productions

The same day that Operation Ariel – the last Allied mission to rescue troops from France – ended, 25 June 1940, the armistice signed three days earlier between France and Germany came into effect. Hitler's forces had achieved in forty-six days what the Kaiser's army had failed to do in over four years of fighting. During the First World War, the Germans had been in sight of Paris twice, but on 23 June 1940 – nine days after capturing the city – Adolf Hitler visited the French capital. The Germans now occupied all of northern Europe – from the French Atlantic coast to their Polish border with Russia. They had not suffered one defeat since invading Poland nine months earlier. Many outside of German-occupied countries were terrified that the German Army and the *Luftwaffe* were simply invincible.

Britain – knowing that the Germans would certainly follow up their capture of France with an invasion of Britain – began preparing. Children were evacuated from southern English towns, beach defences were constructed, and the production of munitions was increased. The Home Guard was also set up on 14 May. Initially known as the Local Defence Volunteers, its ranks were filled with men who were considered too old for enlistment in the army, many of whom were former First World War soldiers (although there were some younger men who had been rejected by the regular forces for having slight medical conditions). However, while 1.5 million men volunteered, they trained with broomsticks due to weapons shortages, and then, once trained, were often only armed with outdated or poor quality rifles and support weapons, 'Molotov cocktails' (glass bottles filled with flammable liquid and capped with a flaming rag that would ignite the liquid once the bottle was smashed), slug-firing shotguns, or at worst, pitchforks. When coupled with the fact that the British Army had been forced to abandon all of its tanks and anti-tank guns in France, this left British ground forces severely underequipped to defend against the German Army.

It is perhaps lucky then that the Germans were not initially intending to land a ground force in Britain. Having identified the need to attain air superiority in modern warfare, the plan was to first allow the *Luftwaffe* to defeat the RAF and dominate the skies over Britain. Then, in mid-September 1940, nine German divisions and two *Fallschirmjäger* (paratrooper) divisions – 200,000 men in total – would invade southeast England using a fleet of 2,000 barges and ships. There were also four panzer divisions earmarked for the overall invasion of the country.

The Germans felt that there was no way they could lose the aerial battle. After all, the *Luftwaffe* had 3,000 bombers and fighters ready for the campaign, while the RAF – severely depleted after the Battle of France – had only 600 aircraft available. The Germans believed that they would beat the RAF in only a couple of days, and on 10 July 1940, the Battle of Britain began when the *Luftwaffe* started attacking merchant convoys in the Channel, along with southern English harbours. The RAF had to patrol constantly above the convoys, which was exhausting for the pilots. Furthermore, operating close to their bases in northern France, *Luftwaffe* bombers were escorted by large numbers of German fighters. The bitter 'dogfights' – aerial combat between fighters – that followed ended up deciding the future course of the war.

After changing tactics several times – attacking coastal airfields and radar stations, then bombing inland RAF bases before finally switching to targeting cities – the Germans were ultimately defeated in the skies over England, but the war in the air did not end there. After failing to defeat the RAF, the *Luftwaffe* began bombing British cities at night. In late 1940, London was bombed seventy-six nights in a row. On 29 December 1940, the Germans dropped incendiary bombs on the city that started 1,500 fires. Fire-fighters ran out of water and simply had to let the fires burn. This period became known as 'The Blitz', and when it finally ended on 10 May 1941 (with a devastating attack that resulted in 3,000 casualties among Londoners), at least 40,000 British civilians had been killed and a further 46,000 wounded in air raids, while hundreds of thousands were made homeless.

Ireland was not immune from The Blitz, with Belfast bombed heavily on 15 April 1941 and Dublin hit on 31 May, but Éamon de Valera was still determined to keep southern Ireland out of the war, and on 7 November 1940 – after British Prime Minister Winston Churchill requested the use of Irish ports for use by British forces – de Valera responded that the British could not be allowed to use Irish ports as long as Irish partition still existed (the so-called Treaty Ports were back under Irish control at this time).

However, from early 1942, RAF Bomber Command began to seriously avenge some of the damage done to Britain by the *Luftwaffe*, while also disrupting German industry and manufacturing. RAF bombers had remained on the offensive throughout 1940 and 1941, but with poor results. The first raids – carried out in daylight – suffered high casualties and forced RAF Bomber Command to fly at night. With pilots only trained for daytime flying, only three percent of bombs dropped actually fell within five miles of the intended target, and by the end of 1941, 700 bombers had been lost and the amount of planes flying in any one mission had been reduced to save aircraft. But 1942 saw a change in tactics, and soon, effective and devastating raids were being mounted deep into Germany. In the meantime, thousands of pilots and airmen were fighting the enemy in skies all over the world – many of them from Ireland.

During the Second World War, serving in the RAF was an attractive prospect for many Irishmen. While the vast majority of Irish volunteers still joined the British Army, and specifically the infantry, many saw the RAF as offering the most glamour and – thanks to the technical training that men received in the RAF – the best chance to get a good job after the war. However, while an infantryman might survive after being wounded if a comrade managed to get him to a medic, wounded pilots and aircrew ran a greater risk of dying. If they could not fly or operate their plane, they might die in a crash landing, while a damaged aircraft often resulted in the deaths of all on board. In fact, during the Second World War, personnel serving as aircrew with RAF Bomber Command had only a twenty-nine percent chance of coming home from every mission (forty-four percent were killed in action and a further twenty-seven percent were taken POW). For the Irish pilots and airmen of 1939-1945, life was extremely dangerous.

THE FLYING SHAMROCK

BRENDAN EAMONN FERGUS 'PADDY' FINUCANE

Born in Rathmines, Dublin in 1920, Brendan Eamonn Fergus 'Paddy' Finucane was the son of Thomas, an accountant, who had been a member of the Irish Volunteers. Thomas Finucane had also studied mathematics under Éamon de Valera, and had served in Boland's Mill under Dev's command during the 1916 Rising. During the War of Independence, Brendan's mother – Florence – had also been caught up in a Black and Tans ambush while pushing the infant Brendan in a pram.

In 1932, having already developed a love of flying from reading about First World War

Flight Lieutenant Brendan 'Paddy' Finucane from Rathmines, Dublin, seated in the cockpit of his Spitfire at RAF Kenley while serving with No 452 Squadron RAAF, 13 October 1941. This Spitfire was known as 'The Flying Shamrock' – due to the shamrock containing his initials that Finucane had painted on the cockpit. Finucane became so famous that models of 'The Flying Shamrock' were sold in shops, while German pilots became worryingly aware of a skilled Irish air ace they called 'Finucane of the Shamrock'.

aces, the young Brendan and his brother Raymond took off from Baldonnel aerodrome after their father paid ten shillings for a flight. Then, in November 1936, the family emigrated to Richmond, Surrey, and Finucane joined the RAF in May 1938 – aged seventeen. Even though his father was from a republican background he did not stop his son joining up, and Brendan's brothers also went on to serve during the war – Raymond as a sergeant and air gunner with RAF Bomber Command, and youngest brother Kevin as an officer in the Royal Artillery (in fact, 1916 Rising veteran Thomas Finucane tried to join the RAF himself in 1939, but his English wife stopped him from enlisting). During flight training, Brendan was considered an average pilot – nothing special – and then on 13 July 1940, three days after the start of the Battle of Britain, Finucane – now a pilot officer – was posted to No 65 Squadron RAF, a Spitfire squadron based at RAF Hornchurch, but which soon moved to RAF Manston in Kent.

At this time, due to the major losses suffered by shipping, convoys sailing through the English Channel had to be cancelled. Then, on 12 August 1940 – the same day that the Germans switched to begin attacking RAF coastal airfields and British radar stations – Brendan Finucane from Dublin had his first victory. After spotting a group of Messerschmitt Bf109s escorting a flight of German bombers above the Channel, the Spitfires of No 65 Squadron RAF dived on the enemy. Finucane attacked the last German fighter in the formation, firing at it from between 250 and fifty yards range. He hit the enemy fighter and it quickly began to trail heavy smoke before crashing into the Channel. Later that same day, he scored a probable kill and damaged another enemy fighter while helping to defend RAF Manston from a wave of German bombers, and then on 13 August, he shot down a Messerschmitt and again damaged another.

The reason that the Germans were now targeting RAF airfields and radar installations was that they hoped to destroy the RAF on the ground before they became a threat in the air. However, radar was Britain's secret weapon, and with a range of 100 miles out to sea, reports from radar stations on the approach of enemy aircraft were quickly relayed by telephone to RAF Fighter Command Headquarters in Bentley Priory, Stanmore, Middlesex, and from there, orders were sent out to the relevant RAF bases. Squadrons could often be scrambled and in the air within five minutes of the radar station having picked up the German planes. Also, the pilots were helped by similar reports from the 30,000-strong civilian volunteer Observer Corps (soon redesignated the Royal Observer Corps) who – using binoculars and simple instruments in their permanently-manned posts throughout the British countryside (which all had landline telephone connections) – could provide information on the number, height, direction of travel, and type of enemy aircraft approaching.

However, after damaging several radar arrays in initial attacks, the Germans soon stopped targeting them. They simply did not understand how RAF Fighter Command were using radar, and also mistakenly believed that the operations centres at radar stations were below ground and therefore immune to bombing. And so, unable to understand the tactical value of radar, the Germans stopped attacking it and instead focused on the RAF airfields.

Pilot Officer Brendan Finucane and No 65 Squadron RAF were withdrawn to Scotland at the end of August 1940, but by the end of 1941, Finucane was now a celebrated RAF 'ace' (five confirmed victories earned a pilot this title). Famed for getting in close and only opening fire when he was sure he would hit the enemy, he often returned with ammunition left over, having fired only when he could guarantee a direct hit. He was awarded the Distinguished Flying Cross because he had 'shown great keenness in his efforts to engage the enemy and he has destroyed at least 5 of their aircraft. His courage and enthusiasm have been a source of encouragement to other pilots of the squadron' (*London Gazette*, 13 May 1941). Around the same time, on 15 April 1941, he was attacked by German *Luftwaffe* ace Adolf Galland. Galland was on his way from Brest to Le Touquet with an unusual cargo – lobsters and oysters for the birthday party of a senior *Luftwaffe* general – but had decided to fly over Dover to do some 'hunting' en route. He came across a flight of Spitfires out on training manoeuvres and attacked. The Spitfires were led by Finucane, and although Galland managed to down three British fighters, Finucane managed to get above him and descended on Galland, firing as he went and badly damaging the German's plane. There are conflicting reports as to what happened next, with the more reliable one claiming that Galland bailed out over the Channel as his Messerschmitt went down in flames near the French coast – he was rescued a few hours later – while Galland himself claimed that he safely landed his aircraft and delivered his seafood cargo intact.

Not long after this dogfight, in late April 1941, Finucane was promoted to flight commander of the newly formed No 452 Squadron Royal Australian Air Force (RAAF) at RAF Kirton-in-Lindsey, Lincolnshire. This was the first RAAF squadron to serve as part of RAF Fighter Command, and their first operational flight was in July 1941. Soon enough, Finucane had been awarded two bars to the Distinguished Flying Cross. The citation for the first appeared in the *London Gazette* on 9 September 1941 and read:

> This officer has led his flight with great dash, determination and courage in the face of the enemy. Since July, 1941, he has destroyed three enemy aircraft and assisted in the destruction of a further two. Flight Lieutenant Finucane has been largely responsible for the fine fighting spirit of the unit.

The second appeared only days later:

> This officer has fought with marked success during recent operations over Northern France and has destroyed a further six enemy aircraft. Of these, three were destroyed in one day and two in a single sortie on another occasion. His ability and courage have been reflected in the high standard of morale and fighting spirit of his unit. Flight

Lieutenant Finucane has personally destroyed fifteen hostile aircraft.

(*London Gazette,* 26 September 1941)

Remarkably, this was followed within a month by the awarding of a Distinguished Service Order for:

Recently, during two sorties on consecutive days, Flight Lieutenant Finucane destroyed 5 Messerschmitt 109's bringing his total victories to at least 20. He has flown with this squadron since June, 1941, during which time the squadron has destroyed 42 enemy aircraft of which Flight Lieutenant Finucane has personally destroyed 15. The successes achieved are undoubtedly due to this officer's brilliant leadership and example.

(*London Gazette,* 21 October 1941)

When Brendan 'Paddy' Finucane received his Distinguished Service Order and the two bars to his Distinguished Flying Cross from King George VI at a ceremony in Buckingham Palace on 25 November 1941, he was now a true RAF ace and a national hero in Britain, with the press actually hounding him whenever he was on leave home in Surrey.

While flying with No 452 Squadron RAAF, Finucane was asked about what it was like to be a fighter pilot.

Before going off on a trip, I usually have a funny feeling in my 'tummy', but once I'm in my aircraft everything is fine. The brain is working fast, and if the enemy is met it seems to work like a clock-work motor. You don't have time to feel anything ... I have come back from a sweep to find my shirt and tunic wet through with perspiration. Our chaps sometimes find they can't sleep ... You come back from a show and find it very hard to remember what happened. Maybe you have a clear impression of three or four incidents which stand out like illuminated lantern slides in the mind's eye. Perhaps a picture of two ME's [Messerschmitts] belting down on your tail. Perhaps another picture of your cannon shells striking at the belly of an ME and the aircraft spraying debris around. But for the life of you, you can't remember what you did ... Later when you have turned in and sleep is stealing over you, some tiny link in the forgotten chain of events comes back. Instantly you are fully aware and then the whole story of the operation pieces itself together and you lie there reliving the combat. The reason is simply that everything happens so quickly in the air that you crowd a tremendous amount of thinking, action and emotion into a very short space of time, and you suffer afterwards from mental indigestion.

In January 1942, Finucane was put in command of No 602 Squadron RAF based at RAF Redhill, Surrey. The following month on 20 February, after fighting German aircraft in the skies above Dunkirk for over an hour, he was wounded for the first time when enemy fire hit his aircraft and tore open his leg from his thigh to his knee. He ordered his wingman –

But now, despite British losses, the *Luftwaffe* was at a disadvantage. Radar and the Observer Corps meant that British pilots were airborne and high enough to engage enemy planes by the time that German aircraft reached them. Also, German pilots were far from their bases in northern France, which meant that they always had to keep one eye on the fuel gauge. A German pilot had, on average, thirty minutes of flight time over Britain, and fuel consumption doubled once he was forced to engage in a dogfight. Many German pilots actually crashed into the Channel on their return flights to France, or were sometimes forced to land on French beaches, and the knowledge that this might happen had a generally demoralising effect on pilots once they arrived in English skies. Also, the Junkers Ju87 Stuka dive-bomber – made famous by its role in German *Blitzkrieg* and easily identified by the siren-sound it made as it dived – was ineffective in destroying British planes on the ground in large enough numbers. British planes were defended by anti-aircraft guns, and were concealed and protected in 'E-bays' – walled parking bays shaped like a capital E – the walls of which prevented bombs dropped nearby from damaging the planes. Also, the G-forces created by the Stuka's dive usually caused the pilot to black out. (The Stukas were actually pulled up out of their dives by an auto-pilot.) This added to the fact that once it had dived, a Stuka would now be flying at 100mph, below 1,000ft and without fighter or ground support, meant that RAF fighters could easily attack and destroy them. By 19 August, the Germans were forced to withdraw the Stuka dive-bomber from the Battle of Britain, replacing it with the *Luftwaffe's* 1,500 medium bombers.

Then, on 7 Sept 1940, the Germans began attacking London, building up to a heavy attack on 15 September (later known as 'Battle of Britain Day'). Believing that they had now exhausted the RAF and reduced RAF Fighter Command to 200 operational aircraft, they targeted the capital, thinking that the RAF would throw in everything it had left to defend the city. Once committed, the *Luftwaffe* planned to simply destroy what was left of the RAF in the air.

In reality, the British had increased fighter production and were now building 250 new planes a month. RAF Fighter Command had 600 planes, not 200, and furthermore, the number of British pilots had been increasing every month since the start of the battle, with the result that there were enough men in training to replace losses. It is a common misconception that the German change of target on 7 September – switching from bombing the RAF airfields to bombing London – saved the RAF, which was allegedly on the verge of defeat. The truth was that, while the switch in target did obviously take pressure off the RAF, the RAF was not only holding its own at this time, but was also growing steadily. Modern research by historian Stephen Bungay also suggests that, even if the Germans had continued to attack RAF airbases and not targeted London on 7 September, they could not have sustained their losses for much longer, and that the RAF would still have ultimately won the Battle of Britain.

By the time Belfast-man Kenneth Mackenzie took to the air with No 501 Squadron RAF in late September 1940, the serious threat to the RAF had passed. Fifty-six enemy aircraft were shot down by RAF fighters on 15 September, and after the *Luftwaffe* were ordered to concentrate on city bombing exclusively, Operation Sealion and the plan to invade Britain was postponed indefinitely on 17 September.

However, while Britain was no longer at risk of being invaded, German bombers were wreaking havoc on British cities. And so, the RAF still had a war to fight in the English skies. It was not until May 1941 that German bombers were finally withdrawn from northern France in order to head east for Operation Barbarossa against Russia. On 7 October – having only joined No 501 Squadron RAF two weeks earlier – Kenneth Mackenzie performed a feat that would earn him the nickname 'Super Mac'. After shooting down two Bf109s already while serving with his new squadron, Mackenzie found himself pursuing an enemy fighter that was trying to make its way back to France. The enemy plane was flying low over the sea, but Mackenzie was completely out of ammunition. He had nothing to fire at the German fighter but he was determined to destroy it. And so, Pilot Officer Kenneth Mackenzie flew alongside the Bf109 and then rammed the enemy's tail with his own wingtip. The tail of the Bf109 was torn off and the enemy aircraft spiralled out of control from the impact, crashing into the sea. However, Mackenzie had broken off six foot of his own wing in the process and when he turned for home he barely made it back to England. He crash-landed only 500 yards inland from the coast in Folkestone, Kent and nearly hit a nearby British anti-aircraft battery. The force of the landing threw him forward and he hit his gun sight, knocking out four teeth.

Within a few days, on 25 October 1940, Mackenzie shot down another enemy fighter and helped to destroy a second. But that same day, Mackenzie's wingman crashed into him as he tried to intercept an enemy plane and Mackenzie was forced to bail out. He was unhurt, and by the end of October he had destroyed three more enemy aircraft and had been awarded the Distinguished Flying Cross. Mackenzie was now an undisputed RAF 'ace'.

The following year, in 1941, Mackenzie – now flying Hurricanes in the night fighter role with No 247 Squadron RAF – shot down two more enemy aircraft before being shot down himself on 29 September. While attacking a German airfield at Lannion, Brittany at night, he was hit by enemy anti-aircraft fire and ended up crashing into the sea while attempting to make it back to Britain. He managed to bail out and escape from his plane in an emergency dinghy, but he was forced to row to the French coast where he was soon arrested by the Germans.

Mackenzie remained a POW for the next three years. However, he tried to escape from the Germans on several occasions. En route to the Oflag VIB POW camp, he managed to escape from his guard in a crowded Paris railway station but was soon recaptured. In the camp, Mackenzie was involved in an attempt to tunnel out under the perimeter wire – he was nearly killed in April 1942 when part of the tunnel's roof collapsed; he managed to get clear just in time – but when rumours started circulating that prisoners would be soon moved to another camp, Mackenzie and his fellow escapees decided to try the tunnel at its current length. Unfortunately, although the tunnel did reach beyond the camp perimeter, it did not reach far enough beyond the view of the guards and as soon as the first man appeared out in the open, he was spotted. Not long after, Mackenzie and another prisoner tried to dig a shallow tunnel under the camp fence from a ditch near the perimeter. However, they had to stop digging when a guard became suspicious. Finally, after being transferred to Stalag Luft III in Sagan, Lower Silesia (now Zagan in Poland), Mackenzie began a long campaign of trying to convince the Germans that he was insane. He acted mad and purposely developed a stammer. Amazingly, the plan worked and the Germans ultimately fell for it. And so, in October 1944, Mackenzie was returned to Britain. He earned a new nickname – 'Mad Mac' – and went straight into an instructor role, passing on his skills to a new generation of pilots.

Mackenzie ultimately survived the war and remained in the RAF afterwards, serving in the Middle East, the Persian Gulf and Africa before retiring as a wing commander in 1967 (he had been awarded the Air Force Cross on 1 January 1953). Strangely, he never lost the stammer that he had developed in the POW camp. He then went on to act as deputy commander of the Zambian Air Force before serving as managing director for Air Kenya, based in Nairobi. After a period spent living in Cyprus, he moved to England, settling in Lutterworth, Leicestershire in 2000 – a street there was named Ken Mackenzie Close in his honour. When the Battle of Britain Monument was opened on Victoria Embankment, London in 2005, Mackenzie said, 'This is a long time overdue. If we had lost, Britain wouldn't be here today.'

Kenneth Mackenzie from Belfast ultimately passed away on 4 June 2009. He was two days away from his ninety-third birthday.

THE LAST OF 'THE FEW'

HENRY 'HARRY' CLARKE & JOHN HEMINGWAY

Referring to the RAF aircrews that saved Britain from the *Luftwaffe* during the Battle of Britain, British Prime Minister Winston Churchill famously said, 'Never in the field of

Spitfires of Sergeant Harry Clarke's No 610 Squadron RAF, based at RAF Biggin Hill, Kent, flying in three 'vic' formations during the Battle of Britain, 24 July 1940.

human conflict was so much owed by so many to so few.' By the end of October 1940, the RAF had lost 544 killed, 422 wounded, and 1,547 aircraft destroyed. Meanwhile, the Germans had suffered 3,336 killed or missing, 967 captured, and had lost 1,887 aircraft. During the battle, 2,946 RAF pilots and aircrew had taken to the air, and these men would now be forever known as 'The Few'. In terms of pilots alone, at least thirty-eight Irish pilots are known to have flown during the Battle of Britain (twenty-eight from Northern Ireland and ten from the south), and at the time of writing, there is only one left.

From Belfast, Henry 'Harry' Clarke was Northern Ireland's last surviving Battle of Britain pilot until his death in 2010. Having joined the RAFVR in July 1939, aged twenty-two at the time, Harry was called up two months later at the outbreak of war. He was stationed at RAF Kinloss, Scotland before joining No 66 Squadron RAF – a Bristol Blenheim squadron – at RAF Biggin Hill, Bromley, London. By the start of the Battle of Britain, Harry Clarke – now a sergeant pilot – was serving with No 610 Squadron RAF at RAF Biggin Hill. This was a Spitfire squadron, and when the Battle of Britain began, No 610 Squadron RAF was engaged heavily against the first waves of the *Luftwaffe*.

No 610 Squadron RAF was withdrawn to RAF Acklington, Northumberland at the end of August 1940 to recover. Then, in September 1940, during a dogfight training flight, Harry and a student were engaging in mock combat when the student crashed his plane into Harry's by accident. The crash killed the student pilot and cut the harness of Harry's parachute, but when Harry bailed out, he luckily got his leg caught in the harness straps – meaning that he was still connected to his parachute. After possibly hitting his head off the tail of his Spitfire as he bailed out, Harry Clarke lost consciousness and then woke up, falling through the air and hanging upside down from his parachute. He managed to turn his body and secure himself a bit better to the damaged harness before passing out again. When Harry hit the ground he miraculously survived, although he suffered injuries to his head and neck.

Henry 'Harry' Clarke went on to serve with No 602 Squadron RAF, No 266 Squadron RAF, and then No 255 Squadron RAF – the latter of which was variously stationed in Tunisia, Sicily, Italy, Malta and Egypt – before returning to Northern Ireland and finishing the war as a test pilot. He retired from the RAF as a flight lieutenant and lived in Saintfield, County Down. He passed away on 26 July 2010, aged ninety-two.

With Harry Clarke's death, John Hemingway became the last surviving Battle of Britain pilot from the island of Ireland (he was already the last surviving southern Irish pilot of the battle). Born in Dublin in July 1919, Hemingway joined the RAF in April 1938 – aged eighteen – and was posted to No 85 Squadron RAF. This squadron, which flew Hawker Hurricanes, was sent to France at the outbreak of war and attached to the BEF, forming No 60 Fighter Wing of the Advanced Air Striking Force. During the subsequent Battle of France, John Hemingway actually helped to shoot down a *Luftwaffe* Dornier Do77 lighter bomber on 11 May 1940. However, he had to make a forced landing later that day after his Hurricane was damaged by enemy anti-aircraft fire.

During the Battle of Britain, Pilot Officer John Hemingway was forced to bail out twice. On 18 August 1940, Hemingway was flying, as he recalled in a recent interview with Dublin-based documentary producer Zampano Productions:

> Twenty or thirty miles off Clacton [Clacton-on-Sea, Essex], we came across these number of airplanes, some flying straight to England, some circling ... I went off after what I thought were Ju88s ... I climbed up to about 18,000 feet ... they were doing circling and I was going to fly around the opposite way but I didn't quite get it right and somebody clobbered me. They came across ... and hit me, stopped the engine and covered the inside of the cockpit with oil. Things got very smelly and very hot. Lucky we were warned always to enter a fight with the cockpit hood open because they did jam ... luckily it opened ... in the meantime I'd spun down from 18,000 feet to about eight or seven and then I thought, full of confidence, I'd set out for England! I'd no hope of getting to England so I thought to land [in the sea] is a dangerous thing so I bailed out. I thought I could stand on the wing but I just got blown off, landed in the sea, shed everything I could shed – jellyfish everywhere – and started swimming.

Two hours later, after rolling in the waves – although Hemingway actually thought he had been swimming the whole time – he was luckily picked up by a rowboat from a lightship.

Then, on 26 August, while diving against a formation of enemy aircraft, 'I eventually managed to get an airplane in my sights, a Dornier, and [fired], and then started – the silliest thing I've ever done, I suppose – started to pull around to have a second go at the formation.' As Hemingway swooped around, he flew across the sights of all the *Luftwaffe* planes in formation. An enemy aircraft opened fire and he was hit.

> Smoke everywhere, and oil. The airplane was, I thought, on fire. It certainly felt like it. So again the hood opened luckily, but because we'd heard tales that German fighters were shooting down parachutists in the air ... I decided on a delayed drop, and knowing that the cloud top was at about 8,000 feet [about 10,000ft below his current altitude] I delayed until I was in cloud and pulled the [parachute release] and landed.

Hemingway had been shot down over Eastchurch in Kent. He landed in the Pitsea marshes in neighbouring Essex and was picked up by the local Home Guard.

John Hemingway and No 85 Squadron RAF were then withdrawn to Yorkshire in September 1940 before swapping their Hurricane aircraft for Douglas A-20 Havocs in October and adopting a new role as night fighters. By 1 July 1941, Hemingway had been awarded the Distinguished Flying Cross, and two months later on 24 September he was mentioned in dispatches.

By 1945, Hemingway was now a squadron leader with No 43 Squadron RAF based in Italy. Now flying Spitfire aircraft, he was forced to bail out for a third time when his plane was hit by ground fire on 23 April 1945 near Ravenna. As Hemingway recalled:

> I was attacking what I thought was ordinary Germans on the ground and suddenly this ack-ack [anti-aircraft fire] opened up, hit me, knocked my engine out.

Hemingway planned to bail out and was flying at 3,000ft when:

> It must have hit the airplane again. I was shot up into the air, tumbling over and
> over and over and the parachute stripped all the skin off my legs ... I landed, left my
> parachute where it was, and the local farm workers took me along and hid me in a
> place where they had some clothing and seed corn and tools and things like that. I
> immediately changed out of my uniform into one of these farm workers' garbs, and
> as I'd just finished changing a voice ran across the entrance. I don't know what it was
> saying, but it was saying something and he was running, so I was going to do some-
> thing about that. So I ran after him along this ditch and at the end of the ditch I settled
> down behind the grass ... and saw two German *Unteroffiziers* [equivalent to a British
> corporal or US sergeant] with their guns running along towards the hole that I'd been
> in. And as soon as they vanished into the hole I ran away in an orchard ... There was
> gunfire then, and I imagine these people were shooting at me – they might not have
> been – but I imagine that they were and somehow or other I got away. I think I got
> away because I was dressed as an Italian peasant amongst Italians.
>
> Eventually [in intense pain] I went to a farm door and knocked on the door and
> in my best pigeon English said, 'Me English'. So they took me in and didn't shoot me.
> Instead of that they put me down another hole in the middle of another field, gave me a
> bottle of wine and a chicken and said, '... stay still until we call for you again.' Then, some
> hours later, they came back and took me to another farmhouse and a lot of talking went
> on and gesticulating ... and then [after being introduced to] this young girl of about six
> or seven ... she then took me by the hand and [we] wandered along, south.

Suddenly, Hemingway and his young guide came across:

> ... all these German troops dug in ... under trees and things like that. I was terrified,
> more for that young girl. I was terrified for her. But we wandered on, and I didn't look
> at them [the Germans], and we wandered on to another farmhouse. People came out
> of the farmhouse and gathered us in and the young girl vanished.

A group of Italians then marched Hemingway south as fast as they could – regardless of
the pain he was in – until they encountered 'the advance column of the 16th/5th Lancers,
where I had a damn good lunch.'

Squadron Leader John Hemingway remained in the RAF after the war, and rose to
serve as base commander of RAF Leconfield, Yorkshire from January 1966 until September 1968. Then, with the rank of group captain, he retired from the RAF after serving on
the Combined Military Planning Staff from October 1968 until June 1969. At the time of
writing, ninety-two-year-old John Hemingway from Dublin is the last surviving Irish pilot
– from anywhere on the island of Ireland – to have flown in the Battle of Britain. He lives
in County Wicklow.

THE BLITZ IN IRELAND

After the Battle of Britain came The Blitz. Night after night the *Luftwaffe* tried to destroy British morale and industry by bombing its cities. However, the bombings were not confined to Britain, and on 15 April 1941, German bombers attacked Belfast in an event that became known as the 'Belfast Blitz'. The city had been attacked previously – on 7 April, six German bombers attacked the Belfast docks, resulting in thirteen killed and some factory damage – but it was nothing like what happened a week later.

On 15 April, 200 *Luftwaffe* bombers – a mixture of Heinkel He111, Junkers Ju88 and Dornier aircraft – attacked the city just after 10.30pm. Wave after wave of bombers flew overhead. Primarily, the Germans were targeting the Harland and Wolff shipyards – this yard constructed 139 naval vessels during the war, converted over 2,500 vessels for naval use, repaired a further 22,000 ships, and also built 140 merchant vessels – along with aircraft, artillery and tank factories, the Belfast power station, the waterworks, Victoria Barracks, munitions works, and the linen industry (which made aircraft coverings).

Belfast's defences had been poorly organised. By April 1941, there were only 200 public air raid shelters throughout the city (although 4,000 private shelters had been constructed). The city had only twenty-two anti-aircraft guns and no searchlights. And out of these twenty-two anti-aircraft guns, only seven were operated on the night of the raid, and even then, only for a short period of time. The reason they stopped firing was that they were afraid they might hit any RAF night fighters that had taken off to defend the city. However, the city had no RAF night fighters to call on, and during the raid itself, not one RAF plane took to the air to fight off the *Luftwaffe*. Also, unlike in other major cities in Britain, children had not been evacuated from Belfast to the surrounding countryside, and there were 80,000 children still in the city on 15 April. When the married quarters in Victoria Barracks took a direct hit, many children living there were killed in the explosion.

The situation became so desperate that the government of Northern Ireland actually sent a telegram to Taoiseach Éamon de Valera asking for the southern government to send any help it could. Seventy-one firemen and thirteen fire engines were immediately sent north of the border from Dundalk, Drogheda, Dublin city and Dún Laoghaire, with the engines and crews remaining in Belfast for three days. It was truly horrific in Belfast, and on one occasion, when rescuers were trying to free a child from under some rubble, they could not lift the weight of the debris and so were forced to amputate the child's arm and leg in order to pull the child free. One report by Major Seán O'Sullivan – an air raid precautions observer from Dublin – also stated:

Rescue workers search through the rubble of Eglington Street in Belfast, Northern Ireland, after a German Luftwaffe air raid, 7 May 1941. The earlier 15 April 'Belfast Blitz' was much worse.

There were many terrible mutilations among both living and dead – heads crushed, ghastly abdominal and face wounds, penetration by beams, mangled and crushed limbs ...

Fires burned all over Belfast and continued for several days while 220,000 refugees evacuated the city. Trains and buses leaving Belfast were crowded with people – many of whom had absolutely no possessions left – and military trucks were soon used to transport survivors to nearby towns. 10,000 refugees were also officially accepted across the border into southern Ireland, and at least 500 of these are known to have received treatment from the Irish Red Cross in Dublin. Following the southern Irish response to the Belfast Blitz, Taoiseach Éamon de Valera said that 'they are our people, we are one and the same people' while Frank Aiken – Minister for the Co-ordination of Defensive Measures – said, 'The people of Belfast are Irish people too.'

In all, 1,000 people were killed in the raid – this was the greatest loss of life in a single night during The Blitz outside of London, and the majority of the dead had been killed by collapsing buildings rather than bomb explosions. A further 1,500 had been wounded and fifty percent of the houses in the city had been destroyed. One of those killed was twenty-six-year-old Able Seaman Samuel Corry from Belfast. Stationed aboard HMS *Quebec* – a Royal Navy shore establishment at Inveraray, Scotland – Corry was home on leave and visiting his wife Martha at their home on Joseph Street (just off the Shankill Road) when the raid started. They both fled to the Percy Street shelter where they were subsequently killed. Able Seaman Samuel Corry now lies buried in Belfast City Cemetery. Other men tragically died alongside their children as well as their wives. Thirty-six-year-old Rifleman (Private) William McGennity from Belfast, of 70th (Young Soldiers Battalion) Royal Ulster Rifles, was killed at his home in Holmdene Gardens along with his wife, Bridget, and their two children – three-year-old Margaret and sixteen-month-old Robert. Today, Rifleman William McGennity's remains lie in Belfast (Milltown) Roman Catholic Cemetery. His wife and children are buried in Belfast County Borough Cemetery.

Sadly, this was not the last raid against Belfast during The Blitz. Three weeks later, during the early hours of 5 May, the *Luftwaffe* bombed the city once more. The southern government again provided assistance, but over 190 people were killed during this third attack on Northern Ireland's capital.

However, Belfast was not the only major Irish city bombed during 1941, and on 31 May, twenty-eight people were killed when Dublin was attacked by the *Luftwaffe*. This was not the first time southern Ireland had been bombed during the war. Three people had been killed in Campile, County Wexford on 26 August 1940. The *Luftwaffe* then dropped bombs on Sandycove, County Dublin and Shantonagh, Carrickmacross, County Monaghan on 20 December causing several injuries but no fatalities. During the period 1–3 January 1941, bombs were dropped in Duleek and Julianstown in County Meath, in the Curragh area of County Kildare, near Enniskerry in County Wicklow, and at Ballymurrin in County Wexford – although there were no casualties from any of these bombs. However, on 2 January, three women were killed when a house in Knockroe, County Carlow was hit, and twenty people were injured when bombs fell on Donore Terrace, South Circular Road, Dublin on 3 January.

On 31 May 1941, however, four bombs were dropped on Dublin. Two fell causing no casualties – one on North Circular Road, and another near Dublin Zoo in the Phoenix

Park (this bomb damaged Áras an Uachtaráin, the Irish president's residence) – while a third fell in Ballybough, destroying two houses and injuring several people. But the fourth – a landmine – was dropped in the North Strand area and destroyed seventeen houses while damaging 300 others (fifty were badly damaged). Twenty-eight people were killed, ninety injured, and 400 made homeless. These figures were nothing like those suffered in Belfast, but the 'North Strand Bombing', as it became known, was still a shock to the people of a neutral country. In response, the southern Irish government made an official protest to the German government.

Two main causes have been put forward for why Dublin was bombed that night. The first claims that *Luftwaffe* navigational error was responsible and that the bombing was a complete accident, while the second claims that because southern Ireland had recently sent help north of the border during the Belfast Blitz, subsequently taken care of many Northern Irish refugees, and then condemned the Belfast bombing in a protest to Germany (the Dáil had also recently condemned the proposed introduction of conscription in Northern Ireland on 26 May; the following day, Churchill had confirmed that conscription would not be extended to Northern Ireland), that the North Strand Bombing was a German warning to de Valera's government. Southern Ireland may have been officially neutral, but that neutrality might have started to seem biased and pro-British to those in Germany.

The North Strand Bombing, however, was not the last time that the *Luftwaffe* dropped a payload over southern Ireland. Arklow, County Wicklow was bombed on 2 June 1941 – only two days after the North Strand – and then bombs fell on Dundalk, County Louth on 24 July, although there were no injuries on either occasion.

BRINGING THE FIGHT TO THE ENEMY

DONALD 'DON' HARKIN

Immediately following the evacuation from Dunkirk and the subsequent Battle of Britain, the RAF was the only arm of the British forces still on the offensive. Having seen what The Blitz had done to British industry and morale, there was a desire to inflict a similar revenge on Germany, and after an initial bad start, RAF Bomber Command changed its tactics in February 1942 and began a programme of 'Area Bombing' at night against targets that were easier to find. Instead of trying to score pinpoint hits on enemy installations, bombers would now attack large targets – cities. Coastal port cities were initially targeted, meaning that pilots and navigators could use the European coastline as a 'handrail' to guide them to their destination. The first attacks using these new tactics were indiscriminate but

Flight Lieutenant Donald 'Don' Harkin (back row, second left) from Delvin, County Westmeath, of No 300 (Polish) Bomber Squadron RAF. This photograph was taken after Don completed the No 91 Flying Instructors Course (7 FIS) at RAF Upavon in June 1946.

devastatingly effective and the RAF was also soon aided by the introduction of a new radio navigation system codenamed 'Gee'.

The industrially important Ruhr region of western Germany was targeted, as were major German cities, U-boat yards, aircraft and tank factories, munitions production, oil installations, transport infrastructure and other war-related industries – but the war in the air was a battle in which both sides had to constantly adapt their tactics. After the Germans began operating

their own radar system and used it to guide *Luftwaffe* night fighters (which were permanently on station over occupied northwest Europe) towards incoming RAF bombers, the RAF countered by developing 'Window' – small, thin strips of aluminium (known today as 'Chaff') – which, when dropped in the air, confused enemy radar and rendered it useless. But German anti-aircraft defences soon improved and overcame 'Window'. With each enemy improvement, RAF losses grew, only for the table to turn once the RAF adapted.

But despite RAF Bomber Command's steep learning curve during 1939–1945, its bombers played a vital role in helping to defeat the German war machine. One Irish pilot who flew with RAF Bomber Command during this time was Donald 'Don' Harkin from Delvin, County Westmeath. From an early age, Don was interested in flying. He used to make toy gliders and model planes, and he followed the exploits of Charles Lindbergh – the first man to fly solo non-stop across the Atlantic from New York to Paris. Don finished his schooling aged twelve, after primary school, and soon began work as an apprentice in a workshop in nearby Clonmellon, fixing bicycles and the odd car. When his mother subsequently passed away and Don's father moved to England to work in the Short Brothers' plane factory in Rochester, Kent, Don soon followed. On 1 April 1940 – aged eighteen – Don emigrated to Kent where he worked in a local mill while waiting for his job with Shorts to begin. Don then started work as a fitter, and he remembered working on the air frames of Short S25 Sunderland flying boat patrol bombers.

On 5 February 1941, the Air Training Corps was set up to prepare young men for entry into the RAF. Don was interested in joining, so he took some time off work and went to Chatham to sign up. But while there, someone suggested he join the RAF 'as aircrew proper'. Don put his name forward and went for an assessment – a medical and written exam – which included an essay on the recent German invasion of France. Don was informed that he was a little weak in algebra, but

An Avro Lancaster four-engine heavy bomber, exactly like the one Don Harkin from Devlin, County Westmeath flew while serving with No 300 (Polish) Bomber Squadron RAF. The Lancaster became one of the most famous bombers of the war and was armed with four defensive machine gun turrets. With modifications, it could even carry the 12,000lb 'Tallboy' and 22,000lb 'Grand Slam' earthquake bombs.

if he was willing to commit to the training, the RAF would still put him forward for pilot school. Otherwise, if he declined, Don would be placed wherever the RAF needed him, as he had now enlisted.

Don decided to continue down the route of becoming a pilot, and so, while waiting to be called up, he stayed in his job with Shorts and was sent to evening classes for six months in a technical college in Maidstone. Here, he found that he was as capable as the other students who had gone on to secondary school. After this, Don was called up and sent to

Newquay in Cornwall for six months preliminary military training, along with courses in maths, navigating and signalling. Finally, it was time to begin pilot training, but Don had no idea where this would take place. The Commonwealth Air Training Plan meant that he could be trained anywhere from Canada to South Africa. Don was sent to Blackpool to be kitted out for his training and he realised that he was not being sent to Canada when the quartermaster handed him a tropical pith helmet.

On 13 February 1942, Don set sail from Glasgow to Durban, South Africa aboard SS *Ormonde* ('a dreadful ship', as he recently recalled). SS *Ormonde* was part of a convoy that included an aircraft carrier, and Don was soon stationed at Lyttelton Camp, in what was then the Transvaal Province. Don trained here from 16 August 1942 – flying de Havilland DH82 Tiger Moth's and different variants of the Hawker Hart – before qualifying as a pilot and receiving his wings on 16 April 1943. However, while Don was sent back to Britain to begin operational flights, some of his class were selected to go on to instructor school straight away.

When Don returned to Britain he was initially posted to No 576 Squadron RAF at RAF Elsham Wolds in Lincolnshire, before soon moving to join No 300 (Polish) Bomber Squadron RAF stationed at nearby RAF Faldingworth. The Polish Squadron no longer had enough airmen from Poland to make up the numbers required, and so Commonwealth air crews were now being drafted into the unit. However, as Don remembered, the traditional Eastern European food in the Polish Squadron's mess was a new experience!

When Don flew his first operational mission, he remembered that 'it felt good to [finally] be involved ... but you were back that night for a pint in the local. It was a very different type of war.' On one occasion, he was tasked to perform a photo reconnaissance mission, and was ordered to fly 'straight and level' over a German V1 'buzz bomb' installation in order to get clear pictures. The installation was defended by anti-aircraft guns, and Don was terrified as he flew overhead – anti-aircraft shells were detonating in the air around his plane – but Don was not allowed to vary his course or speed. Luckily, he survived, and by May 1944, he was qualified to fly Oxford, Wellington, Halifax, and Lancaster aircraft.

Then, on the night of 5 June 1944 – the night before D-Day – Don took off to bomb targets in support of the landings. However, he was not told that this mission was any more important than others he had previously flown, but 'they did hint that this was a special night ... but they never said it openly.' Then, while flying over the Channel, one of Don's crew turned to him and said 'Look down! Look, out in front!' As Don recalled, 'The sea was alive with vessels. Only then we realised what we were actually at.' Don's target on D-Day was a heavy coastal gun emplacement – however, these guns were protected inside reinforced concrete casements that usually withstood even the heaviest bombing. Most remained in operation until they were assaulted by infantry on the ground.

Several weeks later, on 29 June 1944, Don piloted one of 286 Lancasters (accompanied by nineteen de Havilland DH98 Mosquitos) that attacked two launch sites and a store at the Nazi V1 flying-bomb site at Siracourt in northern France. Over the following days and on into early July, he flew missions to Vierzon, Domléger-Longvillers, Orléans, and against the V1 launch site at Forêt de Croc near Siracourt on 6 July (one of 551 aircraft – 550 bombers and one marker plane – to do so). He also bombed Caen on 7 July in support of Operation Charmwood (1,800 tons of explosives were dropped on the city that night), before flying sorties to Émiéville, Kiel in Germany, and then again to Caen on 18 July – this latter mission was a dawn attack against villages east of Caen in support of Operation Goodwood; the RAF dropped 6,200 tons of explosives on the target area and in the vicinity.

By now, Don Harkin was a flight officer and had completed eighteen successful operational flights. However, when he took off, just under a week later, on 24 July 1944 – at 2136hrs aboard Lancaster ND984 for a mission to Stuttgart (the first of four subsequent days of RAF sorties against the city, during which 73,000 bombs would be dropped) – things were about to change. En route to Stuttgart, Don's plane was hit by ground fire from a German 88mm gun. As Don remembered, 'Jimmy [Sergeant James Philpot], the rear gunner, was about to say something. There was a shout.' Normally, after a British plane was initially attacked, the rear gunner would then direct the captain's evasive action, by letting the pilot know what side of the plane was being attacked, by how many enemy fighters, the direction the ground fire was coming from, and so forth, but 'they [the enemy] got us straight away. They were spot on.' After Don's Lancaster suffered an initial direct hit from enemy fire, 'both port engines went on fire. We tried diving, we tried everything else.' Don's crew were actually worried that he was diving so hard he might 'knock the wings off', but with the nose dive having failed to extinguish the fires, the order was finally given to bail out.

However, as crew members began to jump out of the badly damaged plane, it occurred to Don that he had not heard the rear gunner repeat the order to bail out. Worried that Sgt Philpot might not have heard the order, and therefore might still be in his gun turret, Don stayed aboard the plane as its altitude got lower and lower. With two dead engines and the autopilot barely able to cope, Don finally realised that Sergeant Philpot was already long gone – he had bailed out earlier but had never repeated the order to let everyone else know. Having needlessly waited, Don wasted no more time and jumped out of the stricken Lancaster.

Lancaster ND984 subsequently crashed at 0215hrs on 25 July in the vicinity of Ochsenbach, northwest of Stuttgart. The crew of Don's plane were now, along with the crew of Lancaster LM178 – also in No 300 (Polish) Bomber Squadron and also shot down during this mission – the first non-Polish crews to be posted missing from the squadron.

Don's parachute successfully opened, but because he had failed to get a new strap for his boots that would secure them to his feet should he be forced to bail out (he had actually

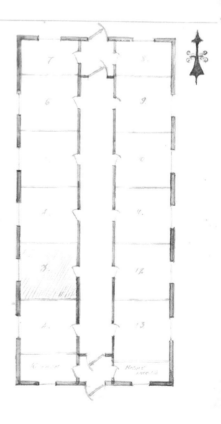

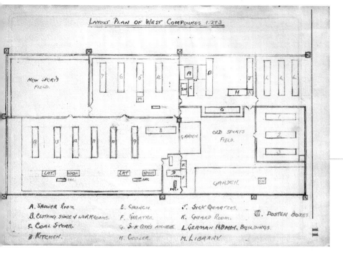

Various drawings made by Don Harkin during his captivity in Stalag Luft I. Clockwise from top left, a drawing of the camp fence and a guard tower (drawn on parachute silk), the layout of Don's room, the position of Don's room (shaded) in the accommodation block, and a plan view of the camp's western compounds.

meant to go to the quartermaster the day before), when his body jerked from the force of the parachute opening, his boots shot off his feet. He then hit the ground hard after falling through a tree. He was winded and in pain at first, but after a while, he finally came to his senses and realised, 'I can breathe. I can move.' He buried any intelligence that he had on his person, including the silk escape map of Europe issued to aircrews, and then wandered around in the vicinity for about an hour 'with no fixed plan' and without any boots. 'Not a good start!' as he recalled. Then, in the dark, he heard a whistle. Don froze, and the whistling sounded again. Don thought, 'Oh Christ, I'm caught already', but then it occurred to him that if it was the Germans out there, they would not be whistling at him. It turned out to be Don's wireless operator – Flight Sergeant David Berrie, a Scotsman – and they teamed up and went on the run together.

After four days in the Black Forest (Don's socks having worn away by now) – trying to make their way to neutral Switzerland by moving at night and sleeping during the daytime – the pair 'became brazen', as Don remembered, and began moving during the day. They took apples from an orchard while being watched by German civilians, who simply waved happily at the fugitives, and then Don and Flight Sergeant Berrie came to an open avenue across their path, darting across it in full view of an old German guard further up the road. At first, the guard seemed confused by what he saw, but then came to his senses and started shouting for the pair to stop. 'That was it,' recalled Don. 'We were caught.'

After being captured, Don was taken to a local army commandant who performed an initial interrogation. Here, Don and his radio operator were questioned side by side, and after a while, when he saw that Flight Sergeant Berrie was looking to Don periodically, the commandant shouted – via an interpreter – that 'He [Don] is not your officer anymore!' The radio operator was then removed from the room and Don was questioned alone. Soon enough, with the commandant getting nowhere, he asked Don if there was anything he could get him. Don was getting 'a bit cheeky', and he replied, 'I wouldn't mind a nice beer.' The commandant got angry and said, 'You should see what you've done to our brewery!' It had recently been bombed and production had stopped.

Don was then sent to a Dulag Luft centre (short for '*Durchgangslager der Luftwaffe*', meaning Air Force Transit Camp). These were where captured Allied aircrews were gathered and interrogated before being sent on to POW camps. Don was taken to the centre at Oberursel, near Frankfurt, and was initially asked to prove that he actually was an officer. Since captured officers and captured other ranks were often treated differently by the Germans, which made Allied airmen frequently pretend that they were officers, the Germans demanded that Don prove his rank.

Don remained in the Dulag Luft for three days, and remembered that you had to be careful who you spoke to and what you said, because – allegedly – German agents had been planted amongst the Allied POWs in order to gather information. Don was particularly suspicious of anyone who acted overly friendly towards him. Finally, Don was given a Red Cross package, containing items like pyjamas, cigarettes and toiletries – which was issued to all new POWs – and sent on to his permanent POW camp, Stalag Luft I, not far from the Baltic Coast near Barth in Western Pomerania, Germany. He arrived there on 8 August 1944.

Meanwhile, back in England, on 25 July 1944 at his home in Snodland, Kent, Don's father – Charles Harkin – had received a letter from Wing Commander Teofil Pozyczka, commanding officer of No 300 (Polish) Bomber Squadron RAF, informing him that Don was missing in action. The letter stated that nothing had been heard of Don or any of his crew since they had taken off the night before, and that while Don might now be a POW, Wing Commander Pozyczka insisted to Charles Harkin that he should 'not raise your hopes too high ... I should like to add that the International Red Cross Society usually takes at least six weeks to obtain any information.' He went on to say:

> During the time that your son had been with this squadron he had grown to be
> quite popular. He had many friends here, all of whom will miss him greatly. During
> his many operational flights he had constantly shown himself to be a skilful and coura-
> geous pilot and you have indeed every reason to be proud of him.

Don's father and other members of the Harkin family in Ireland were soon sending telegrams back and forth as they tried to gather information on what had happened to Don. On 27 July, Charles Harkin wrote, 'Just learned Don missing. Hoping for better news.' However, on 3 August, Don finally managed to get word to his father in the form of a short postcard. It read, 'Dear Dad, no doubt you have all been terribly worried. I am safe and fit – not a scratch, thank God. All the lads also. I shall look forward to letters from you all ...' This must have gone a long way towards relieving Charles Harkin's grief and worry. He soon wrote to his family, 'Don safe. Will [be] prisoner of war.'

In Stalag Luft I, Don met with men who had been POWs since 1940, and also other men that he knew. The billets contained twenty beds to a room with a heat stove in the corner, and Don was actually soon billeted with actor Donald Pleasence whose Lancaster had been shot down on 31 August 1944. Don remembered that the diet consisted of German 'black bread' (rye bread), jam, a poor quality stew, and ersatz coffee, supplemented by Red Cross food parcels which often included cakes, and that a barter system was in operation amongst the POWs. The men showered once a week, and as an officer, Don was excused from having to go out on work parties. Recreational activities included football, table tennis, volley ball, and ice skating in winter (the Germans actually provided the ice skates). Shows were also often performed (many of which were produced by and included Donald Pleasence), along with music recitals. Arts and crafts classes were held, as were religious

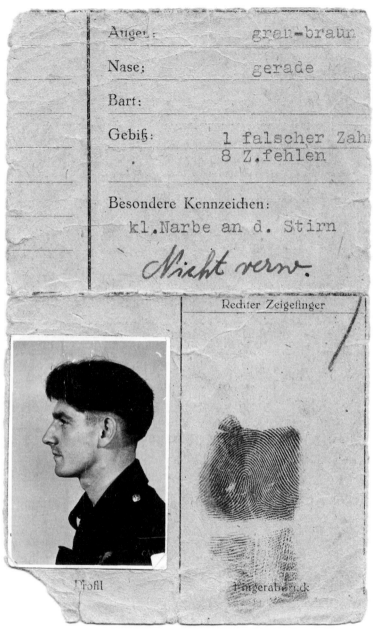

Augen: grau-braun

Nase: gerade

Bart:

Gebiß: 1 falscher Zahn
8 Z.fehlen

Besondere Kennzeichen:
kl.Narbe an d. Stirn

Nicht verw.

Rechter Zeigefinger

Profil   Fingerabdruck

Don Harkin's identity card from his time in Stalag Luft I. Note the fact that Don is not wearing his own RAF pilot's uniform — an airman's wings can been seen on the front of his tunic, and the word 'Canada' is just visible on his upper arm. This is because Don swapped uniforms with a Canadian airman in the Dulag Luft centre in order to annoy and confuse his German captors.

services (the camp chaplain was a padre who had parachuted into Arnhem with the British 1st Airborne Division), and academic courses were organised by the Red Cross — with instructors drawn from qualified POWs in the camp. For these courses, the Germans provided study facilities and a library of books.

Don made Christmas dinner for his billet in 1944, and then, while there were also courses on languages and law available, he studied for a Ground Engineer's Certificate ('C' License Standard – Aero Engines) between January and April 1945. Don also did a course on automobile engineering during this time, his instructor for which was Spitfire pilot and post-war racing driver Robert Cowell (Cowell also held a rare double commission – he was a flight lieutenant in the RAF and a captain in the Royal Army Service Corps – and is also famous for undergoing the first male-to-female sex change operation in British history. He became Roberta Cowell in 1951).

However, while life for POWs in Stalag Luft I was far from unbearable, the men were constantly reminded of the fact that they were prisoners. The camp was surrounded by a double barbed wire fence and electric trip wires, overlooked by sentry boxes containing machine guns and aided by powerful searchlights. During air raids, the POWs initially cheered friendly aircraft as they flew overheard, but then the camp commandant issued orders that, whenever the air raid siren sounded, all POWs were to return to their billets. However, on one occasion during an air raid, a POW was cleaning a cooking pot and, forgetting about the air raid, went outside looking for sand to use as an abrasive to help him clean the pot. A German guard spotted him outdoors and, thinking the POW was trying to escape, shot him. Luckily for the POW however, he was only wounded in the arm.

The POWs also used the codewords 'goon up' and 'goon gone' to warn each other of Germans approaching or leaving the area respectively, especially when they were doing something forbidden, such as listening to a homemade radio for news about the war or working on an escape plan. But the Germans knew about these codewords, and after a German had entered a POW hut and inspected it for about ten minutes (Don had called out 'goon up' as he came near), the German came outside and said to Don, who was standing on the doorstep, 'Now you can tell them goon gone!'

On 30 April 1945, with the Russian Army not far from the camp, the POWs were ordered to evacuate with the German guards. However, they refused, and so a deal was agreed on between the senior American officer in the camp and the German camp commandant. The Germans would leave and the POWs would remain behind. And so, the following day – 1 May – the Russians arrived and liberated Stalag Luft I. Don remembered that, while a row of POWs were sitting with their trousers down on crude seats above a latrine trench, a female Russian officer walked by (800,000 women served in the Russian Army during the Second World War – it was a female officer, Major Anna Nikulina, who raised the Soviet flag over the Reich Chancellery during the Battle of Berlin – but unlike in other countries, most served in combat roles. However, very few ever became officers, and so this was a particularly rare sight). However, while the men were embarrassed at the situation, Don remembered that the female officer 'didn't even bat an eyelid'.

After complaining to the Russians that they had not had fresh meat in a long time, the Russians soon returned – to everyone's complete surprise – with a live herd of cattle and drove them into the camp. Don recalled that the POWs found a few men who were willing to butcher the cattle, and so the prisoners soon had fresh meat back on the menu. However, the Russians also tried to get many of the prisoners to leave, but US and British officers urged their men to stay together as a whole until their own forces arrived. Many of those who refused and who left the camp immediately were never heard from again, while a few joined with the Russians. And so, Don remained in the camp for just over two weeks until he was flown back to Britain on 15 May aboard a Boeing B-17 Flying Fortress as part of Operation Revival.

Following three weeks in rehabilitation, and then after a further few weeks spent drinking with Donald Pleasence ('I remember him bringing me to his crowd, and they were a lovely crowd, the actors.'), Don received a letter on 22 November 1945 from the latest commanding officer of No 300 (Polish) Bomber Squadron RAF – Wing Commander Romuald Sulinski – containing a Polish squadron badge. Sulinski wrote:

> I hope this will be a nice souvenir for you and will always remind you of the time
> during which you had been risking your life Shoulder by Shoulder with us for the
> sake of freedom which to some people means too much, to some others so little.

Don stayed with the RAF after the war and signed on for another four years. He was a student on No 91 Flying Instructors' Course at RAF Upavon, Wiltshire between February and June 1946, after which he began instructing members of the Air Ministry who needed refresher flight training. Most of these were high ranking officers, and Don was not able to openly criticise their mistakes. Instead, as he remembered, it was a case of saying, 'Sir, do you mind me saying but ...' a lot!

In 1946 Don returned to Ireland on leave and went to visit a friend who worked for Bank of Ireland. This friend told Don that Aer Lingus were now looking for pilots, and right away, Don was interested. He travelled straight to the Aer Lingus offices, and when Don got there he found that their chief navigator was an ex-RAF man who had also been in Stalag Luft I. This man recognised Don and brought him to see Darby Kennedy – the head of Aer Lingus. Before long, Kennedy asked Don, 'How soon can you join us?' Don was delighted and wanted to take Kennedy up on his offer, but his renewed RAF contract was a problem. However, after returning to England, talking to an RAF secretary who was dealing with a large number of post-war discharges, and explaining his predicament, the secretary told Don that this was no problem and simply added his name to the list of personnel to be discharged. And so, Don Harkin was no longer a pilot with the RAF.

Don married, ultimately had seven children, and stayed with Aer Lingus until the late 1970s before joining the newly formed Royal Swazi National Airways – the national airline of the Kingdom of Swaziland in southern Africa. The boss of Royal Swazi was an ex-Aer Lingus man, and it was through him that Don heard about the job. Don recalled that the tiny airline seemed to exist to give the king's son ('a very pleasant man') a job 'for the sake of appearances' – he had an office, a secretary, and two planes to take care of.

Donald 'Don' Harkin then retired from flying in 1982 and returned to live in Ireland. At the time of writing, he is eighty-nine years old and lives in County Dublin.

GUARDIAN ANGELS

LAWRENCE 'LARRY' DUFFY

Another Irishman flying raids deep into Germany during this time was radio operator Sergeant Lawrence 'Larry' Duffy from Fyhora – a townland northwest of Arva – in County Longford. Based at RAF Skellingthorpe, Lincoln and serving in No 50 Squadron RAF, Duffy's squadron were flying Avro Lancaster four-engine heavy bombers by the time they set off to attack a German synthetic oil plant at Leuna, west of Leipzig, on 14 January 1945 – by now Duffy was twenty-three years old. During the attack, Duffy's Lancaster – LM 234 – was hit by enemy anti-aircraft fire. When two engines suddenly burst into flames, Duffy's best friend – Australian Pilot Officer Alexander Hunter 'Lex' Nicol – pushed the plane into a nose dive. The plane sped towards the earth and the increase in speed luckily extinguished the flames. Now flying on only two good engines and losing fuel rapidly, Lex Nicol made up his mind to try and limp across the border into neutral Switzerland. He knew there was no way that the Lancaster would make it back to Britain, and so he decided that landing in Switzerland would be the best way to avoid ending up in a Nazi POW camp.

However, Lex was unable to gain altitude and en route to Switzerland, the Lancaster crashed into the side of a snow-covered mountain. Larry Duffy was one of only two men to survive the crash, and the only one who survived relatively uninjured. In a recent interview, Duffy recalled, 'I got out but went back in as another member of the crew had also survived. I managed to get him out.' This second survivor was Sergeant WS McClelland, ironically the only other Irishman onboard – the rest of the aircraft's British and Australian crewmembers had been killed. Sadly, Duffy's best friend – twenty-year-old Lex Nicol – had not survived.

After carrying Sergeant McClelland to a safe distance from the wreckage, Duffy – not knowing if his plane had reached Switzerland or had crashed while still inside Germany – set off to find help. Duffy soon discovered a public house where he was confronted with a man carrying a rifle. The Longford radio officer had to convince this man that he was completely unarmed before the man finally allowed Duffy to come inside. In the public house were several women, but nobody could speak English and so one of the locals set off to bring back someone who could. Duffy recalled, 'When he [the translator] came over he had a swastika in his lapel and I thought, "Jesus, that's it!"'

Duffy now realised that he was still inside Germany (in fact, he had crashed near Reichmannsdorf in eastern-central Germany, nowhere near the Swiss border, and the male population of the town was so low due to German conscription), and the translator – who had learned English while a POW in Britain during the First World War – informed Duffy that he was now going to be executed. Duffy was dragged outside, but then something completely unexpected happened.

> I was bundled out and there were three men with rifles already pointed in my direction. But the ladies got cracking, they screamed, kicked and pulled hair ... There was a fourth woman who was very old, and sitting up in a wicker chair, she was on crutches and she began hitting out with her crutches. Then a crowd assembled on the street, about fourteen yards from the front door, and the other women, when they saw what was happening, they gave a hand too, and stopped them shooting me.

The women of this German town prevented RAF radio operator Sergeant Larry Duffy from being executed by the few local men that remained. Duffy was brought to a military hospital, before being sent to a POW camp near Munich (Sergeant McClelland was also subsequently captured and interred in a POW camp). He remained here for the rest of the war, and when he was released, he met US General George S Patton before returning to his home in London and marrying a girl from Roscommon town, with whom he had three children. In later life, Larry Duffy returned to Ireland and settled near Athlone. Then, in 2005 – aged eighty-three – he returned to Reichmannsdorf with his son Rory and actually met with some of the women who had saved his life all those years ago, along with several locals who remembered seeing his plane crash land. He was taken to the site of the crash, where wreckage from his Lancaster still lay after sixty years, and was also told that there were currently plans to rename the local mountain 'Duffy Mountain' in his honour. As Rory Duffy remembered, 'They had a local band out to meet him and everyone knew the story of the Irishman who survived the crash and the firing squad.'

Lawrence 'Larry' Duffy returned to Athlone after this emotional visit and passed away there on 29 August 2010. He was eighty-eight years old.

FIGHTING ON THE HOME FRONT

JOHN DAVIN POWER

Meanwhile, the fight against the *Luftwaffe* on the British Home Front continued. Organisations such as the Home Guard, the Auxiliary Fire Service (later the National Fire Service), Air Raid Precautions and the Civil Defence did what they could to reduce the damage and loss of life caused by German bombing, and many of the men serving in these organsations were older men, often veterans of the First World War. John 'Jack' Davin Power was one such man.

Two photographs of Sergeant-Major John 'Jack' Davin Power from Kimmage, Dublin, taken during the First World War. The one on the left was taken first while Jack was in camp in Basingstoke before he deployed overseas, while the photograph on the right was taken in Capetown, South Africa after Jack was evacuated from Gallipoli due to an extreme case of influenza – it shows a much thinner, gaunter man.

Born in 1881 in Kimmage, Dublin, Jack's father was an accountant with the City of Dublin Steam Packet Company shipping line, and by 1911, Jack was working as a railway clerk for London, Midland and Scottish Railways and living with his wife – Marguerite, a national school teacher – and their two young daughters at Beechwood Avenue Lower in Ranelagh, Dublin. In 1914, the First World War broke out. The following year – on 4 February 1915 – Jack Power enlisted in the British Army. However, he was given the rank of staff sergeant-major in the Army Service Corps – possibly due to his previous experience in the transportation business – and sent overseas to France immediately. Jack landed in France on 18 February, exactly two weeks after enlisting. He was then thirty-four years old.

A British fireman – one of many volunteer firefighters at the factory where he worked as a fitter – practises using his fireman's hose during a training exercise. Veteran soldier John 'Jack' Davin Power from Kimmage, Dublin would have received identical training.

Staff Sergeant-Major John 'Jack' Davin Power later served during the Gallipoli campaign against the Turks (he was at Suvla Bay at some point) before developing a severe case of influenza and being evacuated back to Britain – in a postcard to his family, he soon wrote that 'this influenza has left me just skin and bone.' According to the family, he then returned home to Dublin on Easter Monday 1916 and – because he was wearing his British Army uniform – he was nearly shot by members of the Irish Volunteers until a neighbour suddenly recognised him. Then, in 1919, Jack was finally discharged from the British Army, having reached the rank of temporary regimental sergeant-major (warrant officer class one).

However, the war had affected Jack Power in ways other than physical. He separated from his wife, leaving her and their three children behind and moving in with his brother Nick who lived at Harold's Cross. Returning to his job with the railway, Jack later went on Mediterranean cruises and travelled around Europe. It is very likely that he was suffering from what would today be described as post-traumatic stress disorder, but unlike today, there were no counselling or other services to help soldiers like Jack Power deal with their wartime experiences.

Then, in 1940 – aged fifty-nine – Jack left Ireland for good when he moved to England. He worked initially for a company in north London and then later as a railway official for St Pancras Borough Council. However, Jack Power also joined the National Fire Service as a fireman.

By now, the worst period of the bombing of London – The Blitz – had ended. However, on 21 January 1944, the *Luftwaffe* began Operation Steinbock – a series of night-time raids against southern England. They were carried out for the sake of Nazi propaganda – so that the Germans could be seen to be striking back at the Allies – and became known as the 'Baby Blitz' in Britain. On the night of 14 March 1944, a hundred German bombers took off en route to London. When they reached the city, they dropped incendiary bombs and high explosives across Cliveden Place, Hyde Park, Knightsbridge, Monck Street, Rochester Row and Westminster. The incendiary bombs were particularly devastating, and as British gunners opened fire with anti-aircraft fire and rockets to defend the city, many London buildings were soon ablaze. That night, Fireman Jack Power found himself trying to extinguish an incendiary bomb at 130 Stanhope Street, Camden Town. He was now sixty-two years old, but he was still helping to fight this new war. However, there was a sudden explosion – sadly, Jack did not survive the blast.

Three days later, Jack's niece's husband wrote to Nick Power – the brother who Jack had lived with before leaving Ireland – to say that 'I need hardly tell you how great a shock it came to us to learn of Jack's sad ending. As I have got all the details of what took place today Frances [Jack's niece] has asked me to write you.' The family had gone looking for a Father Vincent, who was handling the funeral arrangements.

He was a very nice sort of man and was glad to see us. Apparently he had got to know Jack very well and used to speak to him every Sunday after Mass. As Jack's land-lady was also a Catholic she called to Fr. Vincent on Wed. and told him of the tragedy and that all she knew was that an ambulance had taken the remains away the previous (Tues) evening. Then Fr. Vincent made a tour of all the morgues until he came to Univ. College Hospital. On his own initiative Fr. Vincent made arrangements that the funeral would be carried out with full rites and requiem and that the remains would be buried in a Catholic cemetery. If he had not done this the authorities would have gone ahead and buried his remains with other unidentified or unclaimed corpses in a communal grave irrespective of creed ... I cannot go into details as to how death occurred beyond saying that it was caused by one of the explosive types of incendi-ary bombs which he was trying to extinguish. Death was instantaneous ... I am very sorry to have to trouble you with all these details at the present time but I felt there was nothing to do only give you all the facts as soon as possible. As it is now nearly 2 am I will conclude and express my heartfelt sympathy with you in your bereavement. Yours Sincerely, Michael.

The funeral of former regimental sergeant-major, First World War veteran, and Second World War fireman John 'Jack' Davin Power was held in St Anne's, Seaton Place on 18 March 1944. He now lies buried in the Catholic plot of Bethnal Green Cemetery. Having survived one world war, he did not survive another.

A DECENT MAN

RAYMOND WALL

It is easy to forget that the vast fleet of RAF fighters, bomb-ers, patrol, reconnaissance, transport and training aircraft could simply not have kept flying if it were not for the ded-icated and often thankless work of RAF ground crews. One Irishman who served as ground crew during the war was Raymond Wall from

Loughrea, County Galway. Born in August 1918, Raymond – whose older brother Thomas had served as an artilleryman during the First World War – was one of the many Irishmen who felt that they had a moral duty to do something to stop Hitler.

Believing that Ireland would ultimately enter the war on the Allied side, Raymond initially joined the Local Security Force (LSF) in Loughrea on 27 August 1940. The LSF was a police reserve whose duties involved traffic control, crime detection, first aid, reporting of missing persons, transport, providing cordons, communications, protective duties, distributing of ration books, census and survey duties, and also observing for downed combatant aircraft, parachutists, or sea mines. Its members were quite active and regularly required to perform these duties. However, when Ireland did not join the war against Germany, Raymond resigned from the LSF (as it was not a part of the Irish military, he was free to leave at any time) and travelled north of the border to enlist. In the recruitment office, he made it clear that he was willing to be placed wherever he was needed – combat infantryman if necessary, whatever would be of greatest use in the fight against fascism. As he was a motor mechanic, he was advised to join either the Royal Armoured Corps, the Fleet Air Arm of the Royal Navy, or the RAF. He liked the sound of the Fleet Air Arm, where he would work with planes aboard aircraft carriers, but he was then told that he could be waiting quite a while for approval to join this branch of the British forces.

The reason for this was that the British forces operated a vetting policy which required all volunteers to provide references – these references would then be checked by sending letters to the referees, asking them to state that the reference from them was in fact genuine. However, with regards to the letters sent by British recruitment offices to referees in southern Ireland, the IRA had recently been sending letter bombs – that looked like letters of reply from southern referees – to the British recruitment offices, which had made the authorities extremely cautious about accepting letters from southern Ireland and had ultimately slowed down the vetting of all southern Irish volunteers. Furthermore, Irishmen who wanted to serve on aircraft carriers were normally subjected to one of the lengthiest and most rigorous forms of background checking. These two factors combined meant that Raymond would have to wait up to a year to be admitted into training for the Fleet Air Arm, and so, that day – 22 July 1943 – he decided to take the quicker and more trouble-free route of joining the RAF. For six weeks he was put to work in a factory in Belfast, near the Harland and Wolff shipyards, where he made parts for tanks, until his paperwork had been processed and he was called up for training.

Aircraftman Raymond Wall from Loughrea, County Galway. He trained as an FME (Flight Mechanic – Engines) and served as ground crew with No 90 Squadron RAF at RAF Tuddenham in Suffolk.

Raymond Wall (on left in both photos) from Loughrea, County Galway, and some comrades working on the engine of an Avro Lancaster four-engine heavy bomber of No 90 Squadron RAF at RAF Tuddenham in Suffolk, c1944/45.

Raymond Wall did his initial training in RAF Padgate, Cheshire, before moving on to RAF Cosford, Shropshire, to undergo technical training. While stationed at RAF Cosford, Raymond's wife Rita emigrated from Ireland to nearby Birmingham, determined – as the couple's son, Cyril Wall, recalled – to stop her husband being 'stolen by an English hussy'. She worked for several war-industry companies – Imperial Chemical Industries and then DuPont – but 'she naively thought she'd see her husband every weekend, but when Raymond was sent to his permanent station in Suffolk, his wife had to stay behind in the factory in Birmingham.'

On 22 March 1944 Raymond Wall finally qualified as an FME (Flight Mechanic – Engines) with the rank of aircraftman, and he joined No 90 Squadron RAF at RAF Tuddenham in Suffolk. By June, the squadron had finished converting from Short Stirling four-engine heavy bombers to Avro Lancasters, and it was this latter aircraft that Raymond worked on for the remainder of the war.

During his time at RAF Tuddenham, Raymond once experienced a night fighter attack. German night fighters were known to get into formation with British bombers returning from missions and simply follow them back to England, and then, as the British bombers neared their base and the ground crews began lighting fires in oil drums to light up the runways, the German night fighters would attack the landing aircraft, as well as the now-illuminated airbase. On one occasion, Raymond recalled that a British pilot was shot down and killed by an enemy night fighter, only moments before he would have safely landed his aircraft after a successful mission.

However, enemy aircraft were not the only threat to RAF ground crews. Often operating with high explosives, accidents could potentially lead to disastrous results. On another occasion, Raymond and his fellow ground crew were loading a 1,000lb bomb onto an air-craft when the winch lifting the bomb from the trolley up into the belly of the Lancaster began to shudder. As the shuddering became more violent, it quickly became obvious that the winch was about to fail. The crew panicked and sprinted away. However, Raymond and a friend simply stood still and watched the bomb crash to the ground. Thankfully – after several extremely tense seconds – nothing happened. Afterwards, the crewmen who had fled asked Raymond and his friend why they had not tried to save themselves. Raymond simply replied, 'It was a 1,000lb bomb. There would've been no point in running!'

Raymond was also interested in the cinema, and he used to assist the RAF projectionist who would show films to the men. Perhaps unusually, these films were also often attended by POWs. In the local area, POWs – mostly Italians, but some Germans too – had been put to work on the land, aiding local farmers. They were not permanently locked away in a POW camp, and Raymond and his ground crew recalled that they were a cheery, friendly bunch – more than happy to be out of the fighting. One night, the POWs were led by two

Home Guard soldiers into RAF Tuddenham to watch a film. While the film was on, the two Home Guard 'chaperones' went to the station's canteen to have a few drinks. When the film ended, the sentries on the gate were subsequently treated to a bizarre sight. In the darkness, they were approached by a group of smiling Italians and Germans who were helping two drunken Home Guard soldiers to walk. They were let out the gate, and later Raymond learned that the POWs had dropped the Home Guard soldiers safely back to their billet – rifles and all – in the nearby town.

Raymond Wall was promoted to leading aircraftman on 1 May 1945, and after the war ended, he was discharged in November 1946. His discharge papers note that he was 'of very good character; steady, hardworking and willing. Able to accept responsibility.' Driving back to Loughrea, however, he stopped in Athlone to visit his sister Melda, and unfortunately most of his RAF kit and wartime souvenirs were stolen from the back of his car. He also experienced some anti-British sentiment on his return to Loughrea, although apparently it was very little compared to what other local veterans had experienced after the previous war.

He ended up settling in Dublin and becoming a mechanical engineer (later specialising in hydraulics, undercarriage and air frame) with Aer Lingus before retiring in 1980. Cyril Wall – Raymond's son – remembered his father as the 'ultimate pacifist ... he was gentle, sophisticated, and condoned no violence of any kind.' This led Cyril to ask his father why he – an unlikely military man – had enlisted during the war. Raymond replied:

> Those were different times then. They were dark times. There was an insidious evil rampaging across Europe, and decent men were needed to stop it.

And while Raymond never really spoke ill of anyone, if de Valera was mentioned in conversation, he used to say, 'There isn't a confessional box in Ireland that's going to save that man's arse from frying in Hell.'

Raymond Wall – who felt it was his duty to volunteer and fight Nazi fascism – died in 1987, aged seventy-nine.

ADOLPH AND THE KERRYMAN

STEPHEN SWEENEY

While most Irish airmen of the Second World War served with the RAF, there were those who flew with the United States Army Air Force (USAAF). During the Second World War, America's air forces were still a part of the US Army (the United States Air Force was not set up as a separate body until 1947), and one Irishman who flew with them during this time was Stephen Sweeney from Ballagh, an area just south of Kilgarvan in County Kerry – not

The cover of the 7 July 1944 edition of Yank *magazine, showing Technical Sergeant Stephen Sweeney from County Kerry, and his beagle-dachshund crossbreed dog Adolph. During the war, Adolph accompanied Sweeney on every mission he flew.*

far from the Cork border. Born in December 1907, the youngest of a large family, Sweeney emigrated to live in New York City in 1925 – aged seventeen – and lived in Manhattan. When America entered the fight in 1941, Sweeney was then thirty-three years old.

He was initially sent to train in Walla Walla, Washington State, on the west coast of the

US, and it was here that Sweeney met a friend who would accompany him on every flight he would make during the war – a beagle-dachshund crossbreed named Adolph. In 1943, Stephen Sweeney – now a sergeant and radio operator – was posted to 352nd Squadron, 301st Bombardment Group (Heavy) in North Africa (he was one of the first crewmembers of the bomber 'Moonlight Cocktail' during this time). This Squadron flew Boeing B-17 Flying Fortress four-engine heavy bombers, and were a part of the US Fifteenth Air Force. Stephen Sweeney and Adolph were soon a famous pair, and an article about them in *Yank* magazine (20 January 1945) recorded that:

> While Sweeney's squadron was moving to an advanced base in North Africa, 'Adolph', a GI youngster at the time, went AWOL to view the strange country-side. When Sweeney reported his loss his commanding officer held up the train for 30 minutes until 'Adolph' was brought in.

During this time, Sweeney also served as an air gunner. This was a cold and lonely job, where Sweeney would have found himself cramped into a Plexiglas bubble for hours with a frequent risk of developing frostbite. Constantly rotating his turret while looking out for enemy fighters, his position was the most exposed on the aircraft and often the first one targeted by the enemy – in fact, air gunners accounted for more than a third of all RAF Bomber Command personnel killed during the war. Famously, one of the worst jobs that ground crews had to perform was hosing out the remains of dead gunners from turrets that had been hit in order to clean and repair them for new gunners.

Then, in 1944, after flying many missions together – some over North Africa, and the remainder over Europe after the squadron was transferred to Italy – Sergeant Stephen Sweeney and Adolph transferred from the US Fifteenth Air Force to the famous US Eighth Air Force, stationed in Britain.

The US Eighth Air Force had begun operating from British airfields in 1942. Unlike their RAF counterparts, however, the US bombers flew in tight formations (although hundreds of RAF bombers might take off at the same time to attack a common target, they did not fly in group formations, meaning each plane was essentially flying by itself) which allowed for greater protection against enemy fighters and for better bombing concentrations on target. Also unlike the British, the American bombers flew daylight raids, but these missions could often result in disastrous numbers of men and planes lost. One thing they had in common with the RAF, though, was that the US Eighth Air Force also had to adapt to enemy tactics. The Germans soon found a way to overcome the protective formations that the US bombers used – they would simply attack the lead bomber, which would usually make the entire formation scatter, and then the German fighters would attack each individual plane in turn.

The US Eighth Air Force began co-ordinating their missions with the RAF in January 1943, but the losses they suffered from continually flying in daylight meant that – by the end of the year – their forces were badly depleted. It was not until March 1944 that they were ready to rejoin the RAF in the skies over Europe. By then, they had developed a system whereby bombers were defended by long-range fighters, and the destruction of *Luftwaffe* air superiority in the lead up to D-Day meant that daylight raids were no longer as risky as they had been in previous years.

By July 1944, Sweeney had been promoted from sergeant to staff sergeant and then to technical sergeant. He had also been awarded the Air Medal on 12 April 1944 for 'meritorious achievement while participating in aerial flight', and then an oak leaf cluster was added to his Air Medal (ie a second award) on 30 May. He was also the recipient of a good conduct medal, and, on 7 July, he appeared alongside Adolph on the cover of *Yank* magazine. However, while Sweeney was only four missions away from reaching the end of a second tour for which he had volunteered (twenty-five sorties was the length of a USAAF tour; Sweeney had now flown forty-six missions), a problem with records meant that the authorities had no hard proof of his flights to date, and so he was required to begin his second tour again. This meant that Sweeney had to fly another twenty-five missions.

Normally, pilots and aircrew who survived long enough to complete a tour (the length of which varied depending on which type of aircraft a man flew) were given base duty or placed in an instructor role – this promise of rest and relevant safety at the end of a dangerous tour was an important goal for Allied air force personnel and extremely necessary for their psychological wellbeing – but they could, of course, volunteer for another tour, as Sweeney had done. However, in 1943, only fifteen percent of aircrews survived their first tour of missions, and those who started a second tour had only a 2.5 percent chance of survival. Regardless, Stephen Sweeney from County Kerry soon re-started his second tour.

Five missions into his new tour with the US Eighth Air Force in early 1945 (Sweeney was serving aboard a B-17 named *Screaming Eagle* at this time), 'the 20-month-old "Adolph" ... [was put] under observation for rabies. While visiting the Service Club, recently, "Adolph" nibbled on the ankle of Sgt. Faloon. Although it was his first offence, "Adolph" was sent to the Base Veterinary Hospital for a week's observation. If tests fail to disclose rabies the flying-pup will be returned to Sgt. Sweeney. "Adolph," proud possessor of 400 hours flying time, is visited twice daily by his master.'

Adolph ultimately tested negative for rabies, and Technical Sergeant Stephen Sweeney and his dog were soon back in the air. Despite all the odds, the pair completed their latest tour of missions and both finished the war without ever having been wounded.

After the war, Sweeney returned to the US with Adolph, but he never managed to readjust to civilian life. In an interview, Jim Mourne – Sweeney's nephew – said:

> He was in and out of veterans' hospitals. He drank a lot, not that I ever really saw
> him drunk. He just used to drink to calm his nerves. Steve was talented. He was a

good musician but he never made much of a career for himself and he did work as a taxi driver and then as a private chauffeur.

However, Sweeney's health continued to deteriorate, and as Jim Mourne recalled:

> They never quite resolved his problem in the veterans' hospital. They gave him psychological examinations. They gave him physicals. But they pretty much contended it was a case of shellshock. He had been through just too many missions and [they] left that type of injury to his brain. Loud noises [were] upsetting terribly. Anybody bickering would upset him. He still retained a very pleasant personality. And we all loved him, but we knew he had his problems. Finally ... he died. It was a tumour on the brain and I kind of suspect, looking back [on] all his troubles after war, that that might have been the source of the problem all along. Steve always considered himself the black sheep of the family, dark black hair, nice smiling personality.

Having never married, Technical Sergeant Stephen Sweeney from Ballagh, Kilgarvan, County Kerry, passed away in 1965. He was fifty-seven years old.

Ultimately, the war in the air, and the Irish who took part in it, played a vital role in stopping the Axis forces during the Second World War. The Allies flew 337,237 sorties during the war (sixty percent of which were flown between D-Day and the end of the war), dropped 3.4 million tons of explosives (sixty percent of which was dropped in 1944 alone), and destroyed or damaged just under 117,000 *Luftwaffe* aircraft. Frederick Desmond Hughes (later Air Vice Marshall) from Donaghdee, near Belfast, and William MacDonald (later Air Chief Marshall Sir William MacDonald) from County Cork, are just two of the RAF pilots who flew during the war, but both of these Irishmen went on to hold the prestigious position of aide-de-camp to the Queen – Hughes in September 1963 and MacDonald in April 1965.

There was a high price to pay for the war in the air. One out of every four fighter pilots did not complete his combat tour of 300 hours (either by being killed or by being taken POW); nearly one out of every two airmen aboard a medium bomber (whose crews had to complete a tour of fifty missions) were killed or taken prisoner, while a heavy bomber crewman had only a twenty-nine percent chance of completing his tour of thirty sorties.

The RAF lost 22,000 aircraft (over Europe alone) and 70,253 personnel killed during the war (at least seventy-nine percent of which were in RAF Bomber Command), the USAAF lost 41,575 planes and suffered over 88,000 airmen killed and over 17,000 wounded, while the German *Luftwaffe* lost 433,000 killed (although this figure includes their infantry units). Meanwhile, civilian casualties were also extremely high. 60,500 British civilians, an estimated 550,000 German civilians, 50,000 Italians, and 67,000 French citizens (killed by RAF and USAAF bombings) died during the war. In the Far East, Allied bombing also resulted in the deaths of half a million Japanese civilians and 260,000 Chinese in Japanese-occupied territory.

The Allied victory in the Second World War was as a result of a vital combined effort between land, air and sea forces. However, the war could only be ended on the ground. Despite what RAF Bomber Command initially thought, its bombers could not simply blast the enemy into submission. And so, the land war of infantry, tanks and artillery still had to be fought. However, having been initially willing to fight peripheral battles only – such as Norway – and then subsequently, after the end of the Battle of France, unable to strike directly at the German Army, the British were forced to begin another peripheral land battle in summer 1940. Initially fought against Germany's new ally – Italy – and then against one of the most famous German commanders, Erwin Rommel, and his Afrika Korps, the Desert War in North Africa ultimately gave the British a victory they badly needed, while allowing the Allies to follow it up with an invasion of Italy and gain a foothold on the European mainland.

CHAPTER 3

FIGHTING ON THE EDGE

– FROM NORTH AFRICA TO ITALY

8th King's Royal Irish Hussars – Lieutenant Eddie McDonnell's regiment – training with their new Stuart tanks, 28 August 1941.

'It is terrible out here. Nothing but heat and sweat.
I shall be glad when it gets cold.'
**Rifleman Leslie Francis from Athlone, 1st London Irish Rifles.
Letter to his mother, 15 August 1944**

On 10 June 1940 – just days after the end of the Dunkirk evacuation – Italy's fascist dictator, Benito Mussolini, declared war on Britain and France. Germany was at the height of its successes and had not yet suffered the defeat of the Battle of Britain. To Mussolini, it looked as though he was bringing Italy in on the winning side, and he was keen to join forces with Germany before Hitler left nothing for him to take. Italy had controlled Libya since 1912, and having conquered Ethiopia in 1936 (killing 500,000 Ethiopians and wounding 250,000 more in the process), Mussolini now wanted to secure Egypt and the Suez Canal. This was British territory, and on 13 September 1940, the Italians launched an invasion of Egypt.

What followed was two and a half years of war in North Africa, during which the Italians were initially pushed back west to El Agheila in Libya, only to be reinforced by Erwin Rommel and the German Afrika Korps, who subsequently pushed the British back eastwards into Egypt. Several periods of advance and retreat on both sides followed while the desert war became famous for being a tank war, where petrol was as vital as water. With wide-open deserts stretching for miles in every direction, armies of tanks manoeuvred and fought in the sand. Their crews were constantly uncomfortable – cramped in an airless tank, they had to endure the heat and noise of the vehicle's engine – and during a fight, they risked being caught inside the tank if it 'brewed up' (if it was hit by the enemy and set on fire). Many men died screaming inside these 'burning coffins', while there are cases of men escaping their tanks with their bodies on fire – men who subsequently died in agony.

Of course, the desert was dangerous in other ways. British troops were often issued only a cup of water a day to wash and shave in, while the diet was poor and the supply of drinking water was not always fresh, and these unsanitary conditions frequently led to outbreaks of dysentery. Swarms of flies also plagued the men – especially when they were trying to eat – along with snakes and scorpions, and they were constantly bombarded with blistering heat and sunlight. The sand was an enemy all by itself, and aside from clogging up and damaging vehicles and getting into every crevice in a soldier's body, men could literally get lost and die while going to the latrine during sandstorms.

Ultimately, the Axis troops were forced to abandon North Africa due to crippling supply problems. The Allies then secured Sicily, before pressing on to invade Italy – finally gaining a foothold on mainland Europe. These were the first major Allied victories of the Second World War, and many Irishmen and Irish units fought here – including the famous 38th Irish Brigade. During the First World War, three Irish divisions had been raised, but the largest Irish formation during the Second World War was brigade-sized. The 38th Irish Brigade contained 1st Royal Irish Fusiliers, 2nd London Irish Rifles and 6th Royal Inniskilling Fusiliers (although this latter battalion was replaced with 2nd Royal Inniskilling Fusiliers in July 1944), and went into action for the first time in North Africa, before going on to fight in Sicily and throughout the Italian Campaign. Also in the desert were the North Irish Horse and 8th King's Royal Irish Hussars – both armoured regiments – and 1st Irish Guards, while 2nd Royal Irish Fusiliers endured months of being besieged and bombed on the island of Malta, and 1st London Irish Rifles and 2nd Royal Inniskilling Fusiliers entered the fight with the invasion of Sicily. And so, there are many stories of Irishmen fighting on the edge of Europe.

THE ONLY SON OF AN ONLY SON

ROBERT EDWARD 'EDDIE' McDONNELL

One Irishman stationed in the desert when the Italians declared war on Britain was Lieutenant Robert Edward 'Eddie' McDonnell of the 8th King's Royal Irish Hussars. This was an armoured regiment – equipped with a variant of the Vickers-Armstrong Light Tank – part of the newly created Royal Armoured Corps, and one of the units that made up the 7th Armoured Division, the soon-to-be famous 'Desert Rats'.

From Kilsharvan House – just south of Drogheda – in County Meath, Eddie McDonnell was descended from the tenth-century kings of Scotland, and also from a much more recent line of doctors and soldiers. A relative – Doctor James McDonnell from County Antrim – had been involved with the United Irishmen and had lost a grandson in battle in India (George McDonnell was killed, aged twenty-one, in 1825). Meanwhile, Eddie's great-grandfather –

Doctor John McDonnell – performed the first operation under anaesthesia in Ireland in 1847. Inspired by a British and Foreign Medical Review report, he performed an arm amputation in Richmond Hospital on a critically ill girl, Mary Kane, who had previously fallen while carrying hawthorn bushes and pierced her elbow joint with a thorn. John McDonnell designed his own ether inhalation apparatus, tested it on himself, and then performed the operation the next day. The operation was successful. Doctor John McDonnell lived to be ninety-six years old.

Eddie's grandfather – Robert McDonnell – was also a doctor and gave the first transfusion of human blood in an Irish hospital, in the Charitable Infirmary in Dublin in 1865, while Eddie's father – John McDonnell, an only son – became a lieutenant-colonel in the 5th Leinster Regiment. However, during the First World War, while on attachment to 1st Royal Inniskilling Fusiliers, he was killed in action on 29 September 1918, less than a month before the end of the war. He was forty years old, and now lies buried in Ypres Reservoir Cemetery. Eddie, also an only son, was three years old at the time.

As a young man, Eddie was educated in Winchester College. He loved horses and was also a keen sportsman. Eddie was active in the boy scouts, and went on to become a sergeant in his Officer Training Corps unit. Then, in 1933, he entered Sandhurst – the British Army's military academy – as a prize cadet. Two years later, he was commissioned into the 8th King's Royal Irish Hussars.

Just before the Second World War had broken out – in August 1939 – the regiment had been ordered to lay petrol dumps in the desert, in preparation for any potential future actions against local Italian forces. The 30,000 British troops in Egypt were surrounded by 450,000 Italians in Ethiopia and Libya, but on 11 June 1940 – the day after Italy declared war – it was the British who first went on the offensive. Raids were launched against Italian positions in Libya, but these were soon stopped due to the arrival of Italian reinforcements and the high-rate of mechanical failures in British equipment. Lieutenant Eddie McDonnell and 8th King's Royal Irish Hussars,

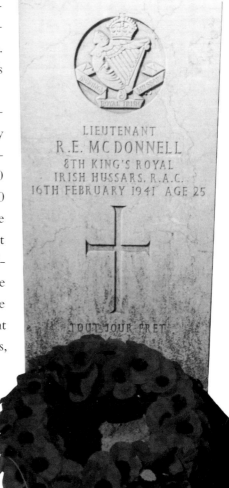

The grave of Lieutenant Eddie McDonnell from County Meath – 8th King's Royal Irish Hussars – in Benghazi War Cemetery, Libya.

along with the rest of the British forces in Egypt, now set up a western line of defence in Egypt. Patrols were frequently sent out to screen to the west and report on the movements of columns of enemy troops and vehicles, but on one of these patrols – while positioned between Sidi Azeiz and Fort Capuzzo – the 8th King's Royal Irish Hussars encountered a force of twenty-nine Italian tanks. By the end of this close range battle, the regiment had lost two tanks and three crewmembers were taken prisoner by the Italians.

On 13 September, the Italians launched an invasion of Egypt. The British were severely outnumbered and were forced to retreat eastwards. Within three days, the Italians had advanced sixty miles, but due to supply shortages, they were forced to stop their advance, with the bulk of the Italian forces digging in around Sidi Barrani. However, in order to defend their newly won territory, they set up perimeter camps that were positioned far apart from each other. These would be easy for British forces to circle around and attack from the rear – which would cut the Italians' supply lines – and so the British prepared to launch a counterattack to strike back at the Italians. Codenamed Operation Compass, it was planned to last only a couple of days.

On 9 December 1940 – the day that Operation Compass was launched – Lieutenant Eddie McDonnell and 8th King's Royal Irish Hussars began harassing the southern flank of the Italians' positions in the desert. Patrols were sent out to make contact with the enemy, and on 11 December – after encountering Italian artillery on top of sand dunes in the vicinity of Buq Buq – tanks from the regiment assaulted the dunes and captured 4,000 prisoners.

Lieutenant Eddie McDonnell and 8th King's Royal Irish Hussars then advanced further west and came within sight of Fort Capuzzo – which the British had initially captured from the Italians during their early raids, only to abandon it later – and helped to cut off Italian troops retreating from Sidi Omar while also defending a gap in the British frontier wire defences. By now, the British had captured 38,000 prisoners and 400 artillery guns, and had only lost 133 killed, eight missing, and 387 wounded. They had never expected to take so many prisoners – which led them to believe that the Italians were not natural soldiers (and also led to the untrue joke that 'Italian tanks had one forward gear for advancing and five reserve gears for retreating') – and thanks to the supplies of food, water, and fuel that the British had captured in Italian camps, Operation Compass could now continue beyond its initial four-day timeframe.

The Italians were pushed out of Egypt, but with 40,000 enemy troops making a stand in the Libyan fortress of Bardia, the British decided to attack Bardia. Lieutenant Eddie McDonnell and 8th King's Royal Irish Hussars were ordered to move to the west of the town on 20 December. The regiment remained here over the Christmas period – which was a relatively quiet time – then on New Year's Eve they moved further west to delay an

Italian force moving east from Tobruk in an attempt to relieve Bardia. Lieutenant Eddie McDonnell and 8th King's Royal Irish Hussars subsequently captured and occupied El Adem airfield far to the west (just south of Tobruk) on 3 January 1941.

Tobruk was the next British target, and after being surrounded on 9 January – by a force that included 8th King's Royal Irish Hussars – it was attacked on 21 January. The following day, Tobruk fell, and the British captured another 25,000 Italians. The enemy were soon in full retreat from Cyrenaica – Libya's eastern province.

In late January, 8th King's Royal Irish Hussars were withdrawn from the desert and sent to Cairo to rest and perform local duties. Unfortunately though, this relief did not come soon enough for Lieutenant Eddie McDonnell. At some point during January, the headquarters of 7th Armoured Division at Aqrdabea had been dive-bombed by enemy planes. Eddie McDonnell had been present at the time of the attack, and he had been badly wounded. He was left behind in a Benghazi hospital when his regiment departed for Cairo, and he subsequently succumbed to his wounds and died there on 16 February.

Eight days after Eddie's death, as the war diary recorded, 8th King's Royal Irish Hussars received the following message from General Michael O'Moore Creagh, commanding officer of 7th Armoured Division:

> The enemy resistance in Cyrenaica has been finally overcome. 7th. Armd Div. have had a large share in the achievement of this success. They have been in contact with the enemy since the outbreak of war [with Italy], and after nearly 8 months have won an outstanding victory. I congratulate all ranks on their endurance and fine fighting spirit. Your skill, energy and courage have alone made this victory possible.

During Operation Compass, the Italians had lost 3,000 men killed and *at least* 115,000 taken prisoner, while the British had lost 494 killed, fifty-five missing, and 1,373 wounded.

Lieutenant Robert Edward 'Eddie' McDonnell from County Meath was twenty-five years old when he died. He passed away only days before the end of Operation Compass – similar to the way his father had been killed only days before the end of the First World War – and, like his father, he was also an only son. Today, his remains lie in the Benghazi War Cemetery.

The British advance ultimately lasted for ten weeks, covered 500 miles, destroyed the Italian Tenth Army (out of an initial force of 150,000 troops, only 32,000 demoralised Italian soldiers now remained in Libya), and reached as far west as El Agheila. Tripoli – the deep water port through which the enemy received their supplies and reinforcements – was now within reach, and if it was captured, it could end the war in North Africa. However, with the British in North Africa preparing to advance on Tripoli, the Germans invaded Greece on 6 April 1941, and so in order to help defend the country, the best British units in North Africa were withdrawn from the desert and sent to Greece. At the same time, the Germans

A mine explodes close to a British truck as it carries infantry through enemy minefields and wire to the new front lines at El Alamein, 1942.

had also decided to reinforce the Italians in Libya – if the war in North Africa ended, it would free up Allied troops to fight elsewhere, and so the campaign had to be prolonged. To do this, the Germans sent General Erwin Rommel and the Afrika Korps to Tripoli. Rommel had already proved himself as a brilliant leader and strategist during the Battle of France, and although he had never fought in the desert before, he was quick to adapt – soon earning himself the nickname 'The Desert Fox'.

Elements of the Afrika Korps attacked the British on the same day that they landed in Libya – 14 February 1941 – and within six weeks, Rommel launched a major offensive against the British at El Agheila on 24 March. In just over three weeks, he pushed the British and Commonwealth troops all the way back to Egypt, capturing thousands of prisoners in the process. The Germans had better tanks and employed better tactics – instead of firing and manoeuvring during battles as the British did, the Germans simply dug their tanks in alongside anti-tank guns and waited for the British to come to them. They also recovered damaged tanks from the battlefield – in order to repair them or salvage parts (something the British did not do initially) – and used tank transporters to move their tanks across the desert when they were not needed, while the British drove their tanks everywhere, which increased wear and tear on the vehicles and led to a high rate of breakdowns.

However, as the British fell back into Egypt, they left behind a pocket of Australian troops in the town of Tobruk. Rommel needed to capture Tobruk in order to advance into Egypt, but the Australians held out and every German assault failed to capture the town. And so, the German troops encircled Tobruk while the *Luftwaffe* tried to bomb the garrison into submission. They bombed it in over 1,000 raids, but the British simply resupplied and replaced the besieged troops by sea. The Germans and the Italians had no naval power in the Mediterranean, and so the Royal Navy could easily sail convoys to Tobruk, while attacking Axis convoys on their way to Tripoli. Unable to capture Tobruk, and with supplies of fuel running low, Rommel could not advance further east into Egypt.

After two failed attempts to counterattack against the Afrika Korps, the Allies launched Operation Crusader on 18 November 1941. Sixty percent of the British tanks – approximately 300 – were damaged or destroyed within five days, but after reorganising, the Allies managed to push the Afrika Korps back the 500 miles to El Agheila, relieving Tobruk in the process. Rommel was now severely low on fuel, and the British were in sight of Tripoli. But, once again, a new campaign against the enemy elsewhere meant that troops had to be taken from North Africa to meet this latest threat. The Japanese were now close to Burma and Malaya, and so units were sent from the desert to the Far East. It prevented the British from pressing on to Tripoli, and allowed Rommel to launch a counterattack on 21 January 1942. By 4 February, the Afrika Korps had reached Gazala, west of Tobruk. Rommel then renewed his offensive on 26 May, captured Tobruk, and entered Egypt, but was stopped by the British during the First Battle of El Alamein in July.

The British were desperate to push Rommel out of Egypt, and on 13 August 1942, Lieutenant-General Bernard Montgomery – better known as 'Monty' – took over command of the Eighth Army and began to reinforce the thirty-mile front at El Alamein while increasing the number of British infantry divisions in the desert and beginning a period of intense training and preparation. Meanwhile, Rommel's units were coming under attack from the RAF, stationed in nearby Egyptian bases, and his supply lines – which led all the way back to Tripoli – were severely overextended. Furthermore, the Royal Navy ensured that only twenty-five percent of Axis supply convoys ever reached Tripoli in the first place, and so, to try and stop the Royal Navy from attacking their shipping, the German *Luftwaffe* began a devastating bombing campaign against the British-controlled island of Malta – home to a Royal Navy base (2nd Royal Irish Fusiliers were also stationed on the island). Malta became the target of a sustained bombing offensive but did not surrender.

On 23 October 1942, the British launched Operation Lightfoot, and the Second Battle of El Alamein began – it would be the largest tank battle of the war so far. One hundred and ninety-five thousand Allied troops faced 115,000 Germans and Italians, and after a twenty-minute barrage of approximately 530,000 shells from 882 Allied light and medium artillery guns across the whole front, the gunners switched to firing on specific enemy targets while the infantry began clearing lanes through German minefields and advanced westwards. Their first goal was to destroy enemy anti-tank guns, and once this had been achieved, a force of 1,029 tanks would follow (the Germans had only 547 tanks available).

The Second Battle of El Alamein turned the tide of the war in North Africa and ultimately succeeded in pushing the Germans back west once and for all. On 23 January 1943 Tripoli was finally captured by the Allies. The Germans were forced to retreat further west into Tunisia, but there was a high price to pay for this victory. The Allies suffered 13,500 casualties, while the Germans and Italians lost 30,500 men. Both sides lost approximately 500 tanks, but this still meant the Allies had over 500 left, while the Germans were reduced to less than fifty.

THE IRISH ARRIVE

WILLIAM UPINGTON

On 8 November 1942, only days before the end of the Second Battle of El Alamein, a large Allied force of 107,000 troops began landing in Algeria, Morocco and Tunisia. Codenamed Operation Torch, its aim was to defeat the 125,000 Vichy French forces in the region, cut off and capture the Germans retreating west from Tripoli, and secure North Africa from the enemy. This force was to include several Irish units – the North Irish Horse (an armoured regiment), 1ˢᵗ Irish Guards, and 1ˢᵗ Royal Irish Fusiliers, 2ⁿᵈ London Irish Rifles and 6ᵗʰ Royal Inniskilling Fusiliers. These latter three units formed the 38ᵗʰ Irish Brigade.

Serving with 6ᵗʰ Royal Inniskilling Fusiliers was twenty-year-old Second-Lieutenant William Upington from Blossomfort, just northwest of Mallow, County Cork. Born in 1922 during the Irish Civil War – the son of Thomas Upington, a poor farmer with very little livestock (who was also a former soldier in the South Irish Horse), and Florence McBryde, a governess from Portarlington, County Laois – he later recalled that, around the time of his birth, the anti-Treaty IRA felled trees on the road not far from his father's farm in order to try and stop and ambush a National (Free State) Army convoy, and that when William was born, a blanket had been hung over the bedroom window in a naive attempt to deflect any rifle fire that might accidentally hit the house. However, due to another tree further down the road being felled too early (it was meant to box in the National Army convoy once they had passed it), the Free State troops turned back, so there was ultimately no ambush outside the Upington farm.

William Upington later wrote a memoir entitled *Sure, It's True Enough*, and in it he recorded that 'I was a delicate, miserable, whinging child, as a baby not expected to live. I was given only one name, no godparents and christened in a hurry.' But William did survive, and at age fourteen, he started work as a men's outfitters apprentice, which made shoes and suits to measure. 'I had to be smartly dressed, collar and tie, never to be seen idle and to [always recommend] something extra to what [the customer] wanted ... I had to go in at 8.00am ... We closed at 6.30pm and 9pm on a Saturday.' His wages were £1 a month.

Then, in September 1939 – one month away from his seventeenth birthday:

> The war started, we disapproved strongly of Ireland being neutral. In the summer of 1940 the government decided to form a local defence force to look out for parachutists. The manager said we should be willing. We attended one parade, I decided if the British landed, I might find myself in the wrong army.
>
> A chap called Ned, who worked in the same firm, and I discussed the possibility of joining up in the British [Army], when it came to the crunch he backed out. As I had made my mind up there was no turning back, I knew very well that it would cause a 'terrible stink' with the family and with the firm who had almost trained me. August Bank Holiday weekend 1940, I finished work on Saturday night. On Sunday morning I caught a bus to Dublin (only Isobel [William's sister] knew of my plans and had given me £5), caught a train to Belfast and headed for the border ... I was through.

William Upington was not the first member of his family to join the British Army. Aside from his father, who had enlisted but not gone overseas during 1914–1918, William's uncle

Captain William Upington, from County Cork, of 6th Royal Inniskilling Fusiliers commands a Captain's Guard of Honour during a Royal Review by Princess Margaret in Belfast on 19 October 1947. Princess Margaret was in Belfast to launch the Union-Castle Line ocean liner RMS Edinburgh Castle. Upington's prosthetic right arm can be clearly seen.

– Sergeant Henry McBryde of the South Irish Horse (subsequently the 7th Royal Irish Regiment) – had fought during the First World War before dying of influenza in Langensalza POW Camp on 8 December 1918, only weeks after the end of the fighting. William's mother also had two cousins – Courtland and Herbert Mitchell – who had served as officers during the First World War, and Herbert Mitchell ended up serving in the Second World War as a colonel in British Army intelligence.

William was soon introduced to army life:

Finally, I was on a train out of Belfast to Ballymena with some very rough young men. During training we were not allowed out for the first few weeks, after that, Saturday nights only if you passed inspection at the Guard Room, then a couple of hours in a packed dance hall, fish and chips and back to the Guard Room for inspection again. We arrived in St. Patrick's Barracks on the Tuesday, reveille at 6am, wash and shave, square your bed space, "bump the floor", first parade at 7am, vaccinations and inoculations and hectic training, marching 180 steps to the minute … Six weeks later we looked like soldiers. We moved to St. Donard's Hall, Belfast. Next day I was on my first sentry of the gate, a 3 ton lorry demolished the gate pier beside me. I had just enough time to jump out of the way.

Now a soldier in 70th (Young Soldiers' Battalion) Royal Ulster Rifles, William Upington was soon promoted all the way to lance-sergeant, after which he was selected for officer training. By mid-1942, having successfully completed the course, he was a second-lieutenant in 6th Royal Inniskilling Fusiliers – part of 38th Irish Brigade – and on 26 October that year, William Upington and his men boarded SS *Strathallan* and set sail for North Africa. William had just turned twenty years old.

On 8 November, Second-Lieutenant William Upington landed at Algiers as part of the Eastern Task Force of Operation Torch. They encountered no opposition from Vichy French forces – the French Resistance in Algiers had neutralised all Vichy coastal artillery guns – and William Upington and his men ended up helping to unload ammunition from Allied vessels. The rest of 38th Irish Brigade joined them on 22 November.

Drenching rainstorms soon gave way to 'a couple of weeks, keeping fit and waiting for orders'. Second-Lieutenant William Upington remained in Algeria as a reinforcement officer – to be called on whenever needed – while the rest of 6th Royal Inniskilling Fusiliers departed for Tunisia on 1 December. Over the following month and into January 1943, the battalion patrolled in various locations – Souk el Khemis, Téboursouk, Medjez el Bab and Goubellat – before setting off for El Aroussa, west of Bou Arada, on 11 January. By this time, as the war diary recorded, 'A possible German breakthrough is contemplated.' 6th Royal Inniskilling Fusiliers were at least 100 men below strength, and after being ordered to take part in their first battle – an assault against enemy positions on Two Tree Hill – the reinforcement officers in Algeria were called on. Second-Lieutenant William Upington was summoned to the front.

As William later wrote:

> In early [January 1943], we receive an urgent message, casualties at the front, 6 officers wanted immediately. We are off in a truck, terrible mountain roads, it took 2 or 3 days, all through Algeria. We arrive at the front and [on 12 January] Capt. Ted [Captain Harold Edward Hooper] takes me to my platoon. 'Sorry,' he said, 'we are going to attack at dawn, your lads in second wave, a chance to get to

know them, 4 tanks in support, breakfast at 3am, rum at 4am, your sergeant will tell you who's who, Good Luck.'

Despite thunderstorms and gales, the attack was not called off, and at 0545hrs on 13 January, 6th Royal Inniskilling Fusiliers advanced against Two Tree Hill. The assault was initially slow due to British shells falling short and thick mud, but then D Company came under enfilading fire from two German machine guns and were pinned down. C Company tried to outflank these machine guns, but came under machine gun and mortar fire, and a report soon came from C Company saying that 'they were held up, only about fifteen men left, all officers out of action and that they wanted ammunition.' 6th Royal Inniskilling Fusiliers could not get their own mortars forward due to the mud, and when A Company tried to reinforce C Company they simply could not advance quickly enough. D Company then tried to advance under cover of 'smoke and shell' but more German machine guns further up the slopes of Two Tree Hill subsequently opened fire on them. It had 'become apparent that the Coys ... had suffered severe losses, were out of ammunition and were being pushed back' and so, B Company – which had been in reserve – was ordered to help cover a withdrawal. 'The enemy did not follow up the withdrawal ... [and it] was marked by orderliness and a keen sense of duty by all ranks to get every man wounded or dead back.'

Regarding the battle, Second-Lieutenant William Upington recalled:

> The attack goes on until 3pm, the tanks are bogged down, heavy casualties. We get away light, the attack is over. My batman is wounded, taken back and I never saw him again.

6th Royal Inniskilling Fusiliers failed to capture Two Tree Hill and lost one officer killed and five wounded, along with eleven other ranks killed, fifty-five wounded, and sixteen missing.

Throughout the rest of January and on into February, after entrenching in their current positions, 6th Royal Inniskilling Fusiliers were subjected to regular attack from enemy infantry, armoured cars and tanks, Stuka dive bombers and artillery and mortar fire, while the rest of 38th Irish Brigade were also in the line with them at this time. Second-Lieutenant William Upington wrote the following about this period:

> I don't propose to say any more about the fighting except, it was continuous night patrols, officers got no sleep, the men were fairly safe in their trenches, officers exposed, moving about in mortar attacks. Capt. Ted briefs me for night patrol [a recce of the area in front of Grand Hand Hill, for which Second-Lieutenant Upington led out a section from B Company], when I get back in the morning he is dead, caught in the open ... killed ... by a grenade thrown by the enemy, who appeared to be surrendering.

Then, on 1 March, 6th Royal Inniskilling Fusiliers came under fire from enemy mortars at 0800hrs. During this attack, William Upington – who had recently been promoted to lieutenant – was wounded by the enemy. It was a wound that changed his future in the army.

> On March 1st, 1943 on a 6 O'Clock "Stand To" I am caught in the open, I think I
> knew it was not fatal. "Stand To" at dusk and dawn, is when an attack may come in,
> Officers are supposed to go around all the trenches, check weapons and see the men
> are alert and issue any orders, this explains why officers are caught in the open as you
> have to get round several positions over 100's of yards.

> It is difficult to explain anything about being wounded, all I can remember is the
> feeling of being hit by an 'iron bar' on the arm; somehow, you just know it is not fatal.
> Most infantry get wounded by mortar fire … when [mortar fire] reaches the target it
> explodes sending shrapnel all over the place causing awful casualties … the Germans
> had multiple 6" [mortars], we called them 'Moaning Minnies'.

William had been badly wounded in the right arm, and he remembered hearing a doctor say:

> We saved your elbow, not much to cover the bone, you lost a lot of blood, don't
> worry you will get free beer in the pub when you get home.

Having had his right forearm amputated, Lieutenant William Upington's first stop after Bou Arada was Thibar Monastery:

> Stretchers all in a row, it is raining, the monks help to carry us in. I don't remember
> much about this place except, 'Your arm is a mess, we will have to operate again.'

After several days travelling by train to 'Bougie' (Béjaïa, near Algiers), William was admitted to a hospital that was 'a sea of marquees'. It was weeks before he was able to stand, and when he was finally able to walk again, it was only with the help of a crutch.

Then, on 13 May 1943 – after three years of war in the desert – the Axis forces in North Africa finally surrendered. Tunis – the capital of Tunisia – had been captured on 7 May, and with that, the remaining Axis forces in North Africa had been surrounded and cut off. Operation Torch and the subsequent Tunisian Campaign had cost the Allies 76,000 casualties, while the Germans and Italians had lost 50,000 killed and wounded, while 250,000 more – nearly all of the Afrika Korps – were taken prisoner. In all, the various desert battles and campaigns since 1940 had resulted in just under 240,000 Allied casualties, and as many as 950,000 German, Italian and Vichy French forces killed or wounded – a possible total of nearly 1.2 million soldiers.

Just over two weeks after the Axis surrender, Lieutenant William Upington was transported back to Britain aboard the HMHS *Newfoundland*, arriving in Bristol on 10 June. Then, after recovering in hospital – which involved 'electric shocks to get my upper arm and elbow working again' – William was fitted for a prosthetic arm in Leeds. However, he was not discharged from the army – despite the extent of his injuries – and he was soon sent back to Palace Barracks in Holywood, just outside Belfast, and promoted to captain. He remained here as a company commander in a holding battalion until the end of the war, after which he 'mounted a 100 strong Royal Guard for the King at the parliament buildings and some months later for Princess Margaret when she launched the *Edinburgh Castle* in Belfast docks, the guard was perfect.'

Captain William Upington was then seconded to the WAFF (West African Frontier Force) and sent to Nigeria, before returning to Britain and taking up the post of weapons instructor to the Royal Army Pay Corps in Devizes, Wiltshire. In 1953 he married and the couple had their first son the following year.

In 1955, William Upington left the army – but not before being granted the honourable rank of major – and ironically, for a man with only one arm, bought a farm in Hampshire and began working the land. Sadly however, his first daughter – born in 1956 – died of cancer, aged only seven years old.

William went on to have two more children and the family moved to a new farm in Devon, and then later to Cornwall, before finally settling to the north of Exeter in Devon in September 1986. At the time of writing, North Africa and 38th Irish Brigade veteran William Upington from County Cork is still active on his farm in Devon. He is now eighty-nine years old.

AIRBORNE

LAWRENCE LEE

Having secured North Africa, plans were drawn up for the invasion of Sicily – the first step on the road to invading mainland Italy. Codenamed Operation Husky, the plan involved the first large-scale deployment of Allied airborne soldiers, the elite 'paratroopers' of Britain and the US. On 13 July 1943, 3rd Parachute Regiment (of 1st Parachute Brigade, 1st Airborne Division) parachuted into Sicily. With them was Private Lawrence Lee.

Born in 1925 in Castlebar, County Mayo, Lawrence grew up in Cavan, and one day – aged sixteen – he decided to join the Irish Army. He was posted to McKee Barracks in Dublin, and soon

Seventeen-year-old Private Lawrence Lee in 1942, around the time that he enlisted in the British Army.

found himself working in the Construction Corps – who assisted the Corps of Engineers – on a job at the Sally Gap in the Wicklow Mountains.

Then, in 1942, after only seven months in the Irish Army – while working on another army-related construction job on an estate in his home county of Cavan – Lawrence's superiors discovered that he was underage. Right there and then, Private Lawrence Lee was discharged from the Irish Army. As Lawrence remembered, 'They kicked me out on the spot ... I wasn't even given the bus fare into Cavan town, so I had to walk the whole sixteen miles.'

Determined to serve in uniform, the seventeen-year-old Lawrence walked into Cavan town and then went straight to a local man who was known to lend money to those who were interested in crossing the border to join the British Army. Lawrence made the trip to Enniskillen and enlisted in the British Army a mere few hours after being discharged from the Irish Army, making him probably one of the few soldiers who could claim to have served in two armies within a twenty-four hour period.

He was sent to Omagh in County Tyrone for six weeks' recruit training. A couple of weeks into the training it was obvious that Lawrence had previous military experience and he was sent on immediately to join the 6th Royal Irish Fusiliers stationed in Scotland. The battalion later moved to Weymouth in Dorset, and then to the Isle of Wight. It was while on the Isle of Wight that Lawrence Lee decided to join the Parachute Regiment.

Any British soldier could volunteer for the elite Parachute Regiment, but you had to pass some of the most physically demanding training that the army had to offer. Lawrence Lee was sent to Hardwick Camp near Chesterfield in Derbyshire for an intense period of pre-jump physical training; he passed all the tests and moved on to RAF Ringway in Cheshire for jump school – this was where all of the 60,000 Allied paratroopers recruited from Europe were trained during the Second World War. Lawrence remembered that, at RAF Ringway, there were only four Nissen huts for troops – two for the paratrooper students in training, one for the women who packed the parachutes, and one for the RAF parachute instructors.

Fully qualified as a British Army paratrooper, Lawrence Lee was sent to join 3rd Parachute Regiment. On 13 July 1943 eighteen-year-old Lawrence found himself taking off from North Africa en route to Sicily. One hundred and five C-47 Dakotas of the USAAF 51st Troop Carrier Wing transported the 1st Parachute Brigade (of which 3rd Parachute Regiment was a part) across the Mediterranean, but somewhere between Malta and Sicily the planes flew off course and were fired on by their own ships. Then, as the brigade flew over the Sicilian coast, Axis anti-aircraft gunners opened fire. Thirty-seven aircraft were shot down and a further ten were badly damaged and forced to abort.

Private Lawrence Lee making one of his qualifying jumps at RAF Ringway in Cheshire, c1943

Private Lawrence Lee and 3rd Parachute Regiment's mission was to capture the 400-foot-long, steel girder Primosole Bridge over the Simeto River (Operation Fustian). They would defend the high ground to the north, 2nd Parachute Regiment would do the same to the south, while 1st Parachute Regiment would secure the bridge. Once the bridge had been taken, they were to hold it until elements of the British Eighth Army arrived to reinforce them. However, initially, the mission did not go to plan.

After the paratroopers exited their aircraft – as the war diarist recorded:

We float down into a world of searchlights, tracer bullets and burning corn stacks ... Unable to find baskets with wireless sets or containers with arms ... Realise we are dropped on wrong D.Z.

Due to the evasive action taken by the C-47 pilots in order to avoid enemy anti-aircraft fire, the battalion was scattered far from its intended drop zone. However, men from 1st Parachute Regiment managed to organise themselves and secure the Primosole Bridge, and by the following day – 14 July – soldiers from Private Lawrence Lee's 3rd Parachute Regiment began to converge on their location. Demolition charges – planted by the Italians – were removed from the bridge, while Italian prisoners were captured and British paratroopers began to dig in in preparation for a German counterattack. Hitler's troops would not surrender as quickly.

While 2nd Parachute Regiment was soon 'heavily engaged' against a machine gun battalion of German *Fallschirmjägers* (paratroopers) to the south, Private Lawrence Lee's 3rd Parachute Regiment – attached to 1st Parachute Regiment at the bridge – were strafed by Messerschmitt fighters. The Germans then attacked the bridge, but the British paratroopers managed to push them back, only for the Germans to start shelling the area again and launch a second, larger assault – this time with anti-tank and 88mm guns. With artillery shells still falling, the enemy continued to put the paratroopers under intense pressure.

The Germans were soon attacking with an armoured car and a heavy machine gun, and then their infantry began to cross the Simeto River, east of the bridge. 1st and 3rd Parachute Regiments were ultimately forced to withdraw, but in their new positions the entire 3rd Parachute Regiment was reunited. By midnight, tanks and infantry from Eighth Army had also arrived in support. With the bridge now in German hands, the British were forced to retake it. It took heavy shelling and several costly attacks by the Durham Light Infantry before it was finally secured on 16 July.

That same day, Private Lawrence Lee and 3rd Parachute Regiment travelled by motor transport to Syracuse, and, on 19 July, they were transported across the Mediterranean back

Men of 2nd London Irish Rifles during the Sicily Campaign. This photograph was taken not long before two of the men pictured – both from Lurgan, County Armagh – were killed in action. Twenty-nine-year-old Rifleman Felix Creaney (second from right without helmet) died on 12 August 1943 and now lies buried in the Catania War Cemetery, Sicily, while thirty-one-year-old Rifleman James Murtagh (the man hugging Creaney) was killed on 15 August 1943 – only two days before the Allies finally secured Sicily – and now lies in Tripoli War Cemetery. Sadly, Creaney's brother Shaun – a gunner with 47th HAA Regiment Royal Artillery based in Northern Ireland – had previously died, aged eighteen, on 24 April 1941 – not long after the Belfast Blitz.

to North Africa. They landed in Sousse, Tunisia. Out of the 1,856 men in 1st Parachute Brigade which took part in Operation Fustian, 141 had been killed, while a further 168 had been wounded or gone missing. At the Primosole Bridge, 295 paratroopers had taken part in the fighting, 115 of whom had become casualties. Private Lawrence Lee had luckily survived.

Men of the 6th Royal Inniskilling Fusiliers, 38th Irish Brigade, searching houses during mopping up operations in Centuripe, Sicily, August 1943.

The Allies finally secured Sicily on 17 August 1943 – a battle during which 38th Irish Brigade also fought, along with 2nd Royal Inniskilling Fusiliers in 5th Infantry Division and 1st London Irish Rifles in 50th (Northumbrian) Infantry Division – at a cost of 5,837 killed, 15,683 wounded and 3,326 captured. The Germans had lost 20,000 men and the Italians 147,000 – mostly POWs.

Private Lawrence Lee and 3rd Parachute Regiment were subsequently sent to Italy when 1st Airborne Division landed at Taranto on 9 September 1943 as part of Operation Slapstick. With not enough aircraft to deploy the division by air, the paratroopers were transported to Italy by the Royal Navy and the only Germans in the area were elements of the 1st *Fallschirmjäger* Division who fought rearguard actions as they withdrew north. Lawrence Lee and his comrades advanced 125 miles to Foggia, and were then withdrawn to Britain in November.

The following year – now a sergeant in 3rd Parachute Regiment (although only nineteen years old) – Lawrence Lee was preparing to jump on Arnhem, Holland as part of Operation Market Garden, when he broke his foot playing football and was forced to stay behind in Britain. He was lucky – the 1st Airborne Division suffered just under 2,000 men killed and over 6,000 captured in the disastrous nine-day battle (this amounted to eighty percent of the division), and Lawrence's 3rd Parachute Regiment was almost completely wiped out.

Lawrence stayed in the army after the war and served in Palestine from 1945 to 1948. Then, when he tried to renew his contract, the army would not let him return to the Parachute Regiment. Instead, they wanted twenty-three-year-old Lawrence to become a regimental sergeant-major (warrant officer class one) in the Royal Pioneer Corps. Lawrence did not want this position, so he resigned from the regular army, moved to Belfast in 1949, and joined the Royal Engineers TA (Territorial Army) there, where he served as a company sergeant-major. Outside of the TA, he began work as a bulldozer/heavy plant driver, a skill that the army had taught him before he had been demobbed.

Company Sergeant-Major Lawrence Lee served in the TA for twenty-two years, and as he recalled, 'they took me out of it in the end', meaning he was forced to retire. During his time with the TA he had trained over 7,000 recruits (one of which was Lieutenant-Colonel SC Kirkwood, who was awarded an OBE in 1992), and in recognition of this fact, the former Parachute Regiment sergeant was awarded the British Empire Medal. As Lawrence remembered, 'After I'd trained them, they [his recruits] were sent over to England for the last bit of their training, and one of my lads would always come back with best recruit [award] or best shot [award].'

Lawrence married in 1952 and had six children, and at the time of writing, he still lives in Belfast. Although eighty-six years old, he regularly goes clay pigeon shooting (he is a very good shot), and also goes hunting and fishing with his sons.

TRAVELLING SOLDIER

CHRISTOPHER 'JACKDAW' JOYCE

On 25 July 1943 – during the Battle of Sicily – the Italian people ousted Benito Mussolini. Knowing that the Allies' next step would be to invade mainland Italy, the Italians tried to join the Allies and prevent the destruction of their country. But the Americans and British would not accept this – they wanted the Italians to surrender, not join forces with them. If they were forced to treat the Italians as allies, then they would have to reveal strategic plans to them, and as far as the Americans and British were concerned, the Italians had proved how undependable they were – since the Germans were still in Italy and fully intending to defend the country (they had actually foreseen an Italian surrender and had subsequently reinforced their units in Italy), any plans revealed to the Italians might quickly make their way into German hands.

It was finally decided that an armistice between the Allies and Italy would be declared, but for the sake of secrecy, Allied soldiers would only be told about this when actually en route to invade. Furthermore, the Americans and British refused to reveal their plans to the Italians until only hours before they landed in Italy – they felt that this would preserve secrecy for as long as possible, while also allowing the Italians to aid Allied forces once they arrived.

The Italians wanted the Allies to capture Rome as their first target, but Allied planes could not support a landing that far north. As a compromise, the Allies agreed to land troops at Salerno in southwest Italy, while the remainder of their forces – which included 2nd Royal Inniskilling Fusiliers in 5th Infantry Division and later the 38th Irish Brigade – would come ashore further south and then advance north to link up with the Salerno troops.

One of the units due to land at Salerno on 9 September 1943 as part of Operation Avalanche was 79th Company (No 21 Beach Group), Pioneer Corps, and with this unit was Private Christopher Joyce. 'Jackdaw', as he was better known, was a member of the Travelling community from Athlone, County Westmeath, where he was well known as a keen boxer.

79th Company departed Tripoli on 5 September and on 8 September, as the war diary recorded, 'Armistice with Italy announced.' The following day, the company landed at Salerno along with the first waves of Allied infantry – not far from 1st London Irish Rifles in 56th (London) Infantry Division. However, while they soon 'suffered casualties chiefly through mortar fire', the war diarist also noted that 'No 4 Section captured enemy pill box & took occupants prisoner.' But it was only one soldier from No 4 Section who silenced the enemy pill box – Private Christopher 'Jackdaw' Joyce.

Jackdaw was soon awarded the Distinguished Conduct Medal (DCM) – junior only to the Victoria Cross – the citation for which read:

> On Sugar Green Beach at 05.00 hrs on 9 September 1943, Pte Joyce who with his section was making his way to Amber Beach spotted a Machine Gun post. Without waiting for instructions he dashed forward, entered the post, and at the point of the bayonet captured the gun and its crew of 4 gunners. Throughout the rest of the day [he] engaged on the extremely important work of laying Sommerfield track [a light-weight wire mesh used as a temporary runway for aircraft] on Amber Beach under continuous mortar fire. This soldier continuously set a fine example of energy and courage which was of immense value.

After also enduring enemy machine gun fire and shellfire, 79th Company were attacked by air throughout the night of 9 September, and over the following days – while working on the beaches – Jackdaw and his comrades suffered enemy artillery and air attacks. Within a few days, as the war diary recorded, 'All sections have worked continuously an average of 14-16 hrs per day.'

Some British units had managed to push seven miles inland by the end of the first day, but on 13 September, the Germans counterattacked at Salerno. The Allies managed to hang on to their beachhead with the help of Royal Navy guns, US artillery, and bomber aircraft, and by 16 September – having failed to drive the Americans and British back into the sea, and with Allied troops also approaching from the south – the Germans withdrew from Salerno. The Allies had lost 2,000 killed, 7,000 wounded, and 3,500 missing in their invasion of Italy, while the German defenders had suffered 3,500 casualties.

The month of September ended with heavy rains and the appearance of malaria among the troops of Jackdaw's 79th Company, but by then, the Allies were firmly ashore. On 1 October, they captured Naples and had soon secured all of southern Italy. However, they were now facing the Volturno Line – the first of many German defence lines designed to slow the Allied advance towards Rome.

Private Christopher 'Jackdaw' Joyce's DCM was one of only four such medals earned by soldiers in the Pioneer Corps during the war, and on 26 April 1946, Jackdaw received a letter from King George VI, inviting him to attend a ceremony at Buckingham Palace in order to receive his DCM. However, Jackdaw was a particularly humble man, and so he declined the offer to attend, feeling that he was not worthy to accept such a great honour. Instead, the medal was sent through the post to him, along with a letter of congratulation.

Christopher 'Jackdaw' Joyce later married Kathleen McDonagh when aged twenty-five, and together the couple had one son and two daughters. Sadly however, Jackdaw's son – Patrick – died young. Then – after many years living in Manchester – Jackdaw passed away when he was seventy-three years old and was buried in his native Athlone. He was not the only member of his family to fight in the Second World War – his first cousin, Martin McDonagh, took part in the D-Day Normandy landings of 6 June 1944 – and according to Traveller historian Michael McDonagh, many Irish Travellers are also known to have served in the US forces during the war. Their story is certainly a forgotten element of Ireland's involvement in the Second World War.

ISLAND PRIZE

EDWARD 'TED' JOHNSON

With the Allies having landed in Italy, the Greek islands in the Aegean Sea were now finally within reach. Greece had fallen to the Germans in late April 1941, and these islands would be vital to any attempt to recapture Greece. Leros, part of the Dodecanese Islands, was heavily fortified and contained a deep water port, so it was an obvious target for the Allies. However, while the British were keen to capture Leros, the Americans wanted to focus on Italy. And so, the British sent a smaller force than initially planned to Leros – a force that barely had any air support.

One of the units involved in the operation was 2nd Royal Irish Fusiliers, and with them was Lieutenant Edward 'Ted' Johnson.

Born in 1922, Ted grew up on a farm in Farnagh (now the Farnagh Stud), just west of Moate in County Westmeath. His father was a sheep and cattle farmer and also bred horses – he was Master of the South Westmeath Harriers and had a good reputation for show jumping. Aged fourteen, Ted left the farm and ended up living in Malahide, County Dublin. Then, in September 1940, he joined the British Army.

As Ted recalled in a recent interview:

Lieutenant Edward 'Ted' Johnson – 2nd Royal Irish Fusiliers – from Moate, County Westmeath, not long after his capture during the Battle of Leros.

> I had been at school in the [south] of Ireland and I travelled to Belfast to join the
> Royal Ulster Rifles. My training took place at Ballymena in County Antrim. We were
> a young soldiers squad, a reinforcing battalion which was meant for home service only.
> I was selected for officer training, and put into a potential officers squad, which meant
> even more training.

After training in Droitwich, Worcestershire and Morecambe, Lancashire, Ted was commissioned as a second-lieutenant in June 1941 and was posted to 2nd London Irish Rifles.

> We were in Arundel, in theory defending the beaches from German invasion. But
> the defences were really only a stretch of barbed wire, and 1 gun per platoon – the rest
> were dummy guns to give the impression we were heavily defended. In the winter of
> 1941 we were moved to Chichester when we were formed into the 38th Irish Brigade
> with the 1st Battalion Royal Irish Fusiliers and 6th Battalion [Royal Inniskilling] Fusiliers. We were sent to Norfolk for further training as a Brigade.

But before the 38th Irish Brigade set sail for North Africa, Second-Lieutenant Edward 'Ted' Johnson was sent to Egypt, as part of a group of forty officers, to serve as replacements in other units – units that had suffered high officer casualties during the North African Campaign. In February 1943 – not long after the end of a vicious two-year siege of the island – Ted landed on Malta as a replacement officer for 2nd Royal Irish Fusiliers. After serving in a coastal defence role, Ted and the battalion returned to Egypt in June.

After a few weeks in Egypt and then a period of further training in Lebanon, the newly created 234th Infantry Brigade (of which 2nd Royal Irish Fusiliers were a part) was given a mission – to invade and capture the island of Leros. On 15 September 1943, the 3,000 troops of the brigade landed on the island unopposed (by now, Ted was a lieutenant in C Company). However, as in Italy, the Germans were not going to surrender Italian territory without a fight. German infantry, *Fallschirmjägers* and marine commandos were quickly ordered to retake Leros (and other Dodecanese Islands captured by the British), and the *Luftwaffe* – which had complete air superiority – began bombing Leros on 26 September in preparation for a German landing.

Regarding this period, Ted recalled:

> The Italians had surrendered by now, but we didn't know what sort of reception
> we would get. We were quite surprised by the complete lack of reaction – we had
> expected a scrap. The Greeks had disappeared, and the remaining Italians were co-
> operative. They were gunners, who were manning the coastal defences ... I was on
> Leros from the 19th September ... During that time we were constantly being bombed
> by the Luftwaffe – JU 87s and JU 88s. As we were so far north ... the Germans had
> air superiority.

After nearly fifty days of bombing, and having secured the islands of Kos and then

Kalymnos to the south, the German invasion of Leros began on 12 November. 2nd Royal Irish Fusiliers were defending the eastern central side of the island, and were positioned on the high ground of Meriviglia overlooking Alinda Bay to the north and Pandelli Bay to the south. Ted later wrote a book about his experiences on Leros; entitled *Island Prize*, in it he recorded that when the German invasion came, his company – C Company – were the battalion's mobile reserve. However, they had no transport with which to perform this role.

From Ted's perspective:

> At about 06.15hours on that calm and dry morning we sensed that all was not quite normal. Not that we could see any enemy craft out beyond Pandelli Bay as the official report alleged at the time. But there was a crescendo of small arms fire building up from the north side of [Mount] Appetici which was out of our line of vision and would have been caused by Italian coast gun battery personnel attempting to repel a landing. The first definite news I had of a landing was hearing Capt Bob Ambrose, an ex Royal Munster Fusilier ... shouting to one of his positions that a landing had been made in the north of the island and on Appetici ... As Battalion Reserve Company we had now been given the order to counter attack and retake Appetici ... a rock-strewn peninsula separating Pandelli Bay from Alinda Bay further north.

As Stuka dive bombers flew overhead, C Company – led by Lieutenant Edward 'Ted' Johnson's No 13 Platoon – advanced slowly and cautiously in order to stay hidden from enemy aircraft and German observers that might be scanning the area. When Ted and his men reached the lower slopes of Mount Appetici, they found that 'the crest was patchily covered with scrub and low windswept trees, with scattered pine trees down the reverse slope.' Ted met with an Italian officer who was supposed to tell him where the enemy were positioned on the slopes, but 'he spoke no English and was very excited and no doubt, like myself, probably very frightened.' So Ted was forced to recce the area himself, and – encountering no enemy – soon had his men positioned on the summit of the hill.

C Company, 2nd Royal Irish Fusiliers were then ordered to retake several heavy calibre Italian coastal guns that were positioned down the reverse slope facing the sea – it had been confirmed that the Germans were now somewhere on Mount Appetici, and it was believed that they had already captured these guns from the Italians. Ted was ordered:

> To take the first and nearest emplacement and thereafter go for the next one if possible ... After much unaimed covering fire I found myself with one of my sections in possession of the first emplacement. Until this moment I had still not seen any of my opponents, nor could any of my men give me any accurate reports of sightings in spite of much hostile fire cracking past us. Suddenly my section commander Lance/ Sergeant John Caldwell, who was beside me and who was trying to get a sight of a target, fell back. He was shot cleanly through the forehead and had died instantly.

My immediate reaction was to push on out of that unhealthy gun emplacement and take John Caldwell's section further down the slope in the direction of the next gun emplacement with all weapons blazing.

Sergeant John Caldwell from Belfast was thirty-five years old when he died, and his body was never recovered after the fighting on Leros ended. Today, he is commemorated on the Athens Memorial. Ted later wrote in *Island Prize*:

He [Caldwell] was a man with a great North of Ireland sense of humour and on many an evening he would keep a few of us at platoon HQ in fits of laughter with his stories and remarks. Another piece of salt of the earth.

Finding the second gun emplacement similarly unoccupied by the enemy, but 'well hit by dive bombing', Ted reorganised his platoon in an area of 'scrub and rocks' and stood fast. Meanwhile, the platoon sergeant of the platoon on Ted's left – Sergeant O'Connell – 'was badly wounded during this action and later died of his wounds. The action as a whole had the effect of taking back the summit area of Appetici and at least two gun positions.'

There were actually two sergeants named O'Connell (they were also both named Daniel) who died while fighting with 2nd Royal Irish Fusiliers on Leros, and so Ted could be referring to either of them. Sergeant Daniel Joseph O'Connell was from southern Ireland, and today lies buried in the Leros War Cemetery, while twenty-five year old Sergeant Daniel P O'Connell from Spangle Hill, Cork has no known grave and is today commemorated on the Athens Memorial.

Having encountered C Company attacking them from the summit, the Germans temporarily withdrew down the slopes to regroup and reorganise. Meanwhile, C Company remained in their current positions for the rest of the day, and while Stukas continually bombed the area, Ted's platoon suffered no further casualties. Then, C Company received an order that started a period of frustration and confusion among the unit – it was an order that changed the outcome of the Battle of Leros.

Completely bypassing the proper chain of command, Brigadier Robert Tilney – commander of the Allied forces on Leros – issued on order directly from himself to C Company, 2nd Royal Irish Fusiliers to withdraw from Mount Appetici all the way back to their pre-invasion positions at Meriviglia. German *Fallschirmjägers* had captured the narrow central area of Leros and had effectively cut the island in two, and Tilney was withdrawing C Company to take part in a counterattack. However, a confused C Company were not told why they were being removed from Mount Appetici – about the German paratrooper landing or about the counterattack – and when they returned to their initial positions, they simply waited for further orders. As a result, the counterattack was never launched, and that night, an even more confused C Company were ordered back to Appetici. By the following morning – 13 November – the Germans at Appetici had seen their opportunity, advanced up the slopes and captured the summit (which had been guarded by only a single platoon of 2nd Royal Irish Fusiliers). The British had lost the vital high ground.

Ted and his platoon were soon positioned:

> On the northwest slopes of our side of the summit. Eventually word came to abandon the feature. My first intimation that all was not under control was when I saw men running down through the trees from the summit towards me, shouting that they were being closely followed by the enemy ... I got the impression they were running for their lives and in doing so were causing panic to those of us whom they passed. It became obvious that my company HQ and 15 platoon had been driven off the summit and that this was the reason that I too was to abandon the hillside. This was done in some confusion and was certainly not a planned and disciplined withdrawal.

After reorganising on the outskirts of Leros village at the base of Mount Appetici, Ted and C Company set off once again for their original positions at Meriviglia, but not before Ted noted that 'I had lost Fusilier James McMaster earlier that morning. He died of an unpleasant wound received from either a grenade or a mortar shell.' Twenty-five-year-old Fusilier James McMaster was from Ballydrain, southeast of Comber in County Down. With no known grave, today he is commemorated on the Athens Memorial.

The following morning, Lieutenant Edward 'Ted' Johnson and C Company took part in a counterattack against the German *Fallschirmjägers* on Rachi – an area of high ground in the centre of the island. The counterattack ultimately failed to drive the Germans from the area, and with the company second-in-command dead and the company commander now wounded, Ted was soon placed in command of C Company. He recalled:

> My training did not equip me for this promotion of necessity. Yet I well remember, as a cadet officer at 168 Officer Cadet Training Unit in Morecambe back in 1941, acting as cadet company commander for a day and managing to lose an entire company of fellow cadets when I routed my company off the map in the Lake District ... Here I was now, the senior subaltern left in the company and a real life situation of the tired but willing remains of C Company needing a leader. I just had to get on with it.

However, more officers from 2nd Royal Irish Fusiliers would die before the battle ended. On the morning of 14 November, while leading two companies of 1st King's Own Royal Regiment (Lancaster) in a counterattack against German forces on Mount Appetici, Lieutenant-Colonel Maurice French – commanding officer of 2nd Royal Irish Fusiliers – was killed. Ted recorded that, after the Royal Navy failed to provide a preliminary bombardment:

> Maurice went forward with two very weak companies, weak both in numbers and ability, and at first light was caught in the open and short of his objective. The Germans quickly saw their chance and counter-attacked down the hill causing severe casualties. Most of the officers involved in this action became casualties, and many of

the soldiers withdrew in complete confusion. Maurice had no thought of withdrawing and like many of the King's Own officers he was killed, fighting to the best of his ability with a rifle to his shoulder. At the end it seems that he was entirely on his own … What a waste of a kind and gentle man and what a loss to the Faughs [the Royal Irish Fusiliers' nickname] … [Brigadier] Robert Tilney wrote afterwards '… we lost the battle when we lost Maurice …'

After the war, Maurice French's adjutant on Leros – Captain H 'Dougie' Dougall – wrote a letter to Maurice's widow, Diana French. In it, he wrote:

> During the entire time of his command, the Colonel worked literally night and day for the battalion. Though he could manage on little sleep, I do not remember him ever giving himself a fair quota of it. This held true during convoy work in Malta, throughout our training in the Middle East and if possible even more so on Leros. On this island, to say that he averaged two hours sleep per night would be rating it high. None could have done a finer job of work than he did … I think that he had a presentiment that he would not come back. Before going out on the operation we persuaded him to rest and he slept for about forty minutes, the first sleep for forty-eight hours. When leaving Battalion HQ he looked at me and said 'Good bye Dougie'. This worried me for our usual greeting when he was going anywhere was 'Well, Faugh-a-Ballagh'. I do believe he knew that something would happen.

In *Island Prize*, Ted also recalled the contents of one of Maurice French's last letters to his wife. Dated 12 October 1943, it read:

> If anything should happen to me, remember that our separation is only temporary … It is cruelly hard that we should have been four and a half years apart, but the remaining separation will only be like a continuation of this and I will be close to you dearest Di – always.

Colonel JC Coldwell Horsfall of the Royal Irish Fusiliers later wrote:

> [Maurice French] had the disposition and faith of a saint, but he was a warrior none the less. And he ran true to form to the end, with all things lost, the island collapsed, and entirely on his own. No Irish Fusilier officer, nor any other in our army, ever died better and he ranks with Leonidas.

Lieutenant-Colonel Maurice French – born in Newbay, just outside Wexford town, but living in nearby Wellingtonbridge – was forty years old when he was killed on 14 November on Leros. Today, his remains lie in the Leros War Cemetery.

Ted was told to gather all of his remaining men – who he had organised into two platoons – and attach himself to 2nd Queen's Own Royal West Kent Regiment for an operation 'in an area of ground between Meriviglia on the left and Santa Marina harbour on the right.' The attack was confused and chaotic and Ted's men did not manage to advance very far.

[That night] I took what remained of my pathetic little band of weary men back to our home from home where stragglers converged throughout the night ... At this stage of the fight I had managed somehow to scrounge some Benzedrine which kept me from succumbing to sleep, but my soldiers were by now very weary and ... had nothing to sustain them from falling asleep wherever they lay down ... We were now at the end of the fourth day of continuous fighting.

Lieutenant Edward 'Ted' Johnson and the exhausted remnants of C Company, 2nd Royal Irish Fusiliers, were again called on the following morning to support another counterattack. But while trying to get into position, Ted and C Company were fired on by the enemy. The men took cover:

At about 10.00hours the rocky position I was on, with about four other ... became bracketed either side with sustained Spandau [machine gun] fire. We had exhausted almost all ammunition and were hailed by our opponents to give up. Our immediate reaction to this suggestion was to let fly a short burst of fire from our one serviceable Bren [machine gun] and its dwindling ammunition and to move ourselves to another hole amongst the rocks, but we soon realised that a move was out of the question as any attempt even by a single man was met by a burst of very accurate and frightening machine-gun fire from our opponents who had us pinpointed ... We could not achieve anything by launching ourselves and our three or four very tired soldiers into some heroic suicide action.

After stripping down their machine guns and rifles, breaking what parts they could break and scattering the rest, and after Ted smashed his compass, binoculars and pistol, 'we eased ourselves out of our rocky position and commenced the sad and shameful trek down the hillside to the point where we could see our captors.' Ted surrendered to men of the elite Brandenburg Division, and, as he also recalled in his recent interview:

The commanding officer said to us in English, 'Hard luck, good fight. Come and have a cup of coffee.'

That day – 16 November 1943 – Lieutenant Edward 'Ted' Johnson's war ended. The war also ended for 2nd Royal Irish Fusiliers, as on that day, the Battle of Leros concluded with an Allied surrender, and the survivors of the battalion became POWs for the remainder of the war – it was an event that completely shocked the British public. Out of an initial force of just under 14,000 troops, the Allies had lost 419 dead, 4,800 wounded, and 8,500 taken prisoner. The Germans had lost 520 dead and as many as 5,000 wounded in the five-day battle, while also buried in the Leros War Cemetery is an Irish soldier who was connected to a famous Irish historical figure.

Lieutenant Hugh Gore-Booth of Lissadell House, Drumcliffe, County Sligo, 2nd Royal Irish Fusiliers, was killed aged thirty-three on 12 November (his brother, twenty-seven-year-old

Sub-Lieutenant Brian Gore-Booth of the Royal Navy, had died aboard HMS *Exmouth* on 21 January 1940 when she was torpedoed in the North Sea by *U-22* with the loss of all hands; with no known grave, he is today commemorated on the Portsmouth Naval Memorial). Hugh Gore-Booth was second in command of C Company – in which Ted Johnson was serving – and Ted recorded in *Island Prize*:

> At one stage during the afternoon Lieut. Hugh Gore-Booth took a small patrol down and around the right flank of [Mount Appetici], presumably to find out more about the strength and location of our opposition but he was never heard of again ... Hugh was a grand chap, the son of an old aristocratic Irish family, who loved nature and wide open spaces. The only consolation I can find in the place of his death is that the natural scenery there is something out of this world, and forty five years after the battle it remains unspoilt and a place where Hugh would love to be.

While Hugh Gore-Booth's name might not be familiar, his aunt's name is known to every Irish schoolchild. Lieutenant Gore-Booth was the nephew of Constance Gore-Booth – better known by her married title and surname of Countess Markievicz. She is famous in Irish history for having fought with the Irish Citizen Army during the 1916 Rising, and for being the first woman ever elected to the British House of Commons. However, while she is well remembered and celebrated, her two nephews – who fought and died to defeat the evils of Nazism – are completely unknown in modern Ireland.

Meanwhile, after being initially taken to Nazi-occupied Athens, Lieutenant Edward 'Ted' Johnson was transported by cattle cart to Stalag VII-A POW camp in Moosburg, Bavaria – the journey took two weeks and Ted arrived into the middle of a freezing European winter still wearing his tropical-issue uniform from the Mediterranean. He was 'soon taken on to Luckenwalde [Stalag III-A in Brandenburg]. We arrived on Christmas Day 1943. I was put in solitary confinement for 14 days with no interrogation. I was eventually taken from my cell in the middle of the night. The interrogator knew more than I did about why we were there. They thought it was a ridiculous operation.'

In *Island Prize*, Ted added:

> The interview ended with a suggestion being made that I join a so-called Free Irish Battalion which, it was alleged, was currently a valued unit in the German army and which, according to my interrogator, was already well up to strength with my comrades. He didn't look too surprised when his offer was refused. Subsequently there was very little evidence that this unit of traitors ever existed.

Finally, in his recent interview, Ted concluded, 'After the interrogation I was taken to Oflag VIII-F at Mahrisch-Trubau, in Czechoslovakia.'

Ted remained there for six months until, in July 1944:

> We were moved from Mahrisch-Trubau. The Russians were advancing, so we were

put into cattle trucks for a 3-day journey to Oflag 79 at Brunswick [Braunschweig] ... The guards at Oflag 79 were mostly elderly and down graded. There were guards who only had one arm, and those who only had one eye. They were very old, and their clothes were poor quality. We all felt sorry for them, especially during the winter of 1944/45, which was very cold.

Towards the end of the war, when US forces were nearing the camp, the camp commandant was ordered to execute all Allied officers before they could be freed by friendly forces. Thankfully for Ted and his fellow officers, the camp commandant refused ('He was an honourable chap', recalled Ted), and on 12 April 1945, the US Ninth Army liberated the camp.

Ted now discovered that he had actually been promoted to captain during the Battle of Leros, but that the submarine carrying the order had been sunk in the Aegean. He initially returned to serve with 2nd Royal Irish Fusiliers – then stationed in Palestine – as battalion adjutant, and obtained a regular commission in the army.

Ted went on to become adjutant of the Army Apprentices School at Arborfield, Berkshire from 1948 to 1950, before serving three years with the Gold Coast Regiment in West Africa. After finally serving as adjutant at Queen's University OTC, Belfast from 1954 to 1956, he retired from the army in 1958. At the time of writing, Edward 'Ted' Johnson is ninety years old, and lives in Bicester, Oxfordshire.

VETERAN

JOSEPH DUNNE

Back in Italy, the Allies were encountering fierce German resistance, and along with the onset of winter, it was making progress slow, dangerous and difficult. After the Salerno landings, the enemy had fallen back on a line of defence – the Volturno Line – destroying railways, bridges and roads and booby-trapping towns as they withdrew. The heavy winter rains then turned the world to muck; pontoon bridges – laid to replace the bridges the retreating Germans had destroyed – were washed away as rivers flooded, and because of the mud, Allied vehicles were unable to drive into the mountains where the enemy had dug in.

As a result, all guns and supplies had to be dragged or carried uphill by soldiers, while the wounded similarly had to be evacuated on foot (It was during this time that 2nd Royal Inniskilling Fusiliers captured the town of Isernia, which US forces were supposed to secure first. When the Americans arrived later, they were confused by drawings of Enniskillen Castle – the Royal Inniskilling Fusiliers' cap badge and symbol – on walls all over the town).

Because of the build-up of landing craft in Britain for the upcoming invasion of Normandy (along with the build-up in the Mediterranean for the supporting invasion of southern France – Operation Dragoon), the Allies could not outflank the Germans by sea, so they were forced to make continual frontal assaults against the enemy's prepared defensive positions. But the Allies did manage to break through the Volturno Line on 6 October 1943 – thanks to the arrival of 38th Irish Brigade at Termoli, on Italy's Adriatic coast, just in time to help beat back a German attack that day – but the Germans subsequently fell back further north to the Barbara Line, once again destroying and booby-trapping as they went. It took until early November before the Allies were through this new defence line, but the Germans simply withdrew once more.

By 15 January 1944, the Allies had finally secured the third German defence line – the Bernhardt Line – and were now facing the Gustav Line. It stretched from just north of the mouth of the Garigliano River on the coast of the Tyrrhenian Sea, across the Apennine Mountains, to the mouth of the Sangro River on the Adriatic coast. However, it was much more elaborate than previous German defence lines. The Gustav Line (also known as the Winter Line) was a fortress of machine guns, artillery emplacements and concrete bunkers, guarded by rows of barbed wire and minefields and manned by fifteen German divisions.

It looked as though the Allies had reached a point where they could no longer advance, but the British refused to accept this, and so a plan was devised to overcome the Gustav Line. While the majority of the US Fifth Army (which contained the 38th Irish Brigade) attacked the town of Cassino at the western end of the Gustav Line to draw German reserves into the area, the US VI Corps (which contained several British divisions) would use the limited amount of landing craft that were still available, sail around the Gustav Line, and land to the north at Anzio – about halfway along the Tyrrhenian coast between Cassino and Rome. 1st London Irish Rifles in 56th (London) Infantry Division would fight in both battles – Cassino in January and February, after which they were sent to Anzio until being withdrawn to Egypt in March.

One of the units detailed to take part in the Anzio landing was 1st Irish Guards in 24th Guards Infantry Brigade, 1st Infantry Division, and with them was Sergeant Joseph Dunne – a seasoned veteran soldier who had already seen his fair share of combat.

Born in June 1914 – just before the start of the First World War – Dunne was from Killurin (just south of Tullamore), County Offaly. After school, he became a labourer in the nearby Clonad forests owned by Lord Digby, where all of his older brothers worked. Then, as Dunne's son – Joseph Dunne Jnr – recently recalled:

> Despite the joys of being close to nature, Joe quickly became fed up planting trees.
>
> He and three friends had ambitions to travel to America and become New York cops.
>
> They were however advised by Dr Kennedy of Tullamore that the best way of achieving

this ambition would be first to do a spell in the British Army. Inspired by that idea, Joe and his two friends, Joe Healan and Jimmy Bennet, decided to join the British Army, and not just the army but the best of the army. They enlisted, in 1936, in the Irish Guards.

After serving in Egypt and Palestine, Sergeant Joseph Dunne and 1st Irish Guards were sent to Norway at the start of the Second World War. On 14 May 1940, while en route from Tjeldsundet to Bodø, the Polish vessel – MS *Chrobry* – aboard which the 1st Irish Guards were travelling, was attacked by German Heinkel He111 bombers. 1st Irish Guards' commanding officer, second-in-command, battalion adjutant and three of the five company commanders were killed. The majority of the battalion's equipment was also destroyed, and a raging fire threatened to detonate the ammunition onboard. Luckily, however, the survivors from 1st Irish Guards – which included Sergeant Joseph Dunne – were quickly rescued by HMS *Wolverine* and HMS *Stork* before being taken to Harstad.

Dunne and 1st Irish Guards went on to fight at Pothus in Norway, where they suffered repeated, heavy German attacks for two days before being forced to withdraw. Many men from the battalion were left behind during this retreat, but they managed to break through enemy lines and rejoin their comrades later that day. Finally, along with all remaining Allied troops in Norway, 1st Irish Guards were withdrawn from the country in June 1940. As Joseph Dunne Jnr recalled, there 'followed a spell in England and Scotland where Joe augmented his soldier's pay by snaring rabbits for local butchers and took the odd salmon from a Scottish stream.'

On 9 March 1943, four months after 38th Irish Brigade had landed in the region, Sergeant Joseph Dunne and 1st Irish Guards arrived in Algeria to help finally defeat the Axis forces in North Africa. The battalion saw heavy fighting in the Medjez region of Tunisia, before taking part in a brigade attack against five hills at Djebel Bou Aoukaz (known as 'Bou') on 27 April where they suffered heavy casualties.

Having entered Tunis on 13 May 1943, following the Axis surrender in North Africa, 1st Irish Guards were then sent to Italy in December. In January 1944, Sergeant Joseph Dunne and his comrades were detailed to take part in the Anzio landings. On 22 January they found themselves, as the war diary recorded:

> [coming] ashore, disembarking on to a sandy beach ['Peter Beach'] some four miles North West of Anzio. It was a clear spring like day and the whole operation went very much according to plan. Complete surprise was achieved and enemy opposition was negligible ... At about 1430 hrs and two hours before dusk the Battalion moved forward to take over a plateau (thickly wooded on the North side) from the Scots Guards ...

However, while the start of the diversionary Battle of Cassino to the south on 17 January

While a piper plays, a special rum ration is issued to men of the 2nd Royal Inniskilling Fusiliers to mark St Patrick's Day in the Anzio bridgehead, Italy, 17 March 1944.

had drawn German troops away from Anzio – meaning the Allies at Anzio were only facing a few German battalions in the region – US Major-General John Lucas, commanding officer of Allied forces at Anzio, refused to advance. He felt it would be better to dig in and wait until the Germans counterattacked, thereby fighting them in prepared defensive positions, rather than press inland and spread his forces thin. As a result, by 25 January, the Allies at Anzio were surrounded by 40,000 Germans troops, while five more German divisions were on their way (by 29 January, 69,000 Allies were facing 71,500 Germans).

Then, as later recorded in *Volunteers from Eire who have won Distinctions while serving with the British Forces (1944)*:

> On January 26th, 1944, [Sergeant Joseph Dunne] was in command of a platoon which held the left flank of the battalion's position at Caraceto. About 8 a.m. a strong German counter-attack was put in. One other platoon was overrun and two anti-tank guns and a machine-gun were knocked out, leaving this platoon's position completely exposed to high explosive and small-arms fire of the enemy tanks. In spite of this heavy fire Sergeant Dunne reorganised his position at once and beat off two determined German infantry attacks, showing complete disregard for the heavy covering fire given by the tanks.

However, this was not the only act of bravery performed by Sergeant Joseph Dunne at Anzio. During the night of 29 January, 1st Irish Guards took part in the first Allied offensive at Anzio. Their mission was to advance and capture Campoleone to the north of their current positions, and, as the war diary recorded: 'It was believed that the ground was only lightly held, and it was not anticipated that he [the enemy] would offer any serious resistance after our artillery had paved the way for the advance.' 1st Irish Guards' objective was to 'capture some high ground which lay immediately to our front', but 'unfortunately these [artillery] concentrations which kept the enemy's head down and secured the initial stage of the advance cannot have caused many casualties and when the fire lifted the Battalion was met by very heavy Machine Gun and shell fire.' During the fighting however, Sergeant Joseph Dunne led 'his platoon with the highest skill and determination. When his platoon was held up by a fixed line machine-gun he dashed forward and destroyed the enemy post single-handed, killing the two Germans who were manning it.'

The following day in their newly-won positions, 1st Irish Guards were counterattacked, but they fought the enemy off using anti-tank grenades. Then, in order to retain the initiative, a patrol from No 3 Company – which included Sergeant Joseph Dunne – was sent forward, 'supported by American tank destroyers, [and] carried out an offensive sweep to clear the ridge on the left flank of the brigade salient of enemy machine-guns and snipers. During this operation Sergeant Dunne led his platoon with the greatest efficiency and courage, destroying three enemy posts with no losses.' Fifty-five enemy prisoners were also captured during this patrol.

The next morning – 31 January – another patrol from No 3 Company was sent out, and during this patrol 'Sergeant Dunne located a German sniper's nest. Armed with a rifle, he stalked this nest and killed five of the six occupants during the morning. Later in the afternoon he completed the job by killing the remaining sniper who had taken refuge in Vallselata farm.'

Then, on 3 February, the war diary recorded:

> Feb 3rd was as quiet as the 2nd had been noisy. As it seemed at the time, and as it was later to prove, it was a bad omen. Throughout the hours of daylight the only interesting event was that about a thousand sheep came in from the enemy lines past No. 3 Coys position. In the light of subsequent events this fact, insignificant at the time, may well have been a deliberate manoeuvre of the enemy to test for A.P. [Anti-Personnel] mines.

At exactly 2300 hrs that night, 'an exceptionally heavy barrage came down, apparently concentrated in the Bn area and in the direction of [Sergeant Joseph Dunne's] No. 3 Company ... It was obvious at once that this must be the prelude to an attack.' 1st Irish Guards immediately tried to call in support from Allied aircraft and artillery, while ordering their own mortars to open fire. Soon, 'No. 3 Company then reported Germans all around them and said that ... at least one battalion ... [of] enemy had broken through the broad gap between their own positions and the Scots Guards.'

Sergeant Joseph Dunne and No. 3 Company were actually facing *two* German battalions. However, the Germans were bizarrely using First World War tactics and advancing in large waves of infantry behind a curtain of artillery fire. This artillery fire was devastating to the 1st Irish Guards, but once it lifted to allow the German infantry to attack, the Irish Guards' machine gunners simply mowed down the advancing waves. The war diary recorded that Guardsmen Flanagan, Nicholson and Maloney – a machine gun crew – 'kept on firing until their ammunition was exhausted, by which time they had expended nearly eight thousand rounds. But nothing appeared to check the enemy who appeared to come on shouting and gesticulating wildly as if doped.' However, 'when three of the Germans jumped into the machine-gun post, shouting "hands up Englishmen"', this angered the three Irish machine gunners, and as the war diarist recorded:

> This was too much for the 'Micks' [a nickname for the Irish Guards; it is not seen as derogatory] and all three let fly with their fists. Momentarily bewildered the Germans were at a loss what to do, and by the time they had recovered their wits, the three Guardsmen had made good their escape.

After jamming the British radio frequency, the Germans then made the mistake of setting nearby haystacks on fire, which lit them up every time they massed for an attack and made it much easier for British machine gunners to fire on them. Meanwhile, the British tried to confuse the Germans by firing different coloured flares every time the Germans sent one up in an attempt to communicate with their own forces to the rear, while a squadron of Allied tanks had been promised to arrive in support by dawn. However, the enemy was now behind British lines and had managed to set up machine guns in several locations, and German panzers soon entered the fight. The situation was getting desperate.

A decision was made to withdraw. The Germans had punched a gap 1,200 yards wide between 1st Irish Guards and 1st Scots Guards to their right, decimating No 3 Company and taking many prisoners in the process, and the British had to reorganise their line of defence. However, while Sergeant Joseph Dunne had seen the worst of the fighting, he had survived to fight another day. 'On the night of February 3/4, this Sergeant was with his company when it was overrun by a battalion of the enemy. Despite being wounded he fought his way back to his own lines.'

Sergeant Joseph Dunne – who was in command of No 13 Platoon, No 3 Company that night – actually ended up writing a far more detailed report about his experiences during the battle, and this was included in the battalion war diary for the period. In it, Dunne recalled:

> While I was standing in my Platoon area on the night of the 3rd February at approximately 2230 hrs I heard the pre-arranged signal from the forward observation post. Knowing that an attack was imminent I immediately ordered the Platoon to "Stand to". As quickly as possible I ran round to the officer i/c [in command] of the 4.2" Mortar O.P. [Observation Post], which was in the house in the rear of my platoon. I informed him that the enemy were attacking in strength and told him that a defensive plan must be laid on immediately. He replied "Surely it isn't necessary", I repeated my order, and left him to return to my platoon position.
>
> On encountering the heavy enemy barrage on my return, I took shelter in a nearby cowshed until I could cross the open ground to my platoon. On reaching my platoon I found Gdsn. Burke to be badly wounded, lying in his trench. I lifted him from the trench and sent another Gdsn for the Stretcher Bearers [Twenty-eight year old Guardsman Edward Burke from Cork city died of his wounds just under a week later on 9 February. Today he is buried in Anzio War Cemetery]. Then Captain McInerney joined me. I explained to him that I had already given orders to the Mortar Officer for the defensive fire to be brought down. He immediately left me to return to Company H.Q., and I did not see him again.
>
> Whatever happened I do not know, but I saw the enemy at the far edge of the gully. My platoon at once engaged the enemy, as did No. 15 platoon simultaneously on my left, joined by the attached machine-guns. The hayricks in front of 14 and 15

platoons positions were set alight and heavy fire was brought to bear upon the front of the [enemy's] positions by the Vickers machine guns.

On my platoon front the enemy seemed to have moved over to both flanks, as only a number of enemy snipers remained. Next I observed the enemy attacking Coy H.Q., from the rear, and after approximately 30 mins the firing quietened down. I then decided to withdraw my platoon to Bn H.Q., to support them in defence of their positions, knowing that 14 and 15 Platoons had been over-run.

After giving orders to my section commanders of my intentions we moved forward, then swung to the right. We made good progress until we reached the railway, then we came under heavy fire, which I thought came from our own troops. I shouted to them and then found that the embankment was strongly held by the enemy, thus making our object almost an impossibility. I left two sections of my platoon in the gully, which runs from the road to the railway, whilst L/Sgt. Ashton, DCM, L/Cpl. Wilson, 5 Gdsn and myself went forward to the high ground.

Dunne and his comrades on the high ground were soon cut off from the men in the gully, and the following morning – now out of ammunition and with Lance-Sergeant Ashton and Guardsman Swift having been wounded by enemy fire – they were forced to surrender to the enemy:

We were later moved to a house, leaving L/Sgt. Ashton, as we were refused permission to carry him with us. Gdsn. Swift was able to accompany us, with help. We had been in the house for about an hour when one of our tanks opened up on it, causing the enemy to seek safety in the trenches outside. We were left under a guard of 2 Germans, whom we overpowered, and made our escape, taking them with us.

We made our way back by the gully, taking two more prisoners. We passed through the Mortar Platoon, who were in the gully under the railway line. On reaching the road we handed over the prisoners, and Gdsn Swift and myself were conveyed by carrier to the M.D.S. [Main Dressing Station]

For all of his incredible acts of bravery and for his devotion to duty, Dunne was soon awarded the Distinguished Conduct Medal (*London Gazette,* 15 June 1944). It was finally noted in *Volunteers from Eire who have won Distinctions while serving with the British Forces (1944)*:

This NCO's record for skill, determination, marksmanship and personal courage during the whole of the battalion's action in the Anzio bridgehead was of the highest order. Sergeant Dunne comes from Tullamore.

1st Irish Guards finally came out of the line at Anzio on 25 February 1944, and after taking part in subsequent fighting over the following months, the battalion – now badly depleted – was shipped back to Britain in April (around the same time that the North Irish

Horse joined the fighting in Italy when they landed at Naples on 18 April). They stayed here for the remainder of the war as a training battalion.

On 18 May, the Allies at Cassino finally broke through the Gustav Line after bitter fighting, having suffered 55,000 casualties, while the Germans suffered 20,000 killed and wounded (the battle became famous for the pointless destruction of the sixth-century Benedictine abbey on Monte Cassino). By 25 May, the Allies at Cassino had linked up with the Anzio forces and punched through the subsequent Adolf Hitler Line, and by 5 June – the day before D-Day in Normandy – Allied forces were through the Caesar C Line and had captured Rome. During Operation Shingle – the Anzio landings – 7,000 Allied soldiers had been killed and 36,000 more were wounded or went missing; the Germans lost 5,000 killed, 30,500 wounded or missing, and 4,500 taken POW.

However, when 1st Irish Guards returned to Britain in April, Sergeant Joseph Dunne was not with them. At some point in the subsequent fighting in Italy, Dunne had been taken POW by the Germans and sent to Stalag VII-A in Moosburg, Bavaria. The veteran Irish Guards sergeant was not content to wait out the war as a prisoner, and so he tried to escape. He managed to get out of the camp, but was subsequently caught and returned to captivity. It was not until 29 April 1945 that the US 14th Armoured Division liberated the camp, and by then, Sergeant Joseph Dunne weighed only 84lbs (6st).

Following his recovery, Dunne married Bridget Monaghan – a Cavan girl who had spent the Second World War driving an ambulance in London and who had lived through The Blitz – in 1947, and the couple started a family in London. Sadly, she died in 1961, leaving Joseph Dunne to care for his five young children alone. However, as Joseph Dunne Jnr recently recalled:

> As a soldier Joe had learnt that the most important motto for a soldier was 'do your duty'. To this motto Joe now returned and arranged his life so as to cope with the raising of five young children with no thought for his own comfort and pleasure.

Dunne began work as a cocktail barman in the Junior Carlton Club – a London gentleman's club with close links to the Conservative Party – and remained working here (and subsequently for the Carlton Club when the two clubs merged in 1977) until he retired in 1979. By then, he had met every Conservative Party Prime Minister, including Churchill.

Ten years after retiring, in 1989, Dunne returned to live in his native Killurin, County Offaly. At the time of writing, former Irish Guards sergeant, veteran of Norway, North Africa and Italy, and Distinguished Conduct Medal recipient Joseph Dunne still lives in Killurin. He is now ninety-seven years old.

THE FINAL PUSH

LESLIE FRANCIS

Having captured Rome, the Allies pressed on to take Florence. Finally, they came up against the last major German defence line in Italy – the Gothic Line – which ran from Pisa across the Apennine Mountains to Rimini. Operation Olive – due to begin on 25 August 1944 – was drawn up to break through this line, and one of the units detailed to help finally defeat the enemy in Italy was 1st London Irish Rifles in 56th (London) Infantry Division.

Serving in this unit was former cycle mechanic Rifleman Leslie Francis from Irishtown House in Athlone, County Westmeath, but he had not started out the war as a rifleman. When he had first enlisted in Omagh, County Tyrone on 16 October 1941, Leslie had joined the Royal Artillery as a gunner, and after his training he was posted to B Troop, 314th Battery, 102nd Heavy Anti-Aircraft Regiment. This was a County Antrim TA unit (the first TA units had been raised in Northern Ireland in 1937), and was also a part of – after the 38th Irish Brigade of infantry – the only other Irish brigade-sized formation in the British Army during the Second World War, the 3rd (Ulster) Anti-Aircraft Brigade.

On 4 May 1943, Gunner Leslie Francis and 102nd Heavy Anti-Aircraft Brigade set sail for Egypt. Their convoy avoided the Mediterranean and sailed down the west coast of Africa, before stopping in Cape Town, and then sailing up the east coast of Africa in order to enter the Suez Canal. While aboard ship, Leslie wrote to his mother, but the letter was – due to censorship – undated and did not mention where he was going:

> I don't want you to worry too much, as I am having a good time ... we are not going where there is any fighting ... It is very warm here, I am sleeping in a hammock. I fell out of it twice ... I may not be very long away, but we are expecting to have a good time ... I was very sorry that I did not get another leave, as I had expected, still I hope to see you all again at Xmas.

By 13 May 1943 – the same day that the Axis forces in North Africa finally surrendered – Gunner Leslie Francis had arrived in Egypt. 102nd Heavy Anti-Aircraft Regiment's role was to guard the Suez Canal, but there was almost no risk involved as there was no longer any enemy threat in the region. Leslie began to receive Athlone newspapers from his mother, which he used to keep himself up to date on events back in Ireland.

On 3 July 1943, Leslie explained a bit about his new life in Egypt:

> I have promised you a long letter. I should be in town today, but I stayed in camp especially to write this letter ... I was in Alexandria for a week before I came here ... [I heard] the house I used to stay at, in Clacton, was bombed lately. This is the first time

The band of the 38th Irish Brigade plays in front of St Peter's Church in the Vatican City, Rome, 12 June 1944. Rifleman Leslie Francis visited the city on 5 August and soon wrote to his mother that 'The people [were] very friendly and life goes on the same as usually. It is a lovely place. I saw the Pope in St Peters. The largest church in the world, it is beautiful inside. I wish you were here to see it. The most beautiful wall decoration and sculpture in bronze. They are building it now for the past four hundred and fifty years, and it is not finished yet ... I could only see the Vatican from outside. I saw many more historical places such as the Colosseum ... and places I never heard of before'.

I had a bed since August 1942 and now I would sooner sleep outside … I am glad to hear the turf is dry and home, did you cut any this year? It would dry in less than an hour, if you had some of our heat … I got very fond of tea, it is on account of the heat. We are not allowed to drink water, unless it is boiled, so when I come home again you shall have to keep the teapot in action all day … It must be over four months since I saw a drop of rain. The sand is something awful when it starts to blow, everything gets full of it …

By February 1944, Leslie was beginning to long for home. By now, he had been gone for over two years. In his letters, he wondered how his younger brothers had changed, and he was saddened to learn of the deaths of old family friends back in Athlone ('I'll know no one when I get back').

In April, Leslie learned that his brother Harold had been hit by a car – although luckily the accident was not serious – and on 8 May 1944, he wrote his last letter as a gunner with 314th Battery, 102nd Heavy Anti-Aircraft Regiment. When he wrote his next letter on 25 May, he was then Rifleman Leslie Francis, D Company, 1st London Irish Rifles. After fighting at Cassino and Anzio, the battalion had recently returned to Egypt, and in order to replace their losses, men from inactive artillery units had been drafted into the battalion.

Leslie soon wrote that 'I am enjoying the infantry and am feeling twice as fit', and also mentioned that 'I see in the paper today that Mr De Valera got in again. I believe things are very bad back home now with the electricity out and no petrol. I don't know what the people are going to do.'

On 12 July 1944, 1st London Irish Rifles left Egypt to return to Italy. It was the first time that Leslie Francis set foot in an active warzone. They landed at Taranto in southern Italy and, as the battalion's official history recorded:

A strangely familiar sight met the London Irish as they lined the sides of their ship waiting to disembark. They saw men already ashore wearing the caubeen and hackle [the London Irish Rifles' distinctive headdress]. They were men of the 2nd Battalion, waiting to return to Egypt. There was only time for a wave and a shout and the ways of the battalions parted for many long weary, bitter months …

On 25 August 1944, Operation Olive was launched in an attempt to break through the Gothic Line, and two days later – as 1st London Irish Rifles continued to advance north in order to join the fight – Leslie Francis wrote a letter from 'under a tree and the branches are touching the ground with the weight of grapes but all this is no good when you are so far away from home.' Regarding the recent Allied offensive, he added, 'The news is very good. You will see. It will all be over by Christmas.'

However, while the Allies managed to get through the Gothic Line in several locations, there was no major breakthrough and the Germans' last defence line held out. As the official history of 1st London Irish Rifles recorded:

> On September 4 the London Irish moved up, and then it became clear that all was
> not going as well as had been hoped ... Some unpleasantly high features were prov-
> ing a nuisance, and the River Conca was ahead ... For twenty-four hours the London
> Irish sat in their troop-carrying vehicles, moving only six hundred yards in daylight. At
> nightfall they started off in a long column, and progress was slow. The London Scot-
> tish and the Irish advance party were ahead, and daylight found the convoy climbing
> and crawling on bad roads in hilly country with the vehicles stretching for miles, nose
> to tail. The battle could be heard, and it was apparent to the old stagers that the shells
> were not all going the one way. Suddenly and unpleasantly the column came under
> shell-fire and everyone debussed and scattered. This was the battalion's first taste of the
> enemy since Anzio, and it was far from welcome because nothing could be done by
> them in response: the Germans were still far away. Heavier and faster came the shells
> and some casualties were caused, but on the whole the battalion was lucky.

Leslie and his comrades soon arrived at Morciano, before crossing the Conca River and advancing towards Croce – a town that was still in enemy hands. However, as they reached a crossroads (later known as 'Stonk Corner') near Croce, they came under German artillery and mortar fire from elevated positions on all sides. The soldiers of 1st London Irish Rifles scattered and took cover, but then the battalion's vehicles – which had been following the infantry – approached Stonk Corner and also came under heavy enemy fire. The drivers managed to turn their large column of vehicles and escape back down the road. 'Not one man or vehicle was lost.'

Orders were soon received to attack San Sevino Cemetery and the high ground at Point 168 'along the ridge to the south and in the direction of Croce'. Rifleman Leslie Francis' D Company prepared to lead the way, but while they were getting into position to advance:

> In the stillness of the evening the surrounding countryside sprang suddenly into
> life. From positions very carefully concealed on their left flank, the enemy opened up
> machine-gun fire and pinned the entire company down ... and after several fruitless
> attempts to go forward there was no alternative but to wait until total darkness. Sup-
> ported by the gunners the company resumed its advance ... and when they succeeded
> in reaching their objective they discovered that some of the enemy had withdrawn.

But some Germans had remained behind, and the enemy soon launched several coun-
terattacks against D Company, 1st London Irish Rifles. However, after the Germans killed Major Terrence Sweeney – commanding officer of D Company (a German officer pre-
tended that he wanted to surrender, and when Sweeney exposed himself to accept the surrender, the German officer shot him) – an enraged D Company charged the enemy in revenge and 'shot up all the Germans in sight'. Due to the risk of being surrounded by the

enemy, however, they soon withdrew and rejoined the rest of 1st London Irish Rifles, but not before thirty-year-old Corporal Thomas Boylan from Rathmullen, County Sligo and Rifleman Samuel McCullough from County Armagh were killed in action. McCullough is buried in Gradara War Cemetery, while Boylan has no known grave and is commemorated on the Cassino Memorial.

The following day, after a preliminary bombardment by Allied artillery, Point 168 was finally captured by 1st London Irish Rifles. However, by this time, Rifleman Leslie Francis was on his way to a field hospital, having been wounded at some point during the fighting on 5 September. Regarding men like Leslie Francis and their first experience of being under fire, the official history noted:

> The majority of officers and men from the gunners took their conversion to infantry extremely well, and tried very hard under trying conditions. On the whole they were a great success considering the short period of training that was available to them.

Just over two months later, on 23 November – having now rejoined his battalion, and with the winter cold, rain and snows having arrived – Leslie wrote another letter to his mother. She had recently received word from the Record Office stating that her son had previously been wounded – a fact which Leslie had apparently tried to hide from her – and so he wrote in his latest letter:

> I did not like to tell you, as it would worry you too much, but now as you know I will explain everything. I am well again and as fit as ever. I spent two weeks in hospital and seven weeks in a convalescent depot. I don't remember getting hit. I knew nothing until I became conscious in hospital and found that I had three slight wounds on my left thigh and one on my head. I was unconscious for six hours. I had to ask the Sister what happened. I learned that I got hit by shell burst.

By this stage, it was clear that Operation Olive had failed to break through the Gothic Line and end the war in Italy. Rifleman Leslie Francis and 1st London Irish Rifles fought at Forli in November, then dug in on the banks of the Senio River – opposite the Germans on the far side – in December. A period of 'static warfare' began, with both sides firing at each other across the river and with the Germans occasionally sending raiding parties across, but no movement took place. 1st London Irish Rifles remained here for several months as Allied commanders in Italy began planning Operation Grapeshot for April 1945 – a second (and ultimately successful) attempt to break through the Gustav Line – and it was during this time that the Irish people donated £100,000 to Italy's starving population on 12 January, the war having finally taken its toll on the Italians.

Then, on 1 March 1945, Leslie wrote to his brother Lionel:

> I just got back ... to find your letter on my bed ... I hope Eric gets home for St Patrick's Day. It is three and a half years since I saw him, so as soon as I get my twenty

eight days [leave], I shall have to go and see him ... No sign of Harold [Leslie's brother] getting tied up. What is Cyril doing? I believe his *signorina* is sick. I suppose you will be the next. Try and hang on for a while. Well, Lionel, I suppose I have said enough. The censor won't have anything to talk about. So Cheerio, give my love to all. Your loving brother, Leslie.

Three days after writing this letter, Leslie Francis was dead. He was killed only days before 1st London Irish Rifles were withdrawn from the line for three weeks rest at Cesena. Lieutenant D Hutchison – commanding officer of D Company, in which Leslie had served – soon wrote a letter to Leslie's mother back in Athlone. It explained what had happened to her son:

No doubt by this time you will have had official notification of the death of your son. And I thought you might like to know something of how it happened. His was a most unfortunate death as it was no enemy shell or bullet to blame, but one of our own shell. The details, such as they are, are these. The platoon was occupying positions on bank of the Senio, your son and another member sharing the same slit trench. One night on locating an enemy position on the opposite side of the river, the tanks which were supporting us, opened up on it, their line of fire being directly over the platoon's positions. One round by some strange mischance, fell short and landed less than a yard from the trench occupied by your son. He was killed outright, the other occupant suffering little more than a few scratches and severe shock. I may say that I was extremely sorry to lose your son as he was a good Bren gunner, and efficient soldier. He was popular in the platoon both with NCO's and men, who wish me to add their consolations with my own. Words are useless things to express one's feelings and I can only say that I sympathise most deeply with you in your loss particularly when it was caused by such an unfortunate accident. Nevertheless you can well be proud of your son despite the fact that he did not die perhaps as he would have liked, for he was with the platoon in many actions where he might well have met his death and did not, in any of them, let down either himself or his comrades.

In one of his letters to his mother in 1943, Leslie had once written:

> We are sitting here planning out what we are going to do when this is all over, when we go and get the boat at Holyhead ... I hope that day is not so far off.

Leslie Francis from Athlone was twenty-four years old when he died on 4 March 1945, and he now lies buried in Forli War Cemetery. Less than two months after his death, the Allies finally broke through the Gustav Line during Operation Grapeshot – a battle in which 38th Irish Brigade also fought – and the war in Italy ended with a German surrender on 2 May.

The Italian Campaign resulted in a further 300,000 Allied soldiers killed and wounded, along with as many as 580,000 Axis casualties. By then, however, the Allied armies had become truly international. The North African Campaign had been fought by British, American, Canadian, Indian, Australian, New Zealand, South African, Free French, Polish, Czechoslovakian and Greek troops, while the Allies were joined by Italians and Brazilians in Italy. The Irish were represented in several of these armies.

On 29 November 1941 – not long after the start of Operation Crusader in North Africa – thirty-six-year-old Private Francis Irvine from Tempo, County Fermanagh, died while fighting with 2/13th (Battalion) Australian Imperial Force (AIF). He now lies buried in Tobruk War Cemetery. When the Germans subsequently pushed the Allies back into Egypt, thirty-four-year-old Driver Frederick Mathews from Lurgan, County Armagh, was killed

BUCKINGHAM PALACE

The Queen and I offer you our heartfelt sympathy in your great sorrow.

We pray that the Empire's gratitude for a life so nobly given in its service may bring you some measure of consolation.

George R.I.

Above: The condolence letter, sent to Rifleman Leslie Francis' mother back in Athlone, after the death of her son on 4 March 1945 in Italy.
Left: Rifleman Leslie Francis – 1st London Irish Rifles – reading an issue of the Northern Constitution *(a newspaper from Northern Ireland) somewhere in Italy.*

in action on 28 June 1942 – just before the First Battle of El Alamein in North Africa – while serving with the New Zealand Army Service Corps. He now lies buried in El Alamein War Cemetery. Just over a year later on 25 July 1943, fellow Lurgan-man Corporal William Lennon of 48th Highlanders of Canada, Royal Canadian Infantry Corps was killed in action on Sicily. His remains are buried in Agira Canadian War Cemetery, Sicily. Finally, on 12 May 1944 near Anzio, PFC Patrick Wogan of the 350th Infantry Regiment, 88th Infantry Division, US Army, was killed in action. Wogan was twenty-four years old and originally from the Cartown/Sandpit area just outside Termonfeckin, County Louth. He had emigrated to America in 1920 and worked as a compositor for the *New York Morning Telegraph* until he enlisted in June 1942. He had entered the fight on 5 March 1944 – the 88th Infantry Division was the first US Reserve Division to go overseas and the first to enter combat – and less than a month after his death, Wogan's regiment was the first Allied unit to enter Rome. Today, PFC Patrick Wogan lies in Sicily-Rome American Cemetery, Nettuno, Italy.

However, the campaign that led from North Africa to Italy was not the deciding campaign of the war, and in the summer of 1944, all eyes turned to France. The British had been forced to abandon France four years earlier, but now, along with US forces and their other allies, they were about to return. The invasion of Normandy was the largest military amphibious invasion in the history of the world, and thousands of Irish helped to defeat the Germans in France and breach 'Fortress Europe'. This was D-Day.

CHAPTER 4

D-DAY

– 6 JUNE 1944

Mulberry Harbour B – later known as 'Port Winston' – at Arromanches (Gold Beach). These artificial harbours were designed by Irishman, and noted communist, John Desmond Bernal from Nenagh, County Tipperary. After Mulberry Harbour A at Omaha Beach was damaged beyond repair in a storm on 22 June, Mulberry Harbour B remained the only one in operation. Over the next ten months, it landed 2.5 million troops, 500,000 vehicles, and 4 million tons of supplies for the Allies.

'The Channel was crammed with all types of naval vessels as far as the eye could see and as darkness approached we set off ... all the fearful might of battleships, cruisers, destroyers and rocket launches was unleashed on the enemy beach positions and further inland. Looking skywards, a vast array of Allied bombers and fighters flying at varying altitudes and formations passed overhead. It was an incredible sight to behold.'

Private Paddy Gillen from Cork city, No 6 Commando

I n 1942, the Allies had identified the need to open up a second front in Europe. The Russians were fighting the Germans in the east, and if a second front could be opened up, Germany would have to deal with two threats to its borders rather than one, while the Allies could also begin the advance to Berlin and end the war. However, America and Britain disagreed about where to open up this second front. The British wanted to fight up through Italy, while the Americans preferred the quickest route to Berlin – through France – from their strongest base in Europe – Britain. Ultimately, while the British managed to secure a campaign in Italy, the Americans insisted on an invasion of France. And so, planning began for the largest amphibious landing the world had ever seen. Operation Overlord was due to take place in the summer of 1944. It took years of detailed planning while enormous numbers of troops, vehicles, supplies and munitions were steadily built up in Britain.

Back in Ireland during this time, the government was criticised by the US on 10 March 1944 – who claimed that Ireland's neutrality was operating in favour of the Germans – and three days later, the British government banned all travel between Ireland and Britain.

Meanwhile, in preparation for D-Day, the Allies also began feeding the Germans misinformation. Through a system of double agents, the Allies convinced the Germans that Operation Overlord would be supported by an invasion of Norway (while also suggesting that other landings would take place in Crete and Romania). To achieve this, they created fictional military formations that existed only on paper, but had these units 'communicate' with each other by radio – which suggested to anyone listening that they actually existed – while also constructing inflatable tanks and artillery made of plywood that, if photographed, would look like equipment belonging to these non-existent units. British commandos also launched raids in Norway, as if they were preparing the way for a larger invasion, while British diplomats began communicating with Sweden in ways that suggested their forces would soon be in neighbouring Norway.

In order to keep the majority of German forces in France away from Normandy – where the invasion was planned to take place – more fictional Allied army groups were invented (all with their own radio traffic), and the Germans were fed misinformation that suggested the Allies were intending to take the shortest route from Britain to France and cross the Straits of Dover landing at Pas de Calais. These deceptions were a success, and when Operation Overlord began, the Germans had kept units in Norway that could have been used to help repel the Allies in France, while in northern France itself, the bulk of German units were gathered around Pas de Calais, and not to the west in Normandy.

As previously mentioned, Operation Overlord was a hugely ambitious amphibious landing. The plan was to invade five beaches along a fifty-mile front. From west to east they were codenamed Utah, Omaha (US forces would land on both of these beaches), Gold (British), Juno (British and Canadians) and Sword (British). 132,600 seaborne troops would assault these beaches while 23,400 paratroopers – jumping from 2,395 aircraft or landing in 867 gliders – would be dropped behind enemy lines further south. At sea, 4,126 landing ships or landing craft, 1,213 warships, 736 auxiliary vessels and 864 merchant ships from eight different navies (along with the 195,700 naval personnel aboard these vessels) would support the operation, while 3,440 heavy bombers, 930 medium and light bombers, 4,190 fighter aircraft or fighter-bombers, 1,070 RAF Coastal Command aircraft, 520 reconnaissance planes and eighty air-sea rescue aircraft would take to the air. It was a gigantic logistical operation.

The first phase of Operation Overlord – securing a beachhead in France – was codenamed Operation Neptune, and the first day of Operation Neptune was known as D-Day. Originally planned for 5 June 1944, it had to be postponed due to bad weather, and so on 6 June – after Allied bombers and warships pounded enemy positions on the beaches and further inland – the invasion went ahead. While 2nd Royal Ulster Rifles landed on Sword Beach as part of 3rd Mechanised Division – the first division to land on Sword Beach that day – 1st Royal Ulster Rifles, now a battalion in 6th Airborne Division, deployed by glider that evening (this made the Royal Ulster Rifles the only regiment in the entire Allied army to deploy by both sea and air on D-Day). The Liverpool Irish – after sailing to Normandy aboard the former Belfast to Liverpool passenger ship *Ulster Monarch* – landed at Juno Beach alongside the Canadians, while 5th Royal Inniskilling Dragoon Guards, 8th King's Royal Irish Hussars, 2nd Irish Guards (all armoured regiments) and 3rd Irish Guards (infantry) landed in Normandy soon after.

D-Day was a massive gamble that would either see the beginning of the end of Nazi power in Europe, or, if it failed, could prolong the war by years.

ONE OF THE FIRST

RICHARD TODD

The first shots fired during the Allied invasion of France took place after 181 British soldiers – mostly from 2nd Oxfordshire and Buckinghamshire Light Infantry in 6th Airborne Division and led by Major John Howard – landed in Horsa gliders just minutes after midnight on 5/6 June and captured 'Pegasus Bridge' (Bénouville Bridge) over the Caen Canal from the Germans, in order to prevent German panzers from crossing the bridge and attacking the eastern end of Sword Beach once the landings began. Thirty minutes after landing, Major Howard's men were reinforced by 7th Parachute Regiment, and with them was Captain Richard Todd from Dublin.

Todd was born in June 1919, and his father – Major Andrew Todd – was a British Army physician and Irish international rugby player who had earned three caps playing for Ireland. After moving to Devon, then India – where he spent several years – then back to Devon, Todd attended Shrewsbury School before preparing to apply to the Royal Military Academy Sandhurst. However, Todd soon decided not to become a soldier, and instead, he chose to pursue an acting career. He began attending the Italia Conti Academy in London, but because of this, he soon fell out with his mother. Sadly, in 1938 – when Todd was nineteen – she committed suicide.

After performing for the first time as a professional actor in 1936, he performed in regional theatres throughout Britain and then co-founded the Dundee Repertory Theatre in 1939. However, after the outbreak of the Second World War, Richard Todd finally joined the British Army. He was commissioned into the King's Own Yorkshire Light Infantry in 1941 before joining the Parachute Regiment and being promoted to captain. By the time he parachuted into Normandy on D-Day to reinforce Major Howard's men on Pegasus Bridge – making him one of the first British Army officers to land in France – Todd was five days away from his twenty-fifth birthday. The Germans counterattacked at Pegasus Bridge not long after he landed, and Todd was subsequently involved in the fighting to push the enemy back.

Transport moving across the Caen Canal Bridge – 'Pegasus Bridge' – at Bénouville. The bridge was re-named Pegasus Bridge after the mythical winged horse on the formation sign of British airborne forces, and was the location where Captain Richard Todd from Dublin met Major John Howard on D-Day.

After the war, his acting career really took off. After being nominated for the Academy Award for Best Actor in 1949 for playing Corporal Lachlan 'Lachie' MacLachlan in *The Hasty Heart* (the film also starred future US president Ronald Reagan with whom Todd became good friends; the pair later had dinner with British Prime Minister Margaret Thatcher in No 10 Downing Street), Todd played Wing Commander Guy Gibson in the well known 1955 war movie *The Dam Busters*. In 1962 he performed in another classic war film, *The Longest Day*, based on the book of the same name by Irish war correspondent Cornelius Ryan. Ironically, in *The Longest Day*, Todd played the role of Major John Howard – who led the initial attack against Pegasus Bridge, and the very man who Todd was sent to reinforce on D-Day (he actually wore Howard's original D-Day helmet during filming) – while Captain Richard Todd's character was played by another actor. Todd had turned down the offer to play himself, feeling that the part would be too small.

In 1993 he was awarded an OBE, but then, in 1997, he suffered the first of two family tragedies when his youngest son – Seamus – committed suicide, aged twenty. After possibly suffering a severe depressive reaction to an anti-acne drug, Richard Todd's son shot himself in the head. Todd was seventy-eight at the time. Then, in 2005, Todd's eldest son Peter also shot himself, aged fifty-three. He had been having difficulties with his marriage. Richard Todd was eighty-six years old when he lost his second son.

He continued acting for another two years – his last role was in 2007 – and then, in December 2009, while living in the small village of Little Humby in Lincolnshire, Richard Todd died in his sleep. He had been suffering from cancer, and was ninety years old. Having been married twice – both marriages ended in divorce – the Dublin-born actor and Second World War veteran was survived by a son and a daughter. He was one of the first Irishmen, if not *the* first, to land in Normandy on D-Day.

LINKING UP

PATRICK 'PADDY' GILLEN

After being reinforced by men like Captain Richard Todd and 7th Parachute Regiment, the soldiers at Pegasus Bridge now waited for British forces coming inland from Sword Beach to link up with them and finally secure their hold on the bridge. The unit specifically detailed to land at Sword Beach and then advance inland to the troops at Pegasus Bridge was the 1st Special Service Brigade of British commandos. One of the units in this brigade was No 6 Commando, and serving in No 6 Commando was Private Patrick 'Paddy' Gillen from Cork city.

Born in March 1925, Paddy had previously served in 4th Royal Norfolk Regiment before volunteering for the commandos in November 1943. As Paddy recalled in a recent interview:

> I was sent with many others to the Commando Training Centre in Invernesshire [sic] and after six weeks of arduous training – including river crossings, abseiling from the camp's old castle walls, cross-country runs with full pack through snow and ice

carrying weapons and wearing steel helmets which never fitted, we qualified. Before the final passing–out parade we were presented with the coveted Green Beret worn exclusively by commando forces.

Paddy was only eighteen years old when he became a British Army commando, and over the following months 'the training continued, concentrating on beach landings from all types of naval craft, troopships and landing-craft.' Paddy turned nineteen in March 1944,

Commandos of 1ˢᵗ Special Service Brigade landing from an LCI(S) (Landing Craft Infantry Small) at La Breche – 'Queen Red' sector, Sword Beach – at approximately 0840hrs on D-Day. This would have been the sight that greeted Private Paddy Gillen from Cork as he landed.

and then, in May, the various commando units of 1st Special Service Brigade – which included Private Paddy Gillen and No 6 Commando – were moved to a camp near South-ampton and 'totally isolated from the outside world'. Secrecy was so important that, as D-Day approached, troops were not allowed to leave their camps. Instead, they memorised their unit's mission and dedicated their time to studying maps, photographs and models of their landing beaches and the inland areas over which they would be expected to fight.

On 5 June, 'after attending religious services, we received our movement orders.' Paddy and his comrades were issued with forty-eight hours worth of rations, and having packed all their kit – which made each soldier's backpack weigh over 80lbs (close to 6st) – No 6 Commando made their way to 'a small port on the river Hamble and boarded the 22 land-ing craft where I was one of eighty soldiers packed into our launch.' However, as Paddy also recalled, 'At least we were given permission to wear the green beret instead of the helmet, which didn't fit anyway.'

The transport vessels carrying Private Paddy Gillen and No 6 Commando then set out across the English Channel, and as Paddy remembered:

> The Channel was crammed with all types of naval vessels as far as the eye could see and as darkness approached we set off – the opening of the Second Front had started. The landing was timed for 0800hrs – termed H-hour – and at 0530hrs all the fear-ful might of battleships, cruisers, destroyers and rocket launches was unleashed on the enemy beach positions and further inland. Looking skywards, a vast array of Allied bombers and fighters flying at varying altitudes and formations passed overhead. It was an incredible sight to behold.

After 8th Infantry Brigade had landed on Sword Beach first, to help clear the way, Paddy and No 6 Commando approached the Queen Red sector – at the far eastern end of the beach – near La Breche. Their mission, along with the rest of 1st Special Service Brigade, was to advance and capture the port of Ouistreham before pressing on to link up with the elements of 6th Airborne Division holding Pegasus Bridge and the nearby 'Horsa Bridge' (Ranville Bridge) over the Orne River. As No 6 Commando neared Sword Beach – watch-ing an advance wave of British amphibious tanks landing in front of them – Paddy recalled:

> Shellfire and mortar-fire rained down on the beaches – and then it was time for us to put our feet on French soil ... Our flotilla started to take direct hits from shellfire and machine guns and of the 22 landing craft four received direct hits and more were disabled. The order was given to lower the ramps and we began to pour out of the landing craft in single file, with weapons kept above our heads to keep them dry. We were moving as fast as our pack-laden bodies would carry us and I saw many bodies floating in the sea and lying on the beach. We didn't find out till later that night who was dead, wounded or missing from our unit. Some [British] tanks were hit but it was

a welcome sight to see how many got ashore and it lifted our morale no-end.

Private Paddy Gillen and No 6 Commando landed on Sword Beach at 0840hrs on D-Day. As Allied warships fired on enemy positions inland, the battalion advanced off the beach as quickly as possible. No 6 Commando linked up with the surviving Sherman tanks that had made it ashore and then proceeded south along tracks through dense forest.

> The enemy had stuck 'Minen' signs all over the place which must have been bluff as no mines were encountered despite the fact that the troop walked over many of the signed areas.

However, No 2 Troop soon came under German mortar fire and machine-gun fire from roadside positions and enemy pillboxes, while No 3 Troop launched an assault against two more pillboxes and a 'strong point ... in the corner of a field'. No 3 Troop attacked their targets and 'cleared [them] by grenades', after which a 'Section then proceeded off to destroy the six-barrelled mortar which had been firing fairly close all this time, in co-operation with two Sherman tanks which had by this time come up with some other infantry.' At midday, No 2 Troop then came across a German gun battery, as the war diary recorded, positioned 'in hedge behind thick scrub'. No 2 Troop immediately attacked, killing and wounding several German soldiers and taking seven prisoners. Another troop of No 6 Commando then captured four more prisoners in the area, but the Germans managed to remove some of their guns before the commandos could assault them all.

No 6 Commando resumed the advance. However, they started coming under fire from concealed German snipers:

> [the snipers] always fired and retired through the undergrowth. On reaching the Bénouville area small arms fire was heard in the village so the Troop Commander decided to by-pass the village and make for the bridges which had been reported captured by the Airborne. On nearing the bridges a group of men were seen through a hedge 200 yards away and these were first thought to be Germans; on looking at them through glasses, however, they were recognised as paratroops. The Troop Commander waved the Union Jack carried for this purpose and shouted. On seeing us the paratroops cheered frantically and moved towards us.

The Allied ground troops had finally arrived to reinforce and support the airborne, and the next step was to cross Pegasus Bridge and Horsa Bridge in order to secure the area on the far side.

However, as Paddy recalled in his recent interview:

> Getting across the bridges was another task. Enemy snipers were firing constantly, and we really had to sprint – first across the canal bridge and then across the Orne bridge.

That evening, Private Paddy Gillen and his troop from No 6 Commando found themselves in an area of 'high ground [near Amfreville]. After digging-in we camouflaged our areas and prepared our first meal in France. During the night we suffered some more casualties through spasmodic shelling.' Here, Paddy, the commandos, and the airborne paratroopers remained for seven weeks guarding the Allied flank, all the while under shellfire. They were supposed to remain in Normandy for only two weeks after D-Day, and even after being moved from this area after seven weeks, they were only moved to join the fight elsewhere. Paddy and No 6 Commando finally left France at the end of August. On D-Day, the unit had lost three while thirty-two were wounded.

When No 6 Commando was disbanded in 1945, Paddy Gillen returned to 4th Royal Norfolk Regiment as an orderly room sergeant. Then, when the war ended, he soon returned to Cork and began working for the Ford Motor Company. However, he also joined the local No 2 Battery of 8th Field Artillery Regiment, FCÁ (Fórsa Cosanta Áitiúil, or Local Defence Force), and ultimately became a commissioned officer in the FCÁ – rising to the rank of commandant and battery commander. When he retired in 1982, he actually handed over command of his unit to his son – Commandant Robin Gillen – and today, Paddy Gillen's No 2 Battery survives through its descendent unit: No 1 Battery of 31st Reserve Artillery Regiment, RDF (Reserve Defence Forces).

Today, D-Day veteran and Second World War commando Patrick 'Paddy' Gillen is eighty-seven years old. He still lives in Cork City.

CLEARING THE WAY

REDMOND CUNNINGHAM

Of course, the Germans had done everything in their power to make the Normandy beaches impossible to assault. They had laid mines on steel frames and anti-landing craft rails below the water line, steel-girder anti-tank 'hedgehogs' and rows of buried mines beneath the sand on the beaches and the surrounding dunes, and built anti-tank ditches and sea walls to prevent invaders from advancing off the beaches – all guarded by reinforced concrete machine gun and artillery emplacements, supported by machine gun and mortar pits and German snipers. These defences would devastate assaulting Allied vehicles and troops if they were not neutralised somehow, and so, combat engineers were sent in ahead of the infantry and armour to clear the way. In Queen Red sector of Sword Beach, 79th Assault Squadron, Royal Engineers had been tasked with neutralising the beach defences, and leading one of the troops in this squadron was Captain Redmond Cunningham from Waterford.

Born in the Ballybricken area of Waterford city on Christmas Eve 1916, Redmond was

A Sherman crab flail tank of 79th Armoured Division being tested, 27 April 1944. Captain Redmond Cunningham from Waterford commanded identical vehicles on D-Day.

named after his godfather – Irish Parliamentary Party leader and Home Rule MP John Redmond, who Redmond Cunningham's father Bryan (a pig dealer and exporter) had worked for as an election agent. The family business was badly affected after the start of the Anglo-Irish Trade War (or 'Economic War') that began in 1932 when Fianna Fáil first came to power, but Redmond – a vegetarian – did not work in the pig trade like the rest of his family. He did not get on with his own father and after showing a talent for drawing, the young Redmond began working as a draughtsman in an architect's office in Waterford while studying to become an architect. Redmond was working here when, as his son – Irish novelist Peter Cunningham – recalled in an article he wrote about his father for the summer 2008 issue (issue thirty-one) of *The Dublin Review*:

> In 1939 de Valera exceeded the Cunningham family's darkest expectations by making the 26-county Irish state neutral in the newly declared war. Neutrality was seen by the Cunninghams as yet another act of nationalist isolationism, a stance that made Ireland a pariah in the eyes of her chief trading partner, England … The people of Waterford were aware of the war, not just from their wireless sets and censored newspapers, but also from the bright flashes of guns and explosions far out to sea at night, and from the thick wads of sticky tar – oil from ruptured vessels – that washed up on the local beaches.

Furthermore, several Allied and Axis planes were shot down in the area, while combatant aircrews often bailed out from damaged aircraft and landed around Waterford.

Then, in 1940, aged twenty-three, Redmond Cunningham travelled to Omagh, County Tyrone and started work as a clerk-of-works on an army building project. Omagh was the Royal Inniskilling Fusiliers' depot, and the British Army were currently updating and expanding their barracks in Northern Ireland. However, Redmond soon began making once-a-week trips to Belfast to report to a Major Moore on any suspected IRA or anti-British activity around Omagh. The British Army trusted Redmond, and as a Catholic from southern Ireland, they felt he was in a good position to gather intelligence for them.

It was while working for the British Army as a civilian that Redmond joined the Officers' Emergency Reserve. This meant that he could be called up for active service when needed, and this is exactly what happened, in June 1943, when he was immediately gazetted as a second-lieutenant in the Royal Engineers, but without having undergone any period of officer training. He was simply granted a commission because – as Redmond's son later recalled: 'he had some experience in supervising building and engineering projects.' Then an officer in the Royal Engineers, Redmond Cunningham was sent to join 79th Armoured Division.

79th Armoured Division was commanded by Major-General Sir Percy Hobart, who was a highly experienced tank warfare officer and veteran of North Africa. Hobart had been given the job of designing tanks with specialist functions that would help overcome the

German beach defences in Normandy, and so he invented several modified tanks to aid the landings – tanks that became known as 'Hobart's Funnies'.

These included the Sherman 'Crab' – which had a spinning chain-link mine flail attached to the front that detonated mines as it passed over them – and the Churchill AVRE (Armoured Vehicle Royal Engineers). One version of the AVRE was armed with the Petard spigot mortar that fired 290mm 'flying dustbin' rounds – containing 28lbs of explosive – designed to destroy concrete obstacles or enemy bunkers and emplacements. Other variants were equipped with bridging attachments – such as the 'Small Box Girder' deployable steel bridge or 'Fascine' wooden pole bundles that could be dropped into anti-tank ditches in order to fill them in – while others carried the 'Bobbin' canvas cloth that, when laid, prevented vehicles that drove on it from sinking into the sand, or the 'Double Onion' demolition charge, which allowed a tank crew to safely lay explosives against obstacles (AVREs also carried 'Bangalore torpedoes' for clearing barbed wire and other obstacles). Then there was the Churchill ARK (Armoured Ramp Karrier) with extendable ramps at either end which turned the tank into a bridge or ramp for other vehicles when needed, the Churchill 'Crocodile' equipped with an 150-yard range flamethrower, and a variety of amphibious tanks that could be deployed from their landing craft when still out to sea and make their own way to shore.

In his new role as a Royal Engineers officer, Redmond Cunningham was soon training for D-Day. He began exercises with landing craft in the Caledonian Canal, south of Lough Ness in Scotland, and while there he witnessed the RAF training with the bouncing bombs that No 617 Squadron RAF – the 'Dambusters' – would later use in Operation Chastise against the Möhne and Edersee Dams. In July 1943 he was sent to Orford, Suffolk where top secret replicas of the German beach defences in Normandy had been reconstructed for training purposes. At this time, he was also assigned to the newly formed 79th Assault Squadron of 79th Armoured Division.

Not long before D-Day, Redmond Cunningham was promoted to captain. Then, on 4 June 1944, as Peter Cunningham wrote:

> When the invasion fleet was assembling at Portsmouth, he and a friend, Geoffrey Desanges, a fellow captain in 79 Assault Squadron, left the military exclusion zone without permission and went to London for the night. Next morning they hitched a lift back to Portsmouth on a milk lorry and turned up as normal for breakfast, their overnight absence undetected. An hour later, they were directing the loading of tanks on to landing craft ... At just after 0700 hours [on 6 June], tanks were unshackled, chocks removed from under tank tracks, tank engines fired up and the four landing craft [of the squadron] made for shore ... Since dawn the heavy guns of British destroyers had been bombarding the German gun emplacements and fortifications.

My father told me half a century later that an RAF Spitfire came low out of the smoke and was shot down by a Royal Navy destroyer.

79th Assault Squadron's war diary recorded that there was 'little enemy interference except one destroyer is seen cut clean in half and sinking amidships.' This was the Norwegian destroyer HNoMS *Svenner* – the only Allied ship sunk by the German Navy on D-Day.

Captain Redmond Cunningham was in command of No 1 Troop – which comprised six tanks and twenty-four soldiers – of 79th Assault Squadron, and they were due to land at Queen Red sector on Sword Beach in order to clear the beach of mines and other obstacles. In fact, 2nd Royal Ulster Rifles were due to land in Redmond's particular section of beach once he had completed his mission, and so, an Irishman was clearing the way for a battalion of Irish troops to follow.

As the landing craft carrying Redmond and his comrades neared the beaches, the war diarist noted, 'It is just possible to pick out landmarks and we believe we are going in dead on our pre-arranged exits.' The combat engineers were exactly where they were supposed to be, but when a salvo of Allied rockets launched at the beach began to fall short, all landing craft had 'to go full speed astern' in order to prevent being hit. Then, at 0725hrs on 6 June 1944, the tanks of 79th Assault Squadron left their landing craft in five feet of water and began wading their way in towards Sword Beach. Redmond was in an AVRE and exited the landing craft after the two Sherman Crab tanks of his troop led the way.

The war diary recorded:

> For a minute there is no fire from the enemy. From the water's edge up to the back of the beach is about 250 yds ... The first 100 yards is thick with obstacles. First two rows of Ramp Type obstacles, every alternate one mined with a 1935 Tellermine on top, is in four feet of water. Then two or three rows of heavy Pit Props sunk into the ground again each alternate one fixed on top with a Tellermine. And inland of these, rows of reinforced concrete Tetrahedra and steel girder hedgehogs with alternate obstacles wired up with Shells with German push igniters.

The tanks began to hit the beach, and the Germans opened up with anti-tank fire. As Peter Cunningham recounted:

> Things began to go wrong immediately. The first Crab of 1 Troop hit an underwater mine and sat in the surging tide, disabled ... My father ordered the second Crab to proceed up the beach and followed in its tracks, in his AVRE, as the Crab detonated mines. He also ordered the surviving crew of the disabled Crab to fire on a German pillbox situated about 150 yards to the left above the sand dunes. As Redmond's tank

Captain Redmond Cunningham from Waterford.

left the water it was hit twice, low down, by high velocity fire, but not disabled.

Several tanks in other troops were disabled, while others were damaged after they drove over buried anti-tank mines. Engineers and supporting British infantry had been raked by German fire and bodies now covered the sand in Queen Red sector of Sword Beach. The enemy knew what the combat engineers were trying to achieve – create safe lanes up the beach for infantry to follow – and so they fought desperately to prevent Captain Redmond Cunningham and 79th Assault Squadron from completing their mission. However, by 0830hrs, the war diary noted that Redmond's '1 Tp is doing well.' (It was around this time that Redmond's friend, Captain Geoffrey Desanges of No 2 Troop, was killed. He was twenty-one years old.)

Then disaster struck. After Redmond called up a bridge-carrying AVRE to help the remaining Crab from No 1 Troop and his own AVRE cross from the top of the beach to the dunes beyond, the bridge-carrier was hit by enemy artillery fire. However, although the crew of the bridge-carrier exited their tank and managed to deploy the bridge while under heavy sniper fire, the Crab was hit and destroyed once it crossed. Refusing to withdraw, as Peter Cunningham recounted, 'Redmond jumped from his tank and ran back down the cleared mine path to the beach.' He found a Crab at the waterline 'doing nothing', and so he ordered it forward. This Crab managed to cross the tank bridge and bypass the previously destroyed Crab tank – which was now on fire – and advance through the dunes. Redmond 'followed in its tracks in his AVRE, but in the process [his tank was] hit multiple times.' Two of the crew were also badly wounded and it soon became obvious that 'The new Crab was making little progress because of persistent enemy fire. Redmond abandoned his crippled tank and, realising that the mines in the dunes were laid too close together to be cleared by flails, decided the job had to be done by hand.' Redmond and his men initially used mine detectors, but, as the war diary recorded, 'Prodding was then resorted to as the shrapnel on the ground made use of Mine Detector impractical.' It actually took four sweeps – all while under enemy mortar fire – to clear the lane, after which logs were dropped on the sand to make a road for vehicles to use.

By 0940hrs, the British were making progress. There were soon five exit lanes off the beach. Redmond remained at his exit for the next few hours, as he wrote in a subsequent report, 'blowing telegraph poles, demolishing the corners of dangerous houses etc.'

At 1200hrs, as the war diary recorded, 79th Assault Squadron, with ten AVREs, was ordered to advance on the lock gates and bridge at Ouistreham. The Germans succeeded in blowing part of the bridge but after an intense battle Redmond's squadron took control of the locks and the bridge.

> Prisoners are marched off to the Beach ... [Captain] Cunningham is placed in charge of the position with orders to hold it, recheck the Bridge and Lock Gates for

Demolition Charges and Booby Traps, count the captured material and feed the men.

He does more and with much energy patrols the locality, killing and bringing in more enemy ...

For this, and his earlier displays of bravery, Captain Redmond Cunningham was soon awarded the Military Cross (*London Gazette*, 31 August 1944). According to Peter Cunningham's research, this was the only Military Cross awarded to an Irishman on D-Day.

The following day, after securing the canal lock and enduring enemy mortar fire, Captain Redmond Cunningham handed over control of the area to Allied infantry. He went on to serve during the subsequent campaign in Normandy, before fighting in Nijmegen during Operation Market Garden and later in the Rhineland. He was also awarded a bar to his Military Cross for leading Allied infantry in two separate attacks against the German-occupied town of Zandpool in Holland and nearby Leuth while serving in the Rhineland in February 1945. Redmond was only supposed to transport the infantry to their targets, but after they arrived with no officers to lead them, he took charge and led the way, capturing 200 enemy prisoners in the process.

After the war he remained stationed on the Rhine, and in 1946 he took one week leave to return to Ireland and marry Mory McIntyre from Sutton, Dublin. Her family were linked to the Lafayette photographic studio and had set up the Sutton Golf Course, and Mory had played golf for Ireland. Then, later in 1946, as Peter Cunningham recalled:

> He was demobbed with the rank of major, gained a qualification as an architect by correspondence course and returned to Waterford, where he set up in practice with his brother Willie, a qualified engineer, as R&W Cunningham, Architects and Engineers.

This was not the only business that Redmond became involved in once he returned home.

> Over thirty years he was at various times the outright owner or substantial shareholder in a dizzying range of ventures, including a chain of hotels, a chipboard factory with 400 employees, a weekly newspaper, a bookshop, a public ballroom, a tyre factory with sales depots across Munster, an ocean trawler, bookmaker's shops, a pub, a fashion boutique and a substantial collection of houses, flats, ground rents and sites scattered around Waterford city and Tramore.

However, the war hero is only one half of Redmond Cunningham's story, and by D-Day, soldiering had already changed him from the man he used to be. Redmond later admitted to his son that he had sunk two boats in the Ouistreham Canal when he arrived there – an act for which he was reprimanded because it prevented Allied vessels from using the canal – because he was bored, and Peter Cunningham believes that boredom was also what made Redmond remain at his beach exit for several hours, 'blowing telegraph poles, demolishing the corners of dangerous houses etc.' The war had turned an 'artistic, gentle individual' into someone who thrived on adrenalin, and on 7 June – after handing over the canal lock to Allied infantry – Redmond actually drove south through 21st Panzer Division's lines into Caen for a beer, only hours before it was occupied by German reinforcements rushing to Normandy, before returning to his men.

Then, during his actions in the Rhineland that earned him the bar to his Military Cross – as reported by Captain Jack Golding – '[Captain Redmond Cunningham] was personally disposing of a Jerry officer when [the infantry commander] arrived', meaning that Redmond was executing a German prisoner.

Peter Cunningham remembered that those who knew his father from before the war 'contrasted [Redmond's pre-war personality traits] with those of the subsequently flamboyant war hero', and that after the war, Redmond 'lived life at a flat-out pace ... the only thing in life that terrified him was boredom.'

He tells of how Redmond began to drink:

> ... outrageously, squandering his many assets in the process ... My father burned out his friendships, one by one, including those with his children. Only my mother, who adored him, stayed loyal to the end ... My father was reinvented by the war ... [he became] a larger than life character, a reckless adventurer of the type so admired by the officer class, a gambler and drinker of champagne, an entrepreneur and a dreamer ... I have no doubt that the war affected him extremely deeply and negatively in terms of his outlook on life, and he almost certainly drank too much to overcome the desperate things that had happened, and he was a young, quite artistic man and brutalised by it. They had to do awful things.

The change in Redmond was summed up in a photograph taken by a street photographer in College Green, Dublin in 1951. After the photographer called out to Redmond and took the photo as he turned, Peter Cunningham recalled:

> [my father] swivels to the danger. In my father's expression at that moment, in his instinctive reaction to the unexpected intrusion, is the story of the war he recently fought. His narrowed eyes seek out the sudden risk, as they might have when he heard the bolt of a sniper's rifle. The set of his mouth is uncompromising, his body is poised to attack ... [seeing this] I grasp the great cost of being a war hero.

Redmond had also been wounded several times in combat. Peter Cunningham described these wounds:

> Embedded in the back of his neck, just above the hairline, was a lump of shrapnel the size of a sixpence. Dad used to let me feel it. At the back of his left knee a stippled arc could be seen, the pattern of a German machine gun. Luckily, the bullets had not damaged the kneecap but had exited through the muscles of the thigh. The third

wound had been caused by shrapnel, probably at the same time as the neck wound: this wound was in Dad's right buttock, and was visible at such times as when he was changing out of swimming togs, or climbing from the bath.

Redmond Cunningham and his wife moved to Dublin in 1987, but after Mory passed away and Redmond grew older, he became:

> Much reduced in physique and bodily functions, trapped in a maze of the brain from which he could find no way out, widowed, dependent on carers, and lonely, he spent his last days … sitting in his armchair in the front room of his house in Dun Laoghaire. He no longer read or watched television. He had not taken a drink of alcohol for years.

In 1999, Redmond Cunningham from Waterford city finally passed away. Having earned a Military Cross and bar, as well as the Belgian *Croix de Guerre*, and having cleared the way for 2nd Royal Ulster Rifles on D-Day, he was deeply scarred by the war after it ended. He was eighty-two years old when he died.

THE NEXT WAVE

JAMES DURHAM

Finally, as troops moved inland from the invasion beaches, waves of fresh soldiers began land-ing in Normandy to reinforce the men who had been fighting since morning. Most landed by sea, but some deployed by air. One such unit – the glider-borne 1st Royal Ulster Rifles in 6th Air-borne Division – landed in Normandy at approximately 2100hrs on D-Day. As they descended towards their

Rifleman James Durham from Rathmines, Dublin, of 1st Royal Ulster Rifles, 6th Airborne Division.

landing zones, they flew over the heads of 2nd Royal Ulster Rifles, who had landed earlier by sea. 1st Royal Ulster Rifles soon touched down and began to reinforce their comrades in 6th Airborne Division.

Serving in 1st Royal Ulster Rifles that day was Rifleman James Durham. Born in Rathmines, Dublin in March 1925, James Durham's father had previously served in the British Army – where he was also an army bandsman – and James' older brother had been born in Egypt while his father had been stationed there. After his father died when James was twelve years old and the family had moved to Cabra, James began work as a fitter/welder. Then, in 1941, he crossed the border into Northern Ireland – along with his best friend – and joined the British Army. James was underage and so he lied in order to enlist. He was only sixteen years old at the time.

While James Durham's best friend ended up serving in Cyprus, James joined 1st Royal Ulster Rifles, a battalion that had yet to enter the war. It had originally been a regular infantry unit, but had been converted into a glider-borne unit and ultimately attached to 6th Airborne Division for D-Day. On that day, James was now nineteen years old, and when 1st Royal Ulster Rifles exited their gliders after landing in the area around Ranville – with some of the gliders having come under enemy machine gun and mortar fire – James and his comrades were sent to secure the nearby village of Longueval on the banks of the Orne River the following morning.

Longueval was secured against little enemy opposition on 7 June, but when 1st Royal Ulster Rifles pressed on to capture Sainte Honorine, they encountered heavy German resistance. The Germans in Sainte Honorine were armed with machine guns and mortars, and enemy tanks and self-propelled guns soon entered the battle. A and B Companies – who had assaulted the town – were pushed back, while C Company – positioned on high ground to the south in order to provide supporting fire – were similarly pounded by enemy artillery and mortars. By the end of the day, 1st Royal Ulster Rifles had retreated back to Longueval. They had lost sixteen killed (at least eight of which were Irish; four from Northern Ireland and four from the south), sixty-nine wounded, and forty missing. Rifleman James Durham was one of the wounded.

Having been hit in the legs and feet by enemy fire, James was helped by a comrade and managed to make it back to Longueval and 1st Royal Ulster Rifles' defensive positions. It would be six days before another British unit attempted to capture Sainte Honorine, and even though this second assault was supported by artillery, it too failed to secure the town.

However, as James Durham's daughter – Rita Harris – recently recalled:

> After some time while he was lying on the [ground] the medical corps van was going around and they were only taking the walking wounded and leaving everyone else behind. My dad was being left behind. Suddenly one of the medical personnel

said, 'Look, there's Jimmy Durham from Rathmines – take him.' And he was rescued from the battlefields in Normandy. He was taken back to the army hospital in England and they were going to remove his leg when the surgeon said that he thought he could save the leg and operated on it.

From what I remember hearing my dad spent almost two years recuperating before returning home. His sister Allie and his mom were sitting home alone one Christmas Eve listening to stories on the radio about people returning home when someone knocked on their hall door. My aunt Allie said to my gran, 'Imagine if that was Jimmy at the door returning home.' When they went to the door there was my dad standing at the door. He was on crutches and he had a broken Christmas candle in his hand

Riflemen of 1ˢᵗ Royal Ulster Rifles, 6ᵗʰ Airlanding Brigade, 6ᵗʰ Airborne Division, aboard a jeep and trailer, driving off Landing Zone 'N' past a crashed Airspeed Horsa glider on the evening of 6 June 1944. Rifleman James Durham from Rathmines, Dublin, landed in France aboard one of these gliders.

that he had carried all the way home as a present. He had travelled all the way home from Belfast, presumably getting dropped back there by the Army and getting a train and hitching lifts and walking the rest of the way home.

Having been discharged from the British Army and with the war now over, James Durham started work as a car assembler for McKearns Motors on Alexandra Road in the docklands, while also marrying and having six children. He loved to camp – the family went camping every weekend and for two weeks in summer – and as James got older he replaced camping with hiking in the Dublin and Wicklow mountains, as well as doing the Kerry Way and the Pennine Way in England. As Rita Harris remembered:

> They [James Durham and his wife] cycled all around Ireland. They cycled with Wicklow 200 and my Dad and brother did 'Co-operation North' and they cycled the Royal and Grand Canal before any of the restoration on the canals started and spoke all the time of how wonderful it was and how it should be preserved.

However, James did not openly speak about the war or about his time in the British Army, and his daughter recalled:

> I remember one day I was in school, when I was very young, and I proudly announced that my dad had been in the British Army. I cannot remember specifically what was said to me, but I remember feeling that it was not a good thing and I should not mention it again, which I didn't. That would have been in the 1960s.

Rita also remembered that her father was:

> Such a devoted husband and father, he didn't frequent pubs and only enjoyed a few drinks at Christmas when all the relatives would get together ... My dad had a great singing voice and enjoyed nothing better than a good sing song with his family at Christmas. It turned out that in his youth he was a regular singer in pubs in Rathmines, where he grew up ...

James Durham – who deployed to Normandy by glider on D-Day and who was wounded on D+1 – lived in Dublin for the rest of his life. He died in October 2000, aged seventy-five.

THE SCREAMS OF THE CHILDREN

JAMES MURRAY

While this chapter has mainly focused on Irishmen's experiences on Sword Beach on D-Day, there are hundreds of Irish stories surrounding 6 June 1944 – enough to fill a book by themselves – and many of them show just how brutal and horrific the fighting was in

Normandy that day and after.

Just to give one example, Private James Murray from South William Street in Dublin fought on D-Day with 2nd King's Own Shropshire Light Infantry. In later life he never openly spoke about his experiences, but one day, when he had a few drinks on him, he once told his nephew – Michael Murray – that on D-Day, a mortar shell had landed between himself and a friend. While James was completely unhurt, the friend was 'vaporised' – all they ever recovered of him was a bit of a rifle and a piece of boot. However, James went on to say that the worst thing about D-Day was 'the screams of the children'. Confused, Michael asked his uncle what he meant. 'The German soldiers', replied James. 'They were only children.' James Murray then explained that he had witnessed fellow British soldiers using flamethrowers against German pillboxes on D-Day. The screams he was remembering were of the young German soldiers as they burnt alive inside.

Endless, detailed preparation had resulted in D-Day being a success. The Allies had fooled the Germans into keeping the bulk of their forces away from Normandy, they had attained air superiority in France and all but destroyed the *Luftwaffe*, and just prior to D-Day, Allied bombers had attacked French infrastructure and the road and rail network to prevent the Germans from moving troops into the Normandy area once they realised what was happening. The Allies now had a foothold in France – however, there was a high price to pay for breaching the walls of Fortress Europe. At

Twenty-three-year-old missionary priest-in-training Patrick O'Connor from Dolphin's Barn in Dublin, taken at Uriage-les-Bains, France in 1943. Patrick was studying at Chartres when the war began, and he remained living in France throughout the Nazi occupation, during which he was interrogated by the Gestapo and suspected of being a British spy. D-Day marked the beginning of his liberation, and after the war he decided that 'I wasn't cut out for it [the priesthood]. See I was older, and the war had an effect on everyone, on your way of thinking … I had a different aspect on [life]'. At the time of writing, Patrick O'Connor is ninety-one years old and still lives in his native Dublin city.

least 12,000 Allied soldiers, sailors and airmen were killed or wounded on D-Day. It is not known exactly how many troops the Germans lost, but it is estimated to be between 4,000 and 9,000 casualties. But the Allies were now ashore, and thanks to the artificial Mulberry Harbours that were soon set up on the invasion beaches – designed by Irishman and noted communist John Desmond Bernal from Nenagh, County Tipperary – and PLUTO (Pipe Line Under The Ocean), fresh supplies of troops, vehicles, supplies and fuel were available to continue the offensive.

The British were soon attempting to break out from their beachheads in the Caen area, while the Americans began advancing towards Saint-Lô and beyond to Avranches. After subsequently encircling the 50,000 German troops trapped in the Falaise Pocket on 21 August, the Battle of Normandy ended on 25 August with the Liberation of Paris. By then, the Allies had lost over 226,000 men killed and wounded since D-Day, while the Germans had suffered anything from 210,000 to 450,000 casualties.

However, this was not the end of the German Army. The Germans withdrew east and the Allies followed. Operation Market Garden – a failed Allied attempt to create a corridor from Eindhoven, through Nijmegen and Arnhem, in order to open up the deepwater port of Antwerp for Allied use – took place in September 1944. If it had succeeded, the Allied supply lines would have been greatly shortened and the Allies would have been able to renew their advance across the Rhine and into Germany. Following Market Garden, Germany launched the Ardennes Offensive (better known as the Battle of the Bulge) in December 1944. Hitler gathered all of his available forces for one last push in an attempt to drive the Allies back, but it too failed. By March 1945, the Allies were across the Rhine, while the Russians were closing in on Germany from the east. On 30 April, Adolf Hitler committed suicide as Berlin crumbled around him, and on 8 May, the German armed forces unconditionally surrendered.

In Ireland, U-boats from the Atlantic were soon after docking in Derry, while on 7 May – the day before the German surrender – students of Trinity College Dublin came out onto the roof of the university and sang the English and French national anthems in celebration. However, this started a local riot that resulted in the burning of the Irish tricolour.

The German surrender ended the war in Europe, and 8 May became subsequently known as VE Day (Victory in Europe). However, VE Day did not mark the complete end of the Second World War. Out of the three Axis powers, one still remained. The Empire of Japan.

CHAPTER 5

A LONG WAY FROM HOME

– THE WAR

AGAINST JAPAN

'It felt odd to be walking barefoot on ashes that used to be human beings …You never forget sights like that.'

Michael Blanchfield from Dublin, Royal Navy,
from 'Barefoot in Hiroshima', published in
Flying, Not Falling: Poems, Stories and Reflections on Life by Older Adults

B y the time that the Empire of Japan launched its surprise attack against the US Pacific Fleet at Pearl Harbour on 7 December 1941, the Japanese people had already been at war for a decade. The country had limited natural resources, and after the Wall Street stock market crash in 1929, Japan had begun expanding its influence in mainland Asia. In 1931 they started a war with Manchuria in order to secure Manchurian coal and iron ore, and then in 1937 they invaded China. Here, they developed a reputation as brutal, vicious soldiers, and in December 1937, the Japanese Army massacred between 200,000–300,000 Chinese civilians in Nanking.

Japan was ruled over by Emperor Hirohito – who the Japanese people viewed as a god incarnate – but Hirohito was, in effect, a puppet of the country's military government. The prime minister was an army general – Hideki Tojo – and he had insured that the Japanese people had received physical and military training from an early age (even basic flight training in mock cockpits), that they believed Japan had a 'divine right' to expand and con-quer, and that each Japanese soldier knew his life belonged to the emperor and could be sacrificed if necessary. There was no greater honour than to die in battle for the emperor, and retreat or surrender were never to be considered. This made the Japanese Army an extremely formidable enemy.

After Japan joined with Germany and Italy in 1940 to form the Axis powers, the Vichy Government allowed Japanese troops to enter French Indochina. The Japanese were then close to the Philippines – US territory – and so America placed an embargo on oil and iron ore shipments to Japan. With no supply of oil to fuel their military, the Japanese decided to capture their own oilfields. The closest ones were in the Dutch East Indies, but for these to be assaulted and secured, British Malaya and the American Philippines would also need to be neutralised, along with the Royal Navy station at Singapore and the US Pacific Fleet at Pearl Harbour.

And so, on 7 December 1941 (or 8 December across the international date line to the west), the Japanese launched simultaneous attacks against Pearl Harbour, the Philippines, Malaya, Thailand, Hong Kong, Guam, and Wake Island, while bombing Singapore. On 15 December, they also invaded Borneo, and in January 1942, they started other campaigns in Burma, the Dutch East Indies, New Guinea and the Solomon Islands. The Japanese advances were swift and successful, and the fighting in the Far East saw some of the most bitter and violent battles fought during the Second World War.

'CALEHAN SAN'

CORNELIUS CAHALANE

One of the places assaulted by the Japanese on 8 December 1941 was Hong Kong – then a Crown colony. 52,000 Japanese troops attacked 14,000 British and Commonwealth soldiers that were supported by only five RAF planes, one Royal Navy destroyer and several gunboats and motor torpedo boats. After seventeen days – in what became the first ever surrender of a Crown colony to an invading army – the Allied troops in Hong Kong were forced to surrender to the Japanese on Christmas Day. The British and Commonwealth forces had lost 2,113 killed and missing, along with 2,300 wounded, while the Japanese had suffered 1,996 killed and 6,000 wounded. Meanwhile 4,000 Hong Kong civilians had been killed, along with 3,000 more seriously wounded.

One of the men present at the Battle of Hong Kong was Petty Officer Cornelius Cahalane from Skibbereen, County Cork. Having joined the Royal Navy when he was only seventeen years old in 1928, Cahalane went on to serve aboard various warships before being posted to HMS *Tamar* on 18 March 1940 – he was then twenty-eight years old and had served in the Royal Navy for twelve years. HMS *Tamar* was a former troopship that had been launched in 1863, and was now the Royal Navy's shore base at Hong Kong. After the Japanese launched their attack on 8 December, HMS *Tamar* was towed out to a bouy, but three days later – when it became clear that Japanese forces might capture Hong Kong along with HMS *Tamar* – the order was given to scuttle the ship. Along with four others – which included a sailor from Union Hall, County Cork – Cornelius Cahalane volunteered

Petty Officer Cornelius Cahalane from Skibbereen, County Cork, with some Chinese civilians in Hong Kong. This photograph was taken not long before the Japanese invasion of the city.

to sink the ship. By the following day – 12 December – the five sailors had scuttled HMS *Tamar*, but because the ship became airlocked, she had to be fired on by the Royal Artillery in order to finally sink.

Later on, during the Battle of Hong Kong, Cahalane was in the lead truck of a convoy when they were ambushed by the Japanese. Cahalane began shouting at the following trucks to stop and turn around, but as his grandson – Conor Cahalane – recalled, none of the British soldiers could understand his strong Cork accent. However, Cahalane obviously managed to escape from this ambush as he later found himself manning a machine gun, along with two comrades, on top of a building in Hong Kong. They were firing on nearby Japanese positions and, as Conor Cahalane recalled:

> There was a lot of smoke and fire in the surrounding area. There was a stray Alsatian

downstairs, and when the firing stopped all of a sudden it started going mad. They [Cahalane and his comrades] were looking over the roof to see what was going on but saw nothing. It turned out someone had planted a satchel charge on the building; it went off and killed one of them, seriously wounded the other and knocked my granddad out. He was concussed, and he had hearing problems in his ear after that.

On Christmas Day 1941, the order finally came to surrender. As Cahalane's grandson recently remembered:

> He [Cahalane] had a bayonet on him that he stashed in a wall. He always intended on coming back in later years to see if it was here but never did. They were all given a piece of paper to sign, promising that they wouldn't escape [it was also made clear to men at the time that if they did escape, ten of their comrades still in captivity would be executed]. He and a few others refused, and were moved to some other cell, and I'm not sure what the Japanese did to them, but they eventually signed a mark. He wasn't happy about it, made a scrawl on the piece of paper, and when the Japanese weren't looking robbed three blank ones off the pad. He sewed them into his battledress and hid them for the rest of the war. Someone robbed one of them off him, but we [the family] still have two originals.

Meanwhile, Cahalane also 'spoke very badly of the [British] officers after the surrender, said they took no care of their men, just themselves'. It must be mentioned however that many officers did continue to look after the welfare of their men, and often received horrible beatings and other punishments for challenging camp authorities about how their soldiers were being treated.

Nine thousand and five hundred British and Commonwealth soldiers became POWs after the Battle of Hong Kong, and the Japanese looted the city, murdering many of its inhabitants and raping approximately 10,000 women. On the day that the Allies surrendered, the Japanese also committed the St Stephen's College Massacre. This building was being used as a hospital, and after breaking in the Japanese

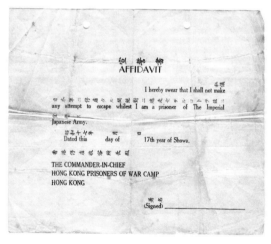

One of the blank affidavits that Petty Officer Cornelius Cahalane from Skibbereen, County Cork, stole from his Japanese captors. Little victories like these often provided a lifesaving boost to men's morale, and helped British prisoners feel that they were succeeding – in some small way – in defying the enemy.

bayoneted wounded soldiers in their beds and gang raped several of the nurses (some on top of a pile of corpses) before murdering them and mutilating their bodies. Sadly, this was to be repeated again and again after the Japanese had captured an area from their enemies.

Petty Officer Cornelius Cahalane was sent to Omori POW camp – an artificial island in Tokyo, Japan. 'He saw lots of the big bombing raids on Tokyo. They got the typical POW treatment from the Japanese; beatings with canes, food with rat droppings in it.'

However, Conor Cahalane recalled that his grandfather also used to tell a humorous story about his time in the camp:

> One day he was down in the showers, and when he came out the whole place was deserted, so he walked up the camp and everyone was at parade, and guards were running around shouting looking for the missing person. He came onto the parade ground in his towel and some guard came over to him, and he was sure that was it [he was going to be punished], but the guard just said to him 'Only you Calehan san [this was how the camp guards pronounced his name], only you' and let him go into the parade!

When the camp was liberated by the Americans in 1945, Cahalane appeared in a newspaper photo of the event. Someone back in Cork recognised him, and brought the photo to Cahalane's mother. But because he was looking down at the ground in the photo, his mother was terrified that her son had gone blind during captivity. Cornelius Cahalane – although a bit underweight – was otherwise fine, and the former POWs soon assembled on a pier near Omori camp to welcome the arrival of a US ship. Cahalane was the senior ranking man in his group, but when he saluted the arriving Americans, their officers refused to return the gesture.

After returning to Europe and being granted leave to visit Skibbereen – where he met a local girl and ultimately got married (he also learned during this time that his brother Joseph had served aboard a submarine in the Mediterranean, had been sunk, and had subsequently spent the remainder of the war in an Italian POW camp) – Cahalane stayed in the Royal Navy after the end of the Second World War.

In 1953, Cornelius Cahalane – by then forty-one years old and a chief petty officer – retired from the Royal Navy and returned to live in Skibbereen. He soon moved with his family to Northern Ireland where he started a job with the civil service, but because he was a Catholic, as Conor Cahalane recalled, 'Someone tried to firebomb their house.' Luckily, only the front porch was burned and the rest of the house was spared, but Cahalane left the Northern Ireland civil service and returned to Skibbereen. In 1995, his wife died, and then, in 1996 – now eighty-five years old – former Royal Navy chief petty officer and Second World War POW Cornelius Cahalane also passed away.

DEFIANT

JOSEPH BARRETT

After the Japanese made a lightning advance through the jungles of the Malayan Peninsula – in a campaign which resulted in 5,500 Allied soldiers killed, 5,000 wounded, and 40,000 taken POW, along with 1,793 Japanese soldiers killed and another 3,378 wounded – the British and Commonwealth forces in Malaya fell back to Singapore. They were poorly equipped and desperate for reinforcements, but the Japanese just kept coming. On 8 February 1942 – having crossed the Jahore Straits onto Singapore Island – 36,000 Japanese troops attacked the 85,000 Allied soldiers in Singapore on 8 February 1942. One week later, after both sides had suffered around 5,000 casualties, the British were forced to surrender to the Japanese. Eighty thousand men became POWs in what was the largest surrender of British-led troops in history, and

Lance-Bombardier Joseph Barrett from St Audoen's Terrace, Dublin, of 9th Coastal Regiment, Royal Artillery. He suffered horrifically after being taken prisoner by the Japanese.

this led the Japanese to believe that Allied soldiers were weak and 'dishonourable'.

Once again, the enemy went on the rampage in Singapore, and in the Alexandra Barracks Hospital, wounded soldiers were bayoneted (at least one while undergoing surgery) or beaten and urinated on, while medical staff were also killed and several nurses were raped. After the murder of 250 staff and patients, hundreds of survivors were imprisoned in confined conditions overnight (those who could not stand or who fell on the march to their cells were also bayoneted) and these survivors were executed the following morning by machine gun fire, rifle fire, were bayoneted, or were hacked to death with machetes while begging for mercy. Despite having signed the Geneva Convention, the Japanese treated their defeated enemies with extreme cruelty, and only a few Allied personnel from the hospital managed to escape to report what had happened. At least two Irishmen are known to have died in the massacre: thirty-nine-year-old Captain Ransome Allardyce – a doctor with the Royal Army Medical Corps from Ranelagh, Dublin; he was bayoneted by the Japanese – and twenty-one-year-old Trooper Patrick Moran of 18th Reconnaissance Regiment, Reconnaissance Corps, from Clonmoyle, County Westmeath, who was ill in hospital at the time. Allardyce is buried in Kranji War Cemetery, while with no known grave, Moran is commemorated on the Singapore Memorial.

One of the Irish soldiers who fought during the Battle of Singapore was Lance-Bombardier Joseph Barrett of 9th Coastal Regiment, Royal Artillery. From St Audoen's Terrace, Dublin, he was in command of an anti-aircraft gun when the Japanese invaded Singapore. When it soon became obvious that his position was about to be overrun by the enemy, Joseph and his gun crew were ordered to dismantle their gun in order to prevent it falling into enemy hands. When the enemy arrived and captured Joseph Barrett and his comrades, they demanded that the Dublin-man reassemble his gun. He refused, and so he was tortured by the Japanese. Joseph refused to give in, and he was ultimately imprisoned in Changi POW camp. He was perhaps lucky, as the Japanese could have easily executed him for such an act of defiance.

In October 1942, 600 officers and men of the Royal Artillery – including Lance-Bombardier Joseph Barrett – were taken from Changi POW camp and crammed into the hold of a ship in Singapore. They had no food, water or ventilation – sanitation was non-existent – and many men died from dehydration, heat exhaustion and dysentery on the voyage. The men had been told they were being taken to Japan, but in reality they were being transported to the Solomon Islands in order to construct Japanese airfields. By the time the ship reached Rabaul, eighty-two men were too sick to work, and so they were left behind when the vessel moved on to its final destination – Ballalae Island. Here, the survivors worked and slowly died off due to lack of food, water, medical care, and also due to disease, extreme heat, Allied air raids and horrendous treatment at the hands of the Japanese. When they finally finished work on the Ballalae airfield, the Japanese executed the remaining survivors, fearing that they might soon be liberated by Allied forces (out of the original 600 that had left Changi, only eighteen survived the war). However, it is unknown at what point Lance-Bombardier Joseph Barrett from Dublin actually died. He may have been murdered during the final massacre, or he may have already succumbed to hunger, thirst or sickness by the time the Japanese executed the remaining POWs.

Back home in Ireland, his family had initially received a telegram – not long after he had been taken POW in February – that Joseph was missing in action, presumed dead. Joseph's family subsequently sent a picture of Joseph to anyone and anywhere they could think of in order to try and get some information on Joseph's whereabouts (they even sent it to the Pope in Rome), but after the war they were visited by one of Joseph's former comrades – who had also been in Changi POW camp – and he finally explained what had happened to their son. Tragically, when Joseph had enlisted in Belfast and then returned home to Dublin to wait for his call up, a row had broken out between him and his mother over his enlistment. During the argument she said 'I don't care if I never see you again' and sadly she never did. This deeply affected her from the day she learned that Joseph was dead until her own death in 1969. She wore black from 1945 until 1969 – she never came out of mourning for her son.

Lance-Bombardier Joseph Barrett from St Audoen's Terrace, Dublin was twenty-five years old when he died on Ballalae Island (one of six known Irishmen to have died there). Initially buried in unmarked graves, the Royal Artillery men were reinterred in a temporary cemetery at Torokina on Bouganville Island after the war, before being laid permanently to rest in Port Moresby (Bomana) War Cemetery in Papua New Guinea – their individual bodies were never identified, and so their names were also commemorated on the Singapore Memorial.

'IT'S A LONG WAY TO TIPPERARY'

TERENCE GLEESON

Also taken prisoner during the Battle of Singapore was Corporal Terence Gleeson from Cloughjordan, County Tipperary. Stationed at RAF Kallang, he was captured on 20 March 1942 and, like most Allied POWs, was initially interned in nearby Changi POW camp. However, in November 1943, he was being transported – along with other Allied POWs – to a new camp in Java when the transport ship *Suez Maru* (known as one of the Japanese 'Hell Ships') was torpedoed by the American submarine USS *Bonefish* off the Kangean Islands. Due to a lack of proper markings, the *Suez Maru* appeared as just another Japanese troop carrier to the US submarine, and at least 300 of the 549 POWs aboard the ship died in the initial explosion or drowned as the *Suez Maru* quickly sank. However, many men – both Allied prisoners and Japanese military personnel – managed to get off the ship and jump into the sea, but after a Japanese minesweeper that had been escorting the *Suez Maru* arrived and rescued the roughly 300 Japanese survivors, the minesweeper's crew began firing on the POWs with machine gun and rifle fire for a period of two hours. They executed approximately 250 prisoners in the water before sailing away, leaving only one survivor – a man named Kenneth Thomas – to be picked up by an Australian ship twenty-four hours later. It was not until 1949 that the *Suez Maru* massacre became known about, after a Japanese witness came forward to tell his story. By then, the war had been over for four years, and Britain and the US were now concerned with repairing relations with Japan in order to gain an ally against communism in Asia. The authorities decided not to pursue the case – also fearing that they would be criticised for having taken six years to deal with the incident – and the decision was purposely made not to tell the families of the executed men how their loved ones had died.

Corporal Terence Gleeson was only twenty-four years old when he was killed on 29 November 1943 – either during the initial explosion aboard the *Suez Maru*, or during the subsequent massacre of Allied survivors in the water. He was not the only Irishman to die during the massacre however, and he died alongside thirty-four-year-old Gunner Alex Morrow of 239th Battery, 77th HAA Regiment, Royal Artillery from Donegal town, who was also aboard the *Suez Maru*. With no known graves, both men are commemorated on the Singapore Memorial.

Tragically, the *Suez Maru* massacre was not an isolated incident. Over one year earlier – on 1 October 1942 – the *Lisbon Maru* had been torpedoed by the American submarine USS *Grouper* while en route from Hong Kong to Japan. However, the ship did not sink quickly, and while the Japanese personnel onboard were rescued by other vessels in the convoy, 1,865 diseased and starving POWs were locked in the cramped, hot and airless hold for over twenty-four hours with no water. The Japanese were planning to leave them onboard as the ship sank and even tried to block the air shafts to the hold in order to suffocate the prisoners at one point, but when the men realised what was happening they finally made an escape attempt. However, many of those that made it into the water – like their comrades aboard the *Suez Maru* a year later – were shot and bayoneted by the enemy. Out of the 1,865 POWs aboard the *Lisbon Maru* when she was torpedoed, only 1,006 survived the sinking to be recaptured by the Japanese. Robert Widders – who has done extensive research on Irish POWs in Japanese captivity during the Second World War – recorded in his book, *The Emperor's Irish Slaves*, that dozens of Irishmen are known to have died during the *Lisbon Maru* disaster. He also quotes from Tony Banham's *The Sinking of the Lisbon Maru: Britain's Forgotten Wartime Tragedy*, which recorded the experiences of Gunner Jack Etiemble – who was aboard the ship and who survived the sinking. As Gunner Etiemble climbed out of the hold after the POWs finally decided to make their escape attempt, the wooden ladder that they were using broke – trapping the remainder of the POWs below. Etiemble recalled that 'Just after the ladder gave way … I heard an Irish gunner shout "We cannot get out, let's give them a song".' And so, as the *Lisbon Maru* sank, the escapees heard the voices of the trapped men – which included at least one Irishman – sing 'It's a Long Way to Tipperary'.

IMPRISONED

CHRISTOPHER GREEN

One Irishman taken prisoner during the Battle of Singapore – and who later recalled his experiences in a Japanese POW camp – was Christopher 'Christy' Green from Bow Street in Dublin. Also jokingly known as 'Bluer' Green, Christy was born in 1903 to parents William – a labourer – and Sarah, a fish dealer. He was one of those few Irish Second World War soldiers who were old enough to remember the 1916 Easter Rising; he had gone out into the streets of Dublin during the fighting. Marshal Law had been declared in the capital and there was a curfew in force, but the family needed something to eat, and so thirteen-year-old Christy snuck outside and managed to return with a 'flitch' (side) of bacon. He more than likely found it in an abandoned butcher's shop.

Although he never learned to read or write, he became a successful sheep and cattle dealer in adult life. He worked by getting a loan from a bank, travelling to the west of Ireland, buying a flock or a herd, and then bringing them back to sell at the Phibsboro/Cabra market in Dublin (he lived on St Attracta Road, Cabra). However, on 6 March 1941, foot-and-mouth disease was announced (cases were rife at the time), and the government ordered the slaughter of 3,800 animals. Then, on 14 May, a further five outbreaks of foot-and-mouth were reported across the country. This devastated Christy Green's business. Christy found himself in debt to the bank and he needed a way to settle his loan. Although he was thirty-eight years old and married with children, he took to train to Belfast and enlisted in the British Army.

Christy Green joined the Royal Artillery as a gunner and was sent out to Singapore, just in time to be captured by the Japanese on 15 February 1942. However, while the prisoners were often badly treated by the guards (Christy later remembered that, after a fellow POW stole and ate a tomato, the Japanese guards force fed the prisoner more tomatoes until he vomited. They then force fed him his vomit until they were satisfied that the man had learned his lesson), the treatment that the POWs received in Christy's camp was nothing like that experienced by men in the Thailand and Burma camps. Christy later recalled that his Japanese guards were 'cruel but honest'. If a POW had something to barter with the Japanese – such as a watch or a fine pen – a price or an object of trade would be agreed on

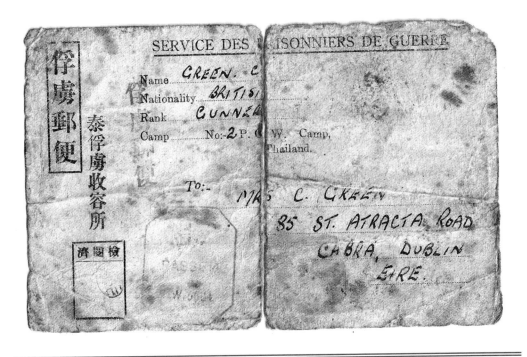

The front and back of a POW postcard sent from No 2 Camp (Songkurai) in Thailand by Gunner Christy Green to his family back in Dublin, 15 January 1944. POWs were often terrified to mention that their health was anything other than 'good', since complaining in any way would almost certainly result in a beating from a Japanese guard.

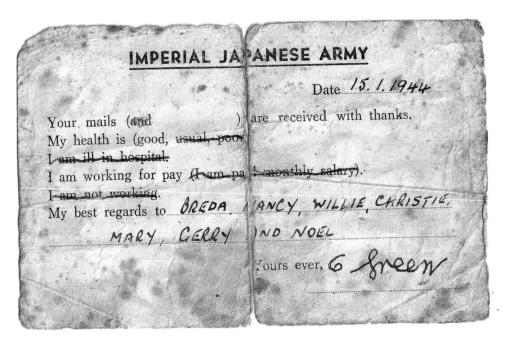

with the guard, who would then take away whatever the POW had to trade and hold on to it for a few days (in order to make sure the watch, pen, etc worked), before returning with the agreed price or object of trade.

Christy put his business skills to good use and set up a secret gambling ring called the 'Shamrock Club'. He started sneaking out of the camp at night to travel to a local village where he bartered for eggs, chickens, and other supplies. On one occasion, on his way back to the POW camp, Christy heard Japanese guards approaching. The only way to avoid getting caught was to dive into a nearby river and swim across – Christy normally forded the river at a shallower spot upstream, but the river beside his current position was much deeper and Christy could not swim. He had no choice but to dive in, and somehow, although in later life he could never explain how, he managed to struggle across to the other bank and return to the camp undetected.

By 1944, Gunner Christy Green *had* been sent to one of the infamous Thailand–Burma POW camps. These were the camps where the Japanese had used slave labour to construct the 'Death Railway' during 1942 and 1943. Allied prisoners had been poorly fed on a diet of terrible watery rice (which often contained animal faeces, maggots, and earthworm eggs that hatched in men's stomachs; the worms would then crawl up a man's throat and exit through his nose or mouth), boiled flour, rotten vegetables and some dried fish, made to work up to eighteen hours a day and had been denied medical care. If a man was too sick to work, he was punished by having half (or sometimes all) of his daily ration of food – which was already tiny – taken away. Lice-infested prisoners often wasted away until they weighed only 70lbs (5st) or went permanently blind from vitamin deficiency, while the Japanese beat men, tortured them and executed prisoners for any number of reasons.

Punishments included the breaking of limbs, pouring buckets of urine or boiling water on top of prisoners or smearing manure on their genitals and leaving them to be plagued by biting insects, or making a man stand to attention for hours in the blazing sun with no water and often while holding up a heavy weight overhead (moving or fainting was punished by beating the prisoner), while worse 'crimes' were punished by tortures including the pulling off of fingernails with a pliers or shoving a running water hose down a man's throat until his stomach was bloated with water (a guard would then usually jump on the prisoner's stomach).

Finally, executions were also carried out with vicious creativity. Firing squads aimed at prisoner's throats – which often resulted in several volleys being needed to complete the executions – while others were beheaded (an act which nearly always required the executioner to hack away with the sword a few times to finish the job), disembowelled alive by having their intestines pulled out, or were even crucified. Men were also often made to dig their own graves before they were bayoneted and then quickly buried.

Emaciated British prisoners of war in a Japanese hospital for POWs at Nakom Paton, Thailand. These men would have been used to construct the 'Death Railway' between Thailand and Burma.

Diseases like cholera, beriberi, malaria and dysentery swept through the camp as men's bodies – which reportedly looked like skeletons wrapped in skin – became covered in ulcers (ulcers often got so bad that men's limbs had to amputated; these operations and others were performed with homemade or poor quality surgical instruments and with no anaesthetic). Sanitation was appalling and latrines were never cleaned, and there are cases of POWs committing suicide by sticking their heads into piles of maggot-infested human faeces in order to suffocate themselves. Out of 250,000 Asian labourers and 61,000 Allied POWs who worked on the Death Railway, 90,000 and 16,000 respectively never survived to see its completion. However, when Christy arrived at No 2 Camp (Songkurai) in Thailand in early 1944, the railway had already been finished. POWs were now being used to maintain the railway, and these maintenance workers thankfully experienced nothing like what their fellow prisoners had gone through during the construction phase. Christy was lucky – Songkurai had been the most notorious camp during 1942-1943, with 3,000 POWs having died here alone.

After the war ended, Christy Green returned to his family on St Attracta Road in Cabra, Dublin. However, he was not impressed by bunting of the King and Queen that neighbours had hung up to welcome him home, and he became deeply upset when he saw how much his daughters had grown up. Similar to fellow Dubliner Richard 'Dicky' Adams (mentioned in Chapter 1), who had brought home dolls as presents for his now-grown up daughters after five years in a German POW camp, Christy Green returned home with chocolate bars for his girls. But they were now young women, and Christy had not seen them for over three years.

Christy – in common with most war veterans – never really spoke openly about his experiences, and while he never stopped going to the pub for a drink with friends, he certainly began socialising less. He now had permanent droops under his eyes and began suffering from recurring bouts of malaria, but then letters from former POWs began arriving at his house. Since he was illiterate, Christy asked his wife to read the letters, and it turned out that they were from men who owed money to Christy – men who had played cards with him back in the Shamrock Club and lost. They felt the need to pay up on their debts, and so they were sending Christy his backdated winnings. With this money, Christy was able to start up his sheep-dealing business again.

In later life Christy Green was known as a very dapper man who wore suits all the time. He contributed a lot of money to have the statue of the Virgin Mary in Cabra near St Attracta Road put up, but then he sadly died of a heart attack in 1960. Christopher 'Christy' Green had been a heavy smoker, and he was only fifty-seven years old when he passed away.

SPIRITUAL COMFORT

CORNELIUS SEXTON

However, it was not just Irishmen serving in the British Army who were taken prisoner at Singapore, but also Irishmen serving in the Australian Imperial Force (AIF). One such man was army chaplain Father Cornelius 'Con' Sexton – raised in Ballyvaughan, County Clare, but who had been born in September 1905 in nearby County Galway. The son of two national school teachers, Father Sexton was ordained in All Hallows, Dublin in June 1930 before he was sent to Sydney, Australia along with two fellow new priests – Father WJ Fahy and Father P McManus – sometime before November that year (as recorded in *The Sydney*

Morning Herald, 8 November 1930).

Then, in July 1940, he joined the Australian military and became an army chaplain with the rank of captain attached to 2/20th (Battalion) AIF. The following year, on 2 February 1941, he sailed to Malaya with his unit aboard HMT *Queen Mary*, and after suffering from chronic cholecystitis – an inflammation of the gall bladder – in May, he was still in Malaya when the Japanese began their invasion on 8 December. Father Sexton was now thirty-six years old.

On 23 January 1942, he fell ill again and was admitted to a field ambulance and later to a military hospital (during this time, 2/20th AIF were involved in heavy fighting against the Japanese in Mersing, Malaya). However, he had returned to his men by the time they had withdrawn to Singapore and by the time the Japanese began their assault on the island on 8 February. That night, with 2/20th AIF having been forced to spread out to cover a wide front, the Japanese attacked the battalion and managed to break through the

On 30 August 1942, the Japanese ordered the 20,100 prisoners of war in Changi Jail, Singapore, to sign an undertaking not to escape. The POWs refused and they were crowded into Selerang Barracks (which had accommodation for only 120) until they signed under duress on 4 September. The photograph shows the crowded Barrack Square during what became known as the 'Selerang Incident'. Irish priest and AIF chaplain Father Con Sexton from Ballyvaughan, County Clare was present at the time.

Australians' lines. However, the Australians succeeded in inflicting heavy casualties on their enemy before withdrawing and digging in along the Lim Chu Kang Road, but because this was a poor defensive position, the men were ordered to retreat further south.

The fighting continued on 9 February, and, as Father Sexton recorded in an interview he gave post-war:

> We had several wounded brought in ... during the night ... from the shelling ... and the colonel of our battalion sent up men to try and stop the [enemy] landing, but it never – it should have never [been ordered] – it was a massacre ... there were so many killed on that particular night that should never have been because their chances were nil from the time that they left their posts until they went up to the Causeway ... they didn't stand a chance ... the first two [wounded] that were brought in, as far I can remember, were Chinese who were fighting with our forces and the doc said, 'Padre, will you go down – take these down to the hospital before dawn.' And we loaded them on to the back [of a truck].

However, en route to the field hospital this truck was hit by enemy mortar or artillery fire and Father Sexton was 'blown out of the truck' along with another soldier – Jack Bowman. When they finally recovered their senses, as Father Sexton later recalled:

> Jack said to me, 'Are you alive, Father?' I said, 'Yes, I am. Are you?' Irish humour, if ever there was one ... and then we looked inside the truck and the two Chinese were dead. And we took them down to the hospital anyhow and unloaded them.

While in the hospital, Father Sexton asked a doctor to look over some wounds he had received to his hand and wrist when his truck had been hit. The doctor examined his injuries and then said, 'I'm sorry ... I'll have to cut off your fingers.' But the priest refused and replied, 'Listen, give me a cigarette and stitch it up if you can and do the same with that [the wrist wound].' So that is exactly what the doctor did and Father Sexton's fingers were saved.

After this, Father Sexton 'went back [to his unit] for another load [of wounded] ... to gather anybody we could that was still at the RAP [Regimental Aid Post].' This RAP was soon moved, and then 2/20th AIF's commanding officer – Colonel Charles Assheton – led a group of men forward towards the enemy. Father Sexton volunteered to go with them but he was refused permission. This probably saved his life, as when the Australians got into position, many of them fell asleep from sheer exhaustion before the enemy arrived, and when the Japanese finally showed up, 'the Japs just crept up on them [the sleeping Australians] and bayoneted one after another.'

Meanwhile, Father Sexton and a convoy of seven trucks with Red Cross markings withdrew towards Selarang Barracks near Singapore. However, the Japanese had blocked the road and – even though the trucks were clearly carrying wounded men – they fired on them. Several trucks were hit and rolled over, but Father Sexton's managed to make it through. At the same time, the Australians and the rest of the British and Commonwealth troops were withdrawing to Singapore city. The Japanese were closing in.

In the confusion of the Battle of Singapore, 2/20th AIF was split up and men fought on in groups of various sizes until the Allied surrender was declared on 15 February. Father Sexton initially found himself interned in Selarang Barracks, but he was soon transferred to nearby Changi POW camp where, in August 1942, he began suffering from dysentery. However, being held prisoner did not prevent him from ministering to his troops, and he later recalled:

> The lads used to come in from the airport of a night time, if we had stole a bit of timber now and again from the Japs, we made kind of a little chapel ... But the last year [1945], through some Chinese who were working on the airport, we got a letter through to the Bishops of Singapore, and we got altar breads and altar wines.

Father Sexton also managed to get hold of red berries that he dried in the sun to make rosary beads. However, 'there was no vestments ... just an old yucky pair of shorts and a pair of thongs that one of the Dutch prisoners had made for me.'

However, it was not just Allied soldiers that Father Sexton ended up ministering to. In an almost certainly unique event, he also received a request for a blessing from a Japanese soldier:

> [One day, while saying Mass] I turned around ... [and] I saw this guard standing just in front with the bayonet on the end of the rifle ... And I said [to myself], Cornelius, you're for it ... and didn't pretend anything, went on. And I asked the lads at the offertory, 'Do any of you boys like to go to Holy Communion?' and quite a few did. And when the Mass was over, they slunk away.
>
> The guard stayed and he put his rifle and bayonet on the ground, and he said in perfect English, 'Father, I'm a Catholic, educated by some Marist fathers in Korea, and I have a wife and two children ... We're leaving for Borneo in the morning. I'll never see them again.'

Father Sexton blessed the soldier, and though the circumstances were tragic, he later remembered this event as 'my most wonderful experience'.

After being liberated in August 1945, Father Sexton was underweight and soon diagnosed with neurotic beriberi – a nervous system disorder caused by vitamin deficiency. Having recovered, he sailed aboard HMAS *Manoora* via Labuan Island and landed at Brisbane on 15 October 1945. He was finally back in Australia.

Father Sexton soon found out that his mother – who now lived in Shrule, County Mayo – had been sent a telegram back in 1942 that he was 'missing, presumed dead'. And so, he wrote to her, letting his mother know that he was still very much alive and well. He remained in Australia after the war and on 25 April 1950 (ANZAC Day), Father Sexton was one of several priests who celebrated a Mass in Saint Mary's Cathedral, Sydney (as recorded in *The Sydney Morning Herald*, 26 April 1950) to remember Australia's fallen war dead. 3,000 people attended the mass and one of the priests in attendance – Father John Roche, a former naval chaplain – said that, 'For the men and women whose memory we revere today we must always have the greatest reverence.'

THE ESCAPE

JAMES FEENEY

However, not every British soldier who fought the Japanese during 1942 became a POW, although in the case of the next man, he very nearly did. Born in Longford town in 1918, James Feeney enlisted in the Royal Inniskilling Fusiliers in Omagh, County Tyrone in January 1935 – aged seventeen. (His uncle, Michael Feeney had served with the Leinster Regiment during the First World War and had been wounded at Ypres in January 1915.) He was posted to the 1st Battalion and sent out to the Far East to join them in February 1936. By 1939, Feeney was now serving in Singapore, but 1st Royal Inniskilling Fusiliers were soon moved to the Wellington Hill Station in southern India. They were still here when Japan entered the Second World War on 8 December 1941. Private James Feeney was now twenty-three years old.

After invading Burma in January 1942, the Japanese succeeded in capturing Rangoon from the British on 7 March. The British then withdrew to the centre of the country in order to try and stop the enemy from advancing any further towards India, while summoning all available reinforcements to Burma. On 9 March, the last of these reinforcements arrived when Private James Feeney and 1st Royal Inniskilling Fusiliers landed at Magwe – on the banks of the Irrawaddy River, just south of the valuable Burmese oilfields at Yenangyaung – having flown all the way from Calcutta, India. They were the only Irish regiment that would serve in the Far East during the Second World War.

On 19 March, having been transported south by truck – as 1st Royal Inniskilling Fusiliers' war diary recorded – 'Bn disembarked in the Prome area. Occupation of defensive position on the eastern outskirts of the town completed.' Here, 1st Royal Inniskilling Fusiliers (part of a force that included 1st Burma Division, 17th Indian Division and 7th Armoured Brigade) remained until 28 March when one company was 'ordered to form part of a small striking force to harass Jap advance on main Rangoon-Prome road.' However, by the following day, the 'Force [was] cut off by the Japs forming a road block in the area of Shwedaung. Force fought its way back through the road block. Bn suffered 13 ORs [Other Ranks] killed 4

ORs wounded'. Twelve of the thirteen killed were Irishmen – ten from Northern Ireland and two from the south.

The Japanese were closing in on Prome, and having bombed the British airfield at Magwe out of action – which had forced the Allies to withdraw all of their planes to Chittagong in India – the Japanese had complete air superiority. On the night of 30 March, they began bombarding Prome, and by midday on 2 April, Private James Feeney and the British were forced to withdraw north to Allanmyo where they established new defensive positions. However, by 6 April the battalion was ordered to withdraw further north and on 10 April they were just south of Alebo and had lost their commanding officer, Lieutenant-Colonel Ralph Cox.

Two southern Irishmen now took over command of the battalion: Major Samuel McConnell from County Dublin as commanding officer and Major Brian Boyle from Abbeyleix, County Laois as second-in-command.

Then, on 11 April – while patrolling south of their defensive line – elements of 1st Royal Inniskilling Fusiliers encountered troops from the advancing Japanese Army. After a fire fight, Lieutenant Patrick Kelly from County Down and several other ranks were, as the war diary recorded, 'Reported wounded [and] missing. Fighting patrols sent out with object of bringing in casualties.' The patrols found none of their missing comrades (Lieutenant Kelly was twenty-one years old when he died. With no known grave, today he is commemorated on the Rangoon Memorial). Encounters between British and Japanese soldiers continued throughout the day, and orders were soon received to withdraw once more.

The Japanese advance proved relentless and, despite attempts at opposition, over the following days Private James Feeney and 1st Royal Inniskilling Fusiliers continued their retreat north. By 16 April, the battalion was forced to march across country due to the fact that Japanese planes were bombing and machine gunning any Allied convoys that used the Burmese roads, and on 17 April they arrived at their latest destination – the Yenangyaung oilfields north of Magwe. Two days earlier, orders had been given to destroy the oilfields and the local refinery in case it fell into Japanese hands, and so the exhausted, thirsty and hungry 1st Royal Inniskilling Fusiliers arrived at Yenangyaung to see clouds of black oil smoke billowing into the air. Along with 7,000 other British soldiers, they were soon surrounded by a similar number of Japanese troops.

After being ordered to launch attacks against the enemy in the vicinity of the oilfields on 18 and 19 April – battles during which Major McConnell and Major Boyle were both killed (McConnell was forty-four years old and Boyle was thirty-six; with no known graves, both men are commemorated on the Rangoon Memorial) – Private James Feeney and his surviving comrades managed to break out of Japanese-encircled Yenangyaung. A further withdrawal of Allied forces in Burma was soon ordered, and on 26 April, 1st Royal

Inniskilling Fusiliers had reached Myingyan. They then had to march twenty-six miles in the extreme jungle heat to reach the ferry at Sameikkon that would take them over the Irrawaddy River – a march described by the war diarist as 'one of the worst during the campaign'.

Over the following weeks, the battalion suffered repeated Japanese attacks – while having to frequently turn and launch their own assaults against the pursuing enemy – as they retreated closer and closer to India. Wounded men often had to be left behind as the British retreated sometimes only hours ahead of the advancing Japanese. The jungle, the heat and tropical diseases like malaria also took their toll, and when 1st Royal Inniskilling Fusiliers arrived at Tamu – an area of Burma right on the border with India – on 17 May, the demoralised battalion had only thirteen officers and 121 other ranks left out of an initial strength of 600. The unit had marched over 500 miles since landing at Magwe on 9 March, and had lost two thirds of its soldiers killed, wounded or sick since that time. However, they had now reached the relative safety of India. They had escaped from the Japanese.

Private James Feeney from Longford was one of the survivors, and although 1st Royal Inniskilling Fusiliers soon took on new drafts of men and later returned to the fight in Burma, James Feeney was sent back to Europe. It is unclear whether he was withdrawn due to injury, or for other reasons, but by July 1942 he was back in Ireland. Then, as Feeney's son – John Feeney recalled – 'while on leave from the British Army in Longford, my father saw a man struggling in the Royal Canal Harbour (now filled in), jumped into the water, knocked the man out and brought him to the quayside. The rescue was, apparently, reported in the *Longford Leader*.'

Sadly, however, James Feeney did not live for very long after performing this heroic act. In 1953 – only eight years after the Second World War ended – he died of heart failure, aged thirty-five, having also suffered from recurring bouts of malaria since 1942. He may have escaped from the Burmese jungle, but it appears to have stayed with him for the remainder of his life.

NO COWARD

RICHARD KELLIHER

The Japanese campaigns of late 1941 and early 1942 were incredibly successful – they secured vast areas of territory, pushed their enemies back everywhere, and captured thousands of prisoners in the process. However, by mid-1942, the Allies had regrouped and were ready to strike back at the Japanese. While the Americans began their campaigns in the

Pacific, the Australians attacked the Japanese in New Guinea. One of the men who took part in the latter was Irishman Richard Kelliher.

Born in Ballybeggan, Tralee, County Kerry, in September 1910, Richard Kelliher went to a technical college in Tralee before starting work in his brother's garage. Then, in 1929 – along with his fifteen-year-old sister Norah – he emigrated to Australia. Kelliher was nineteen when he sent foot in Australia and soon began work as a travelling labourer and farm hand (known locally as a 'swagman'). However, he did not have a particularly strong constitution and he frequently fell ill – on two occasions he contracted typhoid and meningitis. But this did not stop Kelliher from joining Australia's military after the war started.

King George VI pauses to talk to several Australian Victoria Cross winners. He is pictured talking to Private Richard Kelliher from Tralee, County Kerry, of 2/25th AIF. Kelliher and his fellow VC winners had travelled to England as members of the Australian Victory Contingent of 250 to attend the Victory Parade held on 8 June 1946 in London. Some weeks following the parade, and after other members of the contingent had left for Australia, the King officially presented Kelliher with his Victoria Cross medal on 9 July 1946.

On 21 February 1941 – while living in Brisbane and now aged thirty – he enlisted in the AIF and, on 11 October 1941, he joined 2/25th AIF who were serving in Lebanon (he was admitted to the ship's hospital for two days while en route to join them).

However, Private Richard Kelliher and 2/25th AIF did not remain in the Middle East for long, and on 10 March 1942 they returned to Australia aboard the American troopship USS *Mount Vernon*, landing at Adelaide. The Japanese had recently launched their various campaigns against the British, the Dutch and the Americans in the Far East, and they were now threatening mainland Australia. And so, Australian troops were being withdrawn from other fronts to defend the country. 2/25th AIF began training at Woodside Camp near Adelaide, before moving to Caboolture in Queensland. They later undertook weapons training, along with jungle and amphibious landing training, in Enoggera, Brisbane.

While home, Kelliher was fined twice for going absent without leave on two occasions, and was also awarded three days' confinement to barracks for conduct to the prejudice of good order and military discipline on 24 July. On 9 September, Private Richard Kelliher and 2/25th AIF returned to the war when they landed at Port Moresby on the south coast of New Guinea. US forces had invaded the Japanese-occupied island of Guadalcanal in the southern Solomon Islands, and the Australians were also now trying to push the Japanese back on New Guinea. Private Patrick Kelliher and 2/25th AIF took part in the advance towards Gona and then the fighting around Templeton's Crossing and Gorari in October and November. Finally, on 16 November, a combined force of American and Australian troops – which included Private Richard Kelliher and 2/25th AIF – launched the Battle of Buna-Gona against the Japanese beachheads at Buna, Sanananda and Gona. However, they completely underestimated the strength of the enemy defences and many of the 20,000 Allied troops were also sick with malaria, typhus, dysentery and dengue fever. After two months of fighting, they had lost 2,300 men killed and over 12,000 injured.

On 19 January 1943, Private Richard Kelliher and 2/25th AIF returned to Australia from New Guinea. Three days later, the Battle of Buna-Gona ended. It was ultimately an Allied victory, but it nearly changed Private Richard Kelliher's military career forever. On 12 November 1942 – just before the start of the battle – Kelliher was arrested for withdrawing from the front without orders. When his unit later returned to Australia, he was court-martialled in Ravenshoe, Queensland on 27 March 1943 (less than two weeks after being fined £3 for going absent without leave again, for four days this time) for – as his service record stated – 'misbehaving before the enemy in such a manner as to show cowardice' and 'conduct to the prejudice of good order and military discipline'.

The prosecution claimed:

> That approx 1630 hours 12 Nov 42 whilst his section was in a forward position
> held up by and facing the enemy and under the enemy's fire [Kelliher] failed to get

into his allotted position in his section and moved back to Coy HQ saying 'It's too bloody hot for me. I am not a bloody fool' or words to that effect.

Character witness statements were then produced which stated that Kelliher was:

> Generally of good behaviour ... Usually amenable to discipline ... [but] Not particularly responsive to training ... A generally weak character yet strong enough to influence others in the wrong direction ... Lazy, deceitful and greedy: 'all for himself' when his own safety is concerned ... not a satisfactory soldier.

Kelliher insisted during the trial that his platoon commander had selected him to be a runner and had ordered him to the rear for information. However, since Kelliher's platoon commander had subsequently been killed during the battle and he also had no witnesses who could back up his claim, Kelliher was found guilty of the charge of cowardice (although not guilty for the charge of misconduct). He was sentenced to detention for a period of one year, and began his sentence on 22 April when he was imprisoned in 4th Australian Detention Barracks.

Private Richard Kelliher from Tralee did not remain in detention for very long. On 31 May 1943 – just over five weeks after starting his sentence – Kelliher was acquitted and allowed to return to his unit (he did not join them immediately as he was admitted to hospital suffering from malaria). When he finally returned to 2/25th AIF, he apparently swore that he would prove he was not a coward.

On 20 August, Private Richard Kelliher and 2/25th AIF returned to New Guinea when they once again landed at Port Moresby. They were initially sent to Six Mile Valley camp where they trained and took part in exercises at various levels. Then, on 7 September, they flew to Nadzab to join the fight against the Japanese base in the town of Lae. The following day, 2/25th AIF were ordered to advance through the Markham Valley – through plantations on either side of the Markham Road – and help capture Lae. Patrols from the battalion frequently encountered the enemy over the following days (the Japanese also launched an attack against A Company on 12 September), but then:

> During an attack by [Private Richard Kelliher's] platoon on an enemy position at Nadzab, New Guinea, on the morning of 13th September, 1943, the platoon came under heavy fire from a concealed enemy machine-gun post approximately 50 yards away. Five of the platoon were killed and three wounded and it was found impossible to advance without further losses.
>
> In the face of these casualties Private Kelliher suddenly, on his own initiative, and without orders, dashed towards the post and hurled two grenades at it, killing some of the enemy but not all. Noting this, he then returned to his section, seized a Bren gun, again dashed forward to within 30 yards of the post, and with accurate fire [firing from the hip] completely silenced it. Returning from his already gallant action Private Kelliher next

requested permission to go forward again and rescue his wounded section leader [who was badly wounded in the arm, back and stomach]. This he successfully accomplished, though under heavy rifle fire from another position.

Private Kelliher, by these actions, acted as an inspiration to everyone in his platoon, and not only enabled the advance to continue but also saved his section leader's life. His most conspicuous bravery and extreme devotion to duty in the face of heavy enemy fire resulted in the capture of this strong enemy position.

This citation, which appeared in the *London Gazette* (28 December 1943), announced that Private Richard Kelliher from Tralee had been awarded the Victoria Cross – the highest award for valour in the face of the enemy that a British or Commonwealth soldier can receive – for his actions at Heath's Plantation during the Battle of Lae. The war diary for 2/25th AIF also added that 'Position B Coy [in which Private Richard Kelliher was serving] occupied proved to be enemy HQ and a considerable amount of equipment and documents relating to evacuation plans were captured.' Private Richard Kelliher had finally proved that he was no coward, and that he was a soldier worthy of the Victoria Cross.

2/25th AIF was the first Australian unit to enter Lae on 16 September, but Kelliher fell ill and had to be evacuated back to Australia. He landed in Brisbane on 27 January 1944, less than a month before 2/25th AIF also returned to Australia in February. Kelliher remained ill for nearly all of 1944 – spending most of his time in hospitals – before being finally released and joining 11th Australian Advanced Workshop on 6 December (he was considered medically unfit to return to a combat role).

He must have been extremely sick during periods of 1944 – or perhaps the war had changed him in other ways – as on 26 May that year, Kelliher's mother wrote to his commanding officer saying:

Thank you for letter recently received in which you sent me an account of my son. As I have not heard from my son Richard for a long time I shall be deeply grateful to you if you will get in touch with him and ask him to write to me. I am very anxious to hear from him. I do not know his present address. I am an old woman 70 years & will be very thankful if you can inform me if I am entitled to any allowance through my son. Before he joined up he always sent money to support me, since then I have received no help.

The following year, on 8 August 1945, Kelliher marched with 2/25th AIF through Brisbane. Twelve days later – after Japan finally surrendered to the Allies – he was discharged from the AIF. However, the following year he was re-enlisted on 28 March and sent to England as part of the Australian Military Forces' component of the 8 June 1946 London Victory Parade. While in London, he was officially presented with his Victoria Cross by King George VI – an event which his family from County Kerry attended – and he also took time to visit

Tralee before returning to Australia, arriving there on 22 August. He was discharged for a second and final time on 13 September 1946.

Richard Kelliher started work as a cleaner in Brisbane City Hall and in 1949 – now aged thirty-nine – he married nineteen-year-old Olive Hearn. The couple had three children. Kelliher applied for a taxi license but failed to get it, and so he moved to Melbourne and got a job as a gardener. In 1953, he returned to London for the coronation of Queen Elizabeth II, and also for the Victoria Cross centenary celebration three years later (on both occasions he visited Tralee). However, his health worsened and by the 1950s he was badly disabled. Then, on 16 January 1963, he suffered a stroke. Twelve days later, he died of cerebral thrombosis in the Heidelberg Repatriation General Hospital, Melbourne. Richard Kelliher from Tralee, County Kerry was fifty-two years old when he passed away, and he now lies buried in Springvale Cemetery, Melbourne.

THE LAST VC

JAMES MAGENNIS

Private Richard Kelliher was not the only Irishman to earn the Victoria Cross for fighting the Japanese. On 31 July 1945, Leading Seaman James Magennis from Belfast performed an act of bravery that also earned him Britain's highest military honour. He was the only citizen of Northern Ireland to receive the Victoria Cross during the Second World War, and his VC was – chronologically in terms of the action for which it was awarded – the last one awarded during the war (jointly with his commanding officer, Lieutenant Ian Fraser of HMS *XE3*). This means that Irishmen have the distinction of earning the first VC of the First World War (Lieutenant Maurice Dease of 4th Royal Fusiliers from County Westmeath, 23 August 1914) and the last VC of the Second World War.

Magennis – a Catholic from Majorca Street in west Belfast – was actually born James McGinnes in October 1919. On 3 June 1935 – aged fifteen – he enlisted in the Royal Navy and changed his surname to Magennis. Then, on 19 December 1941, the destroyer that he was serving on – HMS *Kandahar* – hit an Italian mine while trying to assist the light cruiser HMS *Neptune* which had previously been damaged by mines. Seventy-three men died in the sinking, although luckily for James Magennis he was not one of them. The following year – in December 1942 – he was transferred into the Royal Navy Submarine Service.

However, James Magennis – now an able seaman – did not go on to serve aboard the Royal Navy's larger submarines, and he volunteered instead for 'special and hazardous duty' and began training as a diver (Magennis later became the first man in Royal Navy history to exit a submarine in a diving suit, perform a military operation, and then return to the same submarine). By September 1943 he had been assigned to the passage crew of the midget submarine – HMS *X7*. These submarines were, as the name suggests, much smaller than their larger counterparts. They could be crewed by anything from one to eight sailors, and were designed to operate in shallower waters (such as attacking targets in harbours). Midget submarines were towed by a larger submarine to their area of operations, where the passage crew would be replaced by the operations crew who would then carry out the mission. During Magennis' time as part of the passage crew of HMS *X7*, the midget submarine took part in Operation Source – an attempt to destroy the German warships *Lützow*, *Scharnhorst* and *Tirpitz* in Kåfjord and Langefjord, Norway. HMS *X7* managed to help disable *Tirpitz*, but she was then attacked and had to be scuttled by her operations crew (only two of the four sailors onboard survived). For his part in Operation

Source, Able Seaman James Magennis was mentioned in dispatches (*London Gazette*, 21 December 1943).

Magennis did not remain as passage crew for the rest of the war. By 1945 he was stationed in the Far

Leading Seaman James Magennis (left) from Belfast and his commanding officer Lieutenant Ian Fraser (right) from London, both of whom earned the last Victoria Crosses of the Second World War for their actions on 31 July 1945.

Ordinary Seaman Reggie Lee from Glenageary, Dublin aboard HMS Plym *in 1945. On 19 October 1946, Reggie was serving aboard HMS Newfound-land when she was ordered to fire on and finally sink* Takao – *the Japanese heavy cruiser that James Magennis had disabled on 31 July 1945. Reggie took a photograph of the event, and after later learning about Magennis' link to* Takao, *he forwarded the photo on to the Belfast VC winner. Reggie thought that Magennis might like to have it – after all, he had tried to sink the ship in the first place.*

East and began serving aboard HMS *XE3*, where there was no changing of crews and all sailors aboard served in an operations role. The XE-class was an updated version of the X-class, and was usually crewed by four sailors, at least one of which had to be a qualified diver. These new midget submarines (there were six XE midget submarines) operated from the depot ship HMS *Bonaventure*, and could carry two large mines which contained two-tons of explosives each, along with six 20lb limpet mines. During operations, it would be the diver's job to attach these limpet mines to the hull of a target enemy vessel, and this is exactly what James Magennis – now an acting leading seaman – did on 31 July 1945.

That night, HMS *XE1* and HMS *XE3* were ordered to find and destroy the Japanese heavy cruisers *Myōkō* and *Takao* respectively in Singapore harbour. HMS *XE3* was towed to the target area by the submarine HMS *Stygian*, after which she sailed the last forty miles alone to reach *Takao*. The crew had to navigate past sunken wrecks and through minefields laid by the Japanese, all while evading detection by enemy listening posts. However, they reached *Takao* and Magennis then exited the midget submarine to begin his work.

A later entry in the *London Gazette* (13 November 1945) described what happened next:

Leading Seaman Magennis served as Diver in His Majesty's Midget Submarine XE-3 for her attack on 31 July 1945, on a Japanese cruiser of the Atago class. The diver's hatch could not be fully opened because XE-3 was tightly jammed under the target, and Magennis had to squeeze himself through the narrow space available. He experienced great difficulty in placing his limpets on the bottom of the cruiser owing both to the foul state of the bottom and to the pronounced slope upon which the limpets would not hold. Before a limpet could be placed therefore Magennis had thoroughly to scrape the area clear of barnacles, and in order to secure the limpets he had to tie them in pairs by a line passing under the cruiser keel. This was very tiring work for a diver, and he was moreover handicapped by a steady leakage of oxygen which was ascending in bubbles to the surface. A lesser man would have been content to place a few limpets and then to return to the craft. Magennis, however, persisted until he had placed his full outfit before returning to the craft in an exhausted condition.

Shortly after withdrawing Lieutenant Fraser [the commanding officer of HMS *XE3*] endeavoured to jettison his limpet carriers, but one of these would not release itself and fall clear of the craft. Despite his exhaustion, his oxygen leak and the fact that there was every probability of his being sighted, Magennis at once volunteered to leave the craft and free the carrier rather than allow a less experienced diver to undertake the job. After seven minutes of nerve-racking work he succeeded in releasing the carrier. Magennis displayed very great courage and devotion to duty and complete disregard for his own safety.

HMS *XE3* then withdrew safely from the area. Meanwhile, HMS *XE1* had failed to find *Myōkō*, and so they placed their charges on *Takao* as well – despite the danger from the explosives already laid by Magennis. Six hours later, the mines exploded, badly damaging *Takao*. For his display of courage and bravery during this operation, twenty-five-year-old Acting Leading Seaman James Magennis from Belfast was awarded the Victoria Cross.

When the war ended, Magennis returned home to his native Belfast where he was hailed as a hero and became well known throughout the city – with the people of Belfast raising a £3,600 'shilling fund' for him. However, due to his working-class Catholic background, the city fathers refused to give him the freedom of the city (only a small photo of him was placed in the council chamber robing room).

Magennis married Edna Skidmore in 1946 and the couple went on to have four sons, but the couple had soon spent nearly all of the £3,600. They had been treated like local celebrities and so they had lived as such – spending and buying well beyond their means. In 1949, Magennis retired from the Royal Navy and soon also found out that he was no longer welcome in Belfast – aside from elements of the Protestant unionist community who had never really accepted him, Magennis was now being shunned by the Catholic nationalist community because he had served in the British forces during the war. On one occasion, when he visited his old school – St Finian's on the Falls Road – none of the schoolchildren stood up from their seats when he came into the room (this was a normal mark of respect for visitors). Then, due to worsening poverty, he was soon forced to sell his Victoria Cross to a pawn shop for £75. In Belfast, the newspapers were outraged and complained how the

Catholic Magennis had disrespected the honour of the Victoria Cross. Magennis began to receive hundreds of angry letters from locals, and so Joe Kavanagh – the pawn shop owner – agreed to give the medal back to him, but only under the condition that a journalist and photographer were present to record the event. Finally, in 1952, Magennis' eldest son David was hit by a bus on the Cregagh Road, Belfast, and killed.

By 1955 thirty-six-year-old Magennis had left for Bradford in Yorkshire and was work-ing as an electrician, initially down the mines in Doncaster and then in Bradford. He later met Queen Elizabeth II at Buckingham Palace in 1977 during her silver jubilee, and on 12 February 1986 former leading seaman James Magennis passed away from lung cancer. Not long after his death, his surviving sons were forced to sell his Victoria Cross – they simply could not afford to insure it. It was bought by Lord Ashcroft, and became the first in his famous collection of Victoria Crosses.

Unlike with other VC winners, Belfast was not quick to build a memorial to Magennis after his death (although Bradford in Yorkshire placed a plaque in his honour in the local Anglican cathedral immediately after his death), and it was only on 8 October 1999 – one year after a commemorative plaque was placed outside his former home on Carncaver Road in Castlereagh, Belfast – that one was officially unveiled in the grounds of Belfast City Hall. Ian Fraser – Magennis' former commanding officer, who had also earned the VC that day – attended the ceremony and said that 'Jim [Magennis] gave me bother from time to time. He liked his tot of rum, but he was a lovely man and a fine diver. I have never met a braver man. It was a privilege to know him and it's wonderful to see Belfast honour him at last.' This was the first memorial ever erected by Belfast City Council to a working-class Catholic, and just to prove that times had changed, the memorial was unveiled by Cllr Robert Stoker – Ulster Unionist Party Lord Mayor of Belfast. Then, in 2005, a mural depicting Magennis was painted on a wall in the loyalist estate at Tullcarnet as a celebration of the sixtieth anniversary of VE Day.

ASHES

MICHAEL BLANCHFIELD

After the Japanese failed to capture Imphal and Kohima in India, the British soon began a campaign in late 1944 that successfully pushed the enemy back in Burma. At the same time, the Australians were defeating the Japanese in New Guinea, while by 21 June 1945 the Americans had advanced island by island through the Pacific and had secured Okinawa. Wave after wave of bombers – sometimes containing more than 2,000 aircraft – were now continually launched against the Japanese mainland. Day and night, Japanese cities were heavily bombed. Over 250,000 Japanese civilians were killed, while a further 8 million were made homeless.

However, the most devastating – and infamous – bomb dropped on Japan during 1945 was a weapon that had never been used in warfare before. Ironically, while Japan was preparing for invasion by training children to fight with bamboo spears and bows and arrows, the US Army Air Force's B-29 Superfortress bomber *Enola Gay* dropped a 13–18 kiloton atomic bomb – codenamed 'Little Boy' – on the Japanese city of Hiroshima on 6 August 1945. Seventy to eighty thousand people were killed instantly, while another 70,000 were wounded. Anything within a one-mile radius of the blast was destroyed – which included over two thirds of Hiroshima's buildings – while 4.4 square miles were set on fire. However, the initial explosion was not the only threat to the people of Hiroshima, and by 1950, as many as 200,000 survivors had died from cancer, leukaemia, or other long-terms effects of exposure to atomic radiation.

According to Robert Widders' *The Emperor's Irish Slaves*, there were at least three Irish witnesses to the dropping of the atomic bomb on Hiroshima – Battery Quartermaster Sergeant Kenneth Cluff from Stradbally, County Laois, Private Michael O'Connor from Ballybunnion, County Kerry, and Sergeant Ernest Williams from Cork – POWs who were serving in local work details.

However, there was another Irishman who witnessed the aftermath of the devastation, and not long after the war ended, Michael Blanchfield from Dublin set foot in Hiroshima. He recently wrote a short account of his experiences entitled 'Barefoot in Hiroshima', which was published in *Flying, Not Falling: Poems, Stories and Reflections on Life by Older Adults*, and in it he recorded that:

> When the war came I was called up to join the Royal Navy. My people were sea-faring folk so going to fight at sea was no big deal. I used to send food parcels to my mother back in Dublin. I travelled every corner of the world with the Navy. You name it, I saw it: Egypt, New Zealand, Guadalcanal, Hong Kong. I especially remember Japan. Our ship went into Hiroshima soon after the atom bomb was dropped on it and Nagasaki. We had to walk around the ruined city of Hiroshima with our boots hung around our necks, as the least vibration would cause the few remaining buildings to collapse. It was a wasteland, like something out of your worst nightmare. A lot of the Japanese who were not instantly incinerated to dust fell ill to diseases caused by radiation and died in droves. It felt odd to be walking barefoot on ashes that used to be human beings …You never forget sights like that. Some of the hardest men in the Navy were never the better of what they saw. It drove some people mad with the things they saw. Hell, it was, and a man-made one at that. How could any person

see thousands of souls destroyed and not be driven mad by it? I wouldn't wish that experience on my worst enemy.

UNDER THE BOMB

JOSEPH AIDAN MacCARTHY

Three days after Hiroshima, on 9 August 1945, the B-29 Superfortress bomber *Bockscar* dropped a second atomic bomb – codenamed 'Fat Man' – on Nagasaki. The bomb exploded with a blast yield of 21 kilotons, and produced 3,900°C of heat and winds of over 1,000kph. Between 40,000–75,000 people were killed instantly, with thousands more dying later from the after-effects of radiation. Once again, there was at least one Irishman at Nagasaki.

Born in 1913 in Berehaven, County Cork, Joseph Aidan MacCarthy (who went by Aidan) attended Clongowes Wood College before studying in the Cork Medical School. In 1938, he qualified as a doctor, and the following year he joined the RAF and became a member of their medical staff. He served in France during the German invasion and was one of those rescued during the Dunkirk evacuation. Then, while back in Britain, he helped to save the lives of two airmen in May 1941 after their aircraft crashlanded into a bomb dump and caught fire – MacCarthy received minor facial injuries and burns during the rescue and was later awarded the George Medal for his bravery (*London Gazette*, 9 September 1941).

In late 1941, MacCarthy volunteered to serve in North Africa, but while docked in Cape Town aboard SS *Warwick Castle* en route, the ship's orders were suddenly changed and she was instructed to sail immediately to Singapore to help stop the recent Japanese invasion of Malaya. MacCarthy managed to avoid being captured when the enemy finally conquered Singapore – he escaped to Java with other British forces – but the Japanese advance continued and he was captured there in March 1942. Doctor Aidan MacCarthy was now a POW.

He experienced the full horrors of POW life in various camps – frustrated by a lack of medical supplies and having to watch men die horribly and needlessly – but he continued to do whatever he could for the soldiers, sailors and airmen in his care. Then, in April 1944, he was selected as part of a draft to go to Nagasaki, but while en route, the vessel on which he was travelling was torpedoed. MacCarthy survived, but later arrived in Nagasaki – as he recalled in his book *A Doctor's War*:

> ... naked on the dock ... covered with cuts and abrasions from the nails and sharp edges of the wreckage. Salt encrusted our bodies and our skins were wrinkled like new-born babies. A few local women gave us water and some makeshift splints and

paper bandages before being chased away by the returning Army personnel ...

MacCarthy was initially put to work in a Mitsubishi steel factory (he was so thin and had so little flesh on his hips that he soon developed pressure sores from sleeping on a straw mattress), but along with his fellow POWs they committed sabotage whenever they could, often by weakening shipbuilding rivets. On one occasion, he and eleven other southern Irish POWs were beaten up by the camp commandant personally, after the Japanese officer discovered where they were from. As MacCarthy recalled:

> We Irish had, it seemed, joined forces with the British to wage war against the Japanese people, who were only defending themselves against the brutal attacks of the American and Commonwealth warmongers.

Soon transferred to a nearby factory and now the POW camp's senior Allied officer, MacCarthy was beaten almost daily as punishment for 'offences' committed by his men.

By Spring 1945, Doctor Aidan MacCarthy found himself working in an opencast coal mine on the outskirts of Nagasaki. After the end of the Battle of Okinawa in June and the beginning of the Allied bombing campaign against mainland Japan, 'we were particularly terrified of being killed by American bombs, and it was with immense relief that we were suddenly told by the authorities that we could dig some air-raid shelters for ourselves.'

However, the coal mines and the air raid shelters were not the only things that MacCarthy found himself digging in 1945. By summer, he and his comrades were digging again, 'this time a pit about six foot deep and about twenty foot square ... It did not take us long to work out that we were digging our own grave.' In fact, this was part of a larger Japanese plan to eliminate all Allied POWs before they could be liberated by friendly forces.

Robert Widders reproduces a section of a Japanese report in his book *The Emperor's Irish Slaves* which stated:

> Whether they [the POWs] are destroyed individually or in groups, or however it is done, with mass bombing, poisonous smoke, poisons, drowning, decapitation, or what, dispose of them as the situation dictates [and] in any case it is the aim not to allow the escape of a single one, to annihilate them all, and not to leave any traces.

By mid-1945, the Japanese knew that they were losing the war, and they were not about to let Allied POWs survive to go home.

However, on 9 August, after seeing a wave of US bombers flying overheard, Doctor Aidan MacCarthy and his fellow POWs at Nagasaki ran to their air-raid shelters. As Mac-Carthy recalled:

> In the shelters we prayed that there would not be a direct hit. A couple of POWs did not bother to go into the shelters, staying on the surface and crouching on the ground in the shadow of the barrack huts. They were gazing at the sky, watching the approaching vapour trails. One of them shouted to us that three small parachutes had

dropped. There then followed a blue flash, accompanied by a very bright magnesium-type flare which blinded them. Then came a frighteningly loud but rather flat explosion which was followed by a blast of hot air. Some of this could be felt even by us as it came through the shelter openings, which were very rarely closed owing to poor ventilation.

The explosions we heard seemed to be two in number and this puzzled experts when later we were debriefed. One possible explanation is that the second sound was a giant echo from the surrounding hills. All this was followed by eerie silence. Then an Australian POW stuck his head out of the shelter opening, looked around and ducked back in, his face expressing incredulity. This brought the rest of us scrambling to our feet and a panic rush to the exits.

The sight that greeted us halted us in our tracks. As we slowly surveyed the scene around us, we became aware that the camp had to all intents and purposes disappeared. Mostly of wooden construction, the wood had carbonised and turned to ashes. Bodies lay everywhere, some horribly mutilated by falling walls, girders and flying glass. There were outbreaks of fire in all directions, with loud explosions recurring as the flapping, live electric cables fused and flared. The gas mains had also exploded, and those people still on their feet ran round in circles, hands pressed to their blinded eyes or holding the flesh that hung in tatters from their faces or arms. The brick built guardroom had collapsed, and the dead guards lay almost naked in a circle around the unlit stove.

We could suddenly see right up the length of the valley, where previously the factories and buildings had formed a screen. Left behind was a crazy forest of discoloured corrupted sheets clinging to twisted girders. Burst waterpipes shot fountains of water high in the air. The steel girders stood like stark sentinels, leaning over a series of concrete 'tennis courts' that had once been the floors of factories. But most frightening of all was the lack of sunlight – in contrast to the bright August sunshine that we had left a few minutes earlier, there was now a kind of twilight. We all genuinely thought, for some time, that this was the end of the world.

Doctor Aidan MacCarthy and his surviving comrades then started to run towards the sea, guessing that this might be the best way to escape the horror of Nagasaki. After struggling through the waters of the Urakami River, and after being 'physically sickened by an endless stream of burnt, bleeding, flesh-torn, stumbling people', he ended up treating wounded survivors in the foothills of the local mountains. Here, as a black rain began to fall, MacCarthy found himself treating some of the most dreadful injuries imaginable, including people who had been hit by glass shards that had subsequently melted through their skin and fused with their bones.

Soon recaptured by the *Kampeitai* (Japanese secret police), MacCarthy was ordered to assist with the cremation of the dead, where 'The smell of burning flesh was overpowering.' However, the attitude of the Japanese towards the POWs quickly changed – they were no longer as violent or aggressive towards their prisoners – and then on 'August 15th, 1945, I woke to find all the guards had seemingly disappeared.' MacCarthy later met with a Japanese interpreter who informed him that Japan had surrendered to the Allies. And so, 'we rang the assembly bell and gathered all the POWs into the compound. In a voice faltering with emotion, I announced the great news.' Doctor Aidan MacCarthy from Berehaven, County Cork – now aged thirty-two – was able to tell his men that the war was over. 'We were all in a state of shock. We cried, hugged each other, shook hands, dropped to our knees and thanked God. A few of us began to sing hymns.'

MacCarthy did not return home to Ireland until November 1945, but he sadly then discovered that his younger brother – Finbar – had been killed, aged thirty on 2 March 1945, by one of the last V2 rockets to fall on London. He died in his home in Parkers Row and today lies buried in Bermondsey, Metropolitan Borough.

MacCarthy later rose to the rank of air commodore with the RAF before developing a brain tumour in 1969 – a result of all the beatings he received while in Japanese captivity. He survived the operation to remove the tumour however, and remained living in England and practising medicine there when he retired from military service. Then, on 11 October 1995 – while having a brandy and listening to his own voice on a taped BBC broadcast – Doctor Joseph Aidan MacCarthy passed away at his home in Northwood, London. He was eighty-three years old, and was later buried in his native County Cork. He witnessed the devastation caused by the most destructive weapon ever created, and lived to tell his story.

The war against Japan was possibly the most gruesome campaign of the Second World War. 650 Irish men and women are known to have been taken POW by the Japanese and at least 148 of these are known to have died in captivity (overall, twenty-seven percent of the 50,000 Allied Far Eastern POWs did not survive the war). They were treated as sub-human slaves and died needlessly, while their Japanese captors stockpiled food and medical supplies that could have saved thousands of lives.

However, Allied prisoners were not the only people treated terribly by the Japanese. Stations containing so-called 'Comfort Women' – women forced into prostitution in military brothels – from China, Indonesia, Japan, Korea, Malaysia, the Philippines, Taiwan, Thailand and Vietnam were set up throughout Japanese-occupied territory. As many as 200,000–300,000 women, many of them only young girls, were forced to perform this work, where they were regularly raped and beaten or otherwise physically abused while being made to serve dozens of soldiers per day. Meanwhile, the Japanese Army also operated Unit 731 – a centre for human experimentation and chemical and biological warfare. Here, doctors performed vivisections without anaesthetic on live patients, purposely infected patients with various diseases to study their effects, amputated limbs to study blood loss, and removed parts of various organs, reattached severed limbs to the other side of the body, or in some cases, removed stomachs and attached the oesophagus directly to the intestines just to see how the body would react. These inhuman experiments were as bad as anything performed by German SS officer Josef Mengele at Auschwitz concentration camp, although they are not as well known.

The war against Japan was a bloody, vicious, dirty war, but it should never be forgotten that the Irish were involved in it too. The Irish also fought to defeat the last of the Axis powers, and finally bring an end to the Second World War.

A view of the devastation caused by the atomic bomb that was dropped on Hiroshima, Japan on 6 August 1945.

CHAPTER 6

DEEP, DARK WATERS

– THE WAR AT SEA

'The ship loudspeakers blared out, "Seven unidentified aircraft approaching off the port bow at a range of thirty-five miles" ... aircraft still unidentified at seven miles. Next, enemy aircraft open fire [and] all hell broke loose as thirty ships [began] firing four guns each at ... the German bombers.'

Radio Officer John O'Sullivan from Ballycurran, Shrule, County Mayo. From his short authobiography: *A Radio Officer's Story*

Britain would not have been able to continue the fight against Nazi Germany without the heroic merchant sailors who risked their lives and braved the harsh conditions of the world's seas and oceans to transport troops and military equipment across the Atlantic, along with the food, fuel, raw materials and other supplies needed to stop the country from being starved into submission. Meanwhile, the Royal Navy guarded these merchant convoys and fought against the Axis navies in an attempt to secure shipping lanes and take back control of the seas from the enemy. This is an often forgotten aspect of the Second World War, but the sacrifices made by thousands of Allied sailors at sea deserve to be remembered.

Service in either the Royal Navy or Merchant Navy had always been popular in Ireland – especially in south-eastern coastal communities such as Cork, Waterford, Wexford and Wicklow – and during the Second World War, Irishmen signed up for a variety of roles at sea. While some were ordinary seamen, others served as anti-aircraft gunners, as radiomen, engineering crew, navy pilots, submariners, or as the crew of rescue ships. They sailed all over the world in some of the harshest conditions imaginable – pounding gale force winds, forty-foot high seas, and subzero temperatures in winter – and held positions along the entire length of the rank structure. From seaman to First Sea Lord, the Irish were represented at every level. And while they often fought the German, Italian or Japanese surface navies, their main enemy was small, silent, and unseen – the U-boat. For nearly six years these sailors ran the gauntlet of U-boat-infested waters, with the Battle of the Atlantic being the longest continuous military campaign fought during the Second World War.

IRELAND'S FIRST SEA LORD

ANDREW CUNNINGHAM

Born in Rathmines, Dublin in January 1883, Andrew Cunningham was a man who went on to have an extremely distinguished career in the Royal Navy. His father – Daniel – was a professor of anatomy at Trinity College Dublin, and while studying at Edinburgh Academy, the young Andrew received a telegram from his father asking him if he would be interested in joining the navy. Although his family had no maritime tradition, Andrew thought about it and replied that 'Yes, I should like to be an admiral.' And so, after attending the Naval Preparatory School at Stubbington House, Hampshire, Andrew Cunningham entered the Britannia Royal Naval College in Dartmouth, Devon in 1897 – aged fourteen – and began serving as a cadet aboard the training ship HMS *Britannia*. The following year he graduated and then, in 1899, he began serving as a midshipman aboard the cruiser HMS *Doris*.

However, during the Boer War, Cunningham left the sea and volunteered to fight in South Africa as part of the Naval Brigade. He fought at Pretoria and Diamond Hill before returning to serve aboard ship. By the First World War – having served aboard several vessels and completed courses that qualified him for promotion – Cunningham was a lieutenant-commander and the commanding officer of the destroyer HMS *Scorpion*. This was one of the Royal Navy vessels that pursued the German battlecruiser SMS *Goeben* and light cruiser SMS *Breslau* through the Mediterranean in the early days of the war, which forced both ships to find safe harbour in Constantinople. Realising that they would never be able to safely get them back to German waters, the Germans then handed the ships over to the Ottoman Empire as a sign of good will, which ultimately played a significant part in bringing Turkey into the war on the German side and resulted in the subsequent Gallipoli Campaign, during which Cunningham and HMS *Scorpion* also served. He later went on to take command of the destroyer HMS *Termagent* which was part of the Dover Patrol.

By 1939 and the start of his third war, Cunningham had served as aide-de-camp to the King, had a CBE, KCB (which made him Sir Andrew Cunningham) and a distinguished service order and two bars to his name, and was now an admiral in command of the Mediterranean Fleet, which he described as 'the finest command the Royal Navy has to offer'.

Photograph of Winston Churchill, Franklin D Roosevelt and Joseph Stalin taken during the Yalta ('Big Three') Conference in February 1945. Admiral Sir Andrew Cunningham from Rathmines, Dublin – First Sea Lord – stands above and slightly left of Churchill.

His flagship was the famous battleship HMS *Warspite*, and his initial task in the region was to defend British convoys en route to Malta and Egypt. Meanwhile, his younger brother – General Sir Alan Cunningham, also from Dublin – who had served in the Royal Horse Artillery during the First World War, soon went on to defeat the Italians in East Africa and return Emperor Haile Selassie to power in Ethiopia.

When the Italians finally declared war on Britain on 10 June 1940, Admiral Sir Andrew Cunningham and the Mediterranean Fleet then had the Italian Navy to deal with. The Italians had six battleships, nine heavy cruisers, seven light cruisers and thirteen destroyers docked at Taranto in south-eastern Italy, and so the British began planning Operation Judgement to destroy this enemy fleet. On 11 November 1940 the attack was launched using Fairey Swordfish torpedo bombers that took off from the British aircraft carrier

HMS *Illustrious*. Twenty-one of these aircraft disabled half the Italian vessels that night, at a cost of two planes shot down, two men killed and another two captured. Operation Judgement (which was allegedly studied in detail by the Japanese when they were planning the attack on Pearl Harbour) effectively destroyed Italian naval power in the Mediterranean, and therefore meant that the Allies could safely transport troops, equipment and supplies to North Africa, while severely harassing any Axis convoys en route to Tunisia.

Admiral Sir Andrew Cunningham later fought in the Battle of Cape Matapan to the south of Greece and Crete in March 1941, not long after being awarded a GCB. After an Italian communication was intercepted, suggesting that the Italians were planning to attack Allied convoys en route to Greece, Cunningham led a combined Royal Navy and Royal Australian Navy force of one aircraft carrier, three battleships, seven light cruisers and seventeen destroyers against an Italian fleet of one battleship, six heavy cruisers, two light cruisers and seventeen destroyers. In order to fool enemy spies in Egypt, Cunningham apparently booked a game of golf and an evening party for the day after he was due to depart, and then on the night of departure, he quietly left the club he was in – making sure no one saw him leave – and headed straight aboard HMS *Warspite*. When the battle ended on 29 March, the Italians had lost five vessels, one other heavily damaged, while over 2,300 Italian sailors had been killed. Meanwhile, Cunningham's fleet had only suffered the loss of one Fairey Swordfish torpedo bomber and three men killed. However, while the Battle of Cape Matapan was Italy's greatest naval defeat of the war, it was ultimately indecisive.

Finally, during the disastrous Battle of Crete in May and June 1940 – when the Allies decided to withdraw from the island – Cunningham insisted that the 'navy must not let the army down.' His fleet remained at Crete – constantly under attack from the *Luftwaffe* – until they had rescued over 16,000 Allied troops from the island. It was a costly decision, and Cunningham lost three cruisers and six destroyers during the withdrawal, while fifteen warships were badly damaged.

By late 1942, Admiral Sir Andrew Cunningham had been made a baronet, and he was then appointed as naval deputy to US General Dwight D Eisenhower (Supreme Commander, Allied Expeditionary Force), who wrote that Cunningham 'remains in my opinion at the top of my subordinates in absolute selflessness, energy, devotion to duty, knowledge of his task, and in understanding of the requirements of allied operations. My opinions as to his superior qualifications have never wavered for a second.'

On 8 November 1942, Cunningham was in command of the fleet that covered the Operation Torch landings in Morocco and Algeria, and on 21 January 1943 he was promoted to Admiral of the Fleet. During the subsequent Axis evacuation of Tunisia, he commanded the naval blockade as part of Operation Retribution – an attempt to stop the enemy from escaping from North Africa to Sicily. During this operation he famously ordered his fleet to

'Sink, burn, destroy. Let nothing pass.' Finally, he commanded the Allied naval element that took part in the invasions of Sicily and Italy.

Admiral Sir Andrew Cunningham from Rathmines, Dublin was now sixty years old. However, he had not yet reached the height of his achievements. In October 1943, he became the First Sea Lord of the Admiralty (the head of the Royal Navy and the Naval Service) and Chief of the Naval Staff. This meant that he could no longer serve as commander-in-chief of the Mediterranean Fleet, but it meant that he was now a member of the Chiefs of Staff committee, with responsibility for the overall strategic planning of the Royal Navy. In this capacity, he also attended the Allied conferences at Cairo, Tehran, Quebec, Yalta and Potsdam.

After the war – having become a baron and then a viscount – Cunningham retired from the Royal Navy in May 1946. In 1952 then sixty-nine years old, he served as Lord High Steward at the coronation of Queen Elizabeth II, and then passed away eleven years later in London on 12 June 1963 after attending a meeting at the Admiralty. Admiral of the Fleet Sir Andrew Cunningham was eighty years old when he died, and he was buried at sea off

HMS Warspite – *one of the most famous battleships of the Second World War – while serving in the Indian Ocean as part of the Eastern Fleet under Admiral Sir James Sommerville, 1942. She had previously been Admiral Sir Andrew Cunningham's flagship, and during the Battle of Calabria – 9 July 1940 –* HMS Warspite *hit the Italian battleship* Giulio Cesare *with a broadside, even though both vessels were travelling at full speed and nearly fifteen miles apart. It is a naval marksmanship record that still stands to this day.*

the Nab Tower, Portsmouth from the destroyer HMS *Hampshire*. On 2 April 1967, a bust of him was unveiled in Trafalgar Square, London by Prince Philip, Duke of Edinburgh, in recognition of his incredible service to the Royal Navy during three wars.

DEFENDER

JOHN GALLAGHER

Born in December 1919, John Gallagher from Derrycassan, Downings in north County Donegal joined the Royal Navy in 1941. His mother had died when he was very young, and after serving at several shore establishments, Gallagher was posted as an anti-aircraft gunner to the Belfast-registered John Kelly Ltd collier SS *Parknasilla* sometime before 1942.

Then, in early 1942 – as recorded in the *London Gazette* of 14 April 1942:

> The ship was sailing alone when she was attacked at night by German aircraft. Two

Senior Second Engineer Jim McCarter – Merchant Navy – from Lurgan, County Armagh, mans a Hotchkiss M1909 Benet-Mercie machine gun mounted on his ship. They were used as anti-aircraft guns aboard Merchant Navy vessels, and it was this type of weapon that Able Seaman John Gallagher from County Donegal used to defend SS Parknasilla in 1942.

assaults were made by bombs ...

The Merchant Navy crew were huddling under cover, but as the German planes circled around to strafe the vessel for the second time, Able Seaman John Gallagher rushed out from under cover – along with comrades John O'Hara, a lamp trimmer from Cushendall on the northeast coast of County Antrim, and Joseph McCleery, a fellow gunner. Figuring that they were dead men anyway, and that they might as well go down fighting:

> O'Hara took the Lewis Gun, firing it lying on his back on the after hatch, without
> any cover. Gallagher and McCleery kept the Hotchkiss gun and the Holman Projector
> in action and drove off the attack. The three men showed courage and resource and
> the ship was brought safely to port.

For this display of bravery, all three sailors were awarded the British Empire Medal (Civil Division), while the captain of SS *Parknasilla* – William Gibson from Garron Point, County Antrim, who had been awarded an MBE for his service aboard SS *Carnalea* during the First World War – was commended 'for brave conduct' during the attack.

Gallagher served on in the Royal Navy until after the end of the war – he was discharged on 28 December 1945. He never spoke about his wartime experiences, but once mentioned that he had met twenty-six other Donegal-men during his time attached to the Merchant Navy, only three of whom survived the war. Gallagher initially became a fisherman in Hull, East Yorkshire, before returning to work as a butcher in his native County Donegal, where he reared his own animals and used to drive around the country selling the meat. In 1993, John Gallagher – who defended Merchant Navy vessels against enemy attack – passed away. He was seventy-four years old.

RESCUER

CHRISTOPHER 'CHRISTY' ROBINSON

However, while some Irish sailors defended their vessels from attack, others had to perform the vital duty of rescuing survivors from ships that had not been so lucky. Born in Limerick in 1925, Christopher 'Christy' Robinson was the son of a former 2nd Royal Munster Fusiliers' private who had served in India before being wounded and taken prisoner by the Germans during the First World War, while his brother – Thomas – joined the Royal Navy in 1937. In 1940 – now fifteen years old and having recently left school – Christy joined the Irish Army. As he recalled in a recent interview with the Limerick branch of the Royal British Legion:

> My pals were joining the Irish Army at that time. I decided to go to Sarsfield

Barracks in Limerick and chance my arm at joining up. I gave my age as eighteen years. I knew I was [meant to be] a soldier. My parents were not happy when I told them but they gave way in the end and I got their blessing.

After his initial training, Christy was posted as a gunner to 4th Light Anti-Aircraft Battery based in McKee Barracks, Dublin. He formed part of the crew of a 40mm Bofors anti-aircraft gun with attached searchlight, and soon found himself manning outposts in Clontarf and along the Bull Wall. He recalled that 'I liked the army life, really made a man of me and I loved the guns [but] I would have loved to be in action ... At times we got red alerts and had to man the guns and searchlights.' Christy served in Dublin with the Irish Army for two years until:

One night and its red alert time again, all the searchlights are on and they pick up [a] German bomber [with] very distinctive markings on it. Headquarters instructed us to fire on it, we couldn't believe it. We let hell go loose with our guns firing away that night. They dropped a bomb on the North Strand and then vanished from view. They did terrible damage that night ... After that bit of action, my mind was made up. It was further afield for me.

Seventeen-year-old Gunner Christy Robinson requested his discharge, and received it by officially admitting that he was underage at the time of his enlistment. Christy immediately travelled to England and joined the Merchant Navy. After a period of training, he was posted to SS *Dundee* – a rescue ship – and as Christy recalled:

The Captain and some Officers were Royal Navy. The crew consisted of Royal Navy and Merchant Navy. We [were] Merchant Navy under Royal Navy orders. We all got on very well together; some were first timers, like myself, but we soon learned the ropes. We sailed down the Clyde, then out to sea at last. We sailed along the coast to meet the convoy. The convoy was heading to Halifax in Nova Scotia, Canada; it consisted of forty ships with three corvettes and one aircraft carrier as escorts ... We were well out into the North Atlantic and it was very cold; off watch you slept with lifejacket and heavy clothing on, just in case of action.

Aboard SS *Dundee* there was:

A small hospital and lots of blankets and beds in case of rescue ... we were soon in action, a U-boat had hit two merchant ships on the edge of the convoy – lucky it was daylight. The corvettes went after it, dropping depth charges everywhere. We headed for the sinking ships to see if we could rescue anyone; we put clinging nets over the side and everyone not on watch had to climb over the side to help the survivors onto the ship. Many lives were lost but we did our best and had to catch up with the convoy or we would have been sunk as well. The Captain gave us a double tot of rum; we were all shaking in our shoes.

An Irish merchant ship, Irish Poplar, *with large markings on the sides to warn U-boats that she is a neutral. However, several neutral and similarly marked Irish vessels were sunk by U-boats during the war, while others were attacked and destroyed by the* Luftwaffe. *This photograph was taken from the destroyer HMS* Viscount *in the mid-Atlantic, sometime between 22 September and 20 October 1942.*

This was my first trip at sea and, for the first time, I shook with fear. I never before saw two merchant ships being sunk. The subs had gone. We had a lot of dead on board and they were buried at sea, because we were too far from land. The convoy reached Canada without further trouble and was dispersed to different ports. We went to Halifax, Nova Scotia; ambulances and the army took the injured to hospitals around the city. Some were in a very bad shape. Let's hope they survived.

Seaman Christy Robinson was only eighteen years old when he first experienced the horrors of the war at sea. On his return journey as part of another convoy SS *Dundee* was attacked by German aircraft. Royal Navy anti-aircraft gunners onboard managed to fight them off. Arriving safely in Glasgow, Christy was given seven days' leave which he used to return home to Ireland and visit his family in Limerick. While there, his mother gave him a 'caul' as a present (a caul is a thin membrane that a very small percentage of babies are born with covering their head). Tradition had it that a sailor who owned a caul would be protected from drowning, and so Christy promised his mother that he would carry it with him always, which he did.

He returned to sea and sailed in 'the North Atlantic run. A bit more experienced ... It was the same procedure. The German Wolfpack submarines were sinking merchant ships and we tried to save as many lives as possible.' These enemy U-boats were extremely hard to spot even when they were travelling on the surface, as they had such a low silhouette, and were responsible for sinking over 16.8 million tons of merchant shipping and thousands of Allied vessels during the war. Christy also remembered:

> During my time at sea, I often met a lone Irish ship sailing close to the convoy. These ships had Eire and Irish flag markings on the side and [were] all lit up at night – we sailed in pitch darkness. We couldn't even light a cigarette on deck. Some of those Irish ships would radio to the convoy and tell us of the position of submarines on our route. Some of those ships paid the ultimate price for this act with all hands lost – very brave men. I often think of them. May they rest in peace.

Also, while Allied convoys often could not stop to rescue the survivors of sunken vessels, Irish-registered ships always did, and during the Second World War, Irish merchant vessels are known to have rescued 534 seamen (both Allied and Axis) from the sea.

In terms of neutral southern Ireland's experience of the war at sea during 1939–1945, southern Ireland had fifty-six registered ships at the start of the Second World War, but bought or leased fifteen more during the conflict. In all, sixteen Irish vessels were lost during the war, some due to accidentally hitting mines, but some due to direct attack (nearly exclusively from German forces). Aside from those Irish vessels which were strafed or bombed by German aircraft and which survived, on 9 March 1940 the Irish-registered ST (Steam Trawler) *Leukos* was sunk with the loss of all eleven crew after she was attacked by *U-38*. The vessel had been fishing near British trawlers which began to flee when the U-boat appeared, and allegedly the crew of ST *Leukos* was trying to ram *U-38* in order to help the British fishermen escape when she was fired on.

On 15 July 1940, SS *City of Limerick* was sunk in the Bay of Biscay, despite having 'EIRE' in giant white letters and the Irish tricolour painted in several places on her hull. On 4 September that year, SS *Luimneach* was sunk in the North Atlantic, while SS *Kerry Head* was bombed and sunk by German aircraft on 22 October and the Irish Lights vessel SS *Isolda* was similarly attacked and destroyed on 19 December off the coast of Waterford. The following day, SS *Hibernia* – the Dun Laoghaire to Holyhead ferry – was bombed while docked in Dun Laoghaire. However, the bombs missed and fell on the nearby Sandycove railway station (while SS *Hibernia* had previously been an Irish-registered vessel, at the time of the attack she was on the British registry of ships).

In 1941, SS *St Fintan* was attacked and sunk in the Irish Sea on 22 March. Then, on 13 June 1941 – having recently sailed from Rosslare – the Irish ferry SS *Saint Patrick* was bombed by the *Luftwaffe* while en route to Fishguard. Although the majority of its crew and passengers were saved, thirty were killed in the sinking, which included seventeen-year-old Deck Boy John Brennan from Wexford and sixty-year-old ticket collector Edmund Roche from Mallow, County Cork. Out in the North Atlantic, *U-564* torpedoed and sank SS *Clonlara* on 22 August, while, in 1942, SS *City of Bremen* was lost in the Bay of Biscay after it was attacked by German aircraft on 2 June that year. SS *Irish Pine* was torpedoed and sunk by *U-608* with the loss of all thirty-three onboard on 15 November 1942, while on 23 February 1943, SS *Kyleclare* was torpedoed by *U-456*. Finally, on 15 May 1943, SS *Irish Oak* – while en route from Tampa, Florida to Dublin with a cargo of 8,000 tons of phosphate fertiliser – was torpedoed by *U-607*. Southern Irish vessels were always clearly marked, but despite this, at least 149 neutral Irish sailors are known to have been killed during the Second World War.

Then there was MV *Kerlogue*, who rescued the crew of the British collier SS *Wild Rose* on 2 April 1941 after she was attacked by German bombers, only to be herself attacked accidentally by the RAF on 23 October 1943. Then, four days after Christmas that year, the crew of *MV Kerlogue* found themselves rescuing Nazi sailors from the water after the German destroyer *Z27* – along with the torpedo boats *T25* and *T26* – was sunk by the Royal Navy. They managed to save 168 Germans, although four soon died onboard. Ironically, *MV Kerlogue* had earlier hit a German mine in Cardigan Bay, Wales on 7 October 1941, which meant she had the unique distinction of having rescued sailors from both sides during the war, while also having been attacked by both sides.

Meanwhile, Seaman Christy Robinson soon found himself 'heading for Russia and we were not happy about this trip; Russia at this time was losing the war. The Germans were near Stalingrad. Our convoy was heading for Murmansk and other ports. It was a terrible trip with snow and terrible seas all the way. At Murmansk, Russian men and women were unloading the cargoes, guns, munitions and raw materials and then they went back to the war front. They were tough people.'

Out of the 95,000 Allied sailors who took part in the Arctic convoys (or Russian convoys as they were also known), roughly 3,000 are known to have died at sea – a much higher casualty rate than that suffered on any other convoy route during the Second World War. As the western Allies tried to send vital supplies and military equipment to Russia, the crews of these convoys had to sail through U-boat-infested waters – where German warships and *Luftwaffe* aircraft also patrolled – while dealing with extremely rough seas and bitterly cold conditions. Ice had to be constantly chipped off vessels while men had to work and fight in subzero temperatures. Winston Churchill later referred to sailing in an Arctic convoy as 'the worst journey in the world'. Sadly though, these brave sailors never received the recognition that they should have. After the war and with the beginning of the Cold War, Britain did not want to officially acknowledge the help that it had given to Russia during 1941–1945, and so no Arctic convoy medal was ever issued (Soviet Russia did issue the Russian convoy medal to Allied veterans in the late 1980s, but the British Ministry of Defence did not recognise this award until 1994). It was only after an eight-year campaign by surviving veterans that a badge emblem, but not a medal, was issued in 2005.

After returning from Russia to Glasgow – having sailed up the Clyde behind a corvette that had also been part of the convoy – Seaman Christy Robinson was returning from Mass the following Sunday when he noticed that the corvette, which SS *Dundee* was now berthed beside, was the destroyer HMS *Ambuscade*. Christy recalled:

> I remembered my father wrote saying that my brother Tom was on that ship. I went on board and inquired if he was still on the ship. I was taken to the petty officers' quarters, I couldn't believe my eyes – there was Tom staring at me. It was the first time we met since the start of the war and [we had been] on the same convoy to Russia. The bottle of rum was opened and we had a great celebration ... We both had seven days leave coming and we headed back to Limerick to enjoy it and to meet our parents. We had a great time in Limerick, but soon the time came for us to go back. We said our goodbyes to our family and it was back to sea again. The next convoy was heading for the east coast of America. I had done twelve months on this ship, a very lucky ship and I was a wiser seaman but it was time to look for another ship in case my time had run out.

After sailing aboard other Merchant Navy vessels during the war, Seaman Christopher 'Christy' Robinson stayed at sea until 1955, 'when my good wife Maeve asked me to get a shore job, which I did.' At the time of writing he is eighty-seven years old and in his recent interview he concluded:

> To all those men who went down to the sea in ships, no matter what nationality – they were all heroes. I salute you.

BENEATH THE WAVES

MICHAEL EDWARD SHERIDAN

While most sailors served aboard surface vessels during the war, there were also those who fought beneath the waves. Born in September 1917 in Portumna, County Galway – although he later lived in Castlepollard, County Westmeath – Michael Edward Sheridan (he

went by Edward) joined the Royal Navy as a boy in January 1933 – aged fifteen. When the Second World War began, Sheridan – then twenty-two years old – found himself training at the HMS *Dolphin* submarine school. On 1 January 1940, Sheridan was posted to the recently launched T-class submarine HMS *Tetrarch* as an acting leading telegraphist.

During his time aboard HMS *Tetrarch*, she torpedoed and sank the German submarine chaser *UJ B/Treff V* on 23 April 1940 in the Skagerrak straits between the southern coasts of Norway and Sweden. On 20 May she sank the Danish fishing vessel *Terieven* while capturing another – the *Emmanuel* – and taking it to Leith, Scotland as a prize, before sinking the German tanker *Samland*

Above: *Petty Officer Telegraphist Edward Sheridan. Originally from Portumna, County Galway, he later lived in Castlepollard, County Westmeath. Sheridan spent most of his wartime service aboard submarines in the North Sea, the Mediterranean, and in the Indian Ocean.*
Right: *British T-class submarine HMS* Truant, *which Petty Officer Telegraphist Edward Sheridan served aboard in early 1942.*

on 16 June southwest of Lista, Norway. HMS *Tetrarch* was then sent to operate in the Mediterranean, and on 4 November 1940 she torpedoed and sank the Italian merchant vessel *Snia Amba* off Benghazi, Libya. However, by 6 January 1941, Sheridan had been transferred to another submarine – the R-class HMS *Regent*. He was lucky, as in October 1941, HMS *Tetrarch* was lost with all hands off Sicily.

Edward Sheridan – who was made permanent leading telegraphist on 3 March 1941 – did not serve aboard HMS *Regent* for long, but during his time aboard this submarine she torpedoed and sank the Italian merchant vessel *Città di Messina* on 15 January east of Tripoli, Libya, before torpedoing and damaging the German merchant ship *Menes* northwest of Tripoli on 21 February. However, after performing this latest attack, HMS *Regent* was depth-charged by the Italian destroyer *Saetta*. Depth charges were barrel-shaped explosives that were dropped from surface vessels. Fixed with pressure-sensitive fuses, they detonated once they reached a certain depth, and were designed to destroy submarines by creating violent shocks underwater that would burst the target vessel's hull. Submariners were particularly terrified of them, as they could also damage or disable a submarine underwater, leaving the crew to die slowly as they ran out of air.

When HMS *Regent* was depth-charged the submarine was damaged, but luckily for Leading Telegraphist Edward Sheridan, she survived the encounter. Then, on 1 April – less than three months after joining the crew of HMS *Regent* – Sheridan left this vessel and was soon posted to the P-class submarine HMS *Parthian*. Once again he was extremely lucky; HMS *Regent* later hit a mine north of Barletta in Italy on 18 April 1943 and was lost with all hands.

On 1 October 1941, Sheridan was again transferred – this time to another P-class submarine, HMS *Perseus*. The next day, she sank the German merchant ship *Castellon* northwest of Benghazi, Libya (while firing on but missing the *Savona* during the same attack), before torpedoing and sinking the Italian merchant vessel *Eridano* off Lefkada Island, Greece on 4 December.

When 1942 began, Leading Telegraphist Edward Sheridan joined the crew of the T-class submarine HMS *Truant* on New Year's Day. This vessel had recently been ordered to sail to the Far East, and travelled through the Suez Canal and sailed past the southern tip of India to reach the Dutch East Indies on 18 February. Six days later on 24 February, HMS *Truant* spotted at least six enemy vessels ahead – three merchant ships and three warships. The submarine dived to attack and ultimately fired six torpedoes at the Japanese cruiser *Nagara*. Four of the torpedoes missed, however, while the other two hit *Nagara* but failed to explode. The Japanese then began depth-charging HMS *Truant*, and two depth charges exploded so close to the submarine that they actually rocked the vessel. It was Sheridan's second experience of being attacked by the enemy in this way.

On 27 February, HMS *Truant* docked at Surabaya, Java. Spare equipment was taken off and several crewmembers disembarked – one of which was Leading Telegraphist Edward Sheridan – before the submarine returned to the sea and began operating off the coast of Singapore. Sheridan then returned, via Australia, to the HMS *Dolphin* shore establishment in England, before later serving at HMS *Valkyrie* – an Isle of Man training base that provided advanced radio/radar courses. Sheridan continued to advance his radio skills when he attended the Royal Naval Communications/Signals School (HMS *Mercury*) at Petersfield, Hampshire from April to July 1944, before returning to the sea as part of the crew of the sloop HMS *Lapwing* on 8 July 1944 with the rank of petty officer telegraphist. He was now twenty-six years old.

However, on 20 March 1945, HMS *Lapwing* was sailing as part of convoy JW65 from Greenock, Scotland to Archangel, Russia when she was torpedoed by *U-968* – they were only one day away from reaching the port of Murmansk. Following the initial explosion the vessel caught fire, and so the survivors began diving into the icy Arctic waters to escape. When escort ships had finally rescued all of the survivors from HMS *Lapwing*, only sixty-one men out of a crew of 219 had survived. Sadly, Petty Officer Telegraphist Michael

Edward Sheridan from Portumna, County Galway was not one of them. Having stayed at his radio to the end – sending out a distress signal and trying to call for help – while his comrades elsewhere escaped, he went down with HMS *Lapwing* that night. Sheridan was only twenty-seven years old when he died. He was one of only two men aboard HMS *Lapwing* to be posthumously mentioned in dispatches (*London Gazette*, 7 August 1945), and with no known grave, today his name is commemorated on the Plymouth Naval Memorial.

EVERYWHERE

EAMONN 'ED' O'DEA

The old saying 'Join the Navy, see the world' was definitely true in the case of this next man. During the Second World War, he seems to have served almost everywhere. Born in Kildimo, County Limerick in March 1915, Eamonn 'Ed' O'Dea sadly had to suffer the death of his mother when he was only four – she died during the so-called Span- ish Flu pandemic of 1919. Raised by his father and two aunts, who all called him Edward or 'Ed' for short – which led Ed to believe that this was his actual birth name – he had a poor upbringing and used to walk to school without any shoes. Having left school at fourteen, Ed worked as a farm labourer or fished along the River Shannon.

Petty Officer Ed O'Dea (right) and his brother, Lieutenant Patrick O'Dea of the Royal Army Service Corps. Patrick served in North Africa and later met and married a German Jew who was working as a translator at the post-war Nuremburg trials. Patrick O'Dea then became a member of the Palestine police force – although there was a rumour that he was secretly gunrunning for the Israelis – before retiring to England where he lived for the rest of his life. Both Ed and Patrick O'Dea came from a poor background in Kildimo, County Limerick.

The harsh conditions of an Arctic Convoy. Able Seaman Thomas B Day standing against the ice-encrusted barbette for 'B' turret onboard HMS Belfast, November 1943.

In 1936, aged twenty, 'Ed' O'Dea left Ireland to find better work and along with three friends he joined the Royal Navy (of the four of them, two died during the war and the fourth, a man named Hayes, ended up running a pub in Cork in the 1960s). Ed signed on as a stoker and when the Second World War began he was aboard the minesweeper HMS *Bramble* (a ship allegedly nicknamed the 'Irish Navy' because of her large number of Irish crewmen). This vessel was a part of 1st Minesweeping Flotilla based at Scapa Flow in the Orkney Islands, and began minesweeping operations in this area in September 1939. However, when *U-47* subsequently sank HMS *Royal Oak* at anchor here, the Royal Navy Home Fleet moved to the River Clyde area and HMS *Bramble* went with them. By November, she was back in the North Sea keeping the gaps in the British East Coast Mine Barrier free of enemy mines (that month, Ed was made an acting leading stoker), and in December she took part in her first Atlantic convoy. By January 1940, HMS *Bramble* was back at Scapa Flow. After a refit during 1940 at Leith, Scotland, HMS *Bramble* resumed her minesweeping duties and was sent to sweep the area off Harwich, Essex, between the Thames Estuary and Portsmouth in February 1942. While here, she was hit by a *Luftwaffe* bomb during an air raid – it was an event that Ed O'Dea never forgot.

Ed used to command a shift in the engine room during this time. The bomb that the *Luftwaffe* aircraft dropped ended up hitting and detonating in the engine room. It had been another team's shift at the time – five men – and when the rescue crews got into the engine room, they found that their five comrades had been blown apart. Ed later recalled that they scooped up what was left and placed the remains in five different body bags – even though they could not identify what belonged to each man – before burying them at sea.

After she had been repaired, HMS *Bramble* was transferred to Western Approaches Command for Atlantic convoy duty in April and later to 3rd Escort Group in May – whenever she was not actually sailing as part of a convoy, she was clearing enemy mines in the Western Approaches. Then, in October 1941 – Ed sailed in his first Arctic convoy (Convoy PQ2 from Liverpool to Archangel). However, while on the return voyage in November, HMS *Bramble* was detached to join a new incoming convoy – PQ3 – meaning that Ed had to return to Archangel instead of Britain. The following month, he was again detached to join the next incoming convoy – PQ5.

After finally returning to Britain in February 1942, it was decided that HMS *Bramble* should be again refitted – this time to 'articise' her for operating in polar waters (up to this point, the ship had not been properly equipped for sailing in the Arctic Ocean). Then, on 26 April, she sailed from Reykjavik, Iceland bound for Murmansk as part of Convoy PQ15. During the first three days of May this convoy was spotted by a *Luftwaffe* reconnaissance aircraft and came under heavy attack from German submarines and aircraft.

However, by 5 May 1942, the surviving vessels of Convoy PQ15 had made it to Murmansk.

HMS *Bramble* was once again detached from an outgoing convoy to join and protect the incoming Convoy PQ16 on 30 May, and, on 10 June, they were ordered to help look for surviving ships from Convoy PQ17 which had scattered after coming under threat from German warships. Out of the thirty-nine ships in this latest convoy that had sailed from Iceland, only fifteen ended up making it safely to Russia.

By September 1942, Ed O'Dea had returned to Britain and was transferred from HMS *Bramble* to the shore establishment HMS *Drake* (three months later on 31 December 1942, HMS *Bramble* was sunk by the German destroyer *Friedrich Eckoldt* in the Barents Sea. All of the 121 crewmembers aboard were drowned in the sinking). However, he did not remain here for long, and on 20 January 1943 – having recently had his promotion to leading stoker made permanent – Ed ended up aboard the frigate HMS *Teviot*. But at some point before Ed joined his new vessel, he was in Devonport docks when the Germans launched a bombing raid against Plymouth. Ed began running for safety when he suddenly saw another sailor just standing there, leaning up against a lamppost. The man was not moving, just leaning, and so Ed rushed over to him. He shouted at the man to see if he was alright, but when Ed touched the man, he collapsed 'like a heap of jelly', as Ed later recalled. The man's bones had been shattered by the percussion of an earlier bomb explosion. He had literally been killed by the blast, only it had left no signs on his body.

Having completed Atlantic convoy duty in April and May, Ed's new ship – HMS *Teviot* – was sent to the Mediterranean and helped to escort and then defend the Allied convoys that took part in the invasion of Sicily in July (they also assisted in the rescue of survivors of the British ship SS *City of Venice*, which had been torpedoed and sunk off Cape Tenez, Algeria on 4 July). More Atlantic convoys followed – but not before Ed met King George VI while still in the Mediterranean. The king was apparently on a visit to the region and so the ship's company had been formed up for a review. Because of his stutter, the king was known for being extremely shy when reviewing troops, and he never generally

Two photographs taken by Ed O'Dea from Kildimo, County Limerick during the war. The first (left) shows two ship's cats aboard a minesweeper docked in Portsmouth, while the second (opposite top) is of a Russian sailor in Murmansk, taken in 1942.

stopped to speak to the men.

However, on this occasion, as he walked past the sailors who were all standing at attention, he stopped in front of a 6'6" Kerryman, Dennis Menihan, who was standing next to Ed. Behind the king was his aide-de-camp – an officer whose job it was, at times like this, to write down everything the king said so it could be used later in press releases.

'What is your name?' the king asked.

'Dennis Menihan, sir,' the Kerryman replied.

'And w-w-w-where do you c-c-c-come from?' asked the king.

Menihan suddenly looked sideways at the king and – confused – replied 'Huh?' in a loud Kerry accent.

Terrified of the king being embarrassed, the aide-de-camp suddenly jumped in. 'Your Majesty, Huh is a small village in Ireland.' Satisfied, the king moved on.

After another brief spell on Atlantic convoy duty, HMS *Teviot* was then attached to the Eastern Fleet and sent to Ceylon (modern Sri Lanka) – arriving there in August 1944 after sailing via South Africa and Yemen. Here, Leading Stoker Ed O'Dea and HMS *Teviot* defended incoming convoys from Britain while helping to support military operations against the Japanese in Burma, including the Allied landings on Cheduba Island which took place on 24 January 1945.

When HMS *Teviot* was transferred to the South African Navy, Ed O'Dea later returned to Britain aboard the heavy cruiser HMS *Cumberland* – not long after the war ended on 12 November 1945. Post-war, Ed stayed in the Royal Navy, and by mid-1947 he had been promoted to petty officer stoker mechanic, going on to serve aboard various destroyers, anti-aircraft frigates and corvettes, as well as the aircraft carrier HMS *Eagle*. Then, on 15 April 1958 – having served for twenty-two years at sea and having gained the rank of chief mechanic – Eamonn 'Ed' O'Dea retired from the Royal Navy. He was now forty-three years old, and later claimed that he had never experienced any anti-Irish sentiment during any of his years with the Royal Navy.

He retired with plenty of stories to tell about his time at sea. During the war, one of Ed's ships (most likely HMS *Bramble*) was attacked by a German Focke Wulf FW 200 (Condor) long-range bomber out of Norway. The Condor was armed with two 500lb bombs and the pilot tried to drop both of these on Ed's ship. The first bomb missed and exploded in the water nearby, but the second was right on target and fell down the ship's funnel into the engine room. Miraculously however, the bomb failed to explode. Ed's ship was immediately ordered to return to England to have the bomb defused – a tense trip for the crew – after which she set sail again. Then, after the war, he was once aboard a vessel that was hit by a typhoon while sailing in the South China Sea. The ship was blown 500 miles off course but miraculously survived.

After leaving the Royal Navy, Ed joined the Hampshire police in 1958. But then, after five years in the police, it was suddenly discovered that he had no British passport, and that he had also never been vetted when joining the police. As a result of this, an MI5 agent was dispatched to Limerick to find out if Ed was an IRA agent. This agent wound up asking questions about Ed in a Limerick pub, where he found out that Ed's father had been an Irish Volunteer during the War of Independence. So, back in Hampshire, Ed was called before a local judge. It was then discovered that his real birth name was Eamonn and not Edward as he had always believed, and so, since he was apparently operating under a false name, the authorities became suspicious of Ed's motives in joining the Hampshire police – they feared he might be an IRA operative trying to establish himself in the English police force. However, after Ed explained that he did not actually know that his real name was Eamonn, and after signing official forms to put the record straight, the matter was settled and Ed continued on in the police.

He soon married Olive Kennington – a nurse from Piltown, County Kilkenny – who had served as a nurse in Britain during The Blitz. On one occasion, she had been in a nursing home that was bombed while she was inside. Miraculously, Olive managed to walk out of the wreckage. Later, on her way to her nursing exam finals in London, she was on a bus that was driving along behind another bus. The bus in front was suddenly hit by a German flying bomb – it was completely destroyed – and Olive's bus was knocked over onto its side by the blast. Again, Olive survived, and actually continued on to attend her exams. She later nursed on Malta, and then post-war in Berlin; during this time she was also sent out to Belsen concentration camp where she saw mounds with numbered posts sticking out of them – '5,000' or '10,000' – signifying the amount of dead buried in these mass graves.

When Olive inherited a farm back in her native Waterford in 1967, Ed O'Dea and his wife returned to Ireland. However, after six months of farming, Ed soon recalled how hard it actually was – it was extremely hard work – and so he travelled down to the employment exchange in Waterford. A staff member took a look at his CV and then asked Ed if he had any experience working with boilers. The Royal Navy engineering veteran of twenty-two years replied, 'I know a little', and so Ed was given the job of getting a boiler up and running in an AnCO factory (AnCO was an industrial training authority – forerunner of FÁS) on a local industrial estate. However, when he arrived for his first day of work, after taking a look at the boiler, he found that all he had to do was press a green button to start the machine working. It was totally automated, and so Ed's services were not required. As a result, he was put to work in stores on the premises.

Chief Mechanic Eamonn 'Ed' O'Dea from Kildimo, County Limerick sailed in the North Sea, across the Atlantic to America, through the Arctic Ocean to Russia, and in African, Indian and Far Eastern waters during his time with the Royal Navy. He passed away in April 1982, aged sixty-seven.

HUNTER

EUGENE ESMONDE

Although aircraft carriers had been around since the end of the First World War, these vessels – and the fighters and bombers that they carried – played a pivotal role in the Second World War. A navy could now attack its enemies far out to sea – or alternatively launch raids against land-based targets – with air support, instead of having to rely solely on their ships' guns.

One Irishman who flew as part of the Fleet Air Arm of the Royal Navy during the Second World War was Eugene Esmonde. Although born in Thurgoland, Yorkshire, in March 1909, his parents were Irish and his father – Dr John Joseph Esmonde, the then-MP for North Tipperary – soon brought the family home to Drominagh near Borrisokane in County Tipperary. However, on 17 April 1915 – while serving as a captain in the Royal Army Medical Corps during the First World War – Dr Esmonde died of 'pneumonia and heart failure consequent on the strain of overwork', as a report later stated. Eugene was only six years old when his father died. Meanwhile, his elder half-brother John Lymbrick Esmonde (an MP and later a Fine Gael TD for Wexford) served in the trenches with the Leinster Regiment and later the Royal Dublin Fusiliers, while another half-brother – Geoffrey Esmonde – was killed on 7 October 1916 while serving as a second-lieutenant with 26th (Tyneside Irish battalion) Northumberland Fusiliers. He was only nineteen years old, and today lies buried in Cite Bonjean Military Cemetery, Armentières.

On 28 December 1928 nineteen-year-old Eugene Esmonde was commissioned into the RAF. He was then posted to the Fleet Air Arm of the Royal Navy and began serving in the Mediterranean. Before the Second World War had even started, Esmonde retired from military service in 1934 and flew for Imperial Airways. With them, he survived a serious

Officers and ratings – who were decorated for the part they played in the sinking of the Bismarck *– standing in front of a Fairey Swordfish aircraft. Lieutenant Commander Eugene Esmonde from County Tipperary is second from the left.*

accident in 1935 when his plane crashed into the Irrawaddy River in Burma, and was later one of the first pilots to fly the large Short Empire flying boats which introduced the first airmail service between Britain and Australia. In May 1939, Esmonde returned to serve in the military, this time taking up a commission of lieutenant-commander in the Fleet Air Arm.

When the war broke out, Esmonde served initially aboard the aircraft carrier HMS *Courageous*. However, this vessel was sunk by *U-29* on 17 September 1939 – only weeks after the outbreak of the war – with the loss of over 500 lives, but luckily Esmonde survived the sinking. He was soon posted to the far more modern Illustrious-class aircraft carrier HMS *Victorious*, and it was while serving aboard this ship that Lieutenant-Commander Eugene Esmonde launched raids against the most famous German warship of the Second World War – the battleship *Bismarck*.

On 24 May 1941 – then leading the nine Fairey Swordfish torpedo bombers of No 825 Naval Air Squadron, Esmonde took off from HMS *Victorious* to attack the *Bismarck*. *Bismarck* had recently broken out into the Atlantic to raid Allied shipping (at the time, the Germans believed that only surface warships were suited to deep-sea raiding, and that U-boats should be restricted to coastal waters) and the British needed to remove her as a threat. Weather conditions in the Atlantic were appalling as the squadron flew towards their target, but Esmonde and his comrades managed to navigate the 120 miles to the *Bismarck* and launch their assault – Esmonde himself managed to hit the German battleship amidships on the starboard side – before the entire flight returned safely to HMS *Victorious*. Two days later, bombers from HMS *Ark Royal* attacked the *Bismarck* again – this time managing to jam her rudder, which meant the battleship could now only sail in continual circles (her crew were later able to stop her from going in circles and put her on a course, but the vessel had almost no way of manoeuvring). A 'sitting duck', the British continually attacked *Bismarck* until she finally sank on 27 May. For his part in helping to sink the mighty German battleship, Lieutenant-Commander Eugene Esmonde was awarded the Distinguished Service Order (*London Gazette*, 12 September 1941).

Six months later, Esmonde was serving aboard the aircraft carrier HMS *Ark Royal* when she was torpedoed by *U-81* in the Mediterranean on 13 November 1941. The torpedo hit the vessel between the bomb store and fuel bunker – beneath the bridge island – while the explosion rocked the ship and threw Fairey Swordfish torpedo bombers off the deck and into the air. Several sections of HMS *Ark Royal* were flooded and the ship began to list. Attempts were made to tow the vessel to Gibraltar, but the list worsened and the order was given to abandon ship. Miraculously – aside from one seaman killed in the initial explosion – the remaining 1,487 personnel onboard were safely evacuated and Lieutenant-Commander Eugene Esmonde was later mentioned in dispatches (*London Gazette*, 16 January 1942) for helping to rescue the vessel's crew. HMS *Ark Royal* finally sank in the early hours of 14 November.

In February 1942, the *Kriegsmarine* launched Operation Cerberus – an attempt to sail their warships in Brest, France, through the British-blockaded English Channel and home to their bases at Wilhelmshaven and Kiel in Germany. The British did not want these vessels to reach German waters, and so attacks were launched.

On 12 February, Lieutenant-Commander Eugene Esmonde was ordered to take off and attack the battleships *Scharnhorst* and *Gneisenau* and the heavy cruiser *Prinz Eugen*, which were approaching the Straits of Dover. Esmonde was now in command of six Fairey Sword-fish torpedo bombers of No 825 Naval Air Squadron based at RAF Manston in Kent, but after higher command failed to confirm if a fighter escort would be provided, Esmonde waited for as long as he could for the confirmation before taking off without any fighter support. En route to their targets, Esmonde and his comrades were finally joined by ten Spitfires of No 72 Squadron RAF, and together these British squadrons soon came under attack from German fighters who were defending the enemy warships.

The Spitfires were forced to scatter and all six Fairey Swordfish torpedo bombers were damaged by enemy fire. However, they continued with their mission alone and soon came under fire from anti-aircraft batteries aboard the fleet of German vessels in the Channel (*Scharnhorst*, *Gneisenau* and *Prinz Eugen* were all being escorted and defended by other smaller ships as well as German destroyers). What happened next was later recorded in the *London Gazette* of 3 March 1942:

> Lieutenant-Commander Esmonde knew well that his enterprise was desperate ... Touch was lost with his fighter escort; and in the action which followed all his aircraft were damaged. He flew on, cool and resolute, serenely challenging hopeless odds, to encounter the deadly fire of the Battle-Cruisers and their Escort, which shattered the port wing of his aircraft. Undismayed, he led his Squadron on, straight through this inferno of fire, in steady flight towards their target. Almost at once he was shot down; but his Squadron went on to launch a gallant attack, in which at least one torpedo is believed to have struck the German Battle-Cruisers, and from which not one of the six aircraft returned. His high courage and splendid resolution will live in the traditions of the Royal Navy, and remain for many generations a fine and stirring memory.

Hit by fire from an enemy aircraft before he could reach his target, Lieutenant-Commander Eugene Esmonde's plane exploded in flames and crashed into the sea. Only five of the eighteen men aboard the Fairey Swordfish bombers survived, four of whom were wounded.

For leading this brave attack against incredible odds, and for dying in an attempt to stop the enemy warships from returning to Germany, Esmonde was awarded the Victoria Cross. His great-uncle, Captain Thomas Esmonde from Pembrokestown, County Waterford, had also earned a VC in 1855 during the Crimean War – but sadly, Eugene's was awarded posthumously.

Lieutenant-Commander Eugene Esmonde from Drominagh, Borrisokane, County Tipperary was only thirty-two years old when he died on 12 February 1942. Today, his remains lie buried in Gillingham (Woodlands) Cemetery.

By the time that the Second World War ended, the Allies had lost over 36,000 military sailors and 36,000 merchant seamen killed during the Battle of the Atlantic alone, along with 175 warships and 3,500 merchant vessels. Meanwhile, the Germans lost 783 U-boats and 30,000 sailors (eighty percent of those who went to sea). Sailors risked dying from enemy attack or drowning if their vessel sank, while having to battle against extreme weather and cold. Their sacrifices often went unacknowledged – but the war at sea was as much a part of the Second World War as any major land campaign. Without the efforts of those thousands of sailors, the Allies would never have won the war.

A telegram received on 8 May 1945 by John O'Sullivan – radio officer aboard the tanker MV Taron *– from Ballycurran, Shrule, County Mayo. The telegram informed the ship that the war against Germany was over. John was nineteen years old at the time, and had previously seen the survivors from SS* Athenia *– the first British ship sunk by German forces during the Second World War – arriving at Galway docks while he had been a student there in September 1939. He was in several convoys that were attacked by the enemy during the war, while on another occasion, 'we hit into a sixty mile-per-hour gale which lasted three days and nights. During that time we were lifted thirty to forty feet on the crest of waves and it was a sight watching the motion of the other ships in convoy. As one ship rose to a crest the other went into a trough – the other ship like a skyscraper towering over us.'*

CHAPTER 7

STRANGER THAN FICTION

'Guide us, dear Lord, in Your great way
We who were not trampled on the way.'
**John 'Jack' Agnew from Belfast,
506th Parachute Infantry Regiment,
101st Airborne Division from his poem:** *A Soldier's Prayer*

Perhaps an unusual source of inspiration for a chapter, but in recent years two television series have gone a long way towards reintroducing the subject of the Second World War to a wide public audience. These shows – namely *Band of Brothers* and *The Pacific* (based on books of the same names by historians Stephen E Ambrose and his son Hugh Ambrose respectively) – are about the wartime experiences of US army paratroopers from Easy Company, 2nd Battalion, 506th Parachute Infantry Regiment, 101st Airborne Division (*Band of Brothers*), and about US marines and their fight against the Imperial Japanese Army (*The Pacific*). Their impact on modern popular culture is undeniable, and they have brought to life the subject of the Second World War – along with the struggles and sacrifices endured by the men who fought it – for many who might never open a history book.

What follows are the accounts of Irish-born men who served in the US airborne forces and fought with the marines in the Pacific.

THE IRISHMAN AND EASY COMPANY

JOHN 'JACK' AGNEW

John 'Jack' Agnew was born on 2 January 1922 in Belfast, Northern Ireland, the son of Presbyterian parents Robert Agnew – an iron turner – and Mary Ann Campbell. Jack's family had deep roots in Belfast – his paternal grandfather, James Agnew, had established the Ashfield Dairy in Strandtown, Belfast in 1878, while his maternal grandfather had worked for Harland and Wolff as a steam fitter on the construction of the *Titanic*.

In 1927, when Jack was five years old, the family emigrated to the US, settling in Philadelphia, Pennsylvania. Just under a year after the US entered the war, Jack – then twenty years old and a naturalised US citizen since 1932 – joined the US Army on 21 September 1942 in nearby New Cumberland. He had worked for the previous two years as a precision grinder operator.

Back in Ireland, Jack's uncle – Norman Agnew – had donated part of the Ashfield Dairy lands in Belfast for the construction of an RAF airfield, and Jack's cousin – Robert Keith Agnew, Norman Agnew's son – had already been

John 'Jack' Agnew from Belfast (left) and other members of the Filthy Thirteen.

killed while serving as a leading aircraftman (pilot under training) with the RAF on 9 December 1941. Ironically, this was the day after the US entered the war, and Robert Agnew was buried in Belfast (Dundonald) Cemetery on what would have been his nineteenth birthday.

As for Jack Agnew, after enlistment he joined one of the most famous units in US military history. On 30 September 1942, Private John 'Jack' Agnew from Belfast arrived in Camp Toccoa, Georgia to train as a paratrooper. Not only was he in the very same camp as the famous Easy Company of *Band of Brothers* fame, he was also in their regiment – the 506th Parachute Infantry Regiment (PIR), commanded by Colonel Robert F Sink – and he came to know many of the Easy Company soldiers quite well. In fact, while Jack became a soldier in HQ Company attached to 506th PIR's regimental headquarters, he served as jeep driver for Herbert Sobel – Easy Company's infamously strict and hated commanding officer – for two weeks while at Camp Toccoa, and recalled that Sobel used to make him park outside the camp infirmary where Sobel would then get out, wait for sick soldiers either entering or leaving the infirmary to pass him by, and then berate the ones that failed to salute him. Later, Jack also drove for Colonel Sink.

At Toccoa, Jack would have experienced the 'three miles up, three miles down' fitness runs of Currahee Mountain. However, Jack's fitness was excellent and he received perfect scores during tests. Also, it was while training in Camp Toccoa that Jack became friends with Brincely Stroup, a corporal and former miner from West Virginia.

After leaving Toccoa and travelling to Fort Benning, Georgia at the end of November for parachute training – having partipated in the famous 156-mile march from Fort MacPhearson to Fort Benning en route – Jack took out a $5,000 life insurance policy on Christmas Eve 1942 and named his mother as the beneficiary. Just over two weeks later, on 15 January 1943, he completed the five parachute jumps that qualified him as a paratrooper and that permitted him to wear jumpwings on his dress uniform. However, further qualifications quickly followed. During 1943, Jack trained as a demolition specialist and qualified on 1 April, before completing advanced airborne training and moving to Camp Mackall, North Carolina later that month for tactical training and night parachute jumps. He then went on to earn a carbine marksman badge. Finally, on 1 June 1943, the 506th PIR was officially attached to the 101st Airborne Division.

In fact, because of his demolition specialist qualification, Jack became a member of the demolitions platoon of 506th PIR's HQ Company. This specialist unit contained several sections of thirteen members each, elite soldiers who were purposely selected and trained in order to demolish targets behind enemy lines, but Jack's particular section – because of their reputation for fighting, drinking, ending up in the stockade, generally misbehaving and not shaving or washing for long periods during training – were soon nicknamed the Filthy Thirteen. Later on, after this unit first went into action on D-Day, a rumour spread that the men were actually criminals recruited from prison. This rumour ultimately inspired EM Nathanson to write a fictional novel *The Dirty Dozen* in 1965, which was followed by a successful film adaptation two years later. But, as Jack Agnew later confirmed, while about thirty percent of the film was accurate:

> We weren't murderers or anything, we just didn't do everything we were supposed
> to do in some ways and did a whole lot more than they wanted us to do in other ways.
>
> We were always in trouble.

Being a member of the Filthy Thirteen demolitions section meant, however, as Jack later remembered, 'We ran all the battle courses. Our platoon taught the others how to fight forest fires.' And so, Jack Agnew became an instructor to the men of the 506th PIR, which included the soldiers of Easy Company.

By now, Jack was a Private First Class (PFC), and after moving to Camp Bragg, North Carolina, and then Camp Shanks, New York, on 5 September 1943 he sailed from New York to England aboard SS *Samaria*, arriving at Liverpool ten days later. It was the first time he had been back across the Atlantic in sixteen years. Stationed in various villages around

John 'Jack' Agnew from Belfast (back row, third from left) and other soldiers from the 101ˢᵗ Airborne Division at Chalgrove Airfield, Oxford, in February 1945. He had recently returned from Belgium, having been in the first plane of Pathfinders to jump into Bastogne. Note the three hash marks above the cuffs of most of the men. The 506ᵗʰ PIR – of which Jack's unit was a part – sailed for England in September 1943, and each hash represents six months' service overseas.

Wiltshire, the 506th PIR began a period of intense training in the lead up to D-Day.

Then, at 2300hrs on 5 June 1944, it was finally time for the 101ˢᵗ Airborne Division to go into action. Eighty-one Douglas C-47 Dakotas (known as Skytrains to the British) of the 440ᵗʰ Troop Carrier Group, USAAF carried the 506ᵗʰ PIR across the English Channel. PFC John 'Jack' Agnew and the Filthy Thirteen were with them – attached to 3ʳᵈ Battalion, 506ᵗʰ PIR – and the demolitions platoon had been tasked with destroying several bridges over the Douve Canal before capturing and securing the main bridge at Carentan. Inspired by the fact that one of their members – Jake McNiece – had Native-American ancestry, the Thirteen had also given themselves Indian-style Mohawk haircuts and had painted their faces with war paint (which led to another myth about the unit that they were all Native-Americans).

As they flew across the Channel, the C-47s came under fire from German anti-aircraft batteries on Jersey and Guernsey, but they were soon over France and the men were given the green light to exit their aircraft. However, due to heavy enemy ground fire, paratroopers were being dropped far from their designated drop zones while units were being scattered and separated. As recorded in *The Filthy Thirteen* by Richard Killblane and Jake McNiece:

> Jack Agnew landed at St. Come du Mont, near a German battalion command post about a mile from his objective. When he landed, the barrel of his bolt-action Springfield [Jack was one of HQ Company's two designated marksmen, which is why he was carrying this weapon] jammed in the mud which drove the butt up into his shoulder. He hid near a hedgerow while Germans ran up and down the road. He then moved across to another field and ran into a mortar man who was scared to death and crying. Jack told him, 'Hey, you better come with me or stop making all that damn noise or I'll shoot your ass right now!' He refused to go with Jack.

Jack soon ran into two of his comrades who had been dropped nearby, and while Jack began blowing local power lines, the three made their way towards their objectives, linking up with more of the Filthy Thirteen as they went. After navigating through the flooded areas around the Douve Canal – the Germans had previously opened the canal locks to slow any Allied advance through the region – the assembled members of the Filthy Thirteen, which included Jack Agnew, reached their target bridges (two wooden bridges northeast of Carentan) at 0300hrs on D-Day. After destroying these, the demolitions soldiers then secured the main bridge in Carentan as planned, wired it in case they were overwhelmed by

The famous brick pile at Bastogne. Pathfinders are seen operating one of the CRN-4 sets which were used to guide supply planes to the 101st Airborne Division's location. John 'Jack' Agnew from Belfast is on top of the brick pile.

the enemy and forced to destroy it, and then set up in defensive positions. They were soon joined by more paratroopers from 3rd Battalion, 506th PIR.

Over the following days, PFC John 'Jack' Agnew and the US paratroopers (numbering about forty) at Carentan suffered heavy German counterattacks but managed to hold on to the bridge. However, after three days of bitter fighting, Jack watched in disbelief as US P51 Mustang fighter-bombers bombed and destroyed the bridge that he and his comrades had fought so hard to protect. Thinking that no Allied soldiers could have held the bridge for three days without reinforcement, the American pilots assumed that everyone in the area must be German, and so they attacked and destroyed the bridge, killing several US soldiers in the process.

It was not long before other German units began approaching Carentan from the opposite direction, from the north – units that were being pushed back as US forces advanced from their invasion beaches. On 10 June, the commanding officer of one such retreating German unit – a battalion containing hundreds of troops – demanded that the few US paratroopers at Carentan surrender to him. The paratroopers refused and so the Germans attacked. However, the handful of paratroopers waited for the Germans to expose themselves en masse in open ground and then mowed them down. The entire enemy battalion was virtually wiped out.

After the battle, however, Sergeant Jake McNiece (leader of the Filthy Thirteen) and Jack Agnew went out onto the battlefield to look for a comrade. Then, as McNiece later recalled:

> I saw this Kraut [German] in one of these deep ditches. Just his head and shoulders were above water. One of those machine gunners had tore his chest clear up. It was like a sponge. He was laying there trying to breath. He was pumping that blood and foam out in that water ...
>
> [Jack Agnew later added] He [the German] was all green and rotten but still alive. I said that was a disgrace and someone should put him out of his misery.

Jake McNiece continued:

> Chaplain McGee said, 'Give him a shot.'
>
> I looked over at Jack and said, 'Agnew, you've got that forty-five. Blow his head off.' Agnew [turned his head so he would not see it] shot at him and missed him. Then he kneeled down and put that Colt against [the German's] temple and just blew his head clear off of him.
>
> That chaplain just screamed. He said, 'You knew I didn't mean to shoot his head off. I meant to give him a shot of morphine.'

That same day, the Filthy Thirteen were relieved from their positions at Carentan, although they later went on to take part in the battle to secure the town on 12 June. By 15 June, Jack had earned the right to wear a combat infantryman's badge, and on 29 June the

101st Airborne Division were relieved from the front line and sent to replace the 4th Infantry Division at Cherbourg before returning to England on 10 July. Out of the original Filthy Thirteen, only five remained – the rest had been killed or wounded, while one soldier had been reassigned. PFC John 'Jack' Agnew from Belfast was one of the remaining five.

Jack remained in England until 17 September 1944, when the 101st Airborne Division took part in its second major operation of the war – Operation Market Garden. Having been brought back up to strength with replacements, the Filthy Thirteen secured several bridges in the vicinity of Eindhoven in the early days of the operation, before advancing north and reaching Nijmegen by 2 October. By then, Jack Agnew was one of only three remaining members of the original Thirteen, and he and his comrades were soon manning listening posts along the south bank of the River Nederrijn (Lower Rhine) after the Allies advanced to within sight of Arnhem.

The Germans had previously defeated the British 1st Airborne Division on the far side of the river at Arnhem, but many men had escaped capture and were being sheltered in Dutch homes. And so, as depicted in *Band of Brothers*, a rescue mission (Operation Pegasus) – which involved soldiers from Easy Company, British engineers from XXX Corps, and Lieutenant-Colonel David Dobie of 1st Parachute Regiment – was mounted across the river to retrieve these 1st Airborne Division survivors during the night of 22/23 October. When the mission was launched, it was Jack Agnew and the Filthy Thirteen who cleared lanes through the German riverbank minefields for the rescue teams and their boats.

PFC John 'Jack' Agnew and the Filthy Thirteen left Holland on 26 November 1944 – having served there for seventy-eight days. They were withdrawn to a camp in Mourmelon, France, but after the Filthy Thirteen's leader – Sergeant Jake McNiece – then volunteered to become an airborne pathfinder in early December, Jack was one of five other members of the Filthy Thirteen to follow him.

Pathfinders were paratroopers who dropped behind enemy lines in advance of a main force in order to mark drop zones, set up guiding radio beacons for aircraft, and then keep the drop zones clear of enemy until the main force arrived. It was an extremely dangerous role – soldiers could only volunteer for this duty, they could not be ordered to become pathfinders – and pathfinders generally suffered eighty percent casualties during missions. However, when Jack Agnew and his former Filthy Thirteen comrades returned to England and were attached to 9th Troop Carrier Command at Chalgrove Airfield in Oxfordshire, they believed that they would never be needed or called upon.

A few days later, on 16 December 1944, Hitler launched his Ardennes winter offensive and subsequently encircled the 101st Airborne Division in Bastogne, Belgium. The Americans needed a way to resupply the cut-off paratroopers, and so Jack and his fellow pathfinders were called on (this mission was expected to suffer eighty to ninety percent casualties).

This was Jack's third combat drop, and after jumping in foggy conditions into the area around Bastogne on 23 December 1944, the pathfinders set up several CRN-4 radio sets in the area – including one on top of a large brick pile on the ground. Jack then stood at the top of this pile and held a Eureka homing beacon up into the air to guide re-supply planes onto his location. This unusual sight prompted Jack's comrades to nickname him 'Moses' – since he looked like the ancient biblical leader standing on top of a mountain with the tablet of the ten commandments in his hands (they also took a photo of the event which appeared in *LIFE* Magazine; this image was later reproduced on a Dutch postage stamp). Over the following days, 846 supply planes – carrying fuel, ammunition, rations and other supplies – dropped their precious cargo around Bastogne. It saved the 101st Airborne Division from defeat.

For dropping into Bastogne and helping to re-supply the men of the 101st Airborne Division, Belfast-man John 'Jack' Agnew was awarded the Bronze Star, the citation for which read:

> Private First Class John Agnew ... Parachute Infantry, while serving with the Army of the United States, distinguished himself by meritorious service in connection with military operations against an enemy of the United States. On 23 December 1944 he was a member of a pathfinder group composed entirely of volunteer personnel selected for outstanding ability and courage. The group was given the hazardous mission of jumping via parachute with homing devices and field markers to guide aircraft to the encircled garrison at Bastogne to drop a vitally needed resupply to the surrounding troops. The group enplaned in the early hours of 23 December and several hours later, exposing themselves to heavy enemy fire, landed by parachute in the immediate vicinity of Bastogne and successfully guided the aircraft to the proper landing zone. The work of this pathfinder group proved of great value to the successful accomplishment of this exceedingly important mission. Private First Class Agnew's actions were in accordance with the highest standards of the military service.

Now stranded with the rest of the 101st Airborne Division around Bastogne, Jack took part in the fight to keep the Germans back and was subsequently wounded in action (he also narrowly survived being buried alive when the chateau that the pathfinders were staying in one night was shelled and demolished by enemy artillery; luckily, the pathfinders had been staying in the basement, and Jack managed to find a way out through the rubble for himself and his comrades). When the paratroopers were finally relieved, Jack initially returned to Chalgrove Airfield in Oxfordshire. But after Colonel Sink demanded the return of his demolitions men, Jack rejoined the 506th PIR in Mourmelon, France. Then, on 21 February 1945, he left the 506th PIR when he was transferred to HQ, 501st PIR. With this new regiment, Jack saw service in Germany and Austria, and a report about Jack from the

CO of 2nd Battalion, 501st PIR during this time stated that:

> Physical stamina is excellent. Emotional stability is excellent. Adjustment in the organisation, excellent. General health appears to be excellent. He makes no visits to sick call. He has no known physical defects.

After the fighting ended, Jack joined the 194th Glider Infantry on 11 August 1945, but not before being awarded an oak leaf cluster to his Bronze Star, the citation for which read:

> Private First Class John Agnew ... Parachute Infantry, while serving with the Army of the United States, distinguished himself by meritorious service in connection with military operations against the enemy of the United States from 6 June 1944 to 31 December 1944. Throughout the Normandy Campaign, operation in Holland, and defence of Bastogne, Belgium, he rendered outstanding service as a Demolitionist. His actions were in accordance with the highest standards of the military service.

Finally, PFC John 'Jack' Agnew set sail from France on 6 September 1945 – two years and one day after leaving New York – and arrived in Boston eight days later. He was subsequently discharged two weeks later with a certificate of merit from the 101st Airborne Division's commanding officer General Maxwell D Taylor and a $100 instalment of his $300 mustering-out pay. Now nearly twenty-four years old, Jack returned to live on Disston Street, Philadelphia, and he was given an excellent character rating and excellent efficiency rating from the army.

After the war, Jack initially suffered from post-traumatic stress disorder, but went on to work for Western Electric, a division of American Telephone and Telegraph. His friend from Toccoa – Brincely Stroup – initially moved in with him, but Jack later recalled:

> We were friends for years, we went fishing together often. [But,] you know, we never talked about it. Even after all those years, yeah, we never talked about it.

Brincely then moved out when Jack got married to Elizabeth Jane Potts – whose mother was from County Donegal – in the late 1940s. Together, the couple had two daughters, Barbara and Lynne, who subsequently became friends with Brincely Stroup's ('Uncle Brince' as he was known) own two daughters. As Barbara – Jack's eldest daughter – remembered:

> We used to go to the mountains each year. Dad and Brince liked to rent a boat and go fishing while the moms and girls played on the beach, especially at Tobyhanna State Park in the Poconos. Brince had a beautiful voice and his daughter used to sing in the talent show in Atlantic City on Steel Pier. Dad never forgave Brince for smoking. He still says that Brince would still be alive if he didn't smoke.

On 6 June 2004, Jack was present on Utah Beach, Normandy at the official sixtieth D-Day anniversary celebrations, where he was interviewed by CNN. He was also present at anniversary celebrations that year in Bastogne, Belgium – along with fellow Filthy Thirteen veteran, Jake McNiece. Here, Jack met a local woman holding a sign that read 'Thank You

G.I.s & Allied Forces, you liberated me from concentration camp in 1945.' The woman had been saved from Dachau, aged fourteen at the time, and Jack's daughter Barbara said, 'I am happy to see that Jack lived long enough to meet someone he had helped liberate. There [was] a tear in his eye.'

In April 2005, aged eighty-three, Jack was invited by the Bay Area Terrorist Task Force to join the team in Moscow, Russia, as part of an international task force to look at terrorism tactics at an international level. Aside from his Second World War demolitions qualifications, Jack had gained a degree in firearms identification and had assisted local police and the FBI after the war. The following month, the National Rifle Association (NRA) opened a new exhibit about the Second World War, and Jack's .45 calibre M1911 pistol – which he carried throughout the war – went on display in the NRA Firearms Museum in Fairfax, Virginia (he was also interviewed for the DVD re-release of *The Dirty Dozen* in April 2006).

In February 2010, he travelled to the Military History Show of Shows convention in Louisville, Kentucky, where he was reunited with Jake McNiece and two other surviving members of the Filthy Thirteen, along with three members of Easy Company. Then, two months later, Jack fell ill at his home in the Maple Village retirement community in Hatboro, Pennsylvania. Diagnosed with heart disease, he was brought to Abington Memorial Hospital in Abington, Montgomery County, Pennsylvania, where he subsequently died on 8 April.

Survived by his wife, two daughters and five grandchildren, Belfast-born Toccoa-man and Filthy Thirteen demolitions specialist PFC John 'Jack' Agnew was eighty-eight years old when he died. He was buried with full military honours and now lies in Forest Hills Cemetery, Huntington Valley, Pennsylvania.

ONE OF THE OLD BREED

THOMAS COLVIN DOHERTY

It is ironic, since the war fought by US paratroopers in Europe and the one fought by US marines in the Pacific were poles apart, that the Marine Corps Irishman in this chapter should come from such a different background to PFC John 'Jack' Agnew – although he similarly had a distinguished career. Thomas Colvin Doherty was born in the townland of Ballybrillighan, just outside the small village of Frosses – northwest of Mountcharles – in County Donegal, on 2 May 1920, and his father – Samuel Doherty, a farmer – had fought with the IRA during the War of Independence. In the early 1930s the teenage Thomas Doherty emigrated to the United States and settled in New York City. On 18 April 1937

– a few days before his seventeenth birthday – Doherty joined the United States Marine Corps (USMC) Reserve at the US Navy Armed Guard Armoury on 1st Avenue and 52nd Street, Brooklyn. While stationed here, Doherty variously served with A and B Companies, 1st Battalion, USMC Reserve and shortly afterwards became an NYPD policeman.

On 6 July 1939, just before the start of the Second World War, Doherty was promoted to corporal, and just over two weeks later on 22 July, he qualified as an expert rifleman. On being called up for active service, on 9 December 1940, and beginning a period of training in Quantico, Virginia, Doherty extended his enlistment for one year. As fate would have it, exactly one year later – only days before Doherty's extended enlistment was due to end – the Japanese launched their attack against Pearl Harbour and the US entered the Second World War. Doherty found himself posted to D Company, 1st Battalion, 5th Marine Regiment (D/1/5), a unit in the 1st Marine Division.

There were only 8,918 marines in the 1st Marine Division after Pearl Harbour, and so, recruitment was started to bring the division up to its full authorised strength of nearly 20,000. Doherty assisted in training D/1/5's new wartime volunteers when the entire 1st Marine Division went into garrison at the New River base – near Jacksonville, North Carolina – in June 1941. Here, the division performed tactical exercises and practised amphibious landings, the latter being the USMC's main role.

By May 1942, it was finally time to deploy to the Pacific and enter the fight against the Japanese. Irish-American Robert 'Lucky' Leckie – a marine in H/2/1, 1st Marine Division – wrote a memoir after the war named *Helmet for my Pillow*. He was present at two of the campaigns that Doherty also fought in, but he also recalled the departure of Doherty's 5th Marine Regiment from New River:

> The Fifth Marine Regiment left before we did. It departed during the night. When
> we awoke, their regimental area was deserted, picked clean, as though not even a shade
> had dwelt there, let alone thirty-five hundred exuberant young men. Not so much as
> a shredded cigarette butt or an empty beer can remained. Clean.

By now a Platoon Sergeant, though only twenty-two years old, Thomas Doherty from County Donegal – along with D/1/5 and the rest of the 5th Marine Regiment – travelled by train from North Carolina to California and then sailed aboard the *USAT* (United States Army Transport) *Wakefield* to Wellington, New Zealand, arriving in June 1942. They were joined several weeks later by the remainder of the 1st Marine Division.

After only a couple of weeks in New Zealand, the marines then re-embarked on their transports – which they had to load themselves due to a strike among Wellington's dock workers – and set sail for their first battle of the Second World War. Having pushed as far west as Burma, as far east as the Midway Islands, and south into New Guinea and the Solomon Islands, the Japanese were now building an airfield on the tiny island of Guadalcanal

Marines hit three feet of rough water as they leave their LST to take the beach at Cape Gloucester, New Britain, 26 December 1943. Platoon Sergeant Thomas Doherty from County Donegal landed on the island three days later.

at the southernmost edge of their occupied territory. If it was completed, Japanese planes would be able to reach Australia, and would also threaten Allied shipping in the South Pacific. And so, the 1st Marine Division were sent to capture Guadalcanal. However, they had no 'deuce and a half' trucks, no 155mm howitzers, no sound- and flash-ranging equipment needed to direct counter-battery fire, no tents, spare clothing or bed rolls, and no insect repellent or mosquito netting.

They landed on 7 August 1942, with Platoon Sergeant Thomas Doherty and 1st Battalion, 5th Marine Regiment (1/5) – one of the first units to set foot on Guadalcanal – taking up positions on the westernmost end of the landing area at Alligator Creek at the mouth of the Ilu River. Although the marines on Guadalcanal were attacked by Japanese dive bombers during their first day on the island, they encountered no Japanese infantry, and when night came, they dug in at their current locations. However, tensions were high among the new troops, and as Robert Leckie recorded:

> I awoke to the tiny twanging of hordes of invisible insects winging over my chest. I realised they were bullets when I heard the sound of firing to my rear. I went back to sleep, sadly convinced that the Japanese had got behind us ... In the morning someone explained that the firing had been two companies of the Fifth Regiment [Doherty's regiment], each mistaking the other for the enemy.

This nervous firing resulted in several casualties among marines.

The next morning at 0930hrs, Doherty and 1/5 – supported by A Company, 1st Tank Battalion – crossed the mouth of Alligator Creek and advanced west towards the Lunga River. They stayed in contact with the beach to the north, and moved slowly and cautiously. Ahead of them was the Japanese airfield – soon to be named Henderson Field – and after passing through the airfield, pressing on to the Lunga River and then crossing it, the marines finally reached the main Japanese camp. It had been abandoned in a hurry – the camp was fully stocked with food and ammunition, and none of its radio, electrical or engineering equipment had been destroyed or even damaged by the retreating Japanese.

However, the demoralised enemy soon turned around and began to strike back at the marines. Marine patrols started to encounter well-armed and well-positioned Japanese units, and then the enemy attacked in force on 21 August in what became known as the Battle of the Tenaru (which was actually fought at Alligator Creek, and not at the mouth of the Tenaru River). However, on 27 August, Doherty and 1/5 were moved by sea to an area around the Matanikau River – west of the Lunga River and Henderson Field. This was the second attempt to destroy enemy forces in this area, and by now, the marines were also combating dysentery and hunger – the US Navy vessels, which contained most of the marines' supplies, had withdrawn from Guadalcanal by 9 August due to a series of Japanese aerial attacks (the marines would not receive reinforcements or supplies until the Navy returned on 18 September).

At 0730hrs, Doherty and 1/5 landed in the target area. They found hot food in an abandoned enemy encampment – suggesting that the site had been abandoned only minutes before. No one knew where the enemy was or how many of them they were facing, and the marines had to navigate dense jungle, coral cliffs, ridges and ravines, and areas of five-foot-high kunae grass as they advanced under the burning sun. Then, at around 1100hrs, while exiting a jungle ravine into an open area of coconut trees, the lead elements of the marines' column were attacked by entrenched Japanese troops. The ravine acted as a bottleneck, and the marines could not advance. Communication between units was extremely difficult, and coupled with the dense jungle and the troops' exhaustion, all attempts to launch a flanking attack failed. The marines were forced to dig in for the night, but by the next morning, the Japanese had once again withdrawn into the jungle, and so Doherty and 1/5 returned east to the marines' perimeter.

On 12 September, the Japanese launched another series of night attacks against the marines that lasted three days, this time to the south. 3,000 Japanese soldiers attacked the marines dug in on Edson's Ridge, and by the end of 14 September, the marines had lost fifty-nine dead and 204 wounded, while the Japanese had suffered as much as 850 killed and 500 wounded. However, the marines were still determined to defeat the Japanese west of the Matanikau River – in order to set up an advanced western patrol base and also push back Japanese artillery that was threatening Henderson Field – and so yet another assault into that area was ordered (the Matanikau Offensive).

On 1 November 1942 – malaria now a serious problem among the marines – Platoon Sergeant Thomas Doherty and 1/5 advanced westwards on the right flank of 2nd Battalion, 5th Marine Regiment (2/5). They crossed the mouth of the Matanikau River on recently constructed pontoon bridges after a preliminary bombardment from marine artillery, air strikes and naval guns. However, the assault soon ran into trouble. Doherty's battalion lost contact with 2/5 to their left, and then began to come under enemy small arms and automatic weapons fire, before C Company was finally attacked by well-prepared Japanese forces in a ravine. They suffered heavy casualties, but this latest assault west of the Matanikau River soon managed to surround a large number of Japanese troops. On 3 November, while Doherty and 1/5 were being relieved to take up defensive positions in the east, other marine units – aided by 1st Battalion, 164th Infantry Regiment, US Army – destroyed the encircled Japanese forces. Approximately 400 Japanese soldiers were killed during the

Matanikau Offensive, at a cost of seventy-one US marines.

US forces continued to press west over the following weeks, and after several decisive naval battles, the Japanese were no longer able to supply their troops on Guadalcanal. By February 1943, they began to evacuate from Guadalcanal, and on 9 February, the island was declared free of enemy forces. However, Platoon Sergeant Thomas Doherty and the rest of the 1st Marine Division had left the island the previous December, having fought against the Japanese for four long months.

On 9 December 1942, just over a year after the attack on Pearl Harbour, Platoon Sergeant Thomas Doherty and the 1st Marine Division were relieved by the 23rd Infantry Division of the US Army and sent from Guadalcanal to Melbourne, Australia, for a period of rest and recuperation – the 5th Marine Regiment (which had been the first regiment to leave Guadalcanal) were billeted in the city's suburbs. During this time, the men received periods of liberty before training recommenced and they began to prepare for their next campaign while absorbing new recruits.

Out of the 1st Marine Division, 650 men had been killed, 1,278 wounded, 31 had gone missing, and 8,580 had contracted malaria. In total, however, (when Guadalcanal was finally secured), the US forces had lost 7,100 men killed – just under twelve percent of their 60,000 men – while the Japanese had suffered 31,000 fatalities (an eighty-six percent death rate) and 1,000 taken prisoner out of just 36,000 troops on the island. Under the Bushido code of conduct, it was a terrible dishonour for a Japanese soldier to be taken prisoner or to take part in a retreat, and so the vast majority always fought to the death.

In 1943, while still in Australia, Platoon Sergeant Thomas Doherty attended a commando course at the Australian Commando School, and then another course on the Japanese language. Finally, towards the end of the year, the 1st Marine Division departed Australia and landed at Cape Gloucester, on the western end of the island of New Britain, on 26 December 1943. They had two objectives – firstly, to capture local Japanese airfields, and then to cut off a larger Japanese base at Rabaul, on the eastern end of the island.

However, Platoon Sergeant Thomas Doherty and the rest of the 5th Marine Regiment did not landed at Cape Gloucester until 29 December. They had originally been detailed to capture two small islands near New Britain – Rooke Island and Long Island – but when intelligence suggested that the Japanese forces in the vicinity of the airfields might be larger than the marines had first expected, the 5th Marine Regiment were sent to New Britain to help capture the airfields immediately. 2/5 led the attack, followed by Doherty and 1/5, but difficult terrain – jungle, kunae grass, ridges, streams and swamps – slowed the advance. However – along with the 1st Marine Regiment – the 5th Marine Regiment secured the airfields by nightfall, in the face of almost no opposition. If there had been a large number of Japanese troops in the area, they had clearly withdrawn before the marines had advanced.

The main Japanese force had, in fact, withdrawn east to the Rabaul area – although pockets of troops had been left behind – and the arrival of the monsoon rains soon made it extremely difficult for the marines to advance beyond the airfields of Cape Gloucester. The constant rain, muck and fear ultimately destroyed the morale of many marines on the island, and Robert Leckie wrote a passage which summed up the attitude of the men:

> The puffing of my lips and eyes symbolised the mystery and poison of this terrible
> island. Mysterious – perhaps I mean to say New Britain was evil, darkly and secretly
> evil, a malefactor and enemy of humankind, an adversary, really, dissolving, corrod-
> ing, poisoning, chilling, sucking, drenching – coming at a man with its rolling mists
> and green mould and ceaseless downpour, tripping him with its numberless roots and
> vines, poisoning him with green insects and malodorous bugs and treacherous tree
> bark, turning the sun from his bones and cheer from his heart, dissolving him – the
> rain, the mould, the damp steadily plucking each cell apart like tiny hands tearing at
> the petals of a flower – dissolving him, I say, into a mindless, formless fluid like the sop
> of mud into which his feet forever fall in a monotonous *slop-suck, slop-suck* that is the
> sound of nothingness, the song of the jungle wherein everything falls apart in hollow
> harmony with the rain … Nothing could stand against it …

Regardless of the terrible conditions on New Britain, the marines continued to send out patrols, and these frequently ran into Japanese troops – encounters that were often swift, violent and bloody. However, it was while out on two such patrols that Platoon Sergeant Thomas Doherty's life in the USMC changed completely.

On 23 January 1944, Thomas Doherty performed an act which earned him the Navy Cross – the highest award for valour that the US Department of the Navy can give (only the Medal of Honour is senior to it). The medal is awarded for 'extreme gallantry and risk of life in actual combat with an armed enemy force and going beyond the call of duty', and Doherty's actions that earned him the Navy Cross are explained in the citation for his medal:

> The President of the United States of America takes pleasure in presenting the
> Navy Cross to Platoon Sergeant Thomas C. Doherty … United States Marine Corps,
> for conspicuous gallantry and intrepidity at the risk of his life above and beyond the
> call of duty in Company D, First Battalion, Fifth Marines, First Marine Division,
> in action against enemy Japanese forces on Cape Gloucester on 23 January 1944.
> During a combat patrol to Talasea, Platoon Sergeant Doherty's patrol came under
> heavy enemy assault … Notwithstanding the intense enemy fire and determined to
> break through the enemy's defences, Platoon Sergeant Doherty crossed 40 yards of
> open ground and, at point blank range, silenced a machine gun with hand grenades.
> He killed four snipers and fearlessly exposed himself to locate and destroy the rest of

the enemy. He then rallied his men and pressed a full attack with an aggressiveness which resulted in neutralizing all resistance and permitted his patrol to continue on their mission.

An inspiring leader and courageous fighter, Platoon Sergeant Doherty's gallant initiative and personal valour were in keeping with the highest traditions of the United States Naval Service.

While earning the Navy Cross was an extraordinary feat in itself, *the very next day*, Platoon Sergeant Thomas Doherty from County Donegal won himself another medal for valour – the Silver Star (junior to the Navy Cross he had just gained). As the citation explained:

For conspicuous gallantry and intrepidity as a Platoon Sergeant in Company D, First Battalion, Fifth Marines, First Marine Division, in action against enemy Japanese forces on Cape Gloucester on 24 January 1944. In charge of a section of machine guns during a combat patrol to Natamo Point, Platoon Sergeant Doherty was quick to act when the patrol became pinned down under heavy machine-gun, mortar and sniper fire from a numerically superior and well-entrenched enemy force on the opposite bank of a small stream. Exposing himself to the intense hostile fire, he moved from one position to another across open ground to direct the fire of his machine guns. When one of the guns was hit by a mortar shell and thrown forward into the stream close to the enemy positions, Platoon Sergeant Doherty, although wounded by the burst of mortar fire, rushed out into the open, recovered the gun and put it back into action while his unit withdrew. By his outstanding courage and inspiring leadership, he contributed materially to the success of the mission. His gallant actions were in keeping with the highest traditions of the United States Naval Service.

To add to Doherty's recent list of achievements, some documents also claim that he actually now held the rank of Gunnery Sergeant – the prestigious position of 'Gunny' – which suggests that he was referred to as Platoon Sergeant in his medal citations because he was either still acting in that capacity (junior Gunnery Sergeants were often the platoon sergeants of weapons platoons, which tallies with Doherty leading a patrol of machine guns to Natamo Point), because his promotion had not yet been made official, or because he was simply an Acting Gunnery Sergeant. Regardless, Doherty had earned two medals for valour in the space of two days, and he was still only twenty-three years old.

Following the end of the Battle of Cape Gloucester in April 1944, while the rest of the 1st Marine Division went on to fight in the Battle of Peleliu and the subsequent Battle of Okinawa, Thomas Doherty returned to the US from the Pacific and arrived in Camp Lejeune, North Carolina, on 1 September 1944. Having distinguished himself in New Britain, he had also been awarded a battlefield commission and was now a second-lieutenant in the USMC. Doherty remained at Camp Lejeune until New Year's Day 1944 – serving as a platoon commander, and then attending a course in infantry tactics – before moving to Quantico, Virginia to attend a platoon leaders' class. On 30 March 1945, he travelled to Washington DC to undergo training in espionage and counter-espionage (which included paratrooper training) with the Office of Strategic Services (OSS) – the forerunner of the CIA. This resulted in Doherty being sent on a mission to China. His plane was shot down over the South China Sea but he managed to bail out. However, his parachute did not open fully and he hit the water hard, seriously injuring his right shoulder. By total chance, he was rescued by an American ship, and although he spent several months in hospital, he subsequently recovered and soon returned to duty.

Doherty became officer in command of the Business and Law School at the Marine Corps Institute in the Washington DC Naval Yard, and, one month after this posting ended, Doherty's period of active service with the USMC concluded on 16 December 1945. With the war now over, Doherty returned to serving in a reserve capacity (although he was frequently contacted on short notice by the OSS/CIA or US Army Special Forces for covert assignments) while working with the Department of Justice and on the staffs of congressional committees in a civilian capacity.

After postings to the 3rd and 1st Marine Corps Reserve Divisions in New York and Boston respectively – between January 1947 and March 1950 – Thomas Doherty was called up for service in the Korean War, and after returning to the US, Doherty attended two staff and command courses at the Naval War College in Newport, Rhode Island and at Quantico between 1957 and 1958, and then a course of amphibious training between 1959 and 1960. During this time he also served at various other stations in various roles (though often as a civil affairs and military government officer).

Furthermore, due to his earlier service with the OSS, Doherty is known to have continued working clandestinely for the Department of Justice and the CIA, and although the details are still classified, he is known to have been involved in the Bay of Pigs operation (the CIA's attempt to invade southern Cuba) of April 1961.

After the outbreak of another war, Doherty served a tour in Vietnam. By late 1961, Doherty – now forty-one years old – was a lieutenant-colonel and a battalion commander, and throughout the early 1960s he commanded the 13th Infantry Battalion of the Fleet Marine Force – a combined, responsive force of naval fleets and USMC forces – before attending the Commando Officers' School in Quantico. It was also during this time that, following the assassination of President John F Kennedy – who Doherty greatly admired – on 22 November 1963, Thomas Doherty from County Donegal actually commanded the USMC battalion that marched in the president's funeral procession. The funeral has a more well known Irish connection – the attendance of twenty-four Irish Defence Forces cadets drawn from the 37th Cadet Class who performed arms drill at the graveside – but the

An exhausted US Marine, carrying a machine gun, after the fighting which followed the landings at Cape Gloucester, New Britain. Many marines remember Cape Gloucester as a completely demoralising campaign and regard it as their lowest point of the war.

Marine Corps troops present were also led by an Irishman. Finally, on 1 July 1974 – aged fifty-four and now a full colonel – Thomas Doherty from County Donegal retired from the USMC after thirty-seven years of service. But his involvement with the US armed forces did not end there.

After the end of the Second World War, Thomas Doherty – posing undercover as an injured patient – had been sent into the Veterans' Administration (VA) hospital in Washington DC in order to assess the level of care they were providing. This experience made Doherty interested in pursuing a civilian career dedicated to caring for armed forces veterans, and in 1950 he joined the VA. He became an administrator with the organisation in 1966, and after earning an MBA from the Harvard School of Business, he managed the Miami hospital's move from the 497-bed Coral Gables facility to the 1,035-bed centre in

Miami's hospital district in 1968. Thanks to Doherty's planning and execution, it was an extremely efficient move and there was no disruption to veterans' services. Six years later in 1974 – after fighting for and obtaining an SCI (Spinal Cord Injury) Unit for the hospital in 1973 – he ultimately became the director of the VA's new Miami facility.

Regarding his time as director of the Miami VA hospital, colleagues recalled in a recent article that 'Doherty's military bearing and crisp formality belied his modest nature. Striding the hospital's hallways at more than six feet tall, he was quick with a smile and a friendly greeting', while chief-of-staff Doctor John Vara remembered that 'With wit, charm and jokes ... told in an exaggerated brogue, Doherty – born in Ireland – could pacify angry people, comfort the ailing and inspire employees.' Susan Ward – Doherty's long-time VA spokesperson – also recalled that, during Doherty's time with the Miami VA hospital, the centre 'established several outpatient clinics and partnered with the University of Miami School of Medicine to establish a jointly funded HIV/AIDS Research Initiative ... He was very proud of what he did for his country. He was a Marine to the end. He really cared about the vets and employees.'

Furthermore, Doherty coordinated VA backup and support during periods of civil unrest in Miami, and he prepared the hospital for the arrival of several hurricanes while dealing with other disasters – when the power went out and the water supply was cut off during the 1992 Hurricane Andrew, Doherty personally went around the hospital to check on patients' welfare; he also dealt with the aftermath of a devastating electrical fire in 2000. His leadership doubled the number of hospital employees and he managed to increase the hospital's budget tenfold. A Geriatric Research, Education and Clinical Care Centre was set up, along with two community-based clinics – one for outpatients and another for substance abuse. The Miami VA hospital also became one of only three NIH-supported General Clinical Research Centres within the VA.

Meanwhile, Doherty served as the chairman of the Policy Board Committee of the Greater Miami Federal Executive Board and served two terms as the Board chairman. Also, having attended the Georgetown University School of Foreign Service in Washington DC, he sat on the Advisory Board of St Thomas University School of Law, Miami, while holding the position of adjunct professor of health administration at the University of Miami Florida's School of Medicine. Aside from all of these impressive achievements, Thomas Doherty was also active in law enforcement and health-care circles, and was a lifetime member of the Legion of Valour, the Marine Corps League, and Disabled American Veterans.

On 3 February 2003 – aged eighty-two – Thomas Doherty finally retired from his work with the VA. He was now the recipient of an award from every major veterans' organisation, and he was honoured by the Governor of Florida for his outstanding service, devotion and dedication to serving veterans. He soon also received the AMVETS Silver

Helmet Civil-Servant of the Year Award at a White House rose garden ceremony (in which former president George Bush received the Special Gold Helmet Award), along with the Four Chaplains' Medal, the Distinguished Catholic Service Award, and the Greater Miami Chamber of Commerce's Healthcare Heroes Award.

Four years after retiring, on 21 August 2007, eighty-seven year old Thomas Doherty passed away in his home in Miami Beach after a short illness. His obituary, which praised his life of service and achievement, also revealed another piece of information about his time with the USMC in the Pacific. Doctor John Vara, chief-of-staff at the Miami VA hospital, said:

> He [Doherty] had a special feeling for prisoners of war because he'd briefly been one ... Doherty was held by the Japanese after a Pacific island battle that only a few in his unit survived. They were tied up and beaten for hours until other Americans rescued them.

Completely unknown in his native Ireland, Donegal-man Thomas Colvin Doherty – who had variously been an NYPD policeman, a highly decorated senior enlisted man and later a colonel with the USMC (with tours of the Pacific, Korea and Vietnam to his name), an OSS/CIA and Special Forces operative, and then the director of a large veterans' hospital – now lies buried in the South Florida National Cemetery. He is survived by his wife, Martha, their four children, and eight grandchildren.

CHAPTER 8

FIGHTING THE FINAL SOLUTION

– IRELAND'S JEWS

AND WWII

Anti-Semitism in Germany and the Occupied Territories: A banner reading 'Jews are not wanted here' hangs over the entrance to the village of Rosenheim in Bavaria.

'The personification of the devil as the symbol of all evil assumes
the living shape of the Jew.'
Adolf Hitler, *Mein Kampf*

W hile past wars had often included what we would now call 'ethnic cleansing', the Second World War also saw the first organised, industrial state-approved slaughter of millions of people. By the time it had ended in 1945, the Nazis had murdered anything between 11 and 17 million people in concentration and extermination camps in an event that became known as the Holocaust. Of course, the largest group of these – numbering 6 million – was the Jews.

When Adolf Hitler and the Nazi party came to power in 1933, Hitler blamed the causes of the First World War on what he perceived as Jewish-controlled capitalism. He began instilling strong anti-Semitism in the German people and started removing Jews – along with other 'undesirables' – from German society. The Jews were publicly abused, their shops were boycotted, they were banned from working in the civil service, their property was seized by the Nazis, they were forbidden from using bicycles or public transport or from going to certain areas within German cities – public places such as swimming pools, sports fields, theatres and cinemas were also off limits – schools were segregated and they were not allowed to enter the homes of Christians. When the war broke out they also received lower food rations than other Germans and were only permitted to shop at certain times and only in certain stores. Furthermore, Jews had to carry identity cards and wear a Star of David on their clothing, they were also not allowed marry or have sexual intercourse with non-Jewish Germans, Jewish women under the age of forty-five were not allowed to work in German homes as domestic servants, and they were forbidden from displaying the Reich and national flag or the national colours. Jews were not even allowed to own pets. Before long, they were also placed in ghettos, where overcrowding, disease and hunger were common.

Then, after a Nazi diplomat was assassinated in Paris by a Jew in 1938, 7,000 German Jewish shops were vandalised while 1,668 synagogues in Germany (nearly every one in the country) were either damaged or destroyed on 9 November 1938. This was *Kristallnacht* – the 'Night of Broken Glass' or 'Crystal Night' – after which 30,000 Jews were interred in concentration and forced-labour camps while being made to pay an atonement tax of more than 1 billion Reichmarks for the damage that had been caused by other Germans against their properties and places of worship. By the time the war broke out, 80,000 Jewish refugees had fled to Britain – in the early 1930s, 2,000 a year had entered Britain; after 1938, it had risen to 3,000 a month (with many ending up in Northern Ireland). Meanwhile,

A member of the Sturmabteilung *(SA) – the Nazi party's early paramilitary wing – gives the Nazi salute whilst barring the entrance to a shop during the boycott of Jewish owned businesses, 1–4 April 1933. The shop windows are covered with notices proclaiming 'Deutsche! Wehrt Euch! Kauf nicht bei juden!' ('German! Defend yourself! Don't buy from Jews!')*

the US refused to change its strict emigrant quota system – in place since 1924 – meaning that Britain was almost the only country which, during the 1930s, increased the number of refugees it allowed in, while southern Ireland only permitted somewhere between thirty and 100 Jewish refugees to enter the country before and during the war.

When the war began, Jews from German-occupied territories were also transported to Nazi-controlled concentration camps, and by the start of 1942 – although 1 million Jews had already been murdered by the Nazis at this point – a programme to exterminate *all* Jews was then put into effect. Called the 'Final Solution', it had been designed by Heinrich Himmler – head of the SS and the *Gestapo* – and saw the construction of the first dedicated extermination camps (the two most infamous being Auschwitz and Treblinka). After killing 500,000 people – mainly Jews – using so-called gas vans, which were vans with sealed rear containers into which gas or the van's own exhaust fumes could be pumped in order to kill the occupants, the Nazis then began developing large-scale gas chambers which ultimately killed 5.5 million more Jewish victims. They died alongside millions more – communists, socialists, anti-Nazi journalists and intellectuals, Eastern Europeans, Slavs, Romani gypsies, homosexuals, physically and mentally disabled persons, Jehovah's Witnesses, Catholic clergy, Russian Army POWs, and other political prisoners who were perceived enemies of the Nazi party. It was the most horrific organised slaughter of human beings in history.

Meanwhile, Nazi surgeons began performing appalling human experiments. The most infamous Nazi doctor of the war was Josef Mengele, and his experiments included injecting dye into victims' eyes to see if they would change colour, amputating limbs and removing organs without anaesthetic, sterilising people, performing shock treatments, killing and then medically dissecting twins to study their internal similarities, sewing two people together in an attempt to create artificial conjoined twins, and vivisections on pregnant women. Most of these experiments were carried out on children, and on one occasion – after he found out that an accommodation block in Auschwitz was infested with lice – he ordered all 750 women living in the block to be gassed. And these were just the atrocities performed by Josef Mengele.

However, one forgotten aspect of the story is the fact that many Irish Jews joined the British forces during the Second World War in order to help defeat the Nazis, while others travelled to the extermination camps post-war in an attempt to assist the survivors in any way they could. Ireland's two largest Jewish communities at the time were, and still are, in Dublin and Belfast, and so the Irish Jews mentioned in this chapter are almost exclusively from these two cities. There was Michael Coleman from Dublin who, after serving in the Irish Local Defence Force based at Griffith Barracks, Dublin during the early years of the war, left to join the RAF. He served as ground crew for the rest of the war before going on to serve in the Israeli Air Force following the formation of the modern state of Israel

A column of Jews, guarded by German soldiers, is marched through the streets of Warsaw, Poland, during the winter of 1940.

in 1948. Age eighty-seven at the time of writing, he still lives in his native Dublin. Also from the Irish capital was Bernard Freeman – a dentist – who, while working in southern England when the war broke out, joined the Royal Army Medical Corps and served in Britain throughout the conflict. He then returned home to Ireland and set up a practice on South Circular Road. These men are just two of the many Irish Jews who joined the British forces, fought to defeat the Nazis, or tried to help refugees escape from Germany during the Second World War.

POLITICAL PRESSURE

ROBERT BRISCOE & GERALD GOLDBERG

Irish-Jewish politicians were also active during the war years, men such as Fianna Fáil TD Robert Briscoe from Dublin. He had been involved with the IRA and Sinn Féin during the War of Independence, had – ironically – been sent to Germany by Michael Collins in 1919 as the IRA's chief arms procurement agent, and had then travelled to America with Éamon de Valera that same year before joining anti-Treaty forces during the Irish Civil War.

Fianna Fáil TD Robert 'Bob' Briscoe in the 1930s (top) and the 1950s (bottom).

During the Second World War – now a TD – Briscoe tried to get the Irish government to allow Jewish refugees to enter the country (however, in order to protect Irish neutrality, he was never too vocal with his requests). At the same time, he was also fundraising for Irgun – a Zionist paramilitary group that operated in Palestine and who wanted to see the formation of a Jewish state – and when Irgun leader Ze'ev Jabotinsky visited Dublin, Robert Briscoe taught him guerrilla tactics.

Then there was Gerald Goldberg – a solicitor from Cork city (who joined Fianna Fáil in 1970 and then became the first ever Jewish Lord Mayor of Cork in 1977) – who set up a committee during the Second World War to help Jewish refugees who were trying to escape from the Nazis. However, the Irish government continually blocked his attempts – it was believed that if Ireland allowed Jews to enter the country, it would be viewed as interfering in the affairs of Germany and could be considered a breach of Irish neutrality. This was despite the fact that, in 1942, Rabbi Yitzhak HaLevi 'Isaac' Herzog informed Taoiseach Éamon de Valera about the existence of the extermination camps (Rabbi Herzog, a fluent Irish speaker, had been rabbi of Belfast from 1916–1919, before coming to Dublin and becoming Chief Rabbi of Ireland from 1922–1936, after which he moved to Palestine). However, while de Valera then proposed to allow 10,000 Jews to enter Ireland – making requests to Berlin that Jews in Vittel, France and others in Holland, Hungary, Italy and Slovakia be allowed to come to Ireland – the Nazis warned him about becoming too involved with their affairs. De Valera ultimately backed down and so no Jews were brought to Ireland.

Gerald Goldberg from Cork. After campaigning to help Jewish refugees during the Second World War, he later went on to become the first Jewish Lord Mayor of Cork in 1977.

HELPING THE FIGHT

PETER & ROBERT CRIVON

Irish Jew, Lieutenant-Colonel Robert 'Ruby' Crivon, of the Intelligence Corps. This photograph was taken in Algeria during Crivon's time attached to the British Eighth Army.

Other Irish Jews joined the British forces in order to help stop the Nazis. Peter 'Billy' Crivon from Dublin joined the British Army at the outbreak of war while living in London. However, during training, a fellow recruit accidentally dropped a grenade near Billy and it exploded, causing severe injuries to one of his legs. Billy was then discharged from the army as medically unfit to serve, but insisted on contributing to the war effort in any way he could. He soon joined the Home Guard, serving with them for the remainder of the war. Peter 'Billy' Crivon died in 1958, aged forty-three.

Meanwhile, Billy's older brother – Robert 'Ruby' Crivon (his family give his first name as Robert but he used Reuben during his time with the British Army) – joined the Intelligence Corps. Having obtained a scholarship to Oxford University in 1923 when he was only fifteen years old (and so too young to avail of it), Robert stayed in school for another year before obtaining a sizership to Trinity College Dublin. After studying classics there and graduating with first-class honours, Robert Crivon then started working as a teacher. In 1939 – now thirty-one years old – he travelled to Britain and joined the British Army. By the following year he was a second-lieutenant in the Intelligence Corps.

During the war, Robert was involved with Operation Ironclad – the Allied invasion of Vichy French-occupied Madagascar which took place on 5 May 1942 – after which he served on the staff of Eighth Army in North Africa when Montgomery took command in August that year. By the time the war ended, Robert 'Ruby' Crivon had become a lieutenant-colonel, and – according to his family – he had been offered the French *Légion d'Honneur* for his wartime services but had refused to accept it from de Gaulle. After being discharged from the army, Robert then returned to teaching. However, when Irish minister

Seán MacBride – a close friend – invited him to help in the setting up of the Council of Europe in 1949, Robert Crivon settled in Strasbourg and served as Director of Cultural Affairs for the organisation (his nephew, Quentin Crivon, recalled how Robert also worked in the United Nations' office in Paris at some point, where he became good friends with Irish playwright Samuel Beckett). Robert 'Ruby' Crivon died in 1968, aged sixty.

FIGHTING AGAINST FASCISM

MAX, MAURICE & SOL LEVITAS

Then there were the Levitas brothers of Dublin – Max, Maurice and Sol. The boys had a poor upbringing and lost another brother, Isaac, in March 1923 before the family moved to Glasgow in 1927 and then to London in 1931. In 1933, Maurice joined the Communist Party of Great Britain and then, on 4 October 1936, he became involved with what later became known as the Battle of Cable Street in London's East End. When Oswald Mosley led his British Union of Fascists on a march through the area that day, he was opposed by up to 300,000 anti-fascist demonstrators who erected roadblocks and barricades to prevent

Maurice Levitas from Dublin during his time as a Royal Army Medical Corps orderly in Burma.

the march. When 10,000 police then tried to clear the obstructions and allow the march to proceed, the demonstrators fought back and the result was a series of local riots that ultimately forced Mosley to abandon the march. The event is commemorated as a triumph over British fascism, and both Maurice Levitas and his brother Max were present (Max later went on to demonstrate inside the Savoy Hotel during the Second World War – an event which succeeded in forcing the British government to open underground air raid shelters to the general public – and at the time of writing he is ninety-six years old and one of the last living witnesses of the Battle of Cable Street).

Continuing his fight against fascism, Maurice Levitas entered the Spanish Civil War when he joined the republican cause in December 1937. However, in 1938 – after fighting at Belchite in January and Teruel in February – Maurice was taken prisoner on 31 March at Calaceite near Gandesa by Italian fascists (he was captured alongside Irish 'Connolly Column' leader Frank Ryan). Initially ordered to dig his own grave, after which the Italians were planning to execute him, the guards then changed their minds and Maurice and his comrades were instead imprisoned in the concentration camp at San Pedro de Cardeña. He was beaten regularly by the guards, and also had his skull measured by visiting Nazis who were performing 'scientific' measurements of Jews. On 6 January 1939 he was transferred to San Sebastian prison before being released on 6 February as part of a prisoner exchange requested by Mussolini.

During the Second World War, Maurice Levitas enlisted in the Royal Army Medical Corps in 1942 (his younger brother, Sol, also enlisted in the British Army and at the time of writing is ninety-three years old) and served as a medical orderly in India and Burma – he finished the war with the rank of sergeant. By then, the Nazis had murdered several of his extended family in Riga, Latvia and in Akmeyan, Lithuania (where the Jewish population were herded into the local synagogue and burned), along with an uncle in Paris who was executed on his doorstep by a *Gestapo* officer. Maurice then began training to become a teacher at Ashridge College in Hertfordshire. Once qualified, he began teaching in London secondary schools and, having completed a degree in sociology, he was appointed senior lecturer in the sociology of education at Durham College in 1966 before retiring in 1982 and teaching English to students in East Germany. Maurice then returned to London in 1990.

Even in his old age he was politically outspoken, and on 4 May 1991 Maurice Levitas was chosen by fellow veterans of Spain to read out the roll of honour of those Irishmen who had died during the Spanish Civil War. This event was marked by the unveiling of a plaque in Liberty Hall by the Lord Mayor of Dublin to commemorate their service. On 12 May 1996 he was present at the unveiling of the James Connolly statue by then-President Mary Robinson, and in November that year Maurice Levitas became a citizen of Spain. Finally, on 14 February 1997 – now eighty years old – a civic reception was held in the Mansion House, Dublin for all five surviving Irish Spanish Civil War veterans, of which Maurice was one. He died exactly four years later in London, on 14 February 2001 – aged eighty-four.

THE JEW WHO CAUGHT HIMMLER

CHAIM 'VIVIAN' HERZOG

Finally, in terms of Irish Jews who joined the British forces, there was Chaim Herzog. Born at Cliftonpark Avenue in Belfast in September 1918, he was the son of Rabbi Herzog who was mentioned previously. He moved to 33 Bloomfield Avenue, Portobello, Dublin, with his family in 1919 and went on to attend Wesley College. Then, in 1935, Chaim Herzog emigrated to Palestine and later served in the Haganah Jewish paramilitary group during the 1936–1939 Arab Revolt, after which he studied law in University College London before becoming a barrister.

On 2 November 1942, Herzog enlisted as a private in the TA Reserve (he was already a member of the Home Guard). However, he was soon called up for active service and posted to the Intelligence Corps. Within a short while, Herzog – who spoke fluent Hebrew and Yiddish, good French, German and Arabic, and was also fair at Italian – was selected for officer training and was subsequently commissioned on 1 October 1943 as a second-lieutenant in the Intelligence Corps. He was initially posted as an intelligence officer to 45th Infantry Division on 17 May 1944 – a second line TA division that remained in Britain during the war – but after several other postings to reinforcement holding units in Britain he was attached to the headquarters of 21st Army Group on 12 November 1944 and sent to Europe. This was just after the Battle of the Scheldt and not long before the start of the Battle of the Bulge. Herzog – who adopted the first name 'Vivian' because Chaim was too hard for English speakers to pronounce properly – remained with 21st Army Group's headquarters until 20 June 1945 when he went to XXX Corps' district headquarters post-war. By this time, he had become well known for intelligence gathering while commanding a tank in one of 21st Army Group's armoured divisions, and had also been promoted to captain.

Chaim Herzog was also involved in the liberation of several concentration camps. When Belsen was liberated on 15 April 1945, the first British units through the gates were 14th Amplifier Unit, Intelligence Corps and 63rd Anti-Tank Regiment, Royal Artillery. With them were three Jewish soldiers – one of whom was Chaim Herzog. He entered a hellish place where there were 50,000 diseased, lice-ridden and starving people begging for help

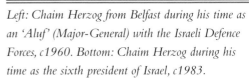

Left: Chaim Herzog from Belfast during his time as an 'Aluf' (Major-General) with the Israeli Defence Forces, c1960. Bottom: Chaim Herzog during his time as the sixth president of Israel, c1983.

– within a few days, 14,000 of these survivors had died despite the Allies' best efforts to help them, and within a few weeks, over 10,000 more had followed. However, what Herzog became most famous for during the Second World War was identifying Nazi war criminal SS and *Gestapo* leader Heinrich Himmler after he was captured and arrested on 22 May 1945. Ironically, the very man who had designed the Final Solution was identified by an Irish Jew. However, the following day, Himmler committed suicide by biting on a cyanide capsule before he could be brought to trial for his crimes.

Herzog remained in Germany after the war until he returned to Britain on 12 December 1946, then a major. He relinquished his commission on 5 March 1947 and was subsequently discharged from the British Army. He returned to live in Palestine, and after the formation of the modern state of Israel in 1948, he fought during the Battles of Latrun during the 1948 Arab-Israeli War. Herzog later became head of the Israeli Defence Forces' Military Intelligence Branch and served as defence attaché at the Israeli embassy in the US before retiring from the Israeli Defence Forces with the rank of major-general in 1962. Aged forty-four, he returned to practising law but covered the Six-Day War in 1967 as a military

Dr Fritz Klein, the camp doctor, standing in a mass grave at Belsen. Klein, who was born in Austro-Hungary, was an early member of the Nazi Party and joined the SS in 1943. He worked in Auschwitz-Birkenau for a year from December 1943 where he assisted in the selection of prisoners to be sent to the gas chambers. After a brief period at Neungamme, Klein moved to Belsen in January 1945. Klein was subsequently convicted of two counts of war crimes and executed in December 1945.

commentator for Kol Israel radio news. After the capture of the West Bank, he was then appointed Military Governor of East Jerusalem, Judea and Samaria.

Between 1975 and 1978 he served as Israel's Ambassador to the United Nations before entering politics in 1981. Then, on 22 March 1983 – aged sixty-four – he was elected as Israel's sixth president, an ironic achievement for a man who had nearly destroyed the synagogue in Lennox Street, Dublin in 1925, aged seven at the time. Along with the three Levitas brothers – who Herzog had been good friends with during his youth – the four young boys had been desperate for the Sabbath to finish so they could go out and play on the street, and in their excitement and impatience they accidentally started a fire. Fortunately, however, it was put out and the synagogue was saved.

During his time in office, Herzog became the first Israeli president to make an official visit to Germany. In 1985, during his State Visit to Ireland, he visited his old school – Wesley College – and opened Dublin's Irish Jewish Museum, while also unveiling a sculpture in Sneem, County Kerry in honour of Ireland's fifth president, Cearbhall Ó Dálaigh, who Herzog had been friends with in childhood.

After serving two five-year terms in office, Chaim Herzog from Belfast retired from politics in 1993. He passed away four years later on 17 April 1997 – aged seventy-eight – and now lies buried on Mount Herzl, Jerusalem.

MURDERED

ESTHER 'ETTIE' STEINBERG

Although born in Veretski, Czechoslovakia in January 1914, Esther Steinberg – known as Ettie – came to Ireland with her family in 1926 after a period living in London. She grew up in a house on Raymond Terrace, South Circular Road, Dublin. Ettie became a dressmaker and embroiderer and on 22 July 1937 – then aged twenty-two – she married Vogtjeck Gluck, a goldsmith from Antwerp, in the Greenville Hall synagogue on South Circular Road, Dublin. The couple initially settled in Belgium, but concerned that they were living so close to Germany, they soon moved to Paris, where their son Leon was born on 28 March 1939.

After the invasion of Belgium, Holland, Luxembourg and France on 10 May 1940, and the subsequent fall of France, Ettie went into hiding. For a long time, they never slept in the same house or lodging for more than one night, but then, in 1942, during a quiet period, Ettie became complacent and decided that the family could remain in their current location for a while. It was at this time that the Vichy Government began permitting the

Ettie Steinberg's wedding photo, taken on 22 July 1937 in Dublin. Her husband – Belgian goldsmith Vogtjeck Gluck – is standing to the right.

rounding up and transportation of local Jews to concentration and extermination camps, and while staying in a hotel in Toulouse, Ettie, Vogtjeck and Leon were discovered and arrested. Sadly however, the Steinberg family back in Dublin had just recently secured visas – thanks to the British Home Office in Belfast – that would allow Ettie and her family to leave France and travel to Northern Ireland. However, the visas arrived in Toulouse the day after Ettie and her family were arrested.

They were initially sent to a transit camp at Drancy, outside Paris, and were then transported on into Germany, leaving Drancy on 2 September 1942. While en route, Ettie wrote a postcard to her family back in Ireland and threw it out the carriage window. By a million-to-one chance it was actually picked up by someone, who then posted it. The message was coded, and read, 'Uncle Lechem, we did not find, but we found Uncle Tisha B'av.' 'Lechem' is a Hebrew word for bread, while 'Tisha B'Av' is a Jewish fast day commemorating the destruction of the temple. Ettie was letting her family know that she had not found salvation, but had instead encountered destruction. The Steinbergs wrote to the Red Cross and even to the Vatican in an attempt to find out what had happened to Ettie, but they only found out after the war had ended. The truth was that Ettie arrived – along with her husband and son – at Auschwitz extermination camp on 4 September 1942 and was put to death immediately. Ettie was only twenty-eight years old. Her son, Leon, was three. It is commonly believed that they are the only two Irish Jewish citizens to have been murdered by the Nazis during the Holocaust, but sadly this is not the case.

In 1942, eighty-year-old Mordekhai Gertzog – a shopkeeper who lived in Szczepanow, Poland – was killed by the Nazis in Berezany, Poland. Mordekhai had actually been born in Ireland in 1860. The same year that he died, fifty-three-year-old Annie Rohrbach – who had been living in Berlin – was killed in Sachsenhausen, Germany. Annie was born in County Kerry in 1889, had emigrated to New York in 1921 (she was still there for the 1930 census), but had then moved to live with and help support family in Germany. Similarly, Philip Watchman from Ireland was deported to Germany after Norway was occupied by the Nazis – he had been living in Oslo at the time and was later murdered in Auschwitz. Then there was Dubliner Afraim/Ephraim Saks who was living in Antwerp, Belgium when the war started – he was killed in 1942, aged twenty-seven. Finally, and perhaps most horrifically, siblings Lina, Adam, Anna and Frida Edinger were also all killed during the Holocaust – they were all born in Dublin, and while forty-nine-year-old Adam was living in Zenzkau, Germany prior to the war, his sisters Lina (aged forty-seven), Anna (aged thirty-nine) and Frida (aged thirty-one) had all married and been living as housewives in Wangerin, Germany. All four of them were murdered by the Nazis.

Meanwhile, other Jews who had lived in Ireland for a period before the war also died in the Holocaust. Twenty-year-old Lea Buchholz from Moszczenica, Poland was killed at Auschwitz in 1942 – she had previously lived in Charleville, County Cork, as had forty-nine-year-old Selman Freimann from Gomel, Belorussia, and fifty-one-year-old Natan Schermann from Szczekociny, Poland who both also died in Auschwitz that year. Finally, in 1939, Professor Isaak Waterman – a widower and teacher who had been born in Manchester in 1863, but who had later lived and taught in Trinity College Dublin for many years – travelled from Dublin to visit family in Vienna. He was subsequently arrested by the Nazis and imprisoned in the infamous Theresienstadt Ghetto when he died in 1943, aged seventy-nine. 144,000 Jews were sent to Theresianstadt during the war – 33,000 died of disease, hunger and of a deadly typhus epidemic that swept through the ghetto in 1945, while 88,000 more were sent to Auschwitz and gassed. Only 17,247 survived the war – which included only ninety-three of the 15,000 children who had also been sent there.

These stories prove that Ireland was not untouched by the Holocaust, and that at least eight Irish-born Jews, two more Jews who were Irish citizens, and four who had lived in Ireland for a time were executed by the Nazis. Furthermore, at the Wannsee Conference – a meeting of senior Nazi officials which took place in Berlin on 20 January 1942 – it was decided that, should the opportunity arise, the estimated 4,000 Jews living in Ireland would also be sent to the extermination camps.

AIDING THE SURVIVORS

JACOB 'JACK' WEINGREEN

In 1946, Jacob 'Jack' Weingreen – a professor of Hebrew at Trinity College Dublin – took a leave of absence from his teaching position and travelled to Belsen under the auspices of the

After returning to Ireland from Belsen, Jack Weingreen (pictured here with his wife Bertha in their Jewish Relief Unit uniforms) resumed teaching in Trinity College Dublin – he later excavated in Samaria and had the Weingreen Museum of Biblical Antiquities in Trinity College's Arts and Social Sciences Building named after him in 1977. By then, he had also written A Practical Grammar for Classical Hebrew, *which is still recognized as the foremost work on the subject.*

Jewish Committee for Relief Abroad and the Jewish Relief Unit in an attempt to help the survivors of the Holocaust. His wife, Bertha, was already at Belsen – she was chief welfare officer responsible for all Jewish displaced persons in the British zone of occupation – and when Jack joined her from Dublin, he became the local director of education. Before long, Jack Weingreen had set up a trade school at Belsen which later became a highly respected technical college – the International Jewish Organisation for Rehabilitation through Training (ORT).

Those under their care included concentration camp survivors, but also thousands of Polish Jews who – having returned home from Germany to Poland post-war – had recently fled back into Germany after anti-Semitic attacks had begun taking place in Polish towns. Then there were the children, and when Bertha once visited a hospital for sick child survivors of the Holocaust in Lubeck, Jack later wrote:

> When she entered the small ward, the faces of the children resembled the faces
> of mummies, which can be seen in museums. Instead of arms and fingers lying on
> the blankets, there were sticks, at the end of which were claws. The shock was over-
> whelming and in the corridor Bertha shed bitter tears at what had been done to these
> children, who were in the last stages of hunger and abuse.

However, the Weingreens were also helped by fellow Jews back in Ireland, specifically the Dublin branch of the Jewish Youth Relief Organisation. Jack and Bertha received a crate of toys to help them set up a kindergarten for Jewish children in Berlin, large bales of Donegal tweed that tailors in the displaced persons' camps could make into winter clothing, and linen from the Northern Ireland mills that could be made into nappies for the babies being born to newly married couples.

Jack and Bertha Weingreen made a great difference to the lives of many Jewish survivors of the Holocaust before coming home to Dublin together in 1947. Jack then returned to teaching in Trinity College before retiring in 1979. He later passed away on 11 April 1995. Professor Jacob 'Jack' Weingreen was eighty-eight years old when he died.

After the war, Jewish groups found it extremely difficult to get permission from the Irish government to allow Jewish refugees into the country. The official reason for this – as given in a 1948 Department of Justice memorandum – was that 'any substantial increase in our Jewish population might give rise to an anti-Semitic problem.' However, adding to the 100 Polish Jewish children who had already been brought to Clonyn Castle, County Meath by a London-based Jewish charity – organised by Rabbi Solomon Schonfeld – in 1946, de Valera overruled the Department of Justice and allowed another 150 Jewish children to enter the country in 1948. But it was still an incredibly small number, and stood in contrast to an earlier request to allow 400 Catholic children to enter Ireland from Germany that had been approved immediately.

However, despite the fact that de Valera was later thanked for his support of Ireland's Jews with the planting and dedicating of the 'Éamon de Valera Forest' near Nazareth, Israel in 1966, the Irish Taoiseach shocked Ireland's Jews – and the wider international commu-nity – when he offered his condolences to German Minister Hempel in Dublin after the death of Adolf Hitler in 1945. It was, however, performed solely to remain in keeping with Irish neutrality, but Sir John Maffey – the British Representative to Éire – referred to it as 'unwise'.

William Solomon 'Ginger' Moiselle. Born in Dublin in 1890, Moiselle came from a well-known Irish-Jewish family of Lithuanian origin who were mentioned in James Joyce's Ulysses. *He ran away to sea when he was fourteen years old – rising from seaman to first mate of a ship – before settling in the US where he started work for the Henney Motor Company in 1930. When America entered the Second World War, Moiselle enlisted as a private – by the time the war had ended, he was discharged as a lieutenant-colonel, having been involved in building railways for the US Army. Moiselle then entered the funeral transportation business and went on to sell hearses all over the US (he even wrote a book on the evolution of funeral transportation). Later, 'Ginger' Moiselle retired to his native Dublin with his wife, Rose.*

CHAPTER 9

MODERN WARFARE

'I'm not here to teach you to hurt.
I'm here to teach you to kill.'
**Dermot Michael 'Pat' O'Neill from Newmarket,
County Cork, 1st Special Service Force, speaking to
1st Special Service Force volunteers at Helena,
Montana, 1942**

While the First World War saw the introduction of many technologies and tactics that play a central role in modern warfare, it was during the Second World War that these were truly developed. During the First World War, massed lines of infantry still walked towards the enemy with bayonets fixed – while mounted cavalry waited in the rear to exploit a breakthrough – almost exactly as armies had done over a hundred years before during the days of Wellington and Napoleon. During the Second World War however, special forces soldiers were deployed in strategic raids against enemy installations, airborne paratroopers were dropped by fleets of aircraft, Allied spies operated behind enemy lines, while technology played a greater role on the battlefield than ever before.

On 15 September 1916 – when the Battle of Flers-Courcelette was launched – tanks appeared for the very first time when twenty-five British Mark I tanks advanced from the start line during the attack. On 12 July 1943, 1,500 Russian and German tanks fought the largest tank battle of the Second World War during the Battle of Kursk (where 6,300 tanks in total were present). Meanwhile, the jet fighter and early cruise and ballistic missiles – the V1 and V2 rockets – were developed by the Germans during the war. Perhaps most famously however, while the First World War started with a pistol shot, the Second World War ended with the dropping of two atomic bombs – thereby ushering in the age of atomic weapons. And so, the Second World War was the first truly modern war.

COMMANDO

EDWIN 'ADRIAN' LEE

Born in Glenageary, Dublin, in 1920, Edwin 'Adrian' Lee attended Blackrock College, Dublin and Stoneyhurst College, Lancashire before travelling to Colchester in 1938 and joining the prestigious cavalry regiment 1ˢᵗ The Royal Dragoons as a trooper (private). The regiment was still horsed at this time, and following training in England, Adrian shipped out to join the regiment in their overseas station – Palestine. 1ˢᵗ The Royal Dragoons had been sent out to Palestine to suppress the Arab Revolt that began in 1936, and Adrian had joined them by the time British Prime Minister Neville Chamberlain gave his famous 'Peace in Our Time' speech on 30 September 1938.

When the Second World War broke out, Trooper Adrian Lee and 1ˢᵗ The Royal Dragoons moved to Cairo, Egypt in November 1940. One month later the regiment was finally mechanised, but by then, Adrian had been selected for officer training. However, although he was offered a commission in 1ˢᵗ The Royal Dragoons, he chose to be commissioned into 1ˢᵗ Dorsetshire Regiment (The Dorsets) of 231ˢᵗ Infantry Brigade, stationed in Malta – officers in 1ˢᵗ The Royal Dragoons needed a substantial private income to support the type of social life that they were expected to lead as part of this regiment, and Adrian was simply not rich enough.

Second-Lieutenant Adrian Lee then served throughout the German siege of Malta before leaving the island in November 1942 when 1ˢᵗ Dorsetshire Regiment and 231ˢᵗ Infantry Brigade were brought to North Africa after the Allied victory at the Second Battle of El Alamein. The unit was subsequently attached to the Eighth Army – then preparing for the invasion of Sicily – but around this time, Adrian Lee volunteered to join the Special Boat Section (SBS). The men of the SBS were the Royal Navy's special forces.

Soon a captain, one of Adrian Lee's first missions with the SBS involved Adrian deploying from a submarine with another soldier for a raid against a railway bridge in Sicily on 17 March 1943. After completing their mission, Captain Adrian Lee and his comrade headed to a nearby beach where they were due to be retrieved by a submarine. However, the submarine never arrived. Realising that too much time had passed and that something must be

Trooper Adrian Lee from Glenageary, Dublin of 1ˢᵗ The Royal Dragoons. This photograph was taken in 1938, not long before Adrian travelled to Palestine to join his new regiment.

Captain Adrian Lee from Glenageary, Dublin of No 41 (Royal Marine) Commando, c1944/45. By this time, Adrian had previously served as a trooper with 1st The Royal Dragoons, as an officer with 1st Dorsetshire Regiment throughout the Siege of Malta, and with the Special Boat Section (SBS) during his raid against a Sicilian railway bridge. More recently he had fought with No 41 (Royal Marine) Commando during the Battle of the Scheldt (Walcheren Island), and he was also parachute qualified.

wrong, Adrian and his comrade then started wandering along the beach. They finally came across a fisherman and his family with a boat, and seeing his chance to escape, Adrian – who spoke some Italian – held up the fisherman and ordered everyone to start rowing.

Adrian later wrote an account of what happened next:

We launched the boat and started rowing. I had previously agreed an alternative arrangement for locating the submarine should anything go wrong by using their attack periscope. We were now a couple of miles off-shore in broad daylight and no contact was made with the submarine. I decided to try to row to Malta, some 153 miles. After 24 hours we had only covered 50 miles and had run into bad weather which blew us onto the beach. The boat turned over throwing the three adults, two children and the Corporal and myself into the sea. I did not wait to see what happened to the Italians and also got separated from my Corporal. I found out later that within the hour my Corporal was arrested and subsequently we were both brought before German and Italian interrogators. The Corporal was taken away but was released within 2 years. I was taken before the Sicilian General and was arrested and advised that I would be charged for ill-treating civilians, but nothing came of this and subsequently I was taken to a POW Camp in the North of Italy.

Six months after being captured, an armistice was declared between the Allies and the Italians on 3 September 1943

The Battle for Walcheren Island: Men of the 4th Special Service Brigade – which included Captain Adrian Lee and No 41 (Royal Marine) Commando – wade ashore from landing craft near Flushing to complete the occupation of Walcheren Island. Adrian and his comrades landed further to the west at Westkapelle.

– the day that the Allied invasion of Italy began. As Adrian Lee recorded:

> There were 500 Officers in [my POW] Camp and the Italian Commandant was known to be pro-British and shortly after the arrest of Mussolini he opened the Camp gates and released all the Officers to avoid the Germans taking them to Germany. I got out and managed to avoid the Germans. I did have one other officer with me and

we walked 600 miles, through mountains and rough country to avoid being caught. Unfortunately, the other Officer was caught because he went through a village. I continued and finally caught up with the South African Division outside Naples, who looked after me for a short while.

Captain Adrian Lee was then taken to Bari in south-eastern Italy to be debriefed, and it just so happened that he was debriefed by an Irish officer in the British Army's Intelligence Corps. When the officer asked Adrian where he was from, Adrian replied, 'Silchester Road, Glenageary, Dublin.' The officer then took a hard look at Adrian and asked him, 'You're not the chap who used to jump into Dun Laoghaire baths for a shilling, are you?' As it turned out, he was. Adrian Lee had apparently made a name for himself during his younger days in Dublin.

Adrian was then allowed to return to Ireland for a period of leave – he weighed only 126lbs (9st), having previously suffered from dysentery. However, he quickly became tired of being home and towards the end of 1943 he began ringing the War Office in London to ask them, 'When are you calling me back?' As a result of this, he was recalled to active service. However, he did not return to the SBS, and after attending a parachute course in Wrexham, Wales, he was posted to No 41 (Royal Marine) Commando on 27 October 1944.

On 1 November 1944, Captain Adrian Lee landed with No 41 (Royal Marine) Commando on Walcheren Island – in the mouth of the Scheldt estuary in Holland – as part of Operation Infatuate. Having recently captured Antwerp, the Allies were attempting to open the city to shipping, but the German Fifteenth Army on Walcheren Island had to be neutralised first – Adrian later recalled that when he landed at the beachhead he started running forward; at the same time, the man next to him was shot and killed only feet away. No 41 (Royal Marine) Commando's specific mission was to land at the western end of the island – at Westkapelle – near a

Adrian Lee was not the only Irish commando to fight in the Second World War. Reginald Valentine 'Val' Clery from Booterstown, Dublin – whose uncle, Reginald Francis Clery, had been killed by rebels during the Easter Rising while serving with British forces – served with No 2 Commando in Yugoslavia, Albania and Italy during the war. Afterwards, he began working with the Canadian Broadcasting Corporation in their offices in Toronto, and went on to create the Canadian radio news show As It Happens, which still runs to this day. He also wrote for magazines and newspapers, co-founded Books in Canada in 1971 – a free independent review journal – and published books on a wide range of subjects. Val Clery passed away on 29 September 1996, aged seventy-two.

gap in a local dyke, neutralise the German threat in the area, and then clear the north end of Walcheren Island in order to link up with Canadians advancing from the east. Enemy resistance in the area was heavy, but by 7 November, No 41 (Royal Marine) Commando had achieved their mission. During Operation Infatuate, the Allies had lost 489 killed, 925 wounded, and fifty-nine missing, while their German opponents suffered 1,200 killed and wounded and a further 2,900 taken prisoner.

No 41 (Royal Marine) Commando remained in Holland for the rest of the war, after which it entered Germany as part of the post-war occupation forces. By then however, Captain Adrian Lee had changed unit several times before returning to Britain. After the war, he then left the regular army but continued to serve in the Parachute Regiment TA (initially 11th Parachute Regiment between 1947 and 1956) while working in the offices of British Airways at Heathrow, going on to become their chief of industrial relations. He later married and had three children, and then parachuted into Arnhem on one occasion as part of Operation Market Garden anniversary commemorations. In 1964 – now a lieutenant-colonel in the 144th Independent Parachute Brigade Group (TA) – Adrian was awarded an OBE (*London Gazette*, 13 June 1964), and he attended a ceremony in Buckingham Palace to receive it, while on 24 April 1965 he was made an honorary colonel of the Montana National Guard 'in recognition of loyal and distinguished service to his Country; in deep appreciation of the personal sacrifice and the long journey he has made to be with us; to signify the bonds of friendship and brotherhood between his Nation and ours, and the British Territorial Army and the Montana National Guard.'

Finally, on 1 August 2005, Edwin 'Adrian' Lee from Glenageary, Dublin – who had variously served as a cavalry trooper, an infantry officer, a special forces soldier with the SBS, and then a Royal Marines commando during the Second World War – died in St Peter's Hospital in Chertsey, Surrey. He had been living in nearby Weybridge for many years, and he was eighty-four years old at the time of his death. He was buried with full military honours.

RAIDER

MILES PATRICK MARTIN

Swift hit-and-run raids were a large part of special forces' duties during the Second World War, and while Miles Patrick Martin was not a commando, he accompanied them on one of the most well-known raids of the Second World War – the Dieppe Raid. Codenamed Operation Jubilee, it was launched against Dieppe on the northern coast of France on 19

Temporary Surgeon Lieutenant Miles Patrick Martin from Killeshandra, County Cavan, around the time of the Dieppe Raid.

August 1942, and involved landings by Canadian troops, US Army Rangers, 'A' Commando of the Royal Marines (later renamed No 40 Commando), and No 3 and No 4 Commando.

Born in Killeshandra, County Cavan in January 1911, Miles Patrick Martin was the son of a local Church of Ireland vicar. He joined the Royal Navy in the 1930s and was stationed in China when he later heard that his father had passed away. Martin then returned to Ireland and attended Trinity College Dublin where he studied medicine. In 1939, he travelled to London where he completed his studies and qualified as a doctor. He married that same year and in 1940 the couple had a son.

On 19 August 1942 thirty-one-year-old Temporary Surgeon Lieutenant Miles Patrick Martin found himself floating off the French coast near Dieppe aboard LCF(L) [Landing Craft Flak (Large)] No 2 – one of several vessels that would support the landing. The aim of Operation Jubilee was to capture and hold a major port for a short period of time – in order to prove that such an objective was possible – gain POWs and intelligence, while destroying enemy defences, strategic targets, and vital port structures and equipment. 10,500 Allied troops faced 1,500 German infantrymen of the 302nd Static Infantry Division in Dieppe. However, other German units in the surrounding area had all possible landing areas targeted with machine gun, mortar and artillery fire, while the *Luftwaffe* still controlled the skies over northern France. When the Allies launched their assault, the Germans were waiting and ready.

No 4 Commando and the US Army Rangers succeeded in neutralising enemy coastal guns west of Dieppe at Varengeville as planned, but No 3 Commando were attacked by German S-boats as their landing craft approached the beaches, and they failed to destroy their targets – another German coastal battery located at Berneval, east of Dieppe. Meanwhile, due to heavy German fire and the dense enemy beach defences, Canadian infantry and supporting tanks failed to advance in the main invasion area. The crews of all twenty-nine tanks that landed were either killed or taken POW. Allied troops were pinned down and massacred on the beaches, while other landing craft were blown off course and landed their troops in the wrong place.

Meanwhile, the captain of LCF(L) No 2 – which Miles Patrick Martin was aboard – brought his ship in as close to the invasion beaches as he could in order to give close support to the Allied troops. However, the Germans targeted the vessel and pounded it with artillery. With the captain soon killed and LCF(L) No 2 and all its guns disabled, the ship finally began to sink.

As Miles Patrick Martin's son – Michael – recently recalled though:

> My father was on board LCF(L) 2 and took over command when the other officers were either killed or incapacitated. With the ship on fire and immovable he gave the order to abandon ship.

Martin ensured that the survivors stayed together, and after a half an hour in the water under enemy machine gun fire, they were rescued by the destroyer HMS *Calpe*.

New Zealander Wallace Reyburn – who covered the Dieppe Raid as a journalist for the Canadian Broadcasting Corporation, and who was nearly killed during the battle – later wrote a book entitled *Rehearsal for Invasion* in which he recalled that, after the battle, he met two badly wounded Royal Navy officers in the ward-room of HMS *Calpe*.

One of them told Reyburn about events after the sinking of LCF(L) No 2:

> There were half a dozen or so of us on the raft. We were all badly knocked about.

The disaster of Dieppe: Scattered dead lie on the beach amongst burning tanks and landing craft after the Allied raid, 19 August 1942.

It's a terrible feeling lying there in agony like that, with all hell popping round you. Some of the men wanted to jump into the water and just swim off – anywhere. But we stopped them. When you're hurt and you've got nothing to do but just lie where you are you get an awfully hopeless, helpless feeling …

But then the M.O. [Medical Officer] came swimming up to us. He climbed on to the raft, and you've no idea what a difference that made to our spirits. We were bucked up right away. He examined each of us and told us what was wrong. There wasn't much he could do about anything; he didn't have any equipment. But I dunno … you seemed to get the reassuring feeling that you were under medical care, that you were being looked after … He's wonderful, that M.O. His name's Martin. He's on the ship here now, practically dropping from fatigue. He and this ship's M.O. are the only doctors on board, apart from sick-bay attendants, and there are hundreds of wounded and dying on board, as you know [there were 278 wounded soldiers onboard, while a quarter of HMS *Calpe*'s crew had also been wounded during the raid]. He hasn't rested a second. He just keeps going back and forth along the decks, up and down the companion-ways, in and out of the sick-bays, looking after the men. He's coming back to have another look at us, see how we're getting along. He'll be here soon, and you'll meet him.

Wallace Reyburn did wait for Miles Patrick Martin to turn up, and he recalled:

Martin arrived in the ward-room in a few minutes. He was dressed in a sports jacket, grey flannels, and white tennis shoes – clothes he'd borrowed from another officer on board. He was small-built, young, good-looking. He sank down on to the bench that stood round the front of the fireplace and talked to the two men on the couch. He was soft-spoken, and there was a warmth about him. A good guy – you could tell it in a second. You didn't need to be told he was tired. He was utterly worn out; his head swayed from side to side as he spoke. Somebody said to him, 'You should rest up a minute or two. Here, let's get you a drink.'

Martin nodded. 'Yes, I think it would be a good idea.' But he didn't pause long over his drink. He soon went back to looking over the condition of the men in the ward-room. When he came to me I said I didn't feel like letting him waste his time looking at the little nick I had in my bottom. 'Let's have a look at it.' He decided it might merely be a nick made by a shell-splinter in passing or the fragment might have gone right in. He advised me to have an X-ray taken when I got back.

The Dieppe Raid had begun at approximately 0500hrs on 19 August 1942. By 1400hrs, the Allies had abandoned Dieppe and evacuated their remaining troops. Out of the 6,086 men who landed and went into action that day, 3,623 were killed, wounded, or taken POW by the enemy (the Germans only suffered 311 killed and 280 wounded).

The Allies also lost 100 aircraft while the Royal Navy lost thirty-three landing craft and one destroyer. Operation Jubilee was a complete disaster, but it was the losses suffered at Dieppe that convinced the Allies that only a large-scale operation with lengthy, detailed planning would be able to breach the walls of Fortress Europe, and that for such an assault to work they must first attain total air superiority and defeat the *Luftwaffe*. It was this realisation that ultimately led to the planning of Operation Overlord and the D-Day landings.

Meanwhile, for his brave and selfless actions on 19 August 1942, Temporary Surgeon Lieutenant Miles Patrick Martin from Killeshandra, County Cavan was awarded the Distinguished Service Order, which he was later presented with by King George VI at Buckingham Palace. The following year, however, he was invalided out of the Royal Navy. Miles Patrick Martin then began working as a GP until he retired in 1984, aged seventy-three. He passed away a few years later.

MARTIAL ARTS MEETS MODERN WARFARE

DERMOT MICHAEL 'PAT' O'NEILL

While the Second World War was also fought with cutting-edge science, there was at least one Allied soldier who mixed ancient tradition with modern warfare. Dermot Michael 'Pat' O'Neill was born in Newmarket, County Cork in 1905. His father, Francis, was a district inspector with the Royal Irish Constabulary (RIC), but after Francis O'Neill died in 1919, fourteen-year-old Pat became a cabin boy on a steamship bound for Asia. For the next few years he sailed throughout the Far East, until he finally decided to leave the sea and return to the land. He settled in Shanghai, China – where his older brother, Frank, had previously worked as a bank teller.

Then, in 1925 – aged twenty – Pat O'Neill joined the Shanghai Municipal Police (SMP). This force contained over 5,000 constables – a mixture of Chinese, Japanese, Sikhs, British, Americans, Russians and others – and was responsible for dealing with Shanghai's notorious criminal underworld. It was the SMP who actually pioneered the study of ballistics, along with the use of body armour, police dogs, police special forces and riot control.

During his six-weeks of recruit training, O'Neill also took courses in jiu jitsu and foreign languages, and then, on his first day as a constable, he was involved in a gunfight with Chinese gang members. However, aside from the very real fights that he found himself involved in on the streets of Shanghai, O'Neill also began to develop his martial arts skills. He took up judo in 1929 (while also studying Chinese Boxing and Chinese foot fighting) and competed in Japan as part of the SMP judo team. In 1934, he was awarded a third dan after a competition in Tokyo, which made him the only foreign non-resident of Japan to hold this rank at the time.

O'Neill ultimately served in the SMP for thirteen years – rising to the rank of sub-inspector and becoming a member of the special branch – while also serving in the Shanghai Municipal Police Reserve Unit (SMP special forces) where he learned combat shooting. In 1938 O'Neill became security chief at the British Embassy in Tokyo, Japan (he became a fourth dan in judo the same year). However, after the US placed an embargo on oil shipments to Japan in July 1941 and it became obvious that the Japanese would soon retaliate, Pat O'Neill snuck aboard a fishing boat due to sail to the Philippines on 5 October 1941. There, he boarded another ship and helped to evacuate women and children from the Dutch East Indies and New Guinea before landing in Sydney, Australia. He remained here – living with his brother Frank – until in early 1942 he received a telegram from William Fairbairn. Fairbairn had previously been the assistant commissioner of the SMP and had commanded the Shanghai Municipal Police Reserve Unit. Fairbairn was currently putting his SMP skills to good use – he was helping to train a new combined unit of American and Canadian commandos that was being set up, a unit that became known as the 1st Special Service Force – and he had been asked to recommend an instructor who could teach similar skills to the OSS (Office of Strategic Services), the forerunner of the CIA. He had recommended O'Neill for the job, and so in May 1942, Pat O'Neill also came to America.

After a period serving as a close combat instructor to the OSS, O'Neill decided that he wanted to help train the 1st Special Service Force. And so, after his request was approved, he joined the unit as a civilian instructor at their camp near Helena, Montana in August. The 1st Special Service Force had been given a seven-month timeframe in which the men had to become paratroopers, skiers and demolitions experts, while also learning advanced weapons handling and close combat, and so O'Neill designed a condensed programme of training for the troops that focused on disarming the enemy, attacking the eyes and throat or kicking the groin or knees in order to throw him to the ground, and then taking him out as aggressively and quickly as possible with kicks to the head. He also taught other classes on knife fighting and combat shooting, and the programme later became known as 'The O'Neill System of Close Combat' (during this time, O'Neill also suggested the blade profile for the famous V-42 commando fighting knife).

In 1943 – following his marriage to Mary Hardin on 12 March – the OSS requested that O'Neill return to them. However, the commanding officer of 1st Special Service Force – Lieutenant-Colonel Robert Frederick – managed to get O'Neill commissioned into the US Army as a captain on 19 June 1943, in order to prevent the OSS from recalling him.

On 10 July 1943, 1st Special Service Force set sail for its first mission – it was due to invade the Japanese-occupied island of Kiska in the Aleutian Islands, off the coast of Alaska. Captain Dermot Michael 'Pat' O'Neill was initially detailed to remain behind in a support role, but he requested permission to accompany the unit into action and it was ultimately approved. However, although Kiska was abandoned by the enemy before the American and Canadian commandos arrived, O'Neill and another officer were swept out to sea during the operation. Freezing and exhausted, they were rescued a day later, having both nearly drowned.

After Kiska, 1st Special Service Force was sent to Casablanca, Morocco, in November. On 19 November they landed in Naples, Italy, and were then ordered to assault two heavily fortified German positions – Monte la Difensa and Monte la Remetanea – in the mountains along the Bernhardt Line.

On 2 December, the attack – during which Pat O'Neill served as both an intelligence officer and Colonel Frederick's bodyguard – was launched in the freezing rain after a heavy preliminary bombardment by Allied artillery. Although the staff of US Fifth Army had expected 1st Special Service Force to take between four and five days to capture Monte la Difensa, they had secured the summit within two hours. The Germans had considered the sheer 200-foot northface of Monte la Difensa to be impregnable. Previous attempts to scale it had failed.

It took longer to capture Monte la Remetanea, however, but by 9 December, it was in Allied hands. 1st Special Service Force continued to fight in the Italian mountains until January 1944. By the time they were taken out of the line, they had suffered ninety-one killed, 313 wounded, nine missing, and 116 cases of exhaustion (a casualty rate of seventy-seven percent).

Captain Dermot Michael 'Pat' O'Neill and 1st Special Service Force then joined the fight at Anzio on 1 February 1944. They took over the Mussolini Canal sector and began sending out aggressive night-time patrols – which O'Neill often went out on – to capture prisoners and gather intelligence. In fact, because of how dangerous the 1st Special Service Force patrols were, the Germans soon withdrew in the area by half a mile, and a note was found on one enemy prisoner – issued by German commanders – which informed the Germans that they were 'fighting an elite Canadian-American Force. They are treacherous, unmerciful and clever. You cannot afford to relax. The first soldier or group of soldiers capturing one of these men will be given a ten day furlough.' This German note had possibly been issued in response to stickers – which depicted 1st Special Service Force's unit insignia along with a slogan in German – that the American and Canadian commandos used to stick on the bodies of enemy sentries that they killed on their patrols. The slogan was '*Das dicke Ende kommt noch*,' which meant 'The worst is yet to come.'

During this time, a German journal was also retrieved that contained the entry: 'The Black Devils are all around us every time we come into the line. We never hear them come.'

And so, 1ˢᵗ Special Service Force was nicknamed The Black Devils, or The Devil's Brigade.

After ninety-nine days at Anzio without relief – during which Pat O'Neill was made a US citizen – 1ˢᵗ Special Service Force were involved in the fight towards Rome after the breakout from the Anzio beachhead began on 25 May. They were then one of the first Allied units to enter Rome on 4 June, having been ordered to secure seven bridges in the city and prevent their destruction by the retreating Germans.

On 14 August, they landed on the islands of Port Cros – where they lost nine men during a battle to capture five forts on the island from the Germans – and Îles d'Hyères off the south coast of France as part of Operation Dragoon. By 7 September, they were positioned in a defensive role along France's border with Italy, while O'Neill became the provost marshal of Monte Carlo, with his headquarters in the Metropole Hotel.

Finally, on 5 December 1944, 1ˢᵗ Special Service Force was officially disbanded, its members being mostly reassigned to American or Canadian airborne units. In its short operational history, 1ˢᵗ Special Service Force – a unit of 1,800 soldiers – had inflicted 12,000 casualties on the Germans and captured 7,000 prisoners.

Captain Dermot Michael 'Pat' O'Neill was not posted to a US airborne or infantry unit however. He was assigned to the provost marshal's section of US Tenth Army and sent to join them on Okinawa. When the Japanese finally surrendered and the Second World War ended, O'Neill then served in Japan as a member of General MacArthur's staff at Supreme Commander for the Allied Powers (SCAP) Headquarters. Now a major and also a recipient of the Bronze Star, O'Neill was finally discharged from the US Army in February 1946. He then returned to the US, but after he and his wife divorced, he decided to settle in Japan.

Pat began work as a police investigator for the Public Safety Division of SCAP Headquarters, and in 1947 he became a 'Godan' or fifth degree black belt in Kodokan Judo – making him possibly the only non-Japanese person in the world to hold this rank at the time. That same year, he helped to introduce standardised close combat training for the Japanese police force, while developing an interest in the Aikido martial art. He worked for the US State Department during this time, and apparently visited Vietnam at some point in the late 1950s.

In 1961, Dermot Michael 'Pat' O'Neill left Japan for the last time and began teaching close combat skills to pilots at the Air Commando School at the United States Air Force Hurlburt Field base in Fort Walton Beach, Florida. His techniques were soon a standard part of US Army recruit training, and by 1971 they were included in the *US Army Field Manual*. In the mid 1960s O'Neill began instructing at the International Police Academy in Washington DC, and was approached by the United States Marine Corps to set up a close combat programme for instructors. O'Neill then became the Head of Development and Instruction of Close Combat at Marine Corps Base Quantico in Virginia. After teaching there for several years, he returned to the International Police Academy before retiring in the early 1970s – although he still frequently acted as a consultant when needed.

Dermot Michael 'Pat' O'Neill from Newmarket, County Cork stayed living in the Washington DC area for the remainder of his life. In 1985, aged eighty, he sadly suffered a fall in his kitchen and was taken to hospital. He developed pneumonia, along with other complications, and passed away on 11 August that year. His body was cremated, and his ashes were interred in Arlington National Cemetery. Having experienced an extraordinary military career and literally fought his way around the world, he is a legend in US military close combat circles, yet completely unknown in his native Ireland.

SECRET AGENT

MAUREEN PATRICIA 'PADDY' O'SULLIVAN

Another aspect of modern warfare was the entry of women into military forces throughout the world. The First World War had seen the setting up of the Women's Royal Naval Service (known as the 'Wrens') in Britain, while nurses had served on the front lines after 1915, but the Second World War saw them fight. Outside of Russia – where 300,000 women served in all of the various combat roles and were often fully integrated with male soldiers – the US and Britain allowed women to volunteer to fight as anti-aircraft gunners on the home fronts. Meanwhile, along with reviving the Wrens, the Women's Auxiliary Air Force (WAAF) and the Auxiliary Territorial Service (ATS) were set up in Britain – these were non-combat organisations but still part of the British Armed Forces – while the Women's Army Auxiliary Corps (later the Women's Army Corps) was formed in the US, along with the US Navy's WAVES (Women Accepted for Volunteer Emergency Service) and the Marine Corps' Women's Reserve. However, in Britain, many women also volunteered to join the Special Operations Executive (SOE), an organisation whose members conducted guerrilla warfare while aiding resistance movements behind enemy lines. During the Second World War, one of the SOE's top secret agents was Maureen Patricia 'Paddy' O'Sullivan.

Born in Dublin, in January 1918, Maureen's father was a journalist and editor of the *Freeman's Journal* – at the time, it was Ireland's oldest nationalist newspaper, having been founded in 1763. However, because of its moderate nationalist opinion, its printing presses were attacked and destroyed by the anti-Treaty IRA in March 1922, just before the start of the Irish Civil War. It managed to resume production not long after, but in 1924 it merged with the *Irish Independent*.

Maureen Patricia 'Paddy' O'Sullivan from Dublin – one of the forty women who joined F Section of the Special Operations Executive (SOE) during the Second World War. She is pictured here with her husband – Walter Eric Alvey – post-war.

In the same year that Maureen was born, her mother – who was from Brittany, France – died of Spanish flu. When her father later remarried, Maureen was then sent to be educated on the Continent around 1925 – where she attended schools in Courtrai, Ostend, Bruges and Brussels in Belgium and another in Paris – and by the time the Second World War broke out in 1939 she had trained as a nurse in London and was now attending the Commercial College in Dublin while living in Rathmines. She had also lost a brother – Paddy – who had fought and been killed while serving with republican forces during the Spanish Civil War, while another brother – Donald – was already a career soldier with the British Army, and a third – John – would later serve in the Palestine police force during the war before becoming a police chief in Nigeria until the country gained independence on 1 October 1960.

On 7 July 1941 twenty-three-year-old Maureen joined the WAAF and was posted to RAF Compton Bassett in Wiltshire as an aircraft handler. On 8 December 1943 she became a section officer (the equivalent of an RAF flying officer) and trained as a wireless operator. Then, on 17 March 1944, she volunteered for the SOE, but due to the desperate need for wireless operators, she was given a mission and parachuted into occupied France in the early hours of 23 March after only six days of SOE training. She jumped near Limoges in dense fog (even though the pilot suggested that they abort the mission due to the bad weather), and according to her son – John Alvey – her parachute became tangled, she landed on top of a cow in the middle of a herd, and then hit the ground and lost consciousness as two wireless sets and bundles of supplies, also dropped from the same aircraft, began landing around her. As recorded in *The Heroines of the SOE* by Beryl E Escott, Maureen later claimed that 'her life [was saved by] the bundles of French bank notes [2 million Francs in total] she was carrying at her back.' When she woke up, she gathered her equipment and headed towards local members of the French resistance who were waiting for her half a mile away.

Maureen, whose codename was 'Josette', was soon sending messages to Britain on behalf of two brothers – Percy and Edmund Mayer – who ran a resistance network named 'Fireman' in Angoulême (she also sent messages for Edmund Mayer's 'Warder' network in south Indre). Maureen's cover story for having suddenly appeared in the region was that she was a '*dame de compagnie*' of a Parisian doctor – she assisted him in surgery and also took care of his children – and that she had come to look in the Creuse area for a lost Belgian parent. She could speak fluent French and decent German and adopted the false name Micheline Marcelle Simonet. Maureen fit right in, and so she began her work of encoding messages for the resistance and forwarding them to Britain using one of seven wireless sets that she had hidden in various locations. However, her work was extremely dangerous and risky. If she was ever discovered by the Germans, she would be tortured and then executed, and Maureen certainly had her fair share of close calls.

On one occasion, Maureen was handling a microfilm message while having some supper when suddenly a German soldier entered the house she was staying in. Maureen pushed the message to the bottom of her soup bowl, but the German did not leave immediately. Instead, he started talking to Maureen, who was forced to keep taking spoonfuls of soup periodically so as not to arouse suspicion. She was terrified that she would reach the bottom of her soup bowl and expose the message before he left, but fortunately the soldier did not stay for too long.

Maureen also used to cycle long distances – up to thirty-seven miles a day – to deliver her messages to various people within the Fireman network. One day, while cycling through the French countryside with one of her wireless sets in a case on her bike, she came across a German check point. The guard demanded that she open her case and Maureen was terrified that she would be found out, but when a German officer arrived, Maureen began flirting with him as best she could – even lying that she would meet him later that night. Luckily, the officer was so taken by her that he simply let her pass. However, he did ask what was in the case, to which Maureen replied, 'Oh! A wireless, of course!' after which they both laughed and she cycled off.

Maureen was, ironically for a special agent, terrible at map reading and she regularly suffered from ill health with her lungs and chest, but on D-Day she was extremely busy sending and receiving messages as part of the Allies' attempt to co-ordinate the activities of resistance groups throughout France. The Fireman network played a large role in slowing the advance of 2nd SS Panzer Division *Das Reich* towards Normandy when the invasion was launched, and later disrupted German attempts to retreat east from France in August. After France was subsequently liberated, Maureen was no longer needed there and so she returned to Britain on 5 October 1944. She was now twenty-six years old, and had sent over 332 coded messages during her time on active service.

By 1945, there were plans to send Maureen into Germany, but when the Allies crossed the Rhine in March that year and her cover was also blown by friends who passed on her story to the press, her mission was aborted. Instead, on 16 June, she was posted to SOE Force 136 in Calcutta, India as a liaison officer with the French. Then, as recorded in the *London Gazette* of 4 September 1945, she was awarded an MBE Civil. It was while serving in India that she met Walter Eric Alvey – a former SOE training officer. The couple married, and soon after they returned to Britain where they settled in Ilkley, West Yorkshire.

The couple went on to have two sons – John and Robin – and while Maureen worked as a wife and mother during their younger years, when her sons went on to boarding school she became a French teacher in a local school. She also gave talks on behalf of the RAF benevolent fund in order to help them raise money. However, as her son John remembered, because Maureen's wartime service was 'more glamorous' than her husband's, Walter Alvey became very jealous of his wife – which led to difficulties with their marriage. John also recalled that – unlike other children at the time – he played pretend parachuting as a child, a game inspired by his mother's wartime adventures, not his father's.

Maureen Patricia 'Paddy' O'Sullivan later appeared on the first episode of an ITV television programme called 'Women of Bravery' in 1957 – she was thirty-nine years old at the time. Her husband died in 1970 and then, in the 1990s, Maureen appears to have developed Alzheimer's disease, after which she ended up in a nursing home. She passed away on 5 March 1994 – aged seventy-six. One of the SOE's most successful spies, she served for five months in German-occupied France when the average life-expectancy of a

SOE agent at the time was six weeks. However, while Maureen Patricia 'Paddy' O'Sullivan had a particularly incredible military career during the war, it must be remembered that thousands of Irish women are known to have volunteered to serve in the British forces during 1939–1945. In fact, while 2,152 joined from Northern Ireland, 3,761 women from southern Ireland also volunteered, making a total of 5,913 – a significant contribution by any standard.

AIRBORNE

SAM KENDRICK

Finally, there were the airborne paratroopers – the elite infantrymen of the Allied armies. Most of the combatant countries that would fight the Second World War began experimenting with airborne units in the 1930s, but it was Germany that led the way when the war began. German *Fallschirmjägers* (meaning 'parachute fighters') parachuted into Norway in 1940, and were also deployed by parachute, plane and glider during the Battle of France. However, after suffering heavy casualties during the Battle of Crete in 1941 – in which 14,000 *Fallschirmjägers* were deployed – Hitler banned any future large-scale airborne operations, regardless of the fact that his forces had actually won the battle.

Ironically, it was the success of the *Fallschirmjägers* on Crete that prompted Britain and the US to begin training large airborne forces for use in the war, with Britain setting up the 1st and 6th Airborne Divisions, and the US the 11th, 13th and 17th, along with the more famous 82nd and 101st Airborne Divisions. (In fact, during the Second World War, John 'Jack' Grier from Granard, County Longford – a US paratrooper with US Airborne Command – held the American record for free parachute jumps with 102 successful landings.) Aside from small raiding parties and limited deployments, the first large-scale deployment of Allied airborne troops took place during the invasion of Sicily, 3,500 paratroopers then jumped in support of the Salerno landings in Italy, and then – most famously – 24,000 airborne soldiers descended on Normandy in the early hours of D-Day. However, it was Operation Market Garden that saw the largest deployment of paratroopers during the war.

At the end of August 1944, the Allies had pursued the retreating Germans out of France and into Holland. However, the Allies were still primarily being supplied from the Mulberry artificial harbours on their D-Day invasion beaches, and since they had destroyed much of northern France's rail network in the lead up to D-Day, the Allies had to transport all of their supplies by truck along supply lines now hundreds of miles long. By 30 August,

A frequently reproduced image of British airborne paratroopers en route to Arnhem aboard a C-47 aircraft, 17 September 1944. In fact, Private Sam Kendrick from Bridgetown, County Wexford is actually in the photograph – eighteen-year-old Sam is fourth from the left (his face is clearly visible just to the right of the soldier with no helmet on). This means that these paratroopers are men of 1st Parachute Regiment, 1st Airborne Division.

they were forced to halt offensive operations due to supply shortages, and even though they soon captured the much nearer deep-water port of Antwerp on 4 September, it could not be utilised as the Germans were still in control of the Scheldt estuary that led from Antwerp to the sea.

Field Marshal Montgomery then argued to General Eisenhower that if he was allocated all available resources and allowed to make one large-scale concentrated attack, he could push through Holland, cross the Rhine into Germany and cut off the industrially important Ruhr region, thereby ending the war by Christmas. Eisenhower ultimately agreed to the operation, but he then insisted that it would only be given 'limited [supply] priority'. Furthermore, Operation Market Garden was approved on 10 September and launched on 17 September. This meant that the planning phase was only one week long, whereas previous operations on this scale had taken months to plan and rehearse. With so little preparation, a lot could potentially go wrong.

The operation was divided into two parts. For Operation Market, three Allied airborne divisions – 34,600 paratroopers in total – would deploy near towns along the Dutch Highway 69 (the Allied axis of advance) and capture bridges over rivers and canals in each vicinity before the Germans had a chance to destroy them. Closest to the current Allied lines, the US 101st Airborne Division would parachute into Eindhoven and secure the bridges in nearby Son and Veghel, the US 82nd Airborne Division would capture bridges further away at Grave and Nijmegen, while furthest from the Allied lines, the British 1st Airborne Division (along with the Polish 1st Independent Parachute Brigade) would land at Arnhem and secure the road bridge there along with the rail bridge at nearby Oosterbeek. Meanwhile, for Operation Garden, the 5,000 tanks and other vehicles of British XXX Corps – which would be led by 2nd and 3rd Irish Guards – would advance up Highway 69 to reinforce the paratroopers at each location along their route and secure the bridges before ultimately breaking out from Arnhem at the end of the line and entering Germany.

When the 1,759 Allied aircraft carrying paratroopers, towing gliders, or transporting vehicles, artillery, ammunition or supplies to Eindhoven, Nijmegen or Arnhem took off on 17 September 1944, aboard one of the planes heading for Arnhem was Private Sam Kendrick of 1st Parachute Regiment from Bridgetown, County Wexford. Born in 1926, Sam travelled to England in 1940 – aged fourteen at the time – and soon started work on a large poultry farm of 16,000 hens and 12,000 table birds in Worchester owned by Hugh Jefferies from Wexford, who had served as a corporal and later risen to the rank of lieutenant-colonel while serving in the Worcestershire Regiment during the First World War. (His only son, also Hugh Jefferies, died in the Second World War on 19 May 1940 – aged twenty-four – while serving as a captain with 1st Royal Irish Fusiliers during the Battle of France. He is buried in Outer Communal Cemetery, Belgium.) Only Sam and another man named

Frank Green were employed there to do all the labouring on the farm.

In 1942, at the age of sixteen, Sam joined the Royal Navy as a boy seaman and was posted to Pembroke where Short Sunderland flying boats took off from to hunt German U-boats at sea – it was Sam's job during this time to take dead and wounded men off the aircraft when they returned from their missions. Then, in 1943 – due to the fact that the Royal Navy had plenty of men whereas the British Army still had a demand for more troops – Sam volunteered to transfer over to the army in Worcester (he was one of many men to do so at the time).

Sam initially wanted to join the Parachute Regiment but – at only seventeen years old – he was too young to do so. Instead, he was posted to 6th (Young Soldiers Battalion) Royal Irish Fusiliers in Ballymena, County Antrim, and took part in an intensive six weeks PT course in Belfast where he had to drag a 6-pounder gun (as part of a seven-man team) everywhere that he went during the course – to meals, to the latrine, everywhere.

Battalions of the Royal Inniskilling Fusiliers and the Royal Ulster Rifles were also stationed in Ballymena at this time, and Sam recalled that he and his fellow soldiers had been warned to be wary of IRA men who had come across the border from southern Ireland to cause trouble. However, following an incident on guard duty when Sam accidently shot and wounded one of his own officers – when the officer refused to halt as he approached in the dark – Sam's earlier request to join the Parachute Regiment was finally approved by his outraged battalion commander.

Sam completed jump school training, advanced map reading and other courses at Hardwick Hall in Chesterfield, Derbyshire and then earned his wings after performing eight qualifying jumps at RAF Ringway near Manchester. He joined a company of 1st Parachute Regiment – stationed at Grimsthorpe Castle, Lincolnshire – as a replacement in their Assault Pioneers Platoon. This platoon was armed with a variety of heavy weapons, including flamethrowers, and it was this weapon which Sam soon began training to use.

In September 1944, 1st Parachute Regiment and the rest of 1st Airborne Division were detailed to take part in Operation Market Garden. Initially, eighteen-year-old Private Sam Kendrick was not selected to go. However, a few hours before the mission was due to be launched, another flamethrower operator went AWOL, and Sam's platoon commander – Lieutenant William Sutton – managed to get approval for Sam to take the AWOL soldier's place.

And so, at 1100hrs on 17 September 1944, Sam took off from RAF Folkingham:

> The whole place was lit up with planes. And about ten past one we came in over Holland – very quiet – but the pilot shouted back down ... that we're in enemy territory. One gun fired at us – that's all, just one – and I don't know what the hell height we jumped because I'd a blinking kit bag on me ... and I'd a flamethrower in there, and a Sten gun.

Sam was supposed to release this kit bag from his body once he jumped and let it hang beneath him on a twenty-foot rope as he descended.

> I jumped out and Christ Almighty I just barely got it off my leg when I hit the ground. I must've been jumping at about 350 feet.

Sam recalled that one comrade broke his leg and another ended up dangling from his parachute in a tree, but 1st Parachute Regiment and 1st Airborne Division were soon on the ground.

> You look at the DZ [Drop Zone], hundreds and hundreds of the troops, and you said how the hell are you going to find your way to your own. But what they done was [they used] coloured lights ... We were a blue light flashing in the woods ... The only thing left on the DZ after we'd cleared it were women cutting up the parachutes to make clothes.

Four British paratroopers moving through a shell-damaged house in Oosterbeek, to which they had retreated after being driven out of Arnhem, 23 September 1944.

Silk was almost impossible to come by in wartime Europe, and thousands of used para-chutes were obviously an extremely exciting sight to many Dutch women!

The drop zone that 1st Parachute Regiment had landed on was DZ 'X', roughly six miles to the west of the centre of Arnhem and near the smaller town of Oosterbeek. While other battalions of the Parachute Regiment advanced to secure Oosterbeek and Arnhem, along with the nearby bridges over the River Nederrijn (Lower Rhine) – the rail bridge at Oosterbeek and the road bridge in Arnhem – Private Sam Kendrick and 1st Parachute Regiment, under the command of Lieutenant-Colonel David Dobie, were initially kept in brigade reserve. However, at 1530hrs they were ordered to head north, cross a local railway line, and secure the area to the northwest of Arnhem.

As dark fell en route, Sam was convinced he could hear foreign voices in the shadows. His commanding officer, Lieutenant Sutton, dismissed his fears:

> 'Don't be silly', he said, 'You're imagining these things. Get on with it.' All of a
> sudden the whole place opened up. Oh my God, the whole place opened up. Mortars,
> machine gun fire, everything.

1st Parachute Regiment had advanced to the Arnhem-Ede road and had run straight into five German tanks, fifteen half-tracks, and enemy infantry. Sam dived for cover into a nine-inch deep ditch at the bottom of the road embankment while German mortars and *Nebelwerfer* rockets detonated on the road above him. Sam was armed with a flamethrower, which meant he was carrying a large quantity of fuel on his back. If a round or a piece of shrapnel hit the canister, Sam and anyone near him would explode in flames. Luckily, this did not happen – although Sam was wounded in the foot by shrapnel and his boot filled with blood.

During the fighting Lieutenant Sutton was also wounded in the head by shrapnel. He survived, but that was the last Sam saw of him. Sam's platoon sergeant – Sergeant John McKnight from Kirkconnel, Dumfriesshire – then took over command of the platoon.

Unable to advance any further north, Lieutenant-Colonel Dobie ordered 1st Para-chute Regiment to turn south and head towards Oosterbeek. 3rd Parachute Regiment had encountered strong German resistance in the town, but 2nd Parachute Regiment had actu-ally managed to make it through to Arnhem and capture the north end of the road bridge. Dobie planned to link up with 3rd Parachute Regiment and press on towards Arnhem in order to reinforce and support 2nd Parachute Regiment at the bridge. It was a plan that was ultimately impossible to achieve.

The poor Allied planning was worsened by the fact that, in Arnhem, elements of the 9th SS Panzer Division *Hohenstaufen* and the 10th SS Panzer Division *Frundsberg* were currently resting and refitting. These were armoured divisions totalling 6,000–7,000 men – many of them veterans of Normandy – armed with approximately 220 tanks each and including

Panzergrenadier (mechanised infantry) units, artillery and self-propelled guns. Furthermore, they were also supported by Dutch SS units (men from Holland who had volunteered for various reasons to serve in the German forces), German SS units, soldiers currently attending the SS NCO School or the 16th SS Training Battalion in Arnhem, Hitler Youth troops, and infantry from the *Luftwaffe* and *Kriegsmarine*.

The Allies had been warned by the Dutch Resistance about the presence of German armour – the greatest threat to a lightly armed airborne force – at Arnhem, but as they feared that the Dutch Resistance had been infiltrated by Nazi spies, these reports were ignored. Decoded German intercepts also suggested that two panzer divisions were stationed at Arnhem, and, allegedly, enemy tanks were even spotted in aerial reconnaissance photographs taken only days before the mission. Regardless, Allied planners sent 1st Airborne Division to fight at Arnhem.

The situation was the same elsewhere – the Allies had believed that the German Army was on the verge of collapse and defeat, and that only poor quality enemy troops were defending Holland – and Highway 69 soon became known as 'Hell's Highway'. Only ten minutes after the tanks of XXX Corps began advancing, they came under intense fire from determined German ambushes and were forced to halt. XXX Corps soon discovered they were fighting *Fallschirmjägers* and other troops from 9th SS Panzer Division *Hohenstaufen* – not third-rate soldiers.

Hell's Highway was also a raised road on top of an embankment, meaning that any tank driving along it was silhouetted against the sky and an easy target, while any tanks that tried to advance through the surrounding fields ended up getting bogged down in the waterlogged Dutch clay, leaving them similarly exposed to enemy fire. The Germans were also armed with anti-tank guns and the excellent disposable anti-tank *Panzerfaust* launcher which could be carried and fired by a single soldier.

The plan was originally for XXX Corps to reach Arnhem forty-eight hours after Operation Market Garden was launched – after that, the 1st Airborne Division would be at risk of running out of ammunition, food and supplies. However, the intense German resistance was slowing the Allied advance – it was turning out to be much slower and bloodier than expected. There was a serious risk that the British troops at Arnhem would all be killed or captured before Allied tanks could reach them.

On the morning of 18 September, Private Sam Kendrick and 1st Parachute Regiment had fought through Oosterbeek to the outskirts of Arnhem. However, almost twenty-five percent of the battalion had been killed, wounded or gone missing, and they were facing a strong German defence line.

2nd Parachute Regiment – although they still held the bridge – were cut off and surrounded in enemy territory, and Allied forces simply could not break through to reach them.

At one point, 1st Parachute Regiment received orders to clear a wood, advance through an open field, and clear another wood on the far side. German self-propelled guns were firing at them, and Sam recalled that he and his comrades crossed the open field by running from dead cow to dead cow and using their corpses as cover.

1st and 3rd Parachute Regiments then tried advancing along the river but were beaten back; the two battalions were reduced to a hundred men. Meanwhile, the Germans were continually being reinforced by forming soldiers from different units into makeshift battlegroups. The Allies were simply outnumbered and outgunned.

On 19 September however – now reinforced by 11th Parachute Regiment and 2nd South Staffordshire Regiment – 1st and 3rd Parachute Regiments tried to break through to the bridge at Arnhem again. Private Sam Kendrick and 1st Parachute Regiment led the way, but became trapped in open ground; under fire from three sides, they suffered heavy casualties in fighting around the St Elizabeth Hospital. Sam recalled that this was the most intense fighting he experienced during the Battle of Arnhem, and during the fight, troops from the Hitler Youth began firing a French artillery gun right at the hospital. However, 'one of our sniper boys got them ... When we passed them by [we saw that] they were only babies.' The Hitler Youth – although young – were one of the most fanatical elements of the German forces, and at Arnhem, these teenagers fought against young men like Sam Kendrick who was only eighteen years old.

By this time, Sam had begun to question why he was still carrying his flamethrower and the extremely dangerous reservoir canister on his back. He was terrified that it would be hit and that he would burn to death. Then, when one of his comrades asked, 'What are you still doing with that flamethrower?' Sam finally decided to get rid of it. 'I don't know by Jesus, I don't want it,' replied Sam. 'Do you want it?' asked Sam, to which the other soldier colourfully replied no.

Sam was still looking for an opportunity to ditch the flamethrower when he and his comrades came across a German command post defended by the Hitler Youth, most of them only sixteen or seventeen years old. An officer turned to Sam, pointed to the flamethrower, and asked the young private if he was intending to use his weapon. Sam replied no, and so the officer asked Sam to pass the flamethrower to him, which Sam did, and then the officer approached the enemy position along with another soldier and 'fired it into the pill box ... I can still hear them screaming,' Sam recalled much later. 'I can still hear them.'

1st Parachute Regiment and the other British units involved in this attack were ultimately forced to retreat – they were not trained in urban combat; there were no defined front lines; the enemy seemed to be everywhere, and they were not equipped to fight German armour – and while withdrawing to Oosterbeek Sam experienced a close call. Enemy bullets impacted a wall beside him, but Sam luckily managed to dive for safety into the cellar of a house.

By the end of the fight, many of Sam's comrades had been killed. With nightfall, the British had no choice but to abandon all further attempts to break through to their comrades at the Arnhem bridge, and so they withdrew to Oosterbeek where they formed a circular defensive perimeter centred on 1st Airborne Division HQ at the Hartenstein Hotel. 1st Parachute Regiment now contained only forty men.

Over the following days the fighting at Oosterbeek continued as the Germans surrounded 1st Airborne Division and launched continual heavy assaults, with Sam finding himself positioned around a laundry and school in the southeast of the town. They were without food and so tired that 'we started taking no notice of bombs and tracer bullets ... all we said was "Oh, that missed us".'

On 20 September, Sam's platoon sergeant – thirty-three-year-old Sergeant John McKnight – was killed while fighting a Tiger tank, 'and I don't mind telling you', recalled Sam recently, 'but I cried. He was like a father to me.' Then, on 21 September (with only 3,600 men left defending the Allied perimeter out of the 10,500 men in 1st Airborne Division who had entered the battle), Sam remembered that one of the corporals in his platoon – twenty-three-year-old Corporal Albert Osborne from Walworth, London – was killed after he was accidentally hit and vaporised by a British 6-pounder shell.

That same day, the survivors of 2nd Parachute Regiment – who had held out at the bridge while under constant attack since 17 September – were forced to surrender at dawn. Now, only the British troops encircled at Oosterbeek remained. Meanwhile, to the south, XXX Corps and the US 82nd Airborne Division had captured the bridge at Nijmegen. However, due to a delay in renewing their advance, XXX Corps faced a strong German defence line at Ressen between Nijmegen and Arnhem. They would not break through in time to save the cut off 1st Airborne Division in Arnhem.

Four days later, Operation Market Garden ended on 25 September 1944 when the survivors of 1st Airborne Division abandoned Oosterbeek and made an attempt to escape across the River Nederrijn to Allied lines in the south. Out of the approximately 10,500 men who had landed, just under 2,000 had been killed, 6,500 had been captured by the Germans, while only 2,000 managed to successfully escape and rejoin the Allies. The Battle of Arnhem – and the wider Operation Market Garden – had ended in defeat and failure, with the Allies having lost between 15,000 and 17,000 casualties along with eighty-eight tanks during the nine-day operation.

As for Private Sam Kendrick from Wexford, he was one of those taken POW by the Germans. He had tried to cross the River Nederrijn, but Sam was not a good swimmer.

He returned to Oosterbeek and was hiding out in a cellar when:

One of these tanks [a German Tiger II, or 'King Tiger'] came up the road ... I

> remember coming up and I had a Sten gun ... and I hadn't fired it ... And this bloody
>
> tank came, and like an idiot I fired the Sten gun at it.

Sam had been told by an officer from 2nd South Staffordshire Regiment not to bother firing at the tank – that it would be a waste of time – but still he did it anyway. However, the enemy tank suddenly started rotating its turret.

> We were standing in a doorway to a house and this poor devil here standing along-
>
> side me – I don't know who he was – he got the full blast of the shell ... it took him
>
> about five or six minutes to die. He was screaming ... The Germans held back there
>
> for a while, they held back. We put all sorts of things around him [the dying man] to
>
> protect him but it was a waste of time.

Soon enough, the Germans moved in. Sam expected them to throw a grenade down to clear the cellar, but instead, they threw stones.

> I suppose they heard the children crying [there were civilians in the cellar too].
>
> Maybe that stopped them? But we all came up and there was a wide road and the SS
>
> were across on [the far] side shouting out 'Raus!' ['Out!'] and they gave us a few kicks
>
> to wake us up.

An SS soldier then 'got hold of [Sam's] chin strap and twisted it as tight as it could go' before dragging the eighteen-year-old private from Wexford up on his feet. The SS took the British paratroopers' weapons, helmets and boots – leaving them with only their wash gear – before marching them past piles of British and German dead in the streets to a POW collection centre in a tennis court next to the Hartenstein Hotel. Sam was kept here over-night before being marched away across the Arnhem bridge.

> There were all these Dutch people and they came out with buckets of water to give
>
> us a drink. And what did the SS do? They shot the bloody buckets! We'd had nothing
>
> to drink, and of course the poor Dutch got scared then.

Sam then saw 'a little Dutch boy, no more than nine, he was all excited, and he had a bike, and this German SS [soldier] said "Come here" and the little lad wouldn't. He went off on the bike and [the SS soldier] shot at him ... He shot the bike from under him.'

Private Sam Kendrick and his fellow POWs were subsequently loaded into cattle carts – fifty men in each cart – 'and the only air you had in there was little slits, and in the middle was a milk churn for [to go to] the toilet. And that was full up – sloshing all over the place.' In the corner of Sam's cart there was also a dead artilleryman who had previously been suf-fering from shellshock; the smell from his corpse was terrible.

The POWs were transported by train to Stalag XI-B POW camp near Fallingbostel – between Hanover and Bremen – in Lower Saxony, Germany. Sam and his fellow prisoners were soon surviving on coffee made from boiled acorns and a loaf of black rye bread per day that was divided up among five men. Each of the five slices were a different size, and the soldiers used to hand out the slices to each other using playing cards – the slice of bread sitting on the ace card was the largest, followed by the king card slice, and so forth. Other than these meagre rations, the only other food that a man might have was dandelions, which many soldiers picked when they were out working as part of a work party.

Sam was later transported to the southeast where he was put to work tunnelling in the Harz Mountains around Bad Grund. A V2 rocket facility was being constructed, and Sam had to operate a large drill that was being used to dig a tunnel leading into the mountain from the west, while another team were digging to meet them from the east.

During the winter of 1944, Sam then found that he was becoming tired and weaker, and then 'this German would come along and he'd give me kicks.' While working here, Sam also came in contact with British POWs who had been taken prisoner during the Battle of France in 1940.

> They were getting Red Cross parcels [but] they wouldn't even give us a fag. Our own men wouldn't give you a fag.

Finally, Sam recalled that after nearby Hanover was bombed by the RAF one night, a German guard started beating him up in the morning – kicking Sam on the ground – while shouting, in English, 'Women and children! Women and children!' Meanwhile, German civilians started walking alongside the POW work parties when they were sent out to work – believing that by doing so, they would be safe from Allied air attacks.

Sam was also witness to one particular incident:

> We were going to work one day down the mine, and a German ammunition train was going down – I don't know where it was going to – but it had these guns with four barrels [Flakvierling anti-aircraft guns], and there were Spitfires overhead, and they shot one down, and the pilot bailed out. The women caught hold of him when he came down – on his legs, on his arms – and pulled him to pieces ... That did make me sick ... God, the roars of him.

However, at the same time, Sam recalled that whenever the air-raid siren went off, the German civilians who worked above ground at the mines would flee into the tunnels for safety. During one air raid, Sam ended up beside a young German girl, and she quietly slipped him a boiled egg to eat. Such was the contrast of war.

Private Sam Kendrick from Wexford was later moved again – this time to a POW camp near Dresden. One night, he came back from being out as part of a work party – having had no food to eat – when 'the SS were outside shouting ... I thought they were going to shoot us. They had wagons, and they took us out down to Dresden.'

This was the night of 15 February 1945. Dresden had just suffered three days of devastating Allied air attacks in which 1,300 heavy bombers from the RAF and USAAF had dropped 3,900 tons of high explosive and incendiary bombs on the city. They caused a

Sam Kendrick from Bridgetown, County Wexford, during one of the recent National Day of Commemoration services at Royal Hospital, Kilmainham, Dublin, where he met former Irish President Mary Robinson. He can be seen wearing the maroon beret and cap badge of the Parachute Regiment.

raging firestorm which destroyed fifteen square miles of the city's centre and killed approximately 25,000 German civilians in a controversial attack that was later severely criticised. Some argued that the historical city of Dresden was not a military target, while the Allies insisted that it was a Nazi transport and communications hub containing 110 factories that supplied the Germany war effort.

Sam and his comrades were brought to Dresden in order to help clear the wreckage of bodies and bury the dead.

> When we got there, it turned your stomach. There wasn't one house; there were no people, nothing – all dead. The houses were all just heaps of rubble ... The only thing living in the town was a slaughterhouse, right up at the end of town. The animals in it were still living, but they were going mad. We let them out, but they were going mad.

Sam was given two paint brushes and different coloured tins of paint – one red, one black – and told that once a building was cleared of dead, he was to paint a black cross with a circle around it on the outside. However, if the POWs could not reach the corpses in a building, Sam was to paint the same symbol in red on the outside.

In April 1945 – back at Bad Grund – Sam woke up in his billet to the sound of gunfire – he recognised it as the sound of an American 155mm 'Long Tom' field gun. The SS then rounded up the POWs in the camp, opened the front gates, and ordered the prisoners to start marching. US forces were approaching, and the SS were abandoning the camp and moving their prisoners elsewhere. And so, the Allied POWs started marching to the northeast, but as they went, 'the German civilians hung sheets out of their windows to surrender, and the SS were tearing them all down – pulling at them and shouting and everything. The German [people] knew they were beat.'

Some time later the prisoner column stopped for a rest in the vicinity of Halberstadt, and as Sam remembered:

> We were having a drop of hot water – a drink – in a wood, and I looked over through the wood and there was a tank with a white star on it. I said, 'There's one of our tanks in that wood there' ... all of a sudden the whole place opened up.

An American armoured unit suddenly appeared and began attacking the SS troops guarding the POWs. Sam and his comrades took cover, and after the battle ended with a US victory, Sam and the others were liberated by these Americans. The US troops gave the former POWs some Hersey chocolate bars, but these immediately made the underfed POWs sick.

Although glad to be finally back among Allied troops, Sam then witnessed Allied soldiers committing their own fair share of war crimes. The American soldiers started taking batches of their recently captured German prisoners into the woods and Sam realised:

> [The US troops] were taking them [the German POWs] into the field and shooting them ... in cold blood. That was the Yanks, they had great cigars in their mouths, and they had these jeeps [with machine guns mounted on them] and they were just lying back there, smoking a cigar, and just pulling the trigger.

This was not the only instance of Allied war crimes that Sam witnessed in the days after his liberation:

> I saw one poor man there, a big tall fella, outside a butter factory when we had been released, and he put his hands up – he had no weapons on him – and a bloody [American] man in a tank just machine gunned him down. And he'd put his hands up. They shot him to pieces – hit him right in the head.

German civilians were soon begging Sam and his former POW comrades to stay in their houses as there were cases of US troops having raped local women and these civilians were hoping that by having an Allied soldier in their home, that their wives and daughters might be spared when the Americans arrived. Sam agreed, and ended up staying for a few days in the home of a man whose two daughters were married to German officers.

Concerned about getting back to Britain, Sam was told by a US major one night that since they were expecting a German counterattack he could not spare any vehicles to take Sam and his fellow POWs to an Allied airfield. However, if Sam wanted to try and make his own way to Hildesheim Airfield south of Hanover, he might be able to board an Allied supply plane for its return journey to Britain. So Sam took his chances and managed to get aboard the first empty aircraft he came across. Within a few hours, he was back in Britain.

Private Sam Kendrick from Wexford of 1st Parachute Regiment was now only 5st 7½lbs (77½lbs) and 'crawling with lice'. When he landed in Oxford he was hospitalised immediately, deloused, and was initially given a bottle of Guinness stout and two raw eggs to help build him back up. He remained in hospital for the next four months. By then, the Second World War had ended.

Sam stayed in the British Army post-war and by 1947 found himself serving in Hanover as a motorbike rider. During the Berlin Airlift of 1948 – a British and American operation to get food, fuel and medical supplies to starving Berliners after the Soviet Union blockaded access to the German capital – Sam was asked to ride down to one of the airfields from where the supply aircraft were taking off. Once he arrived, Sam had 'twelve Germans working for me, and it was my job to make sure that the aircraft were secure.' Sam remained in Germany for two more years before going on to serve in Palestine, Egypt and Cyprus, and he was in Cyprus during the Suez Crisis of late 1956 – again serving as an aircraft loadmaster. Not long after, Sam finally retired from the British Army.

He initially went to live in Farnborough, Hampshire where he worked as a milkman while building a house. Sam then married an Irish girl named Mary and applied for a job at Farnborough Airfield – also known as RAE (Royal Aircraft Establishment) Farnborough, where experimental research and testing were carried out on new aircraft and onboard systems. Sam was successful, and was soon responsible 'for looking after the pilots on the aircraft ... we were in charge of oxygen, air, the safety of the pilots when they got in, we strapped them in and that ... I done that for eight years.' In the mid-1960s, Sam Kendrick then started working for the British Ministry of Transport. Here he remained for twenty-five years (having only two days off sick in that time) – working as a driving instructor – until he retired.

Sam's wife then wanted to return home to Ireland, and so, after over forty years in Britain, Sam Kendrick finally returned to live in his native County Wexford in the late 1980s – where he specifically insisted that he never encountered any anti-British sentiment for having served in the British Army. At the time of writing, he is eighty-six years old and still regularly returns to visit Arnhem – he has been going there since 1947 – where he is now well known locally and is often brought to visit Dutch schoolchildren.

GETTING ON WITH LIFE

Captain William Upington from County Cork commanding a 100-strong Captain's Guard of Honour during a Royal Review by King George VI at the Northern Ireland Parliament Buildings, Stormont, post-war.

'*Quis Separabit*? (Who shall separate us?)'
**Latin motto of the Irish Guards, Royal Ulster Rifles,
London Irish Rifles, and the North Irish Horse**

On 2 September 1945, the Second World War finally came to an end. Over seventy million people had been killed during the conflict, with sixty percent of this number being civilians, not soldiers. Out of the 130,000 (possibly 230,000) Irishmen from north and south of the border who had fought during the war, over 7,500 of them were never coming home. Those who did come home did so without fanfare or acknowledgement. Veterans and their stories were left to fade into obscurity.

Meanwhile, the IRA and the Irish government pursued a more active role. The IRA are known to have forced some Irish Second World War veterans to leave their homes and emigrate – they are also known to have attacked some veterans – while the Irish government actually legislated against one group of Irish Second World War soldiers, namely those who had deserted the Irish Defence Forces in order to join the British military.

However, as always, life went on. On 3 December 1945, oranges went back on sale in Ireland for the first time since the start of the war. On 2 September 1946, the state of Emergency in Ireland ceased to exist. Gas rationing ended on 15 January 1948, and on 18 April 1949, southern Ireland officially left the Commonwealth. Nearly thirty-three years after Easter Rising leader Padraig Pearse had declared an Irish republic from the steps of the GPO on 24 April 1916, the southern twenty-six counties were now totally independent from Britain. A few weeks later, on 3 May, the British government officially recognised the Republic of Ireland, but also passed an act ensuring that Northern Ireland would remain a part of the United Kingdom as long as the majority of its citizens supported this position.

During all of this, Irish Second World War veterans sought to get on with life as best they could.

By the end of the war, many women from Northern Ireland had become so-called GI Brides, having married American soldiers who had been stationed in Northern Ireland during the war. This is the wedding photo of Staff Sergeant Richard Large, US Army, and Ivy Roland from Ann Street, Lurgan, County Armagh, 23 February 1945.

BUILDING A LIFE

GEORGE FRANCIS LOUGHLIN

Sixteen-year-old George Francis Loughlin from Fermoy, County Cork emigrated to England in 1932 to start an apprenticeship as a carpenter with his uncle in Wiltshire; he had previously had a job emptying spittoons in the Fermoy TB hospital. When the war broke out, George saw it as an opportunity to see the world so he enlisted in the army, going on to serve in the 7th Armoured Division (the famous 'Desert Rats') in North Africa. While there,

Gunner Martin Anthony 'Tony' Carolan from Glenvanish, Mountshannon, County Clare (third from left) and several of his comrades in 395/91st HAA Regiment, Royal Artillery in North Africa. Carolan later joined 2nd Royal Scots Fusiliers, and it was after serving with them that he received the thank you note – issued to all soldiers of 21st Army Group in 1945 – from Field Marshal Montgomery. After the war, as his daughter Patricia Brien recalled, 'When dad came back home [to Chelsea] jobs were just as difficult to find. He initially worked as a porter for the Institute of the Blind. He then moved on to work as a drayman for a local brewery – Watney, Coombe and Reid – who had a base in Chelsea. He loved the social side of that. He was an extremely outgoing guy and loved meeting and talking to people. Delivering beer to pubs was great as far as he was concerned. He was a big strong guy and could throw the crates up on top of each other with ease – or so I have been told. He stayed with Watneys until he retired.'

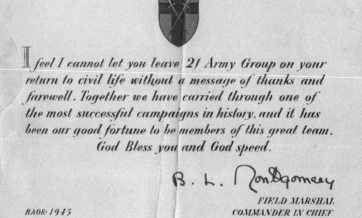

I feel I cannot let you leave 21 Army Group on your return to civil life without a message of thanks and farewell. Together we have carried through one of the most successful campaigns in history, and it has been our good fortune to be members of this great team. God Bless you and God speed.

B. L. Montgomery

FIELD MARSHAL
COMMANDER IN CHIEF

BAOR·1945

his best friend was blown to pieces during a battle right beside him – all that George ever recovered of his friend was his belt buckle. He was later put on a work detail that had to exhume the bodies of comrades who had been temporarily buried – in order for them to be buried properly in a permanent cemetery. George recalled how like 'jelly' their bodies had become. Finally, after contracting malaria and being given light duties in an army hospital while recovering, he saw amputations performed by doctors who lacked supplies of anaesthetic. Injured soldiers were simply held down by orderlies while the doctors worked as quickly as possible.

George married Mary Browne from Fermoy in 1947 and they moved to Woodford, near Salisbury in Wiltshire. Initially, George worked as a carpenter while his wife earned some money as a housekeeper. He cycled eight miles to work every day – and because meat was still being rationed, he set snares to catch rabbits on his way to work and later picked up his catch on the

George Francis Loughlin from Fermoy, County Cork. He served with 7th Armoured Division – the 'Desert Rats' – in North Africa during the war.

way home. The couple then moved to a social housing project in Salisbury – disused army billets on the edge of the Plain – and George set up his own grocery shop in 1948 (as there was no other such shop for two miles in any direction). His wife initially ran it, until the shop was making enough money for George to give up his job as a carpenter and work there permanently. The couple later moved to nearby Bulford Village in 1955 – where they built a house and shop in order to continue the business – and George Francis Loughlin worked hard there until he retired in 1970 to live in Amesbury, Wiltshire. He later passed away in 1989 – aged seventy-two.

A COOL RECEPTION

WILLIAM HOLOHAN

William Holohan was born in Athy, County Kildare in May 1918. William's mother – Christina O'Neill – died in Dr Steeven's Hospital, Dublin from sepsis in November 1920 as a consequence of a beating. She was pregnant at the time. Allegedly, she was beaten by either an 'Auxie' RIC (Royal Irish Constabulary) constable during the War of Independence, or by a family member of her husband's first wife (her relationship with William's father had started as an affair).

When William Holohan's father subsequently fell ill and died in 1927, nine-year-old William was sent to Artane Industrial School along with his older brother John. The two lost contact when John left the school in 1932 (they were not reunited until 1962), and then William was 'farmed out' – as his son, Tommy Holohan, described it – in 1934 to a family named Kelly in Longford.

Two years later they kicked eighteen-year-old William out of the house, so he joined the Irish Army and was posted to Renmore Barracks, Galway. There, he became friendly with a local girl named Peg. When she suddenly emigrated to England with a friend, William was determined to follow her. So he deserted the Irish Army, took the bus to Enniskillen, and joined the Royal Engineers. Within a week, he was back in touch with Peg and soon going out with her.

During the war, and probably because he could speak some Arabic (learned from a priest during his time in Artane), Sapper William Holohan was sent to the Middle East in mid-1943. During this time, he served as bodyguard to Abdullah bin al-Hussein – then-Emir of Transjordan and later King Abdullah I of Jordan. Every morning, William would wake up in his tent and then head into the palace to work, and Abdullah once gave him a decorated brown leather bag to bring home to Peg as a present. William also served in North Africa – where he heard then-Lieutenant-General Montgomery give a speech in Cairo – and later worked at clearing German booby traps in France after D-Day. He recalled that the doors of outhouses were rigged with explosives, as were toilet flush chains, and abandoned *Luftwaffe* aircraft were often left with their cockpit hoods partially open and rigged – anyone who slid them fully open would trigger the bomb. Finally, towards the end of the war, William was sent back to the Middle East and was driving with a Colonel Grey through a pass between Iran and Iraq when they received word that the war had ended. They stopped in a small village where the locals gave them drink to celebrate.

After being demobbed in 1947, William Holohan and Peg – now his wife – returned to live in her native Claddagh, outside Galway. However, the local attitude was that, as an ex-British soldier, William must be extremely wealthy. This was certainly not the case and although he applied for plenty of jobs, nothing ever came of them. As soon as a prospective employer discovered that he was former British Army, that was it. While he once got a delivery job for a fruit vendor, it was temporary and only lasted for a couple of months.

William turned to a local canon who had a nephew in CIE (the Irish bus and rail company). This resulted in a job, but William left it after six months because he got an opportunity to become a trainee linesman with the ESB (Electricity Supply Board). He fought hard to get the job, but was still treated like an outsider for some time after.

One day during the 1960s, while working up a pole in Salthill, William could see into the yard of St Joseph's Industrial School. There was a child being beaten by a caretaker, and so William rushed down the pole and ran up a road towards the school, hopping a fence to get into the yard (he was in his socks as he had been wearing special boots for going up the pole that had to be detached). He stopped the caretaker from beating the child, then gave the man a beating himself. The gardaí were called, but William told them that the caretaker had been beating a child and so they let him go.

William Holohan remained working with the ESB for forty-five years before retiring. The day before he died in 2002, William's son Tommy went to see his father in hospital. William was upset about something, and soon insisted that the very same caretaker who he had caught beating the child all those years ago in Salthill in the 1960s was now working in the hospital. Whether it was true or not, the next day, William Holohan passed away.

The accounts of men such as George Francis Loughlin and William Holohan are just two of the thousands of Irish stories of how returning veterans just had to carry on and live their lives. However, there were others who came home to unwelcome news, some who were unable to cope with life after the end of the war, and others who never came home at all.

FAR FROM HOME

ALEC NIXON & PATRICK O'HARA

After the war, some Irish soldiers returned home only to discover that loved ones had died while they were away. Alec Nixon from Ferguson Road, Drumcondra, Dublin, was one such man. He joined the RAF during the war and was posted to a unit in the Caribbean, but after his brother, Sergeant Charles Nixon – an air gunner with No 166 Squadron RAF – was killed in a mission over Germany on Christmas Eve 1944, Alec was not told about his brother's death. Alec and Charles used to write frequent letters to one another, and when Charles' letters stopped, Alec wrote to his family back in Ireland asking if anything had happened. His family did not have the heart to tell Alec that his brother was dead, and so they continually wrote back to say that Charles must simply be very busy. When Alec Nixon finally came home to Dublin after the war and discovered the truth, he was completely devastated at the loss of his beloved brother.

At the end of the war, Able Seaman Patrick O'Hara from Cork city experienced a similar situation. His father was an old British soldier and, in 1942, he gave the seventeen-year-old Patrick the train fare from Cork to Belfast so he could enlist. Patrick wanted to do his bit, as his father had before him, and after lying about his age, Patrick successfully joined the Royal Navy and served aboard HMS *Teviot* in the Atlantic, the Mediterranean, and in the Far East. On 16 August 1945, docked in Cape Town, South Africa, twenty-year-old Patrick (as his daughter Kathy Bateson recalled):

> Wrote lovingly to his beloved father who had, in fact, died sometime before. The family
> thought it best not to tell my father as they knew it would upset him greatly. When the war
> ended and he went back to Cork the family could not go to meet him with such bad news
> so they sent a family friend. I am not sure my father ever really recovered from the news.

While some men suffered terribly during the war, it was the distance experienced between themselves and their families – especially not being there when a loved one passed away – that devastated other men after the conflict had ended.

STILL DYING

JOHN JOSEPH 'SEAN' COLLINS & ROBERT TURKINGTON

Of course, there were other Irishmen who survived the war but never came home. From Athlone, County Westmeath, Aircraftman 2nd Class John Joseph 'Sean' Collins enlisted in 1945 towards the end of the war and was posted to an RAF unit in India. He was a talented uilleann piper, and by 1947, he was still stationed in India. Then, on 26 February that year, while playing net-ball with some comrades, the ball was knocked out of the court and landed in a nearby lake. Sean waded in to get the

Opposite bottom: Squadron Leader Robert Turkington from Derrytrasna, County Armagh, and (above) the telegram informing his family of his accidental death in Italy after the war in Europe had ended.

ball, and was subsequently sucked under and drowned. He was only twenty-one years old, and had actually been due to come home on leave one month later. It took Indian divers three weeks to recover his remains, and he now lies buried in Ranchi War Cemetery. After an initial telegram was sent to his family and a letter of condolence followed, his uilleann pipes were soon returned to his family in Athlone, not long after Sean himself should have been due home on leave.

Meanwhile, on 29 July 1945, Squadron Leader Robert Turkington from Derrytrasna, County Armagh of No 241 Squadron RAF, climbed into Spitfire MK423 in Italy and took off for a flight to Naples – Turkington was a skilled combat pilot and had previously been awarded a Distinguished Flying Cross with bar and a Distinguished Service Order. The war in Europe was over, and although Turkington was still on operational standby, he expected to be demobbed and home by August. He wrote to his mother to tell her this, and she began to redecorate his room. However, during his flight to Naples on 29 July – as recorded in a later RAF report:

> His engine was heard to cut out and he immediately turned to starboard in an attempt to return to the landing strip. The aircraft began to lose height and suddenly struck the ground with the nose and starboard wing. It then burst into flames. F/ Lieut Jones (601 Squadron) saw the accident from start to finish and stated that S/ Ldr Turkington probably died almost immediately. His body was recovered during the afternoon, after the heat had subsided.

Squadron Leader Robert Turkington was twenty-six years old when he died and he now lies buried in Padua War Cemetery. When a telegram arrived at his mother's house on 2

August 1945, she initially believed it was a telegram from her son saying that he would be home soon. In fact, it was from the RAF, informing her that her son 'is reported to have lost his life as a result of an aircraft accident ... the Air Council express their profound sympathy.'

VETERANS AND REPUBLICANS

MARCUS ERVINE-ANDREWS & DANIEL FINAN

Then there were those veterans who experienced the wrath of the IRA after they returned home. In the 26 July 1940 edition of the *London Gazette*, it was announced that Captain Marcus Ervine-Andrews of 1st East Lancashire Regiment – from Keadue, County Cavan – had been awarded the Victoria Cross:

> For most conspicuous gallantry on active service on the night of the 31st May/1st June, 1940. Captain Ervine-Andrews took over about a thousand yards of the defences in front of Dunkirk ... For over ten hours, notwithstanding intense artillery, mortar, and machine-gun fire, and in the face of vastly superior enemy forces, Captain Ervine-Andrews and his company held their position.
>
> The enemy, however, succeeded in crossing the canal on both flanks; ... There being danger of one of his platoons being driven in, he called for volunteers to fill the gap, and then, going forward, climbed on to the top of a straw-roofed barn, from which he engaged the enemy with rifle and light automatic fire, though, at the time, the enemy were sending mortar-bombs and armour-piercing bullets through the roof.
>
> Captain Ervine-Andrews personally accounted for seventeen of the enemy with his rifle, and for many more with a Bren gun. Later, when the house which he held had been shattered by enemy fire and set alight, and all his ammunition had been expended, he sent back his wounded in the remaining carrier. Captain Ervine-Andrews then collected the remaining eight men of his company from this forward position, and, when almost completely surrounded, led them back to the cover afforded by the company in the rear, swimming or wading up to the chin in water for over a mile; having brought all that remained of his company safely back, he once again took up position.
>
> Throughout this action, Captain Ervine-Andrews displayed courage, tenacity, and devotion to duty, worthy of the highest traditions of the British Army, and his magnificent example imbued his own troops with the dauntless fighting spirit which he himself displayed.

However, when war hero Captain Marcus Ervine-Andrews initially tried to return home to Ireland and settle in his native Cavan, the local IRA threatened him and drove him out, forcing the VC winner to move to Cornwall. Ervine-Andrews ended up staying in the British Army and later retired with the rank of lieutenant-colonel. When he died on 30 March 1995 – aged eighty three – he had previously been the last surviving Irish Victoria Cross recipient of the Second World War.

But while Marcus Ervine-Andrews may have been threatened and forced to emigrate by the IRA, Daniel Finan from Teemana, Ballintubber, County Roscommon, suffered worse at the hands of Irish republicans. He was the youngest son of a farming family, and while his older brothers inherited the farm, Daniel emigrated to England some time before the war to look for work. On 30 July 1941, he enlisted in the RAF and went on to serve as an air gunner aboard a bomber in the Middle East. However, after a spell in hospital (for some unrecorded reason) in July 1943, Daniel was withdrawn from aircrew. He served for the remainder of the war as an FME (Flight Mechanic – Engines) on the ground. He also soon got into trouble twice during 1944 for being drunk, and in 1945 he was admitted to hospital twice, again for an unrecorded cause. Daniel Finan's family maintain that he was now suffering from shellshock – which he developed during his time as an air gunner – and this certainly tallies with the fact that he was removed from aircrew, re-trained in a ground crew role, along with his drinking and periods in hospital.

However, in 1946 – having recently been released from the RAF but not yet officially discharged – Daniel Finan was living in Nottingham. On 12 December he was in a local pub when a row broke out between him and another man – according to the Finan family, the other man was allegedly a member of the IRA. The row turned into a fight that spilled out of the pub onto the street, and it ended with the death of Daniel Finan. He was twenty-six years old when he died, and his death certificate recorded the cause of death as 'fractured skull due to striking his head on a kerb following a fall'.

The story of Daniel Finan is certainly one of the more extreme cases of republican hostility towards Irish Second World War veterans, but this aggression and violence towards men who had served in the British forces helped to create one of the myths of why Irishmen enlisted to fight in the war. As noted in Richard Doherty's *In The Ranks Of Death: The Irish in the Second World War*:

> The years of civil strife in Northern Ireland after 1969 caused many Irish ex-servicemen, particularly Catholics, to claim they had joined up either for mercenary reasons – to put bread on the table – or to avoid personal problems ...

Basically, out of fear of militant republicans and nationalists, many veterans began to make up 'excuses' for why they had enlisted, and this went a long way towards giving the impression that no Irishman fought the war because he felt that it was simply the right thing to do.

REPUBLICAN TIES

PATRICK McDONNELL

At the other end of the spectrum was Patrick McDonnell. Many Irishmen returning from the trenches of the First World War had transferred their military skills to the republican cause and joined the IRA during the War of Independence against the British. In the same way, some Irish Second World War veterans are known to have followed a similar path after their war.

Born on 12 July 1917 on Mountpottinger Road in Belfast (while an Orange Order parade apparently marched at the bottom of the street), Patrick came from a strongly nationalist background. Through his mother's family – who used the name O'Dwyer, but who were originally Dwyer – he was related to Wicklow-man Michael Dwyer, the United Irishmen and 1798 Rebellion leader who, after fighting at the battles of Arklow, Vinegar Hill, Ballyellis and Hacketstown during the rebellion, later fought a guerrilla campaign against the British Army in the Wicklow Mountains from 1798 to 1803. Patrick's mother – Josephine O'Dwyer – was also a member of Inghinidhe na hÉireann and later Cumann na mBan. Prior to the 1916 Rising she worked for the railway in Belfast, and had been positioned there by the republican movement because it allowed her to work as a courier between local republicans and the leadership in Dublin. According to Patrick's son – Gerard McDonnell – Josephine O'Dwyer also met Padraig Pearse and James Connolly during her time sending and receiving republican communiqués between northern and southern Ireland, while Josephine's house on Chemical Street was used as a base by republican agents to sort through material taken from wastepaper bins in a British Army HQ on Royal Avenue.

Meanwhile, Patrick's father – Michael McDonnell – was a member of the IRB (Irish Republican Brotherhood), and it was through this organisation that he met and later married Josephine O'Dwyer. Perhaps strangely then, during the First World War, Michael McDonnell enlisted in the British Army and went on to fight in the trenches (as did his brother Jack, who was killed during the war) before returning home to Belfast in 1918. However, although he had survived the war, Michael did not live for very much longer. In 1920 – following the shooting of an RIC (Royal Irish Constabulary) detective in Lisburn during the War of Independence – 7,000 Catholics were forced out of the Harland and Wolff shipyards while sectarian riots broke out across the city. Clashes between the IRA and the RIC then followed in 1921, and on 10 July that year – in an event that became known as 'Belfast's Bloody Sunday' – sixteen people were killed, more than seventy were wounded, and 161 houses were destroyed (150 of them belonging to Catholics) in a sectarian riot

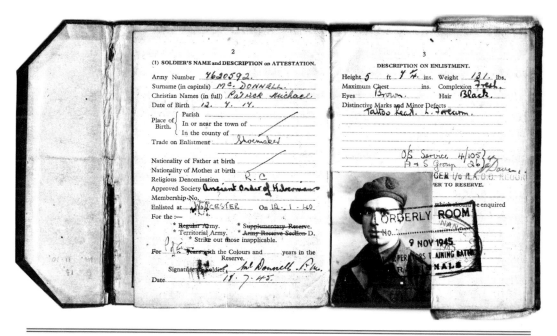

Two documents linked to Private Patrick McDonnell from Belfast of the Royal Army Ordnance Corps. Above, the profile page from his soldier's pay book, and below, his POW information card from Stalag XX-A (which Patrick took from the camp's files before he returned home). Note how much weight he had lost after five years in captivity.

involving rifles, machine guns, hand grenades and petrol bombs. Twenty more people died in late August, and violence continued in Belfast until 1922, but by then, Michael McDonnell was dead. His grandson, Gerard McDonnell, recalled that Michael tried to help a fellow Catholic who was being attacked by Protestant unionists at some point during this period, but the gang turned on Michael and badly beat him too. He suffered a burst ulcer and died of a subsequent infection.

This meant that, by 1922, five-year-old Patrick McDonnell had lost his father. Patrick later went on to become a shoemaker, and in 1934 he emigrated to England prior to the outbreak of the Second World War and was managing a shoe shop by 1939. Then, on 12 January 1940, twenty-two-year-old Patrick McDonnell enlisted in the British Army in Worcester. He joined the Royal Army Ordnance Corps as a private and was sent to France to join the BEF, where he was attached to the 51st (Highland) Infantry Division.

He was still in France when the Germans invaded on 10 May that year, and after the retreat was ordered, Private Patrick McDonnell found himself on the beaches of northern France. He later told the story to his son Gerard:

> Those who could swim were assisting the wounded out to the ships and boats, and he [Patrick] was saying he did lots of runs where they swam and helped people get on board who were wounded … he was going back and forward helping people … [However], a group of them were then put together to try to act as some type of a rearguard while others were trying to be evacuated.

Private Patrick McDonnell from Belfast was one of the men ordered to form the rearguard at Saint-Valéry-en-Caux, west of Dieppe, but during a subsequent battle he was wounded in the arms and legs on 10 June and later woke up in a German field hospital. Private Patrick McDonnell was now a POW.

He was initially interred in Stalag XX-B near Marienburg, East Prussia (now Malbork, Poland) – from where POWs were sent out on work parties to local farms, factories and mills – but after a failed escape attempt, Patrick was sent to the much more secure Stalag XX-A in Torun, Poland. He remained in captivity for the rest of the war, and by the time Private Patrick McDonnell was finally liberated by the Russians and returned home to Belfast, five years had passed. He was then twenty-seven years old.

Patrick McDonnell became very ill not long after he returned home and developed TB. It was initially unclear whether he would survive or not, but he did survive, and after being discharged from the British Army as being 'medically unfit for further service', Patrick married and returned to working as a shoemaker while also working as a part-time telephonist in the evenings. He lived on the predominantly Protestant and unionist Donegall Pass, and when a friend named Clarke – who had a shoe shop on the

Hajo Buth
Germany
Krs. Gandersheim
Ackenhausen No.4

20/9/47
7/10/47

Mrs.

M. FEE

7 Waterford St.

Belfast.

N Ireland

Meine liebe Freundin!

Haben Sie meinen besten herz-
lichsten Dank für Ihren so lieben
Brief vom 15.8.1947, den ich hier-
mit bestätigt und noch reicher be-
schenkten Sie uns mit Ihrem recht
reichhaltigen Paket. Meine kleine
Tochter Hannelore (5 Jahre alt)
jubelte laut vor Freude und läßt
schon jetzt nichts über ihre Tante
aus England kommen. Weiter treibt
sie grosse Propaganda im hiesigen
Ort betreffs Ihrer rührigen Für-
sorge.

Ihre mehr als bescheidene Bitte
erfüllen wir jeden Abend. Ebenfalls sind Sie im Gebet meiner
Tochter eingeschlossen, was sich
immer so niedlich anhört. Die
Schokoladen und Bonbons nahm sie
gleich in Beschlag, wovon sie
dann in rationierten Mengen zu
sich nimmt. Der Zucker ist so wunderbar fein, wie man ihn hier z.Zt.
nicht findet. Ebenso gleicht die
Margarine der hiesigen Butter, die
im Geschmack ausgezeichnet ist.

Das schöne weisse Mehl und das
Backpulver und den Zucker haben
wir für den Weihnachtskuchen auf-
gehoben.

Den schwarzen Tee kennen wir
seit Jahren nicht mehr und ist uns
heute besonders kostbar. Das Pud-
dingpulver und Griess werden ebenfalls die Kinderherzen erfreuen.

Ganz besonders neu waren für uns
Deutsche die "Briskies", die dem
hiesigen Knäckebrot ähneln und in
Milch wunderbar munden.

My dear friend !

I have received your nice
letter of 15/8/47 and I want
so much to give you my best
and heartest thanks, still more
you have presented us with your
rich parcel. My little daughter
Hannelore (5 years old) has
shouted loudly and she loves
her aunty in England very much.
Further she makes propaganda
in this village about your active care.

Your more than modest request
we like to fulfil every night.
Also you are in the daily prayer
of my daughter, what is always
nice to hear. She took the chocolate and the sweets in her posse-
sion, and now she takes of it
with rationed quantities. The sugar is marvellous fine, as we
can not have it here at present.
As well the margerine like our
butter, the taste is wonderful.

We have saved the wonderful
white flour and the "Backpulver"
(force of motion for pastries)
and the sugar for our X-mas-cake.

Since the last years we have
not had the "black" tea and so
it is a particularity to-day.
The pudding-powder and the groat
will enjoy also the children hearts

We Germans do not know the
"Briskies" they are like our
"Knäckebrot" and have a wonder-
ful taste when putting into milk.

P.t.o.

Liebe Freundin, Sie glauben gar
nicht, wie nahe Sie uns gekommen
sind mit den göttlichen Gaben, die
uns so sehr erfreuen.

Ja, liebe Freundin, mein Vater-
land ist grausam zugerichtet und
es bedarf grossen Lebensmutes,
hier noch zu verweilen.

Letztens war ich in meiner Ge-
burtsstadt Berlin und war wieder
tiefstens erschüttert. Ebenfalls
sind die Städte Bremerhaven, Wesermünde, Hannover, Braunschweig
und Hamburg sehr zerstört. Millio-
nen Menschen sind tot, obdachlos
krank – und wenn man fragt "warum"
weil ein Mensch so unvernünftig
rücksichtslos war! Dem deutschen
Volk allein darf keine Schuld ge-
geben werden, denn wir hatten zu
gehorchen und lebten dann herr-
lich und in Freude. Widersetzten
wir uns der Staatsgewalt, wander-
ten wir ins KZ. War es da nicht
verständlich zu folgen, um seine
Familie erhalten zu wissen.

Sehr gütig und lieb ist es von
Ihnen zu schreiben, dass ich evtl.
spezielle Wünsche geltend machen
soll. Dies zeigt mir immer wieder
wie gross Gott in Ihnen ist. Haben Sie meinen innigsten Dank
hierfür – aber ich bin wunschlos
glücklich – wenn ich weiss, dass
meine Mitmenschen gesund, froh
und zufrieden sind.

Ich freue mich weiter, dass
Sie, meinem Freund Ernst solch
grossherzige Kameradin waren
und sind, denn er hat es ver-
dient, wo ihm doch keine Heimat
verblieben ist. Ich versuche
nun, ihm eine zweite Heimat zu
schaffen und freue mich dann,
wenn es ihm hier gefällt. Für
eine passende Beschäftigung
werde ich schon sorgen und er
wird wieder froh und stolz werden. Wann wird ihn Gott endlich
zu uns senden, damit er teilhab-
ben kann an dem grossen deutschen Wiederaufbau.

Ihr Foto war schon in so vie-
len Händen und wurde allgemein
bewundert, denn Sie sind darauf
gut getroffen. Darf ich Ihnen
ebenfalls einige Aufnahmen bei-
fügen und zwar:

Dear friend, you do not
know, what you have done
with your godlike presents,
about which we are so glad.

Yes, dear friend, our home-
land has been dressed cruelty
and we must have great courage
of life to stay still here.

In the last time I have
been in my town of birth Berlin and I was chocked strongly again. As well the towns of
Bremerhaven, Wesermünde, Hannover, Braunschweig and Hamburg
had been terribly damaged.
Millions of people have dies,
have become homeless, sick
and when you are asking "why"
only becuse one man had become
irrational and unfeeling. The
German people alone are not
guilty, because we had to obey
and then we lived splendid and
with pleasure. Did we oppose
against the executive power we
were ordered into a concentration
camp. It is quite intelligivle
that we did obey in order to be
able to earn the living for the
family.

It is very kind of you to
write, I may tell you my special
wishes. This will inform us
that God is alwayse with you and
in you, I want to give you my
heartest thanks for it, but I am
quite happy when I can see, that
my other people are healthy, glad
and satisfied.

Further I am very glad that you
have been and that you still are
such a magnanimous fried to my
friend Ernst. I want also this for
him, because he has no home now.
I am trying to make ready for him
his second home and then will be
glad, when he is satisfied here.
I will look for a suitable job
for him and I will do all my best
in order to make him glad and self-
conscious. When will God send him
to us, that he can help for the
great rebuilding of Germany.

Your nice foto came into several
hands and had been admires of all
you look very nice on it. May you
allow me to add some pictures of
my family and that:

P.t.O.

- 2 -

Nr. 1 der Tag unserer Hochzeit am
10.8.1946. Rechts neben meiner Frau, meine Schwester
Hannelore, dann meine Schwie-
germutter, dahinter meine
Mutter mit Brille, daneben
meine Tante Lieschen. Neben
meiner Schwester linksmein
Stiefgrossvater. Vor uns
unsere Tochter Hannelore.

Nr. 2 Hannelore 8 Monate mit
ihrer Mutti

Nr. 3 Hannelore mit Mutti Sept.45

Nr. 4 unser Heim.

Mein Sohn – Joachim – schreit
gerade kräftig und verlangt sein
Recht. Darf ich Sie herzlichst
einladen, wenn Sie es mal mit Ihrer
Zeit vereinbaren können. Meine
Tochter fragt andauernd, wann kommt
die Tante Fee und besucht uns. Viel-
leicht begleiten Sie Ernst in die
neue Heimat.

So, für heute habe ich wohl ge-
nug geschrieben. Meine Familie
grüsst Sie ebenfalls herzlichst.
Möge Gott Sie weiterhin beschützen
und beschirmen und Ihre Liebe und
Güte tausendfach vergelten.

Mit den freundlichsten Grüssen
bin ich
                                    Ihr

No.1 the day of our wedding on
10/8/1946. At the right hand
side peer my wife my sister
Hannelore, then my mother-
in-law-, behind her my mother
with glasses, near by my aunty Lieschen. Near my sister
at the left hand side my
step-grandfather. Before us
our daughter Hannelore.

No.2 Hannelore 8 month old with
her Mammi

No.3 Hannelore with Mammi Sept.45

No.4 our home.

Just this moment my son –
Joachim – is loudly crying and
with this he ask for his eating.
May I invite you, if you have
time to do to come to see us. My
daughter is always asking, when
does aunty Fee come to see us.
May be it is possible and you are
able to accompany my friend Ernst
into the new home.

So for now, I mean I have
written enough. My family send
the heartest greetings to you.
May God protect and save you
and return all your love and kind-
nes thousandfold.

With the kindest regards I am
always yours
                            respectfully

Hajo Buth nebst
Familie.

---

*The letter – written in German and English
– sent by former German soldier Hajo Buth
to Patrick McDonnell's mother in Belfast,
7 October 1947. During the war, Hajo had
been taken POW and interred in Northern
Ireland, but during one Christmas period, the
British authorities had given German POWs
temporary release and allowed them to spend
Christmas with local Irish families – many
of which were republican or nationalist – who
were willing to invite the POWs into their
homes. Hajo ended up with Patrick McDonnell's
mother, and they stayed in touch after the war
ended.*

Newtownards Road – subsequently developed cancer and became too ill to stay working, Patrick then started running the business for a wage, and when Clarke passed away, Patrick McDonnell moved in next door and set up his own shoe-repair business. However, in the years that followed, Patrick's business started to fail, and then finally, the premises were taken over by the British Army as a billet for their troops. By now though, Patrick – in keeping with his family history – was becoming involved with the republican movement. His son Gerard later discovered that there was an IRA arms dump in Patrick's shoe repair shop, but once the British Army moved in, the IRA could no longer get at the weapons.

Patrick McDonnell then found himself working in another shoe shop on Sandy Row. This – like the street on which Patrick lived – was a strongly Protestant and unionist area of Belfast, but although the owner of the shop did not mind that Patrick was a Catholic, when many of the shop's customers discovered his religion, Patrick received a threatening note that told him to either 'go or stay permanently'. The shop's owner was therefore forced to let Patrick go – both to protect his business and to protect Patrick's life – and Patrick later became a caretaker working for St Joseph's teacher training college in Trench House. He remained working here until his death in 1984 – aged sixty-seven.

Patrick's son Gerard recalled that his father did not really discuss politics when the children were around, but they were told that while they were British subjects, they were Irish, and should be proud of being Irish. Gerard also frequently came across arms in the house while he was a boy – proving that his father stored weapons for the IRA when needed – and he later learned that his father drove members of the IRA leadership around Ireland for many years and that 'he was on call twenty-four hours' during this period. Patrick McDonnell was actually the personal driver for Billy McKee – commanding officer of the IRA's Belfast Brigade during 1962–1963, and later a member of the Provisional IRA's Army Council and commanding officer of the Provisional IRA's Belfast Brigade following the IRA split in December 1969. Others he drove for included Joe Cahill and Corkman Dáithí Ó Conaill, and whenever he was driving for these IRA leaders, Patrick McDonnell used to carry his British Army pension book with him. Whenever he was stopped at British Army roadblocks and asked for identification, he would hand this over and as soon as the soldiers at the roadblock saw that they were dealing with a Second World War veteran, they assumed that Patrick would be the furthest thing from a republican sympathiser, and simply let him pass. However, while he was driving and storing weapons for the IRA, Patrick McDonnell would still wear a poppy on his jacket every 11 November and go to the Belfast cenotaph to remember all the comrades he had lost during the war. As his son Gerard remembered, 'He seen all that stuff as just being respectful of the dead.' Patrick believed that once a war had ended, politics should go out the window and soldiers should be able to remember proudly the fallen.

That said, Patrick McDonnell's loyalties lay firmly with the republican movement, and when his son Gerard became involved in the IRA and was interned without trial in 1972, Patrick sent his war medals back to the British Ministry of Defence with a letter of protest. In fact, Patrick's son – Gerard McDonnell – is likely to be familiar to readers. Gerard was involved in the 1976 'Blanket Protest', where hundreds of prisoners – who became known as 'Blanket Men' – refused to wear prison uniforms and were forced to wrap blankets around themselves after the prison authorities denied them any other form of clothing. Gerard was then one of the thirty-eight people to escape from the Maze during 1983 – he had served eleven years in prison at this point – after which he was told by Provisional IRA command to disappear. He was offered safe passage to America, but instead insisted on remaining active. He took up republican activities immediately, and although Patrick McDonnell wanted to see his son during this time, he never made any attempts to reach Gerard, out of fear that he would lead British forces to him. As a result, when Patrick fell ill in 1984 and died, Gerard did not find out that his father had passed away for five days – not until after the funeral had taken place. It was Kieran 'Header' Nugent – another IRA blanket man – who ultimately told Gerard that his father had died, and Gerard recently said that, because of his time spent in prison and then on the run, 'I'm really sorry I never had the chance to sit down and talk to him [my father] more … I've an enduring sadness because of how life had taken me out of circulation. I never got to talk to my father about himself and myself. We lived parallel lives … I always say now that people should tell others that they love them whenever they can. A time might come when you can't.'

Gerard McDonnell then began operating in England, but was arrested in Glasgow on 24 June 1985 (only weeks after his mother's funeral in May, which he also missed) – along with Brighton Hotel bomber Patrick Magee and other IRA members – and sentenced to life imprisonment. This he served in various English prisons before being transferred to Northern Ireland, firstly to Maghaberry Prison near Lisburn and then the Maze. However, under the terms of the 1999 Good Friday Agreement, he was released from prison, having served a further fourteen years in jail.

His story, and the story of his father Patrick McDonnell, serves to show that Irish families with incredibly strong links to Irish republicanism were often also linked to service in the British Army during the world wars.

OFFICIALLY TARGETED

PHIL FARRINGTON

Sadly, however, most Irish Second World War veterans did not only have disinterested public opinion or IRA aggression to deal with once they started returning home after the war. In the case of one group of veterans, that were officially targeted and directly attacked by Irish government legislation – an assault that began even before the war had ended.

It is estimated that about 5,500 men deserted the Irish Defence Forces during the Second World War, and on 8 August 1945, Emergency Powers Order No 362 was passed in the Dáil resulting in a 'List of personnel of the Defence Forces dismissed for desertion in time of National Emergency' being distributed throughout the country. It was 133 pages long, contained the names of 4,983 men who had deserted the Irish Army, Navy or Air Corps during the war, and stated that these men had lost all pension rights earned during the years they had served, were no longer entitled to unemployment benefits, and were not allowed to work in the public sector for the next seven years. At a time when Ireland was in economic recession and government jobs were often the only ones available, this effectively prevented many of these men from obtaining any work at all (resulting in Order No 362 being nicknamed the 'Starvation Order'). They were also court-martialled as a group – on the same day that Order No 362 was passed – but with none of them present, and although the Order was condemned by Fine Gael (then in opposition), some politicians felt that the punishments placed on deserters were not harsh enough.

Robert Widders, in his book *Spitting on a Soldier's Grave*, deals with the treatment of Irish deserters by the Irish government post-war in greater detail, but desertion is a military crime and under military law it carries a punishment. However, what is perhaps telling about the government of 1940s Ireland and its attitude towards Irish citizens serving in the British forces, is that the crime of wartime desertion was not punished uniformly. Deserters who were caught and sentenced to a period in an Irish military prison did not have their names included on the 'List of personnel of the Defence Forces dismissed for desertion in time of National Emergency', while those who were not caught did have their names included. Also, deserters who never left Ireland were given lesser punishments than those who joined the British forces, and while Irish officers who deserted were also not included on the list – along with ordinary soldiers who deserted but did not join the British forces – those men who did go on to join the British forces were specifically singled out. It seems that a deserter from the Irish Defence Forces during the Second World War was punished, not for the crime of desertion, but for what he did after he deserted. And for those men caught during the war and convicted of desertion, those that had joined the British Army often received brutal treatment in Irish military prisons.

There were several main reasons why men deserted the Irish Defence Forces during 1939–1945. Many had answered Éamon de Valera's call to arms in 1940 and enlisted throughout the country. However, when thousands of these same men – many of whom had been motivated by patriotism, or a desire to protect Ireland from the evils of Nazi Germany – were put to work cutting turf on the Irish bogs (as many soldiers were), they felt that perhaps serving in the British forces would be a more active way of stopping Hitler. For others, the (often only slightly) higher rates of pay offered in the British forces, the poor Irish barracks accommodation, or the unfair system of Irish Defence Forces marriage allowances prompted men to desert and travel to Britain or north of the border to enlist.

However, long before Order No 362 was passed post-war, the Irish government was already striking out at southern Irish soldiers in the British Army, and not just those who had deserted the Irish Defence Forces. Two years after the start of the war, the 1941 Children's Act was passed. It permitted the State to place a child in an industrial school if one of its parents was absent from home. These industrial schools were run by religious orders, and were places where children frequently suffered horrific physical, mental and sexual abuse. But while the children of fathers who had emigrated to Britain or elsewhere to look for work were rarely affected by the Act, the children of soldiers who had joined the British Army were specifically targeted and many were placed in industrial schools while their fathers were denied the right of appeal. Furthermore, the Irish government demanded that the family allowance payments – paid by the British government to the wives of soldiers in Ireland – should be paid directly to the Irish State, and no longer to the soldiers' wives, in order to fund the 'care' of the soldiers' children who were now in industrial schools. The Act was considered unconstitutional by some, but, regardless, it was the beginning of a tragic, systematic attack on Irish soldiers serving in the British forces.

For those deserters who were captured, the treatment they suffered in Irish military prisons was often horrendous. One man who received this treatment was Phil Farrington. In later life, he wrote a short account of his Second World War experiences. Titled 'To Hell and Back', it was published in *Flying, Not Falling: Poems, Stories and Reflections on Life by Older Adults*. Phil grew up in inner-city Dublin and joined the Irish Army in 1941, aged nineteen.

> As life in the Irish Army wasn't very exciting, to say the least, I deserted our army and joined the British Army.
>
> On my way back to Dublin from leave I was caught and sent to a Cork military detention centre for being a deserter …
>
> It was truly like going to Hell. We weren't allowed to speak a word, not even to another prisoner. We had to sleep on three bed boards for weeks before they gave us

a mattress. We all went to Mass in winter, all with shaven heads and freezing. We were always cold, as there was no heat in the place. I've spoken to other men who were there since, and we all remember that awful hunger, and the freezing cold there.

We got up at six in the morning, got a little block of bread and butter and that was it for breakfast. We became so hungry that we would eat anything. If I got an egg I would eat the shell and all, even fish bones and raw potatoes, if you found them. Not a bit of any kind of food, raw or cooked, went wasted, as we were barely able to live on what we were given in that place. At half past four in the afternoon we were given a small block of bread and butter and that was our last meal. Often they just threw the food at us, as if we were animals.

In the prison yard during the day we were made to run around, and if we weren't running fast enough they loaded more bricks into our packs. They would have us stand in the yard for hours at a time, wearing just a pair of fatigues, freezing to the bone. We were given a hosing down with cold water once a week, and we couldn't afford to complain as that would only bring more punishment down on us. Hell it was.

Some tried to commit suicide. One man in the cell next to mine cut his own throat. Another man took such a beating that he was taken to hospital and never seen again. ... The Sergeant in charge said to us, 'If you want to cut your throat, do so. And if you want to swallow the brass buttons on your coat and choke, do so.' He also said that the Minister for Defence didn't give a care what happened to us and that we were to receive no mercy – and they showed us none.

We were made to scrub these long concrete floors. A scrubbing brush was held outstretched by both hands and we had to keep our feet clear of the ground, just on our hands and knees, and if your feet touched the ground they kicked you really hard.

That kind of thing destroyed my knees forever.

After his release from military prison, Phil was so weak from hunger that he was admitted to hospital in Dublin and remained there for two weeks, after which he was sent back to his Irish Army battalion. Within a short while, Phil deserted again. Back in the British Army, Phil was then a soldier in the Pioneer Corps when he came under fire while 'working with the engineers who were building a Bailey bridge to cross the [Rhine] river' in western Germany. '"Keep Working", I told myself. When I finally raised my head and looked around all I saw were bodies. Our men had been cut to ribbons by the Germans and the Rhine flowed a deep red past my frozen, wet feet. I told myself, "If this was bad, then Cork had been worse". At least here I could fight back and die.'

Phil Farrington would ultimately go on to be one of the first men through the gates of Belsen concentration camp – the 11th Armoured Division, of which Phil's unit was a part, liberated the camp on 15 April 1945; to this day Phil refuses to ever speak about what he saw there – before retiring from the British Army in 1947. He acknowledged:

> I met other men who were caught as deserters and sent to Arbour Hill in Dublin, and they got better treatment altogether. The people in charge of the Cork detention centre were much more cruel.
>
> I do think we deserved to be punished for deserting the Irish Army, but no one deserved the brutal treatment that was handed out down there. We were deserters, but not criminals. There is a big difference.

In terms of the treatment of deserters in Second World War combatant armies, the punishment for desertion varied from army to army. During the Battle for Normandy in 1944, 7,022 British personnel were court-martialled for this crime. The US forces convicted and court-martialled 21,000 men for desertion during the war, and by the end of 1945, there were 19,000 US personnel hiding in France – so many that they became known as the 'Lost Division'. However, in terms of the punishment given to convicted deserters during the Second World War, the US did execute one man – twenty-four-year-old Private Eddie Slovik from Detroit – for this offence (although forty-eight more were sentenced to death but were commuted). The Canadians also shot a man for desertion – Private Harold Pringle. Meanwhile, the British had abolished the death sentence for desertion in 1929 (the Australians had effectively ended execution as a punishment for desertion even before the First World War in 1903), while the Germans executed 15,000 deserters during the war and the Russians 158,000. It is very difficult to find information on exactly how convicted deserters were treated in British military prisons – since the treatment by guards who had no respect for these men was often unofficial, illegal, and unrecorded – but perhaps a comparison can be made with the treatment of RAF bombers' crews who were labelled 'LMF' (Lacking in Moral Fibre). This was the term applied to 4,000 men of the RAF who were said to have displayed 'cowardice' in the face of the enemy (many of these men, already decorated for bravery, had simply broken down under the intense pressure of continual combat missions). In 1944, 2,000 of them – NCOs and airmen – were imprisoned in a Sheffield prison, while 'LMF' officers were either asked to resign or transferred from combat status to a desk job. In Sheffield, these men were put to work shovelling coal, peeling potatoes, and in some cases sent to work underground in the coal mines.

And so, it was not unusual, however terrible, for men in other armies – considered 'undesirable' by their military authorities – to be forced to perform hard, manual labour. That said, the additional mistreatment suffered by Phil Farrington and the other deserters in Cork went beyond the concept of 'acceptable punishment', although similar unrecorded abuses almost certainly occurred in other Allied military prisons. However, the fact that deserters who joined the British Army were specifically targeted for this punishment and for inclusion on 'The List' after the war – as opposed to all deserters – shows that the Irish government's attitude at the time to Irish citizens joining the British Army was extremely biased.

Finally, to give an example of just how negatively certain elements of the Irish government viewed service in the British Army, there was no similar list circulated to prevent Irish Nazis, or the few Irishmen who had actually served in Nazi uniform during the war, from getting jobs in the public sector after 1945. In fact, Wexford republican Stephen Hayes returned to his clerical position in Wexford County Council after the war.

Hayes had served as commandant of the Wexford Brigade of Fianna Éireann during the War of Independence, fought on the anti-Treaty side during the Civil War (as an active GAA member, he helped Wexford win the Leinster Senior Football title in 1925 and served as secretary to the county board for ten years during the 1920s and 1930s), before joining the IRA and becoming a member of the IRA Army Council by the time it declared war on the British government in January 1939. In 1940, Hayes became IRA chief of staff and sent a proposed plan (described as 'completely useless' by the German *Abwehr* agent Hermann Görtz) for the invasion of Northern Ireland by German troops to Germany in April that year. It was called 'Plan Kathleen', and called for 50,000 German troops to perform an amphibious landing at Derry while the IRA would advance north from Leitrim to link up with them. When Görtz parachuted into Ireland soon after on 5 May 1940 – landing at Ballivor, County Meath as part of a different mission (Operation Mainau) to forge links with the IRA – Hayes met with him and requested funds and weapons to start a campaign in Northern Ireland. Plan Kathleen soon fell into the hands of the Irish and British governments, and together they developed Plan W – a joint Anglo-Irish response to any possible Nazi invasion of Ireland.

Meanwhile, in 1941, Hayes was arrested and sentenced to five years' imprisonment by the Special Criminal Court (given powers under the 1939 Offences Against the State Act to deal with the threat that IRA members posed to Irish neutrality). But after his release – regardless of the fact that he had worked with the Nazis and actually tried to bring about a German invasion of Northern Ireland – Stephen Hayes returned to his civil service job, while 4,983 Irishmen who had fought against Nazism were blacklisted. Éamon de Valera did pardon all of these Irish deserters post-war, meaning that they could safely come home and not have to risk facing military imprisonment. However, it is acknowledged that this move had more to do with the lack of space in Irish jails than with actually forgiving these men, as proved by the existence of 'The List'.

However, similar to how the Irish Shot at Dawn Campaign managed to secure a pardon for the twenty-six Irish soldiers executed for various military crimes while serving in the British Army during the First World War, the Irish Soldiers Pardons Campaign (WW2) finally succeeded – in 2012 – in securing the announcement of an 'amnesty and pardon' for those Irishmen who deserted the Irish Defence Forces during the Second World War to join the Allied cause. On 12 June 2012, Alan Shatter – Minister for Justice and Defence – announced in the Dáil that 'the Government apologises for the manner in which those members of the Defence Forces who left to fight on the Allied side during World War Two, 1939 to 1945, were treated after the war by the State. The Government recognises the value and importance of their military contribution to the Allied victory and will introduce legislation to grant a pardon and amnesty to those who absented themselves from the Defence Forces without leave or permission to fight on the Allied side ... Members of the Defence Forces left their posts at that time to fight on the Allied side against tyranny and, together with many thousands of other Irish men and women, played an important role in defending freedom and democracy. Those who fought on the Allied side also contributed to protecting this State's sovereignty and independence and our democratic values.'

PERMANENT SCARS

MARTIN GAFFEY

Finally, I was inspired to write my previous book, *A Coward If I Return, A Hero If I Fall: Stories of Irishmen in WWI*, because my great-grandfather – Martin Gaffey from Athlone – had fought in the trenches of the First World War. However, I subsequently learned that his son – Martin Jnr (my great-uncle) – had served during the Second World War.

The two men had very different wartime experiences. While Martin Snr was wounded and evacuated during his war, Martin Jnr deserted the Irish Army and joined the British Army on 3 April 1942. Initially posted to 7th The Queen's Own Royal West Kent Regiment in Maidstone, he was later sent to India – departing Britain on 12 March 1943 and arriving at the transit camp in Deolali, India on 11 June that year (Deolali was a terrible place where malaria was rampant, and this is where the phrase 'gone doolally' – meaning to lose your mind – comes from).

On 12 November 1943 – the day after his twentieth birthday – Martin was then posted to 1st King's Regiment (Liverpool). This battalion was currently a part of the 77th Indian Infantry Brigade, and they soon took part in the Second Chindit Raid against the Japanese in Burma – codenamed Operation Thursday. The Chindits were a special force of British and Indian troops that deployed by aircraft to landing zones behind enemy lines in Burma, harassed the Japanese by mounting raids, and then withdrew by air. They had to march great distances through tropical jungle while under-supplied, under-fed, and while suffering high casualty rates from illnesses such as malaria, but they managed to successfully attack and

Martin Gaffey from Athlone, County Westmeath. Both he and his father were named Martin, both were from Athlone, both were born on 11 November (Armistice Day), and both fought in a world war.

disrupt the Japanese on many occasions.

When Operation Thursday was launched on 5 February 1944, Private Martin Gaffey and 1st King's Regiment (Liverpool) landed at Landing Zone 'Broadway'. However, while other Chindit units advanced to harass the Japanese and set up fortified positions elsewhere, Martin remained at Broadway and was still there when the enemy launched a vicious assault against the landing zone on 27 March that lasted for several days – the Japanese were only pushed back after the British flew in artillery and raised local Kachin irregular troops to help them. During the battle – on 28 March – Private Martin Gaffey was wounded and evacuated back to India. His service record does not record exactly how he was wounded.

He returned to 1st King's Regiment (Liverpool) on 31 July 1944, but it was soon apparent that his wounds, and the malaria that he had also contracted, had left a permanent scar on Martin Gaffey's mind. On 12 October that year, Martin went illegally absent until he was apprehended twenty-eight days later on 10 November at Barlowganj, near Dehradun in northwest India. However, he was not court-martialled, and all mentions of his going illegally absent were subsequently crossed off in his service record and the punishment cancelled, suggesting that the army knew there was another reason for him going AWOL. Then, on 11 January 1945, he was admitted to hospital again, and although he was released and returned to his unit within thirteen days, he was in and out of hospital several times over the next year. On 28 February 1946 he was transferred into 1st Wiltshire Regiment and was soon promoted to lance-corporal, but by 3 June that year he was back in hospital. He was reduced to private twelve days later and was then finally sent back to Britain, arriving on 7 July and being posted to 2nd Infantry Holding

Battalion. However, Martin soon went illegally absent again – for four days between 11 and 15 August – and then finished his period of service with the British Army by serving as a prisoner of war guard at No 168 Brookmill PW Camp at Woodlands, Kirkham in Lancashire. He was subsequently discharged on 3 December 1946, and the discharge testimonial from his last commanding officer stated that his service was 'exemplary' and that 'After 3yrs 4mths service in India & Burma this soldier has shown good service in this unit as a P.W. guard. He is conscientious, and can be relied upon to do a job to the best of his ability.'

What had happened to Martin during the war soon became apparent after he returned home to Athlone. He began suffering from extreme bouts of recurring malaria, during which his mood, temperament and behaviour would change drastically – he would also generally drink heavily, spend recklessly, and then disappear for days on end – and these events plagued Martin for the rest of his life. He suffered one attack just before he was due to be married, and as a result of his subsequently going missing, the wedding never happened and he lost his job as a chrome applier in a bicycle factory, just before he was due to be promoted for his good work. On another occasion, Martin Snr bought his son a suit to help him get a job in an Athlone hotel, but the malaria returned when he was due to go to the interview. When he finally came round, Martin Jnr insisted that he wanted to see his father, and while 'roaring crying' (as the family recall), he told his father that a doctor wanted to perform a brain operation to try and stop the malaria attacks. Martin Jnr was absolutely terrified, and he felt that his father was the only person who could understand.

Martin Jnr later moved to Birmingham and met a woman named May, who he remained with for twenty years. She was a very understanding woman, and whenever Martin took one of his 'turns' she always took him back in. They travelled around the world together ('she was the love of his life' as one family member recently put it), but when May developed cancer and died, Martin went into a decline. On 19 November 1984 he was found unconscious by the roadside near his flat in Birmingham – he later died in the local General Hospital. His death certificate recorded that the cause of death was 'Hepato renal failure ... cirrhosis of the liver associated with alcohol abuse and recent overdose of paracetamol ... took tablets ... killed himself'. When he died, Martin Gaffey Jnr had turned sixty-one years old only eight days previously. Having served in India and Burma for three years during the Second World War, those three years cursed him for the remainder of his life. It could be said that he never really survived the war.

AUTHOR'S FINAL WORDS

Today, most of Ireland's Second World War veterans are gone. Even the youngest remaining ones are, on average, in their mid-eighties. These men and women lived during a time when great moral and physical courage was demanded of them, and at least 130,000 Irish answered the call to fight against the Axis forces. For us, now living in twenty-first century Ireland, it is almost impossible to imagine what it must have been like to live in a world where your home was under the very real threat of being invaded by a fascist army led by a brutal dictator. It is almost equally impossible to imagine the fear and uncertainty that people throughout Europe experienced during those troubled times, but despite this, so many men and women from across this island signed up to fight – knowing that they would have to see terrible things, do terrible things, and perhaps never come back to their loved ones.

My time interviewing surviving veterans – or their families – for this book, was an eye-opening, moving, and intensely personal experience for me. To see an old soldier cry – remembering the death of a best friend over sixty-five years ago – or shrug modestly after recounting how he saved the life of a comrade and say 'Sure what else could I do?' really puts life into perspective. When faced with the stories of men who experienced suffering, pain, and hardships – the likes of which we, who have not seen war, cannot possibly comprehend – it makes us realise how lucky we are that so many brave Irish men and women fought so that our future would be better than their present. We can never thank them enough, but perhaps in some small and humble way – by learning and passing on their stories – we can honour and commemorate their lives. And so I would advise anyone who is interested to do so. If your relatives fought in the war, ask them about their experiences – preserve their memories – because when they are gone, those memories will otherwise be gone forever. The Irish played an extremely significant part in the Second World War – it is a part of our history – and it is vital that we remember that.

Finally, possibly the highest praise for Irish Second World War veterans comes from one of history's greatest figures. In his 'Five Years of War' speech – delivered on 13 May 1945 – British Prime Minister Winston Churchill said:

When I think of these days I think also of other episodes and personalities. I do not forget Lieutenant-Commander Esmonde, V.C., D.S.O., Lance-Corporal Kenneally, V.C., Captain Fegen, V.C., and other Irish heroes that I could easily recite, and all bitterness by Britain for the Irish race dies in my heart. I can only pray that in years which I shall not see, the shame will be forgotten and the glories will endure ...

Hopefully, now, that is exactly what will happen. They were decent men in a dark time, and that is how they should be remembered.

Adleman, Robert H, and Walton, George, *The Devil's Brigade*, Philadelphia: Chilton Books, 1966.

Ambrose, Hugh, *The Pacific*, Edinburgh: Canongate Books, 2010.

Ambrose, Stephen E, *Band of Brothers*, London: Pocket Books, 2001.

Ambrose, Stephen E, *Citizen Soldiers: From the Beaches of Normandy to the Surrender of Germany*, London: Pocket Books, 2002.

Ambrose, Stephen E, *D-Day: June 6, 1944 – The Battle for the Normandy Beaches*, London: Pocket Books, 2002.

Ambrose, Stephen E, *Pegasus Bridge: D-Day – The Daring British Airborne Raid*, London: Pocket Books, 2003.

Ambose, Stephen E, *The Victors: The Men of World War II*, London: Pocket Books, 2004.

Arthur, Max, *Symbol of Courage: A Complete History of the Victoria Cross*, UK: Sidgwick and Jackson, 2004.

Arthur, Max, *Symbol of Courage: The Men Behind The Medal*, London: Pan Books, 2005.

Ballantyne, Iain, *Warships of the Royal Navy: Warspite*, Barnsley: Leo Cooper, 2001.

Barrington, Brendan, ed., *The Dublin Review: Number Thirty-One – Summer 2008*, Dublin: The Dublin Review, 2008.

Barron, HJ Pat, *At the Going Down of the Sun*, Canada: Loonbook, 2000.

Beattie, David, *Interesting, Maybe*, Australia: Meni Publishing and Binding, 2006.

Beevor, Antony, *Berlin: The Downfall 1945*, London: Viking (Penguin Books), 2002.

Beevor, Antony, *Crete: The Battle and the Resistance*, London: John Murray, 1991.

Beevor, Antony, *D-Day: The Battle for Normandy*, London: Viking (Penguin Books), 2009.

Beevor, Antony, *The Battle for Spain: The Spanish Civil War 1936–1939*, London: Phoenix, 2007.

Binney, Marcus, *The Women Who Lived For Danger: The Women Agents of the Special Operations Executive*, London: William Morrow & Co, 2003.

Bradford, Roy and Dillon, Martin, *Rogue Warrior of the SAS: The Blair Mayne Legend*, London: Mainstream Publishing, 2003.

Bryant, Arthur, *The Turn of the Tide*, New York: Doubleday, 1957.

Burhams, Robert D, *The First Special Service Force: A Canadian/American Wartime Alliance – The Devil's Brigade*, Washington DC: Infantry Journal Press Inc, 1947.

Calvocoressi, Peter and Wint, Guy, *Total War: Causes and Courses of the Second World War*, UK: Penguin Books, 1972.

Chorley, WR, *Royal Air Force Bomber Command Losses of the Second World War: Volume 6 – Aircraft and Crew Losses 1945*, UK: Midland Counties Publications, 1998.

Cunliffe, Marcus, *The Royal Irish Fusiliers 1793–1950*, Oxford: Oxford University Press, 1952 (expanded & reprinted, 1970).

Cunningham, Andrew, *Admiral AB Cunningham: A Sailor's Odyssey*, London: Hutchinson & Co, 1952.

Delaforce, Patrick, *Marching to the Sound of Gunfire: North West Europe 1944–5*, UK: Wrens Park Publishing, 1999.

Doherty, Richard, *Clear the Way! A History of the 38th (Irish) Brigade 1941–47*, Dublin: Irish Academic Press, 1993.

Doherty, Richard, *In the Ranks of Death: The Irish in the Second World War*, Barnsley: Pen & Sword Military, 2010.

Doherty, Richard and Truesdale, David, *Irish Winners of the Victoria Cross*, Dublin: Four Courts Press, 1999.

Doherty, Richard, *The North Irish Horse: A Hundred Years of Service*, Staplehurst: Spellmount Publishers, 2002.

Escott, Beryl E, *The Heroines of SOE: F Section – Britain's Secret Women in France*, Gloucestershire: The History Press Ltd, 2010.

Evans, Roger, *The Story of the Fifth Royal Inniskilling Dragoon Guards*, UK: Gale & Polden Ltd, 1951.

Ferriter, Diarmuid, *Judging Dev*, Dublin: Royal Irish Academy, 2007.

Fisk, Robert, *In Time of War: Ireland, Ulster and the Price of Neutrality 1939–45*, Dublin: Gill & Macmillan Ltd, 1996.

Fitzgerald, Desmond, *A History of the Irish Guards in the Second World War*, UK: Gale & Polden, 1952 (reprinted 1986 & 2000).

Fox, Sir Frank, *The Royal Inniskilling Fusiliers in the Second World War*, UK: Gale & Polden, 1951.

Gardner, WJR, ed., *The Evacuation from Dunkirk: Operation Dynamo, 26 May–4 June 1940*, London: Routledge, 2000.

Girvin, Brian, *The Emergency: Neutral Ireland 1939–45*, London: Macmillan, 2006.

Gray, Tony, *The Lost Years: Emergency in Ireland 1939–45*, London: Time Warner Paperbacks, 1998.

Harte, Jack and Mara, Sandra, *To the Limits of Endurance: One Irishman's War*, Dublin: Liberties Press, 2007.

Holmes, Richard, *Acts of War: The Behaviour of Men in Battle*, London: Cassell, 1985.

Holmes, Richard, *Soldiers: Army Lives and Loyalties from Redcoats to Dusty Warriors*, London: Harper Press, 2011.

Horrocks, Lt-Gen Sir Brian, ed., Henry Harris, *The Royal Irish Fusiliers*, London: Lee Cooper, 1972.

Johnson, EBW, *Island Prize: Leros 1943*, UK: Kemble Press, 1992.

Keegan, John, *Six Armies in Normandy*, London: Jonathan Cape, 1982.

Killblane, Richard and McNiece, Jake, *The Filthy Thirteen*, Berkshire: Casemate, 2003.

Keogh, Michael (author) and Keogh, Kevin (compiler), ed., Brian Maye, *With Casement's Irish Brigade*, Drogheda: Choice Publishing, 2010.

Leckie, Robert, *Helmet for my Pillow*, UK: Ebury Press, 2010.

Lunt, James, *16th/5th The Queen's Royal Lancers*, London: Leo Cooper, 1973.

MacCarthy, Aidan, *A Doctor's War*, London: Grub Street, 2006.

Mackenzie, KW, *Hurricane Combat: The Nine Lives of a Fighter Pilot*, London: William Kimber and Co Ltd, 1987.

Mason, David, *Raid on St Nazaire*, London: Macdonald & Co, 1970.

Mortimer, Gavin, *Stirling's Men: The Inside History of the SAS in World War II*, London: Cassell Military Paperbacks, 2005.

Murphy, David (author) and Embleton, Gerry (illustrator), *Irish Regiments in the World Wars*, Oxford: Osprey Publishing, 2007.

Neillands, Robin, *The Battle for the Rhine 1944: Arnhem and the Ardennes – The Campaign in Europe*, London: Cassell Military Paperbacks, 2006.

O'Connor, Patrick, *France 1939–1946: Lest We Forget*, (Privately Printed), 2002.

Orr, David R, and Truesdale, David, *The Rifles are There: 1st and 2nd Battalions The Royal Ulster Rifles in the Second World War*, Barnsley: Pen & Sword Military, 2006.

Plevy, Harry, *Battleship Sailors*, London: Chatham Publishing, 2001.

Richards, Denis, *RAF Bomber Command in the Second World War: The Hardest Victory*, London: Penguin Books, 1994.

Robertson, David Sinclair, *Deeds Not Words: Irish Soldiers, Sailors and Airmen in Two World Wars*, Ireland: Wholesaler Unique, 1998.

Ross, Hamish, *Paddy Mayne*, Gloucestershire: The History Press Ltd, 2004.

Smyth, Jack, *Five Days in Hell: The Battle of Arnhem*, London: Kimber Pocket Editions, 1956.

Snape, Michael, *The Royal Army Chaplains' Department, 1796–1953: Clergy Under Fire*, UK: Boydell Press, 2007.

Stevens, Gordon, *The Originals: The Secret History of the Birth of the SAS in their own words*, UK: Ebury Press, 2006.

Stewart, Graeme, *Silent Heroes: The Story of the SAS*, London: Hodder & Stoughton, 1997.

Stirling, JDP, *The First and the Last: The Story of the 4th/7th Royal Dragoon Guards 1939–45*, UK: Art and Educational Publishers, 1946.

Thomas, David A, *Crete 1941: The Battle at Sea*, London: André Deutsch, 1972.

Truesdale, David, *Brotherhood of the Cauldron: Irishmen with the 1st Airborne Division from North Africa to Arnhem*, Newtownard: Redcoat Publishing, 2002.

Upington, William, *Sure, It's True Enough: 1922–Present Day*, (Privately Printed), 2000.

Widders, Robert, *Spitting on a Soldier's Grave: Court Martialed After Death, The Story of the Forgotten Irish and British Soldiers*, Leicester: Matador, 2010.

Widders, Robert, *The Emperor's Irish Slaves: Prisoners of the Japanese in the Second World War*, Dublin: The History Press Ireland, 2012.

Willis, Clair, *That Neutral Island: A Cultural History of Ireland during WW2*, London: Faber & Faber, 2008.

Winters, Major Dick, *Beyond Band of Brothers*, UK: Ebury Press, 2011.

North Irish Horse Battle Report: North Africa–Italy 1943–1945, UK: W & G Baird Ltd, 1946.

The London Irish at War: A history of the Battalions of the London Irish in WW2, London: London Irish Rifles Old Comrades Association, 1949.

The 8th Hussars: A History of the Regiment, UK: Maritime Publications, 1964.

SERVICE RECORDS

Service Record of Agnew, John; 13115157; National
Personnel Records Center (USA)

Service Record of Clery, Reginald Valentine; 1127936;
Army Personnel Centre (Historical Disclosures
Section)

Service Record of Doherty, Thomas Colvin; 39459;
National Personnel Records Center (USA)

Service Record of Finan, Daniel; 1394330; RAF
Disclosures

Service Record of Fleming, William Joseph; R165640;
The Board of Trade/Ministry of Transport

Service Record of Francis, Leslie Lionel; 11410042;
Army Personnel Centre (Historical Disclosures
Section)

Service Record of Gaffey, Martin; 6355411; Army
Personnel Centre (Historical Disclosures Section)

Service Record of Gallagher, John; JX249490; Royal
Navy Records Management

Service Record of Herzog, Chaim; 14410170; Army
Personnel Centre (Historical Disclosures Section)

Service Record of Lee, Edwin George; 321545; Army
Personnel Centre (Historical Disclosures Section)

Service Record of O'Dea, Edward; KX88642; Royal
Navy Records Management

Service Record of Sexton, Cornelius Gerald; NX35108;
National Archives of Australia (also: Sound Collection Transcript S04056, Australian War Memorial)

WAR DIARIES

1st East Kent Regiment; Dec 1941; UK National
Archives; WO169/1708

1st Irish Guards; Mar–May 1943; UK National Archives;
WO175/488

1st Irish Guards; Jan–Feb 1944; UK National Archives;
WO170/1354

1st Royal Inniskilling Fusiliers; Feb–Jul 1942; UK
National Archives; WO172/863

1st Royal Ulster Rifles; Jun 1944; UK National Archives;
WO171/1383

2nd Royal Ulster Rifles; Jun 1944; UK National
Archives; WO171/1384

2nd Royal Warwickshire Regiment; May 1940; UK
National Archives; WO167/839

2nd South Lancashire Regiment; May 1942; UK
National Archives; WO174/31

2nd The Queen's Own Royal West Kent Regiment; Nov
1943; UK National Archives; WO169/10239

2/20th Infantry Battalion, AIF; Jun 1940–Sep 1941
& Jan–Jun 1942; Australian War Memorial; AWM52
8/3/20

2/25th Infantry Battalion, AIF; Jul–Dec 1943; Australian
War Memorial; AWM52 8/3/25

3rd Coldstream Guards; Jun 1944; UK National Archives;
WO170/1348

No 3 Commando; Aug 1942; UK National Archives;
WO218/34

3rd Irish Guards; Sep–Oct 1944; UK National Archives;
WO171/1257

3rd Irish Guards; Mar 1945; UK National Archives;
WO171/5148

3rd Parachute Regiment; Jul 1943; UK National
Archives; WO169/10345

No 4 Commando; Jun–Sep & Nov 1944; UK National
Archives; WO218/66

5th Royal Inniskilling Dragoon Guards; Jul–Oct 1944;
UK National Archives; WO171/839

5th Royal Inniskilling Dragoon Guards; Jan–Apr 1945;
UK National Archives; WO171/4686

No 6 Commando; Jun 1944; UK National Archives;
WO218/68

8th King's Royal Irish Hussars; Aug–Dec 1940; UK
National Archives; WO169/219

8th King's Royal Irish Hussars; Feb–Aug 1941; UK
National Archives; WO169/1388

12th Royal Lancers; Mar 1943; UK National Archives;
WO169/9326

14th Sherwood Foresters; Oct–Nov 1942; UK National
Archives; WO169/5064

79th Assault Squadron, Royal Engineers; Jun & Sep 1944;
UK National Archives; WO171/1807

79th Company, Pioneer Corps; Sep 1943; UK National
Archives; WO169/12793

INTERVIEWS

Adams, Richard – interview with Richard Adams Jnr

Agnew, John – interview with Barbara Maloney

Barrett, Joseph – interview with Josie Cole

Blanchfield, Michael – interview with Paddy Reid

Briscoe, Robert – interview with Carol Briscoe

Cahalane, Cornelius – interview with Conor Cahalane

Carolan, Martin Anthony – interview with Patricia
Brien

Clery, Reginald Valentine – interview with Noelle Clery

Coleman, Michael – interview with veteran

Collins, John Joseph – interview with Tom Collins

Craig, Mark – interview with Pat Casey

Crivon, Peter – interview with Quentin Crivon

Crivon, Robert – interview with Quentin Crivon and Gail Sackloff

Cunningham, Redmond – interview with Peter Cunningham

Duffy, Lawrence – interview with Rory Duffy

Dunne, Joseph – interview with Kevin Hynes

Durham, James – interview with Rita Harris

Fahy, Joseph – interview with Carmel Lynch

Farrington, Phil – interview with Paddy Reid

Feeney, James – interview with John Feeney

Finan, Daniel – interview with Richard Finan and Frances Farrell

Fleming, William Joseph – interview with Edward Fleming

Francis, Leslie Lionel – interview with Lorraine Francis

Freeman, Bernard – interview with Howard Freeman

Gaffey, Martin – interview with Tony Gaffey and Eileen Kavanagh

Gallagher, John – interview with Sarah McBride

Gleeson, Terence – interview with John Feeney

Green, Christopher – interview with Sarah Cassidy and Donal Cassidy

Harkin, Don – interview with veteran

Holohan, William – interview with Tommy Holohan

Johnson, Ted – interview with veteran

Joyce, Christopher – interview with Michael McDonagh

Kendrick, Sam – interview with veteran and Kenneth Martin

Larney, Owen 'Tony' – interview with Cyril Wall and Richard Adams Jnr

Lee, Edwin George – interview with Reggie Lee

Lee, Lawrence – interview with veteran

Lee, Reggie – interview with veteran

Lehane, Michael – interview with Gordon Revington

Levitas brothers – interview with Ruth Levitas

Leyden, Mattie – interview with Richard Adams Jnr

Loughlin, George Francis – interview with Anne Loughlin

Lynch, Martin – interview with veteran (conducted by Limerick branch, Royal British Legion)

Martin, Miles Patrick – interview with Michael Martin

McCready, William John – interview with Jim McIlmurray

McDonagh, Martin – interview with Michael McDonagh

McDonald, William – interview with Henry Mooney

McDonnell, Patrick – interview with Gerard McDonnell and Jim McIlmurray

McDonnell, Robert Edward – interview with Lucita Shorter and John McCullen

McLoughlin, Christopher James – interview with Colm Connaughton

Moriarty, Anthony – interview with John Moriarty

Murray, James – interview with Michael Murray

Nixon, Alec – interview with Olivia Callan

Power, John Davin – interview with David Davin-Power

Raymond, Seamus – interview with Mike Moriarty

Robinson, Christopher – interview with veteran (conducted by Limerick branch, Royal British Legion)

Rogers, Michael – interview with James Rogers

Sexton, Cornelius Gerald – interview with Tadhg Sexton

Sheridan, Michael Edward – interview with John Kirke

Sweeney, Stephen – interview with Padraig Sweeney

O'Connor, Patrick – interview with veteran

O'Dea, Edward – interview with Ronnie O'Dea

O'Hara, Patrick – interview with Kathy Bateson

O'Sullivan, John – interview with veteran and Colman Shaughnessy

O'Sullivan, Maureen Patricia – interview with John Alvey

Wall, Raymond – interview with Cyril Wall

Wogan, Patrick – interview with Alex Wogan

Photograph credits

The author and publisher would like to thank the families of the soldiers in this book who provided precious photoraphs and memorabilia for publication. Acknowledgement is also due to various archives and museums:

Front cover: Imperial War Museum (MH2011). Back cover: top, Imperial War Museum (CH740); centre right, Neil Richardson; bottom left, Gerard McDonnell; bottom right, Pat Casey. Jack Agnew and Casemate Publishing pp240, 242-243; John Alvey p294; Australian War Memorial p196 (P08489); Patricia Brien p314; Carol Briscoe p265 (top right, centre right); Conor Cahalane pp178-179; Pat Casey pp23-24; Sarah Cassidy p186; Noelle Clery p284; Josie Cole p181; Bridget Connolly pp118, 120; Peter Cunningham p164; David Davin-Power p91; Department of the Taoiseach p14 (centre row, bottom middle, bottom right); Fennell Photography p2 (top); Lorraine Francis pp148-149; Don Harkin pp78-79, 83, 86; Rita Harris p169; Imperial War Museum p8 (MH11040), p17 (HU34709), p28 (O161), p37 (C1115), p42 (HU1137), p47 (HU21013), p57 (H25074), p61 (CH3757), p70 (CH740), p75 (H9476), p92 (D4361), p104 (E3467E), p110 (E18542), p122 (NA5388), p137 (NA13057), p144 (NA16179), p151 (A24371), p155 (B5288), p157 (B5103), p161 (H38080), p171 (B5205), p175 (MH29437), p188 (HU4569), p190 (HU43339), p201 (A26940A), p210 (MH29437), p211 (A11787), p214 (NAM236), p216 (A11787), p220 (A13398), pp224-225 (FL22602), p228 (A20689), p234 (A5826), p238 (NYF14749), p250 (NYF14749), p257 (NYF18409), p260 (MH13348), p262 (HU6312), p264 (IA37578), p271 (BU4260), p278 (BU1121), p283 (BU1244), p287 (HU1904), p298 (K7586), p301 (BU1121); Irish Jewish Museum pp265 (bottom left), 270, 273, 275, 277; Eileen Kavanagh p334; Sam Kendrick p308; John Kirke p224; Reggie Lee pp202, 281-282; Ben Levitas p267; Anne Loughlin p315; Carmel Lynch p33; Michael Martin p286; Gerard McDonnell pp323, 325; Jim McIlmurray pp10-11, 121, 217, 313, 318-319; John Moriarty p22; Patrick O'Connor p173; Ronnie O'Dea pp227, 230-231; Neil Richardson p14 (top row, bottom left); Gail Sackloff p266; Anne Sands pp114, 311; Colman Shaughnessy p237; Lucita Shorter p107; Padraig Sweeney p99; Ted Johnson p126; Cyril Wall pp1, 80, 94, 96.

Text credits

Tony Banham and Hong Kong University Press for quotations from *The Sinking of the Lisbon Maru: Britain's Forgotten Wartime Tragedy* (reproduced in Robert Widders' The Emperor's Irish Slaves, The History Press); HJ 'Pat' Barron and Loonbook for quotations from *At the Going Down of the Sun*; Choice Publishing for quotations from Michael Keogh's *With Casement's Irish Brigade*; Peter Cunningham & the Dublin Review for quotations from issue 31, summer 2008; Richard Doherty and Pen & Sword Military for quotations from *In the Ranks of Death: The Irish in the Second World War*; Ebury Press for quotations from Robert Leckie's *Helmet for my Pillow*; Beryl E Escott and The History Press for quotations from *The Heroines of SOE: F Section – Britain's Secret Women in France*; WJR Gardner and Routledge for quotations from *The Evacuation from Dunkirk: Operation Dynamo, 26 May–4 June 1940*; George G Harrap and Co for quotations from Wallace Reyburn's *Rehearsal for Invasion*; Grub Street Publishing for quotations from Aidan McCarthy's A Doctor's War (reproduced in Robert Widders' The Emperor's Irish Slaves, The History Press); Edward 'Ted' Johnson & Kemble Press for quotations from *Island Prize: Leros 1943*; Richard Killblane, Jake McNiece and Casemate Publishing for quotations from *The Filthy Thirteen*; Limerick branch of the Royal British Legion for quotations from Martin Lynch's 'A Middle Eastern Holiday' and Christopher Robinson's 'Convoy Trips'; John O'Sullivan for quotations from *A Radio Officer's Story*; Paddy Reid for quotations from Michael Blanchfield's 'Barefoot in Hiroshima' and Phil Farrington's 'To Hell and Back' from *Flying, Not Falling, Stories and Reflections on Life by Older Adults*; William Upington for quotations from *Sure, It's True Enough*; Robert Widders and Matador for quotations from *Spitting on a Soldier's Grave: Court Martialed After Death, The Story of the Forgotten Irish and British Soldiers*; Robert Widders and The History Press for quotations from *The Emperor's Irish Slaves: Prisoners of the Japanese in the Second World War*; Zampano Productions for quotations from their interview with John Hemingway. *Every effort has been made to trace holders of copyright material used in this book, but if any infringement has inadvertently occurred, the publishers ask the copyright-holders to contact them.*

INDEX